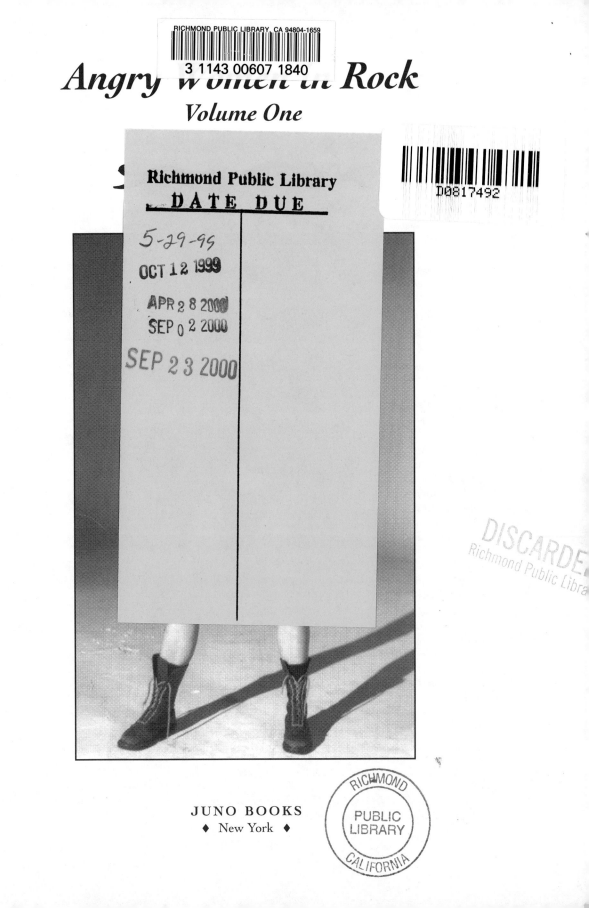

Angry Women in Rock

Volume One

JUNO BOOKS
♦ New York ♦

Editor-in-Chief: Andrea Juno
Project Editor: Jessica Lustig
Production Managers: Lisa London & Susan B.A. Somers-Willett
Production Assistant: Sarah E. Carnevale
Border illustrations: Jodi Lekacos
Women in Rock Map: Abby McGanney Nolan & Pat Redding
Project Photographers: Chris Buck, Kate Simon, Chris Toliver

Special thanks to: Calvin Johnson and K Records, Slim Moon and Kill Rock Stars, Steak, Andrew Bennett, David I.F. Miller (herbalist)

◆

Copyright © 1996 by Juno Books, LLC
ISBN: 0-9651042-0-6

Angry women in rock / interviews by Andrea Juno.
     p.   cm.
     Includes indexes.
     1. Women rock musicians--Interviews. 2. Feminism and music.
  I. Juno, Andrea.
  ML82.A54 1996
  781.66'082--dc20   95-30171

BOOKSTORE DISTRIBUTION: Consortium, 1045 Westgate Drive, Saint Paul, MN 55114-1065. Orders: 1-800-283-3572, phone: (612) 221-9035, fax: (612) 221-0124.

For a catalog, send SASE to:
Juno Books, 180 Varick Street, 10th Floor, New York, NY 10014; phone: (212) 807-7300, fax: (212) 807-7355.

Typesetting by Quadright, New York, NY.
Printed in the U.S.A.

10 9 8 7 6 5 4 3 2 1

Cover Art: Phoebe Gloeckner
Back Cover Photo of Leslie Mah, Tribe 8: Chris Toliver
First Page Photo of Leslie Mah: Erika P. Martin
Back Page Photo of Joan Jett: Photo: Chris Buck/Hair: Paige Smitherman/Makeup: Linda Mason/ Stylist: Andrea Lee Linett/Satin top by Love NYC.

Contents

Introduction

When I was a teenager in the early 1970s a chance encounter in the record bins led me to an album by the group Fanny. The cover was a stark black and white photo of four unadorned strong-looking yet attractive hard-rocking women, a unique novelty in those days. Women would sing, but it was rare for women to drum, play lead guitar and write their own material without being depicted as pin-up girls. Fanny defied society's heavily made-up, artificial ideal manufactured and constructed for male viewing pleasure. They projected a self-assuredness and self-defined sexuality and libido without the typical constraints and manipulations.

Born in 1955, I was part of the first generation of women who grew up with the expectation of becoming anyone I wanted—yet the cultural images surrounding us only reinforced hopelessly restrictive rules. The rhetoric swirling around feminism in early '70s was fueling women to expand their cultural, social and economic horizons. But this exciting dialogue failed to manifest itself in media representations and many social realities. I would watch James Bond movies or a *Star Trek* episode, but was faced with an insurmountable dilemma when I tried to translate the stories to my internal fantasy images: I wanted to identify with the unemotional and much admired secret agent, but it was clear that the only role for me in that world was as one of Bond's interchangeable powerless women, who could be distinguished, like Barbie dolls, only by the color of their hair and bathing suits. Even *that* role was unobtainable for all but the select few women born with the right genetic combination to fit the tall, anorexic, WASP ideal. I would listened to Blue Oyster Cult, the Rolling Stones, Led Zeppelin and T-Rex (along with women like Joni Mitchell and Dusty Springfield), which heightened gender divisions and created a tsunami wave-crash of identity confusion. Those male rock bands screamed out a litany of puerile projections and derision towards women whose only role seemed to serve the male ego. So, for me, the inevitable task was to dissociate and shove aside the contradictions. The worst alternative was to identify with the female (not a "real" female but an idealized female constructed by male desire), resulting in the inevitable implanting of self-doubt and condemnation for not looking or acting like an air-brushed poster of Jerri Hall.

A little crack of clarity and affirmation in the adolescent blur and collision of identity was represented by the four women in Fanny. Rock has always professed (although

many times hypocritically) to ally itself with rebellion and to the dismantling of the status quo. The male hard-rocking, hard-drugging lifestyle of irresponsible and uncommitted abandon seemed more about a rebellion against Dad then a reevaluation of the problems of the world. The members of Fanny and other women rockers expressed a heresy, challenging the fundamental assumptions of gender and jarring loose centuries-old narratives of male dominance and narrow gender definitions (much like David Bowie and bi-sexual/gay rockers did later). The image of the macho rocker icon, wanking away on his guitar and taking his pick of the groupies glides effortlessly into the parody image of an underwear-clad, air-guitaring Tom Cruise in a movie that championed the Republican ideal of the Ivy League MBA-entrepreneur. Given that so many of these geriatric "Rock Gods" were the flag bearers of the middle class, who better to carry on the myth of rebellion than women and queers? Rock'n'roll has always been a haven for the image of the outlaw, making it a natural place where the boundaries of proscribed femininity can be transgressed. Girls can be bold, brash and loud; all the things they were taught not to be.

Feminism in the early '70s was just getting its sea legs, attempting to redress thousands of years of political and economic inequities, and to consolidate a nascent identity to address these inequities in respect to a body politic. As many newly emerging political movements seeking identity, early feminism could be quite rigid, imposing narrow definitions of who or how one could be a "true" feminist. My first rude awaking to this fact was in college, when I went to a women's studies class and was ostracized for the crime of wearing makeup. I didn't discard my feminist identity because of a few humorless bad apples, but I did breathe a sigh of relief when feminism and feminists began to lighten up. There is a natural cycle of growth that feminism, like many political movements follow: burgeoning from the strident and radical early beginnings when women were emerging from a literal slavery (the right to vote and own property was only won in this century), and circling to the present when, having solidified a political power base, women can expand feminine definitions, reflect on expectations with humor and irony and begin to enjoy the fruits of partial victories. Today there is a blossoming of options open to women—despite our society's predilection for ossifying political cycles into petrified forests of dogma with statements like "Feminism is dead," or the manifestation of humorless political correctness and straitjacketed essentialism. From a more secure position won on the back of identity politic movements such as gay, minority and civil rights, new alliances can now be forged and a more *inclusionary* politics can—and should—emerge. The critical dialogue initiated by feminism was a significant key that opened up a world of political issues relevant to men *as well as* women: sexuality and how we view the body, reproductive rights and overpopulation, economic hierarchies of power and inequities, our relationship to the Earth (conceptually a "dead" planet) and how we deal with ecology, waste disposal, destruction of forests and wetlands.

The changes undergone in rock 'n' roll reflect the thriving and flowering of feminism, despite the perpetual media-pronounced deaths and backlashes. A decade after the original punk rock permutations in the late '70s, a new generation re-defined punk in the mid-'80s to include women, gays and a broader acceptance for multi-cultural experience (although in practice, "alternative" punk rock is predominantly white). The political methods of the '60s and '70s—the march, the rally, the cries of "revolution"—had grown stale and clichéd as the older generation grew into smug self-indulgent yuppies. A segment of the younger generation attempted to revive ways in which to infuse their small pocket of culture with fresh radical ideas. Independently-owned record labels such as K, Kill Rock Stars, Thrill Jockey, Touch & Go, Discord and Queenie revived a do-it-yourself philosophy, allowing artists to bypass exploitive major corporations and their tentacles of distribution. Rock music has always been a vector for social change, binding people together in ritual social gatherings in small clubs, where ideas can be broadcasted and the seeds of change can be spread. In the '80s the advances in computer technology (desk-top publishing, access to the Internet and cheap xeroxing) directly contributed to a *samizdat*-like network of fanzines, tapes and records that rippled across the nation, giving voice to an alternative from mainstream ideas and creating a communication network. This helped birth the Riot Grrrl movement and groups like Homocore—allowing women and gays to communicate directly with each other, their conversations unfiltered by the conservative media and major corporate record moguls.

These alternative discourses and economies become increasingly vital as our information age attaches profit and power to information-based, magnet companies—such as Microsoft, Viacom (owners of MTV and Blockbuster) and Time-Warner—and are of the sort which threaten not only artistic expression, but culture and community at large. As has happened in most decades of this century, corporations have packaged, marketed, advertised and capitalized on "alternative" cultures (let us not forget the transformation of the blue jean from rebel hippie culture to its present status, or the Beats now firmly ensconced at the Whitney Museum). Today it's being done through a variety of media: CD-ROM, cyberspace, film, video, radio—all which sell back products designed to sedate people into the illusion of rebellion and transgression. Rock music has become both the umbilical cord and the feedback loop of capitalistic culture, whose shocking economic greed and excess is disguised by the large dose of glamour that society attaches to stardom.

This red-herring approach (repeated in every generation) lulls people away from the harder and riskier work of fundamentally changing these corporate/economic systems where profits and technology have far more value than the quality of human life. It's easier for shareholders to inject into the public the notion and desire that if they invest in the "cool" computer system, buy a "rad" car or purchase the CD of a "transgressive" band as a "lifestyle" choice, they will improve their lives—rather then having them imagine organizing to prevent "downsizing", lobbying for healthcare or more equitably distributing the obscene wealth of the multi-nationals.

As the options for women have grown and more avenues of expression open, is there really anything to be "angry" about? The answer is a resounding "yes." Despite the protestations of some women who have bought the line that to be angry—or to be powerful—is equal to being an unattractive, de-sexualized bitch. In a world careening down a suicidal path, when unchecked greed runs rampant and the distance between the haves and the have-nots becomes wider, anger can be a sane, creative and cathartic option for those conscious enough to see around them. We live in a society where every woman lives under the threat of rape, where being openly homosexual means running the risk of being gay-bashed, where legislation is passed that restricts and could very well do away with our right to abortion (which we've already functionally lost when doctors who perform them are murdered), where women still earn less than men for equal work. Our society is still uneasy with the idea of women getting together, alone, to discuss their concerns—although no one minds if they go shopping together. Just because many of the more overt manifestations of sexism such as sexual harassment, domestic abuse, and the "glass ceiling" have begun to be targeted and addressed (but not done away with), sexism seems to have wormed its way insidiously into more subtle places. We cannot be lulled into thinking that the goals of feminism have been won.

We are currently at an interesting stage in the history of rock with the recent influx of women entering as a steady and unstoppable force. Perhaps, like a Trojan horse or a mutating virus they can't help but change the status quo in, as yet, unknown ways. The best of these musicians choose to address a plurality of issues rather than dualistic and static sound-bites. They embrace paradoxical thinking, birthing new ways of expressing creativity, politics, humor and poetics. Women now occupy simultaneously the male territory of "neutrality" that accompanies power while still retaining an "otherness" — a place alive with risk-taking creativity. This will not last long. Already "women in rock" is not a novelty and in another generation their commonplaceness will hopefully mean creativity is finding avenues other then gender to inhabit. I look forward to a future where gender is no longer a glaring issue, defused from the territory of power, and we can then address more central concerns to our planetary survival and play.

— Andrea Juno, 1996

Women in

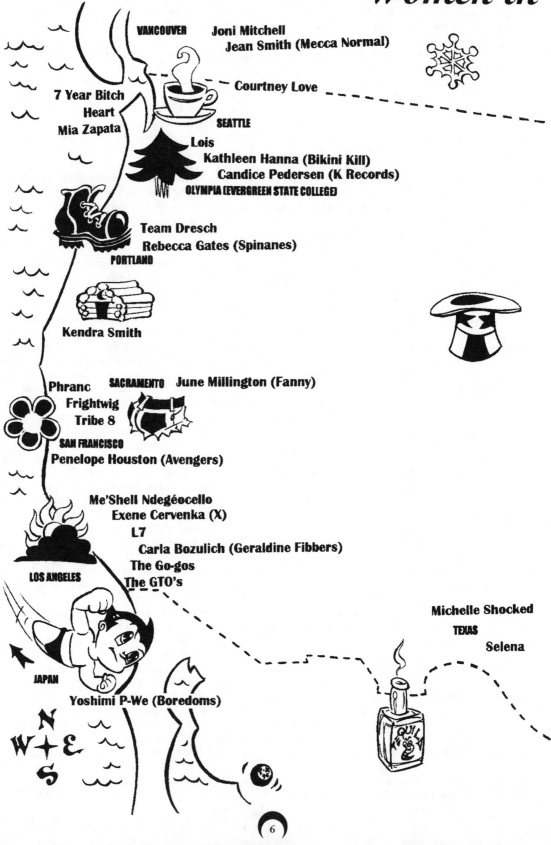

VANCOUVER Joni Mitchell
Jean Smith (Mecca Normal)

Courtney Love

7 Year Bitch
Heart
Mia Zapata

SEATTLE

Lois
Kathleen Hanna (Bikini Kill)
Candice Pedersen (K Records)
OLYMPIA (EVERGREEN STATE COLLEGE)

Team Dresch
Rebecca Gates (Spinanes)
PORTLAND

Kendra Smith

Phranc   SACRAMENTO   June Millington (Fanny)
Frightwig
Tribe 8
SAN FRANCISCO
Penelope Houston (Avengers)

Me'Shell Ndegéocello
Exene Cervenka (X)
L7
Carla Bozulich (Geraldine Fibbers)
The Go-gos
The GTO's

LOS ANGELES

Michelle Shocked
TEXAS
Selena

JAPAN

Yoshimi P-We (Boredoms)

N
W + E
S

Rock Map

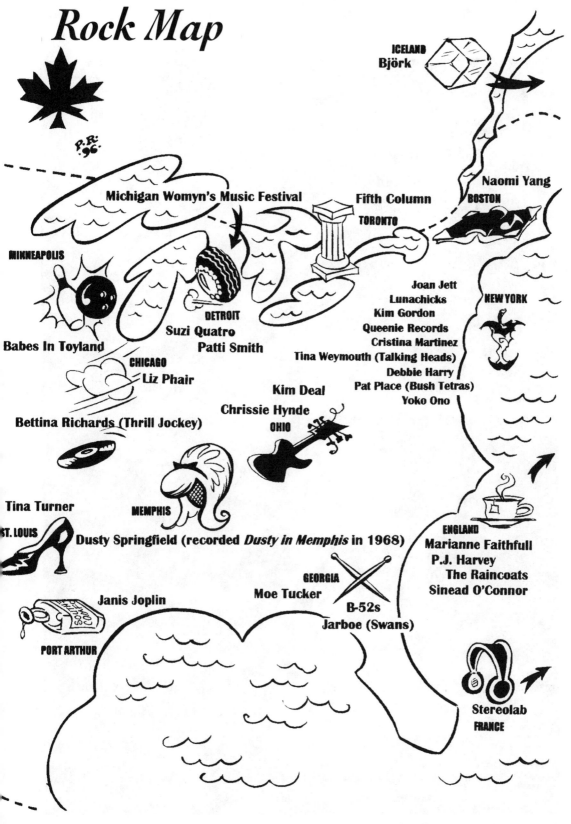

ICELAND
Björk

Naomi Yang
BOSTON

Michigan Womyn's Music Festival

Fifth Column
TORONTO

MINNEAPOLIS

Joan Jett
Lunachicks
Kim Gordon
Queenie Records
Cristina Martinez
Tina Weymouth (Talking Heads)
Debbie Harry
Pat Place (Bush Tetras)
Yoko Ono

NEW YORK

DETROIT
Suzi Quatro
Patti Smith

Babes In Toyland

CHICAGO
Liz Phair

Kim Deal

Chrissie Hynde
OHIO

Bettina Richards (Thrill Jockey)

Tina Turner
ST. LOUIS
Dusty Springfield (recorded *Dusty in Memphis* in 1968)

MEMPHIS

ENGLAND
Marianne Faithfull
P.J. Harvey
The Raincoats
Sinead O'Connor

GEORGIA
Moe Tucker

B-52s
Jarboe (Swans)

Janis Joplin

PORT ARTHUR

Stereolab
FRANCE

Map by: Abby McGanney Nolan & Pat Redding

7

Photo: Monica Curtin/Collage: Creole Blood

Jarboe

Jarboe, a singer and multi-faceted musician, has been a member of Swans since 1984. Her experimental side projects include *World of Skin* and *Beautiful People Ltd.* with Swans bandmate Michael Gira.

♦ **ANDREA JUNO: Were you in Swans from the beginning?**
♦ JARBOE: Oh, no. My background is a bit twisted. I've always loved music, and throughout college I was singing in lounges—I actually was part of a Holiday Inn lounge act! We did all the standards, like "Feelings." I had to memorize all these tunes; it was very difficult work. At the same time I was working in a studio in Atlanta that was affiliated with some people in Nashville. I did demo work, pitching songs to country-and-western singers. I did a demo pitching a Coca-Cola jingle; later, "real" people recorded it. Doing this taught me a certain discipline. When I was told to imitate Julie London and Linda Ronstadt, I realized, "I'm doing everybody else; I'm trying to sound like other people. But what's this doing for me? Do I want to go through my whole life doing cover versions? This isn't fulfilling *me* at all."

♦ **AJ: This is refreshing to hear. So much of the alternative music scene is populated by privileged dilettantes, slumming it after college. *You* were a working stiff like Weegee, going out to do a job. I respect people who have come out of a truly disciplined profession and then find and create their own art—with that rigorous and unglamorous background as a foundation.**
♦ J: At the time I *had* to do that. I was working my way through college with this skill: I could sing. By the time I could walk my father was teaching me music; he wanted me to be able to sing. My parents enrolled me in formal singing classes, and I was in every church choir

there ever was. I had no say in the matter; I was *forced* to do this. I remember being really tiny and my father sitting at the piano, hitting a note and making me sing that note. My parents crammed all this down my throat.

♦ **AJ: Were your parents musicians?**
♦ J: My father wanted to be one. He had a beautiful voice; he played piano and guitar—I think he was in the glee club in college. My father is a whole other topic. I don't really know how it happened, but he wound up working for the F.B.I. in Washington, D.C., under J. Edgar Hoover, and that's where he met my mother—in the basement of the F.B.I. building at the pistol range. She was a secretary at the F.B.I., and she worked her way up to being the personal secretary of the man directly under Hoover. She also was a sharpshooter; she loved shooting guns. So my dad was an F.B.I. agent who was a frustrated musician!

♦ **AJ: What was your childhood like? Were you in Georgia?**
♦ J: Actually, we moved a lot because my dad went undercover. He took on a lot of weird personas. He was from Chicago, but he learned all these rural dialects so he could "mingle." Once he grew a beard. It used to traumatize me as a child, because I didn't know who my father was! [laughs] It was very strange growing up with someone who was constantly changing his appearance, and disappearing for months at a time. He was in Mississippi doing something with the Civil Rights movement; I think he was tracking down an arson ring. He also spent a lot of time in San Francisco involved in some strange

9

Red (1991).

investigation. He was always traveling; he was away a lot.

His office phone downstairs had a "bug" on it. As a young girl I used the phone, and, unbeknownst to me, my dad was listening to my conversations: with boys, girlfriends, talking about what happened on a date. I may have exaggerated when I talked about sex; I probably was a virgin at the time! But my father heard all that. Some of the tapes we've been using in our recordings were originally surveillance tapes from my childhood phone.

◆ **AJ: How did you find out about the tapes?**
◆ **J:** When he died, I got the key to his desk. I was just looking for memorabilia, but I found all these bugging devices, like one enabling you to hear through walls. I found weird little cameras that could fit in the palm of your hand. And I found tapes on little open reels. A friend had an old open-reel tape player, and I started going through them — it's amazing what's on them. Swans are going to release a faux soundtrack album, *Soundtracks For The Blind*, and we're going to use a few of these surveillance tapes.

◆ **AJ: Is this also a record of your life?**
◆ **J:** Not just me, but others, too — people who were bugged in hotel rooms. The tapes are not identified; I don't know who the people are or how top-

secret their business was.

◆ **AJ: This reminds me of Michael Powell's movie *Peeping Tom*, which is basically about this kid who's been filmed all his life by his scientist father, and then becomes a murderer. This seems to be an amazing destiny, that now here you are, as a public performer onstage, being captured *again* by cameras and recording devices — once again under surveillance.**

◆ **J:** I hadn't thought of that before. I did become very paranoid as I grew up; my father hated how I was developing. I really wanted to be this crazy flower child, and when I was 13 I actively sought out drugs and started taking them all the time. I would procure the LSD or psilocybin and take it in my bedroom alone, by myself, and it had nothing to do with partying or to get a kick; it was very *scientific*: wanting to put myself through the most extreme experience. And my dad *had* to have known, just by looking at me! Having a father like this — Mr. Law Enforcement — affected my whole development.

> **Throughout college I was singing in lounges — I actually was part of a Holiday Inn lounge act! We did all the standards, like "Feelings."**

◆ **AJ: Did he ever mention anything you'd said on the phone?**
◆ **J:** No — I never *knew* he was recording me. When I finally found somebody with that antiquated recorder capable of playing back these tapes, I was horrified at what he had heard. When I was 13 I had a boyfriend who was 16 — that was a big deal, having an older boyfriend. He was really handsome, with wavy blond hair,

and I couldn't figure out why he was interested in asking me out—I couldn't believe it. I had a long relationship with him, and told him everything and did drugs with him. He'd pick me up after I'd had a night of "tripping" and drive me around with his friends. He was one of the first boys who tried to touch me, and I let him do it—I kind of idolized him. Then his family moved away, and I found out that my father had approached this boy's father, and had hired the boy to report back to him on my activities!

♦ **AJ: Unbelievable—this is almost entrapment, in that this boy may have been leading you to do things you wouldn't necessarily have done otherwise. And what's truly mind-boggling is that your father was complicit in causing you to do the very things he was *most* afraid of you doing.**

♦ J: It's very odd. My father was such an oppressive force in my life that it wasn't until I finally moved to New York that I was able to experience freedom—get away from it all.

♦ **AJ: How did you join Swans?**

♦ J: When I moved to New York, I was already a big fan of Swans. In Atlanta, I had listened to music all the time; I had about 3,500 record albums. I met a group of people who had a radio show and were playing Throbbing Gristle, etc., and that made me see things in a different way...in terms of possibilities where I could begin creating something original. I started performing in galleries, and before I knew about Diamanda Galás I was using contact microphones and putting my voice through different gadgets and delays. It sounds naive now, but then, being nude and smearing my body with liver and blood and doing all this in a gallery setting seemed kind of *innovative*! [Laughs.]

I probably would have continued doing that and become a performance artist if I hadn't heard Swans' *Filth* album. Hearing that made me decide I wanted to be in Swans. I thought it was amazing; it sounded tribal, scary, creepy, and really intense. I played that record all the time: a steady diet of Swans plus Bach's *Goldberg Variations*, and Whitehouse—that's all I listened to. I was starting to body-build 4-5 hours a day, and listening to Swans really made me sweat and move weights—this brought out a savage side I didn't know I had: a voracious, animalistic side. I *had* to move to New York and contact Swans.

♦ **AJ: How old were you then?**

♦ J: Late twenties, around 1983-84. I went to the address I had and—I'd never seen anything like the Lower East Side or Avenue A [laughs]—it looked like a no man's land. Back then it was totally deserted, compared to the trendy bar and café and boutique area it is today. It was scary as hell—frightening.

> **I would procure the LSD and take it in my bedroom alone. It had nothing to do with partying; it was very *scientific*— putting myself through the most extreme experience.**

I initially contacted Swans under slightly false premises. I was working for an art magazine, and I said I was going to interview them for an article—when really I wanted to join them. I did meet them and interview them and went to a rehearsal; they wouldn't allow me in the room but I could sit outside the door and listen—it was incredible, the walls were shaking and thundering. On my first visits to the East Village I met Swans, Lydia Lunch, Jim Thirwell, Sonic Youth (Kim Gordon and Thurston Moore). When I returned to Atlanta I couldn't stop thinking about moving there. It was definitely the strongest compelling force I'd ever known.

♦ **AJ: And you were doing lounge music then?**

♦ J: That had ended and I was doing those gallery performances, hanging around a small group of weird, creative artists and students. I was married to a corporate systems analyst; I had a very proper kind of life during the day, and went to the symphony with him at night. Then back home I'd put on overalls and Doc Martens and go out to join my other friends who were into hardcore and noise music. So I had this secret life late at night; I had two different personas.

For a long time I tried to have both lives balanced. A friend even gave me a time clock—like what hourly wage-earners use to punch their cards on the job—saying, "This is for one life, but you also have your secret life, and you can have it all." But I found that you *can't* have it all. You can't be married to a corporate guy and go to the symphony and meet his friends and go on sailboat trips on weekends, and also wear Doc Martens and go to Circle Jerks concerts. At least *I* couldn't do this for very long.

My blood was getting hot; I had to get back to New York and be with people who were *doing something* with their lives. My best friend said I must need to be challenged.

So I destroyed my whole life. I had a high-rise apartment with a lot of beautiful furniture, nice clothes, and gourmet cookware, but I sold everything I owned and ended my life there. I divorced the person I was married to, said goodbye to my family and all my friends. I also had a lover at the time, and I said goodbye to him, too. I destroyed it all and came to New York.

◆ **AJ: Then what?**
◆ **J:** I hung around New York for about a year trying to get into Swans—that was my goal. It took a year: making people realize I wasn't a flake, that I had some kind of integrity, that I meant what I said...that I could be strong.

Finally Swans gave me an audition. At the time the question was: "What do we need in the group? We could use another bass player." Or, "Instead of playing tapes with noises, we could get some kind of sampling device and re-create those sounds live onstage." I said, "Name it—I'll learn either one; I don't care." It was Michael Gira who said, "Well, do sampling, because we can expand the sound of the group if we have someone doing samples." I went out and bought a sampling keyboard, learned how to sample, and created this barrage or wall of sound to augment the standard instrumentation of bass, drums and guitar.

At one point I was burned with a cigarette on my left breast; I still have the scar. I was bound and gagged, with a group standing around spitting on me. This had nothing to do with sex; it was about using you as an object; treating you like shit.

◆ **AJ: What about your singing?**
◆ **J:** I was on tour with Swans for a couple years before I used my voice; I didn't try to tell them I could sing—I had to audition to do *that*. The audition was the most nervous night of my life. The band members were intimidating: big, tough-looking men. They rehearsed without their shirts on, and it was all sweat and macho tough guys. I auditioned, they had a meeting, they said, "Okay." I was thrilled, but I knew it wasn't over yet.

I discovered my ability to take a certain level of—not necessarily *pain*, but humiliation, and I tested my breaking point.

I did a long, grueling tour with Swans, and recorded with them, too, just doing sampling. We were ridiculously loud, and I was stupid to not wear earplugs. I remember blowing the sound system in places like Vienna, Austria: there were distorted speakers a foot from my head and my ears were almost *bleeding*. It's amazing I'm not deaf.

I had to be macho, I had to be tough. I had to lug my own equipment and everything I owned myself; I couldn't ask for any help. I had to put up with being in an enclosed bus with everyone chain-smoking and not say anything, even though I didn't smoke or drink or do drugs then; I was completely "straight" in every sense of the word. I had to put up with almost constant drunkenness from nearly every member of the group, constant chain-smoking, and a whole behavior system that was counter to my way of thinking, which involved body-building and vegetarianism.

◆ **AJ: Back in the early '80s it seemed like there was a much more macho, male orientation in the underground arts scene.**
◆ **J:** There was a period in my life, up to my mid-twenties, when I wanted so desperately to be performing and creating that kind of energy and power myself. And at the time there were no doors open to me whatsoever. I can't tell you the sexism I've encountered. The things I've come across in music have been overwhelming; so closed, so negative against females—right in your face, right in the room. And you have to go through that yourself. Maybe it's different with these young groups starting now, but I know that I went through the *wringer* with that. There was a time when the only way I knew how to get close to that power was to have sex with those people.

In Atlanta, I was involved with some people who organized "sexual entertainment" for visiting celebrities. It was just a job: I never hung around backstage. I worked for a guy who was very professional, and when these "big-name rock'n'rollers" came to town, I was one of the people who would go to their hotel and provide "services" for them. So I can understand women who do that, because I did it for a brief period of my youth.

I didn't use "Jarboe"; I used a different name. I was on certain groups' tour riders, which listed things to be provided in different cities—

Photo: Wim Van De Hulst

♦ **AJ: Big groups?**
♦ J: Very big, yes. I would be on a rider [of a band's contract]; I would be requested. There was a difference between me and the girls and women I would describe as groupies, or hopefuls; they would try to get backstage, even just to be with the lighting man, whereas in my case it didn't matter who it was. I was hired because I had the ability to endure, and to provide for the peculiar needs of some of these people. It was me and about a dozen other women, and eventually we were very specific in what we were specializing in, and for me it was this incredible endurance. I didn't even know I had it in me.

When I first got involved in this work, it was sort of mild. But it evolved to where I was the one who was probably involved in *the* most peculiar, *the* most extreme activities; I wound up doing things like being urinated on, being tied up, and otherwise mistreated, but generally nothing that would damage "the plaything." It was, after all, just "games" to them. At one point—I don't really want to name a lot of names—I was burned with a cigarette on my left breast; I still have the scar. I was bound and gagged, with a group standing around spitting on me. A lot of this activity really had nothing to do with sex; it was about using you as an object; treating you like shit. It was very intense. I discovered my ability to take a certain level of—not necessarily *pain*, but humiliation, and I tested my breaking point.

It was interesting for me, because mentally I was able to get myself to another place, and do it. I don't know if I want to say that I *enjoyed* it, but in a way I enjoyed it more than some phony intimacy. There was no warmth involved; it was an athletic experience. That's the best way I can describe it: athletic endurance, which I've always enjoyed. That's what I like about being tattooed, about any number of things: the athletic endurance and the mental challenge that's involved. Rather than breaking me, it's like there's a little seed inside my brain so that I'm *really* tough now, I don't experience stage fright, I can do anything in front of any group. I don't know what it means to have stage fright, to feel "less" than or afraid of an audience, because I think of these past experiences—I could do anything! I'm just *there*. And anything someone could do to me wouldn't hurt me. It's hard to be self-conscious in front of a concert audience when you've performed in a much more revelatory arena.
♦ **AJ: This is so much like what I found when I did the book** *Modern Primitives*: **these explorations of difficulty where pain is transcended.**

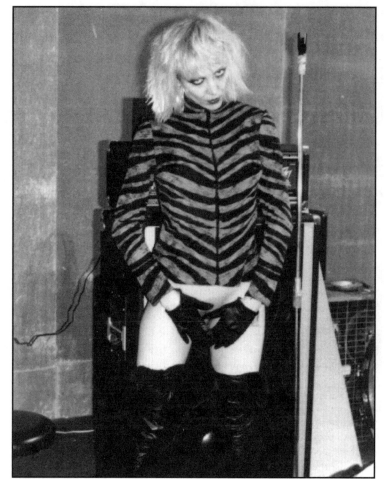

Self-portrait: early persona.

♦ J: It's a discipline.

♦ **AJ: This is intense, because what you're describing in your encounters with these rock groups is the *male* end of things. Contract riders that include a woman as if she were part of the liquor allotment are a perfect example of the need to control and objectify. You had a glimpse of what most people don't see—the world of these male rock'n'roll figures.**

♦ J: Oh, yeah. It's more ridiculous than the average person would even think, especially in those days. Now the media isn't giving those kinds of groups as much attention anymore; things like MTV and the magazines are mostly geared more towards a strange variation of alternative rock. Whereas I'm talking about the era of Judas Priest, AC/DC, Kiss, and Van Halen: the heyday of a whole different mentality. That's when I was involved in the arena-rock world—I've heard it called "hairspray metal." Of

course, that's almost passé, at this point—

♦ **AJ: Not really!**

♦ J: These people were very excessive, spoiled beyond belief, and fetishistic to the point of being just spoiled little babies. That was the kind of world that I saw: very pompous, money-is-no-object, excessive drug use, very exploitative of tremendous numbers of women. Flying here, flying there—a lot of money being wasted, indulgence that I think is really vulgar and *pornographic*.

♦ **AJ: It's truly perverse. And that's not something I would ever say about someone like Bob Flanagan, or you— you embody, to me, something that's very spiritual; You've gone deep into your core and rechanneled it. To me, those guys you've described, who are so *unconscious,* are perverse. You were paid?**

♦ J: —a lot of money. Unfortunately, at that time I had a cocaine habit, and I drank a great deal, so a lot of the money went to that. I regret not tucking it away and investing it in a money market fund or something. But it was "easy money," and it went away easily. It culminated when I had to put myself into a private clinic. I got off the alcohol, I got off the coke, I cleaned myself out and I changed my life. I started bodybuilding, gaining weight, exercising, shaved off all my hair; real athletic.

After that, I came up to New York and met Swans. When I first moved to the city, I worked for a while on 49th Street; I worked in one of those booths, on the phone.

♦ **AJ: Phone sex?**

♦ J: No; just being in a bedroom setting, and men would come in and you'd pick up the phone and talk to them, and they'd look at you. I did that temporarily. I couldn't do it; *I could not do it*. It just was a way to make money, because when you first move to New York it really hits you—you've got to make a lot of money really fast.

♦ **AJ: You had changed so much you couldn't do that kind of work anymore?**

♦ J: No, I couldn't. I couldn't deal with the people running that operation; they were awful, really sleazy. I could not handle it. I realized I could no longer even *pretend* to do it—I didn't have it in me anymore.

I was in this phase of being a teetotaling vegetarian. It was a complete backlash; I became the complete opposite of the person I had been before, who was now unrecognizable to me: bleached blond hair, a lot of makeup, high heels, traditional rock 'n' roll clothing. When I first met Michael I referred to anything in my past as *"She"*—that's how radical the transformation was. I have very foggy memories of the person that I was, of those experiences she had. I'm amazed at that person. Because to be that extroverted, just hurling yourself into dangerous situations, is something that now I don't have in me. Now I'm very tight, I'm very organized, very directed. All that matters to me is my work. I'm very businesslike in how I do my work. I don't spend my energy on anything like what that person did anymore; I don't have time for that.

> **I would be on a rider [of a band's contract]. I was hired because I had the ability to endure, to provide peculiar needs. I didn't even know I had it in me.**

I think she was sort of silly, that other person. She was looking for something, and I don't think she knew what it was. *Now* I know what it is: it culminated in being an artist, and those grueling experiences were research for my artwork! Now that I look at it that way, I can live with it. But I experienced so much humiliation and shame for so long. I never talked about it to anyone. I knew that if it was understood at all, it would be laughed at, or sensationalized, or trivialized, and it's not trivial. It's a hell of a lot to endure, when a woman puts herself in those positions, and it does alter you forever.

But reading about this shouldn't hurt any-one who loves me or cares about me, because it didn't hurt *me*: I just absorbed it. I really identify with the Clive Barker films, when different creatures pull themselves up from the blood matter and become a form—I know that well. I absorbed all this *destruction*, and became someone else. I just hope that even beyond the music and the lyrics, I can do something more with my viewpoint, whether it might be a novel, or an autobiography, something that would dwell more on what I learned. So many times those sorts of experiences are trivialized, and seen as indicating the limitations of what a woman can be. But I don't fit into the mold of some sleazy strung-out person: I've attended operas, and I have a tremendous interest in gourmet cuisine. In fact, inside I feel quite elegant, and yet what people want to do is describe someone who's been through those experiences as trashy.

♦ **AJ: Your work is still taking those risks that you used to take; they're channeled now into your art.**

♦ J: There's a song on *Sacrificial Cake* called "Surgical Savior," and that song says so much about what I went through. I read an article recently about bloodletting and this whole movement in San Francisco, and I understood all that. I was amazed: "Oh, now it's in the magazines, so many years later, when I knew about those sorts of things over 15 years ago."

♦ **AJ: People have unconscious ways of trying to get life back in when their bodies are numb. There are people who do things such as cutting the skin compulsively; that impulse comes from something like an inner gyroscope that's trying to shock the system back to life. But we don't have many "legitimate" avenues in society for how to accomplish that.**

♦ J: That's true; you have to provide that for yourself. Like you say, it seems like a lot of American society has become numb. I'll never be that way now.

At 25, I didn't even know what I was looking for. I just knew that I had to get close to what I thought was "power" (which is almost a clichéd word for me to use); I just knew I had to get close to *something*, and that's what was out there. The way I fell into doing that sex work was very accidental; it was never my career plan. It started out very casually, and then I started getting more involved in that role-playing, and gradually I underwent a severe personality change. The cockiness, and confidence, and everything about me—even my voice—was very different in those days. I absorbed an iden-

Jarboe with Michael Gira (1987).

tity, and then made it my own. It was a mask. At one time I was drinking Scotch when I first got up in the morning; it was nothing to use $150 worth of cocaine in a day. I was on a fast track, never slowing down—until I pretty much just passed out.

♦ AJ: How do you connect this with your childhood, and your father, and your family?

♦ J: I think perhaps, in some ways, it was the ultimate rebellion. It definitely showed me a face I hadn't had. In school I had been the perfect little A student, the teacher's pet, very reliable and always turning my homework in on time; and then in this phase it was just like I was *screaming* against all of that. When I visited my family, they saw me in every kind of bizarre phase: with bright red hair, bleached-blonde hair, a mohawk...I looked ridiculous, and I'm sure they must have been embarrassed, and thought that I was just going through some kind of phase—which I was, but I don't know if they understood how severe a phase it was. I wasn't much in contact with any of my childhood friends or family. I was too lost.

♦ AJ: But not exactly lost; it's more like you went into the woods to get to the other side, to *find* yourself. It was also a journey that was about power. When you described your father, and then these arena-rockers—it was

really about that same sort of wall of control and power.

♦ J: Oh, My father was the same thing. He was incredible. I've never met anyone like him. I suppose some of the men who are in Washington, or work for some of these big companies must be like that. But I don't know anyone like that now; he was really *all-encompassing.*

♦ AJ: We all have to deal with this question of power, which for you was manifested early in your father. Confronting it through these rock'n'roll figures seems to have been a way to actually involve yourself in the extremes of experiencing such power: by being in a situation of subjugation.

♦ J: Yeah; that's the perfect way to describe it. I willingly allowed myself to go through that to get closer to the power I wanted.

♦ AJ: So many women do similar things. The problem is that until recently, nobody really talked about it.

♦ J: I don't feel comfortable talking about this. I can talk about it to you because I really respect the books you've done. I would not feel comfortable talking about this for some article in a rock'n'roll magazine.

♦ AJ: I believe that the transparency of this kind of conversation reflects a kind of revolution of women taking power back for themselves. So many women can relate to what you're saying; it's just that this kind of story has been closeted even in feminist rhetoric. It's important that our history be *available.* There are almost no oral or film or any basic media records that disclose this material— conversations like these have remained secret, outside of public forums of intelligent conversations, relegated to trashy sensationalism. And what we're discussing is a key issue: a woman trying to get close to power, experiencing her own pain and humiliation, and then being able to talk about it.

It's amazing how one-sided the groupie's shame is. Does Mick Jagger or Wilt Chamberlain—celebrities who have publicly bragged about their thousands of conquests— feel ashamed? A woman's shame over sexuality is used by the status quo to maintain and reinforce its power. Shame is planted in our psyches for us to internalize, so that we don't rock the social boat—iron manacles are replaced, in effect, by the mechanism of shame.

Shame has to do with who owns power. If people are made to feel ashamed of physical traits like dark skin, kinky hair, or facial hair like Frida Kahlo's, well, why? Because the power system has created standards of beauty based on blatant racism and sexism: that some races are inferior, and that genders have to conform to narrow constraints. By the same token, why should women be ashamed of their sexuality? Once shame starts to unravel, then power starts to unravel. Openness diffuses shame, and in fact transfers the power of it to one's own creative ends.

♦ J: I've tried to look at my past that way. I've kept notes and memorabilia on my experiences, and have thought about writing a book, although I don't want to be just another one of those women who drop names—

♦ AJ: **You have taken your own experiences and transcended them. You've embarked on the journey of your own transformation—and it's not just *yours*! It's a women's journey; we can all relate.**

♦ J: I've found out what happened to some of the women I knew during that time frame, and I'm pretty lucky! Some of them turned to hardcore, dangerous, painful activities: flogging, torture and other sadism. They turned their backs on so many options. They're living that life and can't do anything else. Some are completely messed up on drugs. Some are dead.

I don't know what it is that keeps hope alive inside. No matter how depressed or black I feel, an inner drive just keeps me going. I think Michael has that also. Sonic Youth were good friends of Michael's. He used to see them almost every day. Both groups started out from the same place, and now they've gone on to a level of commercial success that's astronomical, compared with Swans. Yet we've continued to work without that kind of recognition, or that kind of teenage audience. Maybe what we're after isn't what other people, who might give up, are after. That actual spark inside can't be taken away.

♦ AJ: **It's very difficult to keep one's creativity in the spotlight. Too much publicity can be a curse—although I think Sonic Youth has managed to preserve their creativity and edge under that media glare; they seem to have a very healthy attitude. Society picks certain types and rockets them upward, but often just to shoot them down. It's the hardest task to keep being creative under that kind of pressure.**

♦ J: As far as pressure goes, what comes to mind is Kurt Cobain.

♦ AJ: **Media fame can provide a psychic journey into your own hell. You have to sort out** your masks, and people have many masks. You know how people talk about you at a party; when you become famous that gossip and defamation becomes what people say about you in the press. Our society has such limited and puerile language with which to discuss the complex and different selves one has. So the media describes Kurt Cobain in a certain way, and he starts to identify with that representation.

♦ J: I think it's best not to read those kinds of articles in magazines. I know *my* feelings have gotten hurt, especially after doing an interview for 3 or 4 days with some journalist who seems to be treating you with a lot of respect, and then all that appears in the article is, "Jarboe was wearing a green dress." That happens all the time: my work, my input which I care about, is continually glossed over. All people see is some facade.

> **I really identify with Clive Barker films, when different creatures pull themselves up from the blood matter and become a form. I absorbed all this *destruction*, and became someone else.**

My first solo album came out, and it was totally eclectic; I was taking chances presenting a wide variety of material. I don't care what anyone says; I'm going to keep doing work like that. And *Alternative Press* didn't review my record or interview me, but in their photo issue they printed a photo of me which was provocative. They wouldn't present any of my *work*, just show my body. And that just says it all.

♦ AJ: **That's a typical way of dismissing somebody.**

♦ J: We did an interview on the Internet recently, and out of the blue came all these questions about a latex dress I wore at a concert in the early '80s! I thought: why are we talking about this dress—I don't know why I wore that. Wearing that dress onstage had nothing to do with trying to look sexy; it was more: I liked the way it felt under the hot lights! Years ago I went through this phase of liking rubber. Anyway, I certainly didn't think the interview should fo-

cus on a latex dress I wore ten years ago.

♦ **AJ: So much of the media is superficial— and superficiality is rewarded handsomely in our culture. Crass people, who haven't touched the depths of pain or love or anything significant, are content to exist merely on that surface level. But I have an incredible faith that creativity does go out like a beacon, even though only a small number of people might notice. There is a transmission of knowledge, and it isn't necessarily through the linear process of mailing out your press kit or by record sales; somehow, your thoughts will get out. It's important to have faith in your work, and not get caught up in what the current big hypes are—as if they're the only** *reality.*

♦ J: Besides the media issue, in the music business the question is: Who can you trust? The music business is full of people who don't understand anything to do with honesty or trust. People say one thing and don't mean it, or something is always right around the corner. You don't know what words are true. For that reason I wanted to be really careful about who was going to release my current solo album. I did the work; I prepared for it; and I suffered tremendously to get it out. Then it's: "Can I trust you with this?"

We did one album with a major label, MCA, where all the power was taken away from us. We had to use a producer (we weren't allowed to produce it ourselves), and everything down to the publicity photos was determined by someone else. People were flying in from Los Angeles to oversee a photo shoot, and then flying out. They didn't trust us on any level. While this album was being recorded I was thinking, "Well, these guest musicians are great, but what does this have to do with us?" Everybody was coming in and doing their song-and-dance. The producer has done some great recordings, but as to whether or not this was a good Swans album...

♦ **AJ: It's funny: they come to you for your unique sound, and then they want you to sound like somebody else!**

♦ J: That producer said he loved the *Children of God* album we did in Cornwall, England. *The Great Annihilator* picks up where *Children of God* left off. Everything done in between, while we bounced around on some tiny independent labels, involved finding our footing again—that's how I look at it. You know when it's working; when the album's saying what you want it to say. And to have somebody you don't even know produce your work—that's ridiculous. I can't imagine having some stranger mix your song; the mix is everything.

I think those corporations look at each other's balance sheets. If a big company comes along and invests a lot of money in you and they don't recoup their investment, it affects another company's decision to pick you up. It's rare that they care about your artistry. They look at the bottom line: "Can we market this, can we package this, can we sell this?" And they don't look at the circumstances: they don't care that there was no publicity; they don't care that your record wasn't sent to radio stations; they don't care that the A & R person quit the week your record came out.

My father would force me to touch [the snakes] because he didn't want me to have fear. So I got a huge snake tattoo that wraps around my body.

All that happened to us. We were left in a situation where we'd get on the phone, and we didn't know who we were talking to; it was a total bureaucracy. They didn't have a *clue* as to who we were. The whole department that had known about us was gone—they all left. We were left in this corporate void, where we were just a tax write-off. To go with one of these major companies you need to have a clause—it might be called a "one-man" clause—that says that the representative who "discovered" you, signed you, and understands your concept has to stay there. If that person leaves, it's null and void.

♦ **AJ: This is the whole mythology about the major labels somehow giving you wealth and fame, and somehow being so mighty and powerful—and artistic—and it's just not true.**

♦ J: I don't want to act as the spokesperson for Swans, because that's Michael's project. I can speak for my solo work, but as far as Swans go, he's the visionary. But Michael has gone so far as to say that our major-label disaster ruined his career. It was that severe a blow. We would have been better off staying on the indie labels and just quietly building our momentum.

♦ **AJ: I think it's amazing that you had the force of will to say, "I want to be in Swans,"** and then followed through. **Swans was a very "male" group before you came in.**

♦ J: I had to prove myself. It took a year to get in the group, and during that year I did everything: I cut out press clippings, I pasted them up, I made the press kits and took them to get photocopied. I answered fan mail, I made calls, I was an office go-fer. The first tour I went on was in '84, as a roadie—the most difficult thing to lift up and carry being Michael Gira himself, every night when he was drunk. I had the solid biceps to do it, then. Of course, that was before bodybuilding became such a fashion. And it was also before my physical makeup and immune system were so severly damaged by years of vegetarianism.

♦ AJ: I remember seeing photos of Lisa Lyons [the weight lifter] in the early eighties and being shocked. Our perceptions have changed so radically, by regular exposure to female muscles, that at this point Lisa Lyons wouldn't really shock anyone—look at Madonna's muscles, or Linda Hamilton's in *The Terminator*. That physique is perceived as sexy, not freakish anymore.

♦ J: I still love free weights; I do reps with fifty pounds when I'm not travel-

Photo: Monica Curtin

ing. But I used to do serious body-building. I loved it so much that I think I could have gone into competition body-building. Henry Rollins says, "Fifty pounds is *always* fifty pounds." Reliability. Constancy. You know what you're dealing with.

♦ AJ: **When you were first around Swans, were you sexualized?**

♦ J: I remember being looked over like a piece of meat! Ultimately it was through a *mental* alignment that Michael and I got involved. I saw that he shaped the images and the sound. The other people were basically doing what he told them to do. The essence of the group wasn't necessarily the thundering bass or the heavy drums, it was the creative spark behind it. And that was what I really was after. But the way we became involved was gradual; we slowly built. It's been really hard; we're very different.

♦ AJ: **The whole issue of the links between mind, body, sexuality and creativity—there is a fusionary attraction to another creative**

person, and sexuality does enter into it—is not to be taken lightly. But too often women get dismissed if they're sexually involved with another person in the group, as though that's all there is. That kind of reduction serves to trivialize sexuality and the kind of creativity that's sparked by sexuality; in our culture, women and sexuality in general are shunted off to a realm of "inferior" expression—

♦ J: I see that. When I got involved with Michael, one of my best girlfriends now (and her friends), who had followed Swans from the beginning, hated it after I joined. They just perceived me as "the girlfriend getting into the group," or something like that. She said that I was hated. I was really shocked to hear this. Of course, now she says they all know they were wrong, because I've contributed something *tangible*. Michael is so particular about his work that he would never permit any involvement that wasn't important.

♦ AJ: **People are suspicious of such involve-**

Beautiful People Ltd. (1992).

ments, and of course it's impossible to imagine the opposite situation: a man joining an all-woman band through his relationship with one of the members.

♦ J: In my own life, going from the position I was in (and again, I wasn't part of any slave trade). I was 25 and on my knees getting piss in my face—I did that willingly without anyone coercing me into it. It's strange, because I did develop a tremendous strength from doing that. It didn't break me at all; if anything, it made me incredibly strong internally. At one time I regretted those experiences, but I don't anymore—I'm distanced enough. I even think I *had* to put myself through a kind of ordeal, to reflect back my own creative potential.

And now I've almost come full circle, to the point where, for example, I can remember one night in Austria when four young boys came to my dressing room with roses, and followed me back to my hotel. They stood underneath my hotel room window all night, calling up, hoping to get into my hotel room [laughs]. My feet have been kissed while onstage. I get letters containing nude photographs of boys, with piercings in their genitals (they think I'm interested in that), and all kinds of sexy letters. People give me their beeper numbers… .

♦ AJ: Now you're the rock star—

♦ J: I don't want to call myself that! But it really has come full circle: here are people wanting to have sex with me, selling *me* their bodies: "I will give you pleasure. Whatever you want, I'm available for you." I find this really funny: in the span of a decade, I've gone from one end of the spectrum to the other.

♦ **AJ: And now you're in a position of creative power.**

♦ **J:** Sometimes I wonder…. When I did that "fetishistic entertainment," I had bleached blonde hair and wore spandex pants [laughs] and I don't think any of those people would recognize me now. I wonder if they ever go, "Hey, it's *that* girl!" This gives me a secret thrill.

♦ **AJ: It is a thrill to transform oneself. When I was young I remember being so disconnected from my self, from *everything*—I was like this waif being used by one man after another. But, really, it was a *search* for my self; I was searching for my *own* creative power. Until you get that spark of recognition: "Oh, I can do this!" you may impose that search on other people, looking for that fusional experience. Of course, any humiliation and abuse you encounter drives you further back to your own self.**

I regard this as a heroic journey, one that's rarely discussed. Recently I read Pamela Des Barres's book, *I'm With The Band*. Previously I had dismissed it as the story of a flighty Valley Girl groupie, but she also had this spark of creativity—within her own terms: being in a band, the GTO's, and being involved with Frank Zappa. There are embarrassing parts to her story, but still…

I don't know what it is that keeps hope alive inside. No matter how depressed or black I feel, an inner drive just keeps me going.

♦ J: I don't want to read that, because I have my own perspective and until I write something myself, I don't want her perspective infiltrating or altering my thoughts. I know that during that whole phase of my life, the humiliation and indignity that I experienced made me stronger. I confronted and conquered a level of fear and ego. Actually, Michael incorporated some of my experiences into the early stories in his book *The Consumer*.

When I first decided to get a tattoo (and I have a lot, but they're not anywhere you can see them when I have clothes on), I didn't get them for fashion or to have someone comment on them; I got them as indelible stamps marking experiences. The first one I got is a nude woman kneeling with her hands tied behind her back, looking down with her hair falling around her face. That was my way of leaving that life behind, yet I wanted to remember "that woman" and those experiences (I've also taken this kneeling posture on stage, and then risen from it to sing). That started the whole idea that every tattoo I got would have some kind of personal meaning. Now I have quite a few, and every one is a commemoration.

♦ **AJ: The body as history, marking *true* rites of passage because they are moments of transition in your life.**

♦ J: When I first started getting tattoos, I had to go to a place that was less than sanitary, frequented by bikers and rednecks. I was tattooed by two bearded, fat, crazy guys (one was doing it and the other was an apprentice) who were leering at me. Over the years I watched this tattoo scene explode to the point where fashion models were having it done. Eventually I wound up with this artist who would only tattoo for spiritual reasons; if you came into his shop and wanted some tacky design, he'd kick you out! [laughs] From one end of the scene to the other.

I did an interview for the now-defunct *Creem* magazine; the actual interview was great, but the article ended up as a big photo plus a few soundbites. I had said I was studying Buddhism, and it is something I enjoy studying; I read Buddhist texts and have participated in ceremonies. But I don't like calling myself *anything*. And the text read: "Buddhist. Modern Primitive." I looked at that and yelled, "Hey, Michael—I'm a Modern Primitive!"

♦ **AJ: To be so reduced—**

♦ J: I can't take it seriously, but I found it highly amusing. I didn't know I "was one" until I read that! I was at a coffee shop on Avenue A in the East Village—these coffee bars are everywhere now; that's a change—and a gang of kids came in. One guy had a piercing here, studs there, and bolts in his ears—they *all* had 'em, plus braids or dreadlocks. I think that look

started in San Francisco, via Africa of course.

♦ **AJ: It's even in the suburbs now. I have tattoos, but very few people have seen them. They're not for fashion, but for a combination of reasons: protection, marking, my personal history, occult meaning…**

♦ J: Some people may wonder why someone would have tattoos where they can't be seen…as if one would only go through that to show off? That's missing the whole point.

> **The Dalai Lama was [in New York]… we were outside of the Jumbotron in Times Square, viewing an animated Green Tara. I wondered, "What is going through their heads?"**

I have Tibetan and Buddhist symbols. I thought that if I were killed in an accident, they would provide some sort of identification as to what I'm truly about. Earlier in my life—not so much now—I had a connection with snakes. When I was a little girl—three or four—living in rural Mississippi, I would go down to the swamps where there were all these snakes everywhere, hanging from trees. My father would force me to touch them because he didn't want me to have fear. So I got a huge snake tattoo that wraps around my body—it was unbelievably painful having it done. It's very textured and detailed, with many scales and different colors. That took days of solid work. Actually, that was a wonderful experience: the slicing into the raw flesh, the blood everywhere. The endorphins that kicked in were tremendous. That was a real rite of passage. When you're being cut over your stomach again and again and again, forever—that was overwhelmingly painful, but euphoric.

♦ **AJ: So you're not afraid of snakes?**

♦ J: My mother has always been scared of them; my father wasn't and he didn't want me to be either. I remember going to tent revival meetings in Mississippi and Louisiana when my dad was undercover—he was unbelievable in disguise; he had an old beat-up truck and took on a completely different persona. He grew up in an urban environment, had an M.A. in psy-

Photo: Laura Levine

very tiny. Again, I was asked to perform, so I would stand on this platform and sing these songs and people would like it.

The other side of the family was in New Orleans, which has all these wonderful graveyards. I would go visit the family and attend the Mardi Gras festival. I vividly remember being up on my father's shoulders and watching the masks and magnificent costumes going by, and all the beautiful, colorful, glistening glass beads being thrown out — not cheap stuff like now. I had a box of all these jewels I'd collected. I remember getting lost in the middle of a huge crowd. On one hand, I'm terrified of crowd environments, and on the other hand I find myself in those environments all the time! That's what a rock club is like, and in our early days we played clubs where you had to walk through the crowd to get onstage (there were no dressing rooms). I remember feeling all this fear as I went through those crowds — all the faces, all the noise, all the lights... .

♦ **AJ: That is a kind of modern ritual of communal ecstasy — the only place we can experience that. Most clubs and underground music involve a nod to death and the darker sides — which is what Mardi Gras and the Day of the Dead acknowledge and celebrate.**

♦ J: I have so many memories and experiences involving snakes wherever we moved. Finally we moved to Georgia and rented a house in the middle of a huge field, with woods and a creek nearby, and again there were snakes. I remember my father holding me while we watched a snake devour a mouse; I was afraid he was going to drop me on top of them! He collected rattlesnake rattles, and had a huge box of them on top of a dresser. Sometimes I would wander into his room and reach my hand up and just feel them. I think he'd killed a lot of them and chopped off the rattles himself.

♦ **AJ: Did you keep them?**

♦ J: I want to know what happened to them. After he died there was a feeding frenzy: people were beating down the doors and stealing souvenirs from his apartment. I didn't know who many of these people were — they were coming out of the woodwork — but they were ringing the doorbell and saying, "Well, you know we were good friends, and I sure would like to have this." It's amazing how many people wanted mementos while my mother was still grieving. I was lucky to find those tapes and get them out of

chology, and was very sophisticated. I also remember him burning incense and reading Buddhist texts when I was a child! And yet he could do that — get the accent down, really fool you; infiltrate any group.

As a little girl I remember going with him to those tent meetings and handling serpents; they wanted "a little child to come forth." I remember I had to sing songs about how I had sinned, even though I didn't know anything about sin. My father had to infiltrate these snake-handlers.

♦ **AJ: What was he investigating?**

♦ J: Arson, moonshining, various conspiracies in the region... I don't know all the places he infiltrated. I know about some of them, but I wouldn't be surprised at what it might have extended into; possibly the KKK, or groups like that. We lived in places where there were only dirt roads, stuck out in the middle of nowhere.

♦ **AJ: Would the snakes bite?**

♦ J: Sometimes members of the congregation were bitten, but I never was. And they were poisonous. When I think about that experience, I get a sense of cacophony all around me: people speaking in tongues, weeping — what I would describe as a madhouse. Things were swirling around me; everyone seemed like giants — I felt

there before those were taken. People came from all over the country wanting to get things.

♦ **AJ: But your father had this whole other existence—**

♦ J: It was just amazing how many people showed up after his death; he did have quite a network. He died of brain cancer in the early '80s, before I went to New York. I don't think I could have moved to New York if he hadn't died; if I had tried to go, he probably would have had somebody drag me back. He wanted to oversee and direct my every move, and thought he understood what I was supposed to do with my life. So a lot of the things I did in my twenties were trying to rebel against being under that thumb; I'd had such a proper upbringing in all these churches, religious choirs, and masses (we went to a variety of churches, depending on what undercover role my father was in). I was a really good student, and then, when I started taking acid in my room at night, I was also engaging in really wild sexual experimentation. It's interesting: my father was very repressive and controlling, yet at the same time he'd try to scare me and force me to confront fear and the dark side.

Wearing that dress onstage had nothing to do with trying to look sexy; it was more: I like the way it felt under hot lights! Years ago I went through this phase of liking rubber.

World of Skin [a side project with Michael Gira] shot a video involving snakes, and the snake owner came in with about forty snakes, including some huge pythons. I said, "Let me hold a snake and wrap it around my body"—I don't know what made me say that, but I guess I wanted to see if I could do it. And it was great; I'll never forget that sensation. Several snakes were wrapped around my body and my ankles, and they began to explore me under the hot lights. They crawled through my braids and were writhing all over my body, everywhere, and the *sound*—the rustle of scaly skin on my body—I felt incredibly connected with them. It was like taking a drug and forgetting where

you stopped and something else began. I felt a real communion with those creatures, and now I almost feel like I've been one.

♦ **AJ: What do snakes mean to you, mythologically?**

♦ J: The shedding of the skin: rebirth and eternal life. Snakes glide across the ground in a very elegant way; they're strong—it's like they're one solid muscle. They're very sensual, but I would never have one as a pet. I don't think they should be kept in captivity.

♦ **AJ: The snake is a part of the medical symbol, the caduceus. The ancient Greeks used snakes in early healing rituals. Healers used a certain snake venom as a hallucinogenic to enhance their oracular and psychic powers.**

♦ J: A woman gave me a denim jacket with my name on it, and an elaborate Medusa painted on the back. I wore it to the grocery store, and it attracted so much attention—people coming up to me and asking, "What's that?"—that I thought, "I'm not wearing this anymore." But it's beautiful.

After that video came out, for a while it seemed like everybody was giving me rings with snakes on them, and talking to me about snakes, and sending me snake memorabilia. It was getting out of hand, so I chose to not continue developing that theme in my work.

♦ **AJ: That's healthy, because most people don't know when to end something—especially when it becomes a cliché, devoid of its original life.**

♦ J: I want really rural experiences to be part of the identity around me; the tent revivals and snakes and Mardi Gras were much more formative influences than any kind of New York experience.

The Dalai Lama was here at Madison Square Garden a few years ago and *that* was wonderful. All these monks were participating in front and I went up and stood with them. Later, at midnight, we were outside in front of the Jumbotron in Times Square, viewing an animated Green Tara. I wondered, "What is going through their heads? They've all come from a life in monasteries, and now look where they are. That's real flexibility." That was a very privileged experience, and there weren't all that many people who went up and stood with the monks.

♦ **AJ: How did you get into Buddhism?**

♦ J: Through initially hearing Tibetan ritual music, which was used in a soundtrack for a Ken Russell film—*Altered States*. Those 8-foot-long horns sound so intense, and I like the

chanting. I was attracted by the color of the robes, which is *dark red*. When I first heard the music of Swans, it sounded dark red to me. Then I saw some very elaborate paintings involving demon creatures and skulls, and they tapped into my imagination. I started reading and attending lectures and ceremonies, which involve some very elaborate visualizations. And the more you practice them, the more they get into your mind. To me, that takes the place of taking a hallucinatory drug, because the images are very, very detailed—horrific, sometimes. All the varied sexual positions are explicitly detailed. In particular I started to visualize Maha Kala—she's the wrathful protector.

During this last tour, I began menstruating while performing "Yum Yab" and the blood exploded down my legs—I was screaming with such intensity.

◆ **AJ: Do you start visualizing from an image?**
◆ J: Yes. You close your eyes and start seeing it. After several years' practice, I'm very much still a novice. I think the practice of visualization hones my imagination and sharpens my perception; I'm obsessed with keeping the creative mind sharp. As for my general interest in Buddhism, I'm unclear as to whether my motives are selfish, or whether the goal is to help other people.
◆ **AJ: But you can't help anyone else unless you've healed yourself.**
◆ J: Right, that's the idea. I'm not good at "Nice to meet you" and "Have a nice day." I get in these moods. Rather than saying the right words to someone I meet, I might make them an elaborate meal and present it beautifully, or decorate their home as sensitively as I can. It's a way of doing things that's a gift, and that's what I try to keep doing: proving my sincerity by actually doing something for others. My tendency to be "withdrawn" is potentially misunderstood.
◆ **AJ: But it's a gift to the greater society when you find yourself and express that through creative channels like music. Each per-**

son has their own individual path as to how to be true to your self and best express your gift.
◆ **J:** In doing what I do, the expectations of family and friends are always being let down. My family would like me to be more involved with them, but I can't, because I don't have enough to be two people. I try to maintain a balance between my creative lifestyle and being a member of my family, but I think I've shocked the hell out of everybody. The damage is done now; I can't turn back.

That's a big, courageous step to take if you come from *my* background. It's been a big source of tension, but I've resolved it now. It's my life, and if I'm not appreciated when I'm alive, maybe some descendent looking at my scrapbook will appreciate it. For example, I had a relative who performed song-and-dance on Broadway—her name was Minnie. Maybe no one else at the time respected her for that, but I do now!
◆ **AJ: The nuclear family ideal of Western society is extremely constrictive. Part of being human and evolving creatively and spiritually involves stepping out of the family system that serves to maintain a stasis, a status quo. The xenophobic, small-town system which the Republicans are trying to revive (with talk of "family values") can sometimes be deadly to the evolving soul.**
◆ J: Lately I've been agonizing about the question of having children. I never saw myself as having children, but...it's ego, thinking that the world really needs your child.
◆ **AJ: But ironically, I think more people like you should be having the children, instead of the conservatives or fundamentalists.**
◆ J: I would want to be everything my parents weren't, and I would want to cultivate all creativity. I would want a child to be as free as possible to express themselves, and experiment, and be everything they're capable of being, without the baggage of guilt. I think of all the guilt that was crammed down my throat. But these aren't good reasons. Probably a good reason is: "I'm having a child...come what may! This person's going to be anyone they want to be, and I have to live with that."
◆ **AJ: Children often manifest themselves as your own shadow, no matter what your intentions are—**
◆ J: —and no matter how you guide them? So ultimately I could have a dentist or a lawyer, or the daughter on that TV show, "Absolutely Fabulous." I look at that show and think,

"That's what would happen to me."

♦ AJ: I grew up with very liberal, no-rules parents. If, at the age of 14, I wanted to stay out all night long, they never said anything. This was not necessarily an expression of "love" but an abdication of true parental responsibility. I think a lot of young people have experienced this "all rules gone to the wind" mentality, and they're having to discover what is really valuable, what is discipline, what is care, and what is love. It's a lot of work to actually set rules and get involved with your kids. Growing up, I could do anything, anywhere, at any time, and that was just as damaging as a strict upbringing.

♦ J: Probably all of your friends envied that.

♦ AJ: Of course, they saw it as: "Oh, what cool parents." This younger generation has a lot of casualties; a lot of parents now are very lazy, and use the dogma of the relaxation of rules as a way of not doing the very hard work of parenting. Of course, there's the opposite situation: parents—like your father—who just want to use their kid for their own controlling and self-centered reasons… you were the extension of your father's ego and power. Whatever powerlessness he felt in the outside world, he took out on you, the one place where he *had* some power.

♦ J: I did the most drastic thing when my father died: I came to one of the most "dangerous" places in New York City to align myself with total strangers! His death liberated me. My brother did what was expected of him, and is still doing it. When he visited me in New York, he was angry and jealous: "I wish I could do that, but of course I'm being responsible." [laughs]

> [Men] want women that are weak and submissive—that's the key to so much male sexuality. They can't handle women who are just: "All right; take it out."

♦ AJ: You're actually being *truly* responsible...for being an evolving human.

♦ J: I hope so. I think of myself as an artist, or at least as someone reflecting and asking questions about life. I don't feel any special alignment with the music world, the music busi-

Photo: Laura Levine

ness. For me, it's all about making a work of art, but that kind of talk doesn't translate well to rock music circles. I think about learning songs and singing them with that lounge group. Those people were *musicians;* they could read charts. It wasn't about quirky personal expression or "creating"; it was about being a good instrumentalist or vocalist—

♦ AJ: A technician.

♦ J: I was surrounded by people like that, but now my world is different. This world is about art. Michael has an art background; he went to art school in California with Kim Gordon. Both of them came out here looking for some form of new art expression. They never thought of themselves as just "musicians."

When I hear the term "indie rock" I have to laugh. What's that? Nobody is more independent than we are; we are completely self-funded. Yet now "indie rock" refers to these bands with mega-budgets. Do people have any idea how many thousands of dollars it takes to make a video that airs on MTV? Do they know how many people are in studios working on them? MTV is actually just a lavish corporate commercial for marketing a product—cultivating conformity. Making those videos is big business; there's nothing "indie" about it.

The way I work, I have to be so flexible, just to get access to people and places so I can do what I want to do. I have to work in different cities. I got access to a musician-run studio in an office park out in the middle of nowhere, and worked there for a while, then took the tapes somewhere else to do something different. That would drive a lot of people crazy. It's never: everything's all in one place. The actual *getting the work out* is agony. It takes massive amounts of effort; a lot of wheeling and dealing and going here and going there and doing favors for different people. I have to use my imagination and think of ingenious ways to do things, because I don't have a budget.

♦ **AJ: But sometimes that can produce really creative results, instead of having everything handed to you.**

♦ J: On my album *Sacrificial Cake*, there's a very warbly, distorted, warped voice on the song "Surgical Savior." While my vocal was being recorded, the engineer actually pulled and stretched the physical tape to get that result: "Well, if the tape breaks, we'll try it again." It wasn't done by some expensive, high-tech processor. That's the way I have to work: "How can I accomplish this result?" And a lot of times people ask, "What effect did you use?" I didn't use an effect—that was *me* creating a weird voice as I "became" a character or "became" another creature.

This has taken years of experimenting—just

White Light from the Mouth of Infinity,
Swans (1991).

knowing how to turn that ability on. I'm finally able to sing that way in the context of Swans and projects with Michael. On his solo album it sounds like my voice was altered electronically, but no—it was just me using my throat and actually squeezing my vocal cords and manipulating my neck and putting my hands in my mouth and manipulating my face while being recorded. It's not gadgets!

> **All those guys are just going to have to *die*, over time, before [recording sessions are] going to get much better.**

♦ **AJ: How have you changed Swans?**

♦ J: It would have changed anyway, but when I first met Michael, he wasn't listening to any other music at all. I started playing music around him, and he'd ask, "What's that?" I'd play "world" music or dissonant classical music or string quartets or Maria Callas—nothing contemporary. Just by exposure to a lot of different music, and by getting a sense of musical history, he changed. So perhaps I contributed in this way to a development in the sound of Swans.

♦ **AJ: As more women have come into the music scene, there seems to have been some kind of change or shift. A group like Swans, which started out so archetypically male, has changed significantly since you joined.**

♦ J: Of course, again, it may not be easy to define what is archetypically male. Norman [band member] once referred to Swans as "sensitive guys." There are now organized groups like Riot Grrrls. I tried to comment on this in songs such as "Volcano," which appeared on *A Far Cry*, a compilation CD of women in music and will also be on *Soundtracks For The Blind*. I was being ironic while also understanding the kind of role-playing that is taking place, and the persona you become onstage… the way that male thrust (that's an appropriate word) infiltrates what women do. That song also comments on all I've gone through in making music for ten years and still being essentially ignored or invisible. It's a kind of eulogy, and a word of caution to other women.

On the other side of the coin are these women with fey, soft little voices, playing the flirty, coy girl role and doing "innocent" music—they're part of it, too. When you pose with your legs spread, or wear a tight dress, or smear your lipstick, it all has to do with flirtation and seduction—making a kind of commentary about sexuality. But everything is always viewed through the eyes of *men*. And what's the price you pay for doing that? What message are you sending out? In my case, my message has been so fierce onstage that I've even terrified people—or so they've written me. They thought I was dangerous!?

I was never a "flirt." During the days when I was promiscuous—which I'm not at all now—and interested in sexual conquests, it was to the point where I was so un-coy, or not flirtatious, that any number of times a man, who thought he was just a real stud, would be so intimidated that he couldn't even get it up. I mean, I used to just be so aggressive: "Okay. You want to do it? Let's do it." And they couldn't handle it!

Photo:Wim Van De Hulst

♦ **AJ: You emasculated—**

♦ J: —so many men. I really did; it was to the point where it was hilarious. And I realized that it's a game on us. They want women that they feel are weak and submissive—that's the key to so much male sexuality. They can't handle women who are just: "All right; take it out."

♦ **AJ: A lot of times you almost wonder whether they really want the sex; what they want is to have their egos boosted. Men are taken aback when they're confronted with a woman who doesn't give them the expected submission, who's more like: "Okay, put your money where your mouth is—you want to have sex? Fine!" When a woman actually *wants* sex, she takes it out of the currency of power that men have defined—that somehow it's a conquest, and shameful. She subverts the notion that only men like sex, that women just want love and protection. When women demand sex too, and divorce it from shame ("Will he still love me tomorrow?") then men are scared to death.**

♦ J: Exactly. It's very disappointing when you discover that. If so inclined to spend the en-

ergy, I've always been the kind of person who could go up to anyone, male or female, voraciously—Michael says I'm Swans' attack dog. I'm amused by the idea of a secret-weapon attack dog; I see what I want, I go after it. I'm not interested in being coy. I have a tendency to be serious and blunt.

♦ **AJ: Coy, seductive manipulation in women comes from being powerless, and trying to get power around the edges. But once there's a sense of power that isn't derived from the approval of men, that girly coyness can be discarded. Some women are growing up in a post-feminist environment and actually making their own rules, instead of trying to please the boys.**

♦ J: My original lyrics for "Deflowered" went, "You're a post-feminist rocker girl," but I changed it to, "You're one bad bitchin' whore." Because I thought, "What am I really saying?" I like the idea of women taking back words like "bitch," "slut," and "whore"—using them to have power. Instead of being afraid and letting people call you those names, enabling them to make you feel bad, it's shoving those words back in their faces.

I'm interested in female artists and what they're doing and saying. I really feel an alignment with P.J. Harvey's lyrics, because she has used some of that vocabulary, in a straight delivery with a lack of artifice. When I saw her,

Jarboe at a show in London (1988).

♦ **AJ: This is a dicey area. Media-wise, it's perenially The Year of Women In Rock—this weird tokenism that is easily turned into superficial topicality. In a lot of ways this is a minefield. How can we weave a richer brocade, so to speak? On one level, "Women In Rock" seems a bit tiring—okay! But on another level, rock music has been a bastion of male values. Of course, it's a mirror of the larger society's sexual relations, which are undergoing tumultuous, exciting changes. I've met a lot of younger kids who appreciate the fact that they grew up without having to constantly deal with sexualized power polarities. A lot of sexual power issues (for me) have diminished: you'll see a band, and it's no longer an issue that the drummer happens to be a woman. In my Pollyannish way, I'm looking for the positive, and in clubs now, people seem to be a lot *nicer* than they were in the '70s and early '80s, when there was a much harsher, male edge.**

♦ J: I went to a lot of intense hardcore shows featuring groups like the Circle Jerks, and it was totally male, especially the mosh pit. I would stand on the outskirts and watch. This would be after wearing a business suit all day, so it *was* exciting, but I was an outsider.

I thought about writing a survival guide for women who want to get into music. I've been through so much shit, being the one woman with up to eight guys traveling around in a group. It is very different now; I feel like I *did* attempt to open some doors for women, if only in a small way.

Years ago, Swans had a hardcore crowd. I've had everything happen to me: things thrown at me, every word said to me, gobs of spit on my body. I've had my blouse or dress pulled down by people yelling, "Show us your tits!" Michael, being perverse, wanted me to open or break up the set by singing alone, as a sort of sacri-

she wasn't acting coy or shaking her butt around; she stood and played guitar. To me she projects a strong female image. Some of the others are sending mixed messages—that's what Madonna has always done.

♦ **AJ: I think of Madonna as a kind of stage in women's evolution. She's still stuck in having to address male notions of desire, but she's also tweaking them—like you said, a mixed message. The next evolution of female identity isn't even going to bother with either pleasing men or attacking men; it will go beyond those polarized responses with the grounded self-confidence that will come from not automatically having men as the reference point for women's identity.**

♦ J: And on that day, the ERA will become law!

As far as the icon or wooden idol in question, to me that's just her calculated image. Let's look at her work, by itself. If you just listen to the lyrics—well, they don't say anything to me as an artist. The only thing that interests me at all is her constant trying to be in-your-face, and not be a lady. To me it's like: she must have known Lydia Lunch years ago. In a way she is almost using Lydia Lunch's vocabulary, turning around the questions: "What is feminine?" "What is sexual?" To be in Madonna's position of power and do such predictable music—that's always disappointed me.

fice. So I thought, "I'm going to *really* be a sacrifice. I'll get on my knees, praying to them, right on the edge of the stage"—and the audience was all male; skinhead boys. I was singing "Blackmail," a kind of seductive song with a trance-like quality, and I put myself right there on the edge. Al [band member] would come over and scream at people, "I'll kick your fuckin' face in if you don't leave her alone." Experiences like that are very valuable.

On Eastern European tours we played Ljubljana, Slovenia—we went over there a number of times before it changed. We were the headliners at a festival, and there was broken glass all over the stage. I was always barefoot onstage, and I stepped in some glass as I opened the set *a capella* to prepare the crowd for the barrage of sound to come. I was singing in front of this drunken, drugged mob of boys, and I was pummeled by mushy tomatoes right at my vagina—right there. It left a *stain* (an image I used in the song "Volcano"), but I didn't even blink. And when the song was through, I looked right into their eyes and blew them a kiss and walked back to my position behind the keyboards.

◆ **AJ: In your survival guide, what would you say about experiences like these?**

◆ J: I would say, "Don't have a 'victim' attitude about them. Look at other people's behavior as showing how weak they are." I would talk about when to fight back—although *I* don't recall ever doing that literally. I would emphasize working on your own attitude. Since I was getting this shit, I felt sure that other women were getting it too. And then there are practical aspects: I learned to tour with a massive bag of baby wipes! Because frequently there's no bathtub, no shower, and the sink is stopped up in the club. For sanitary reasons, a female has to wash once in a while, so these baby wipes have been a lifesaver for me.

◆ **AJ: Of course, men have to wash, too, but they just don't.**

◆ J: "They don't care. They'll never bathe," a woman promoter once told me.

◆ **AJ: It's not like women *have* to wash; we could be just as dirty.**

◆ J: I think women want to, just so we don't get sick, but I should emphasize that I am a meticulous person by nature.

◆ **AJ: But we don't have to for some *biological* reason—women's bodies are like self-cleaning ovens! Newt Gingrich said that military women were unfit to serve in the trenches because they'd get infections. That's ridiculous; we don't have to wash any more than men, it's just that culturally, some women *want* to be clean.**

◆ J: That person is so revolting that I can't stand his name being on the same page as my printed words! Of course, I see your point, but I'd like males to use baby wipes, too. I also know all about the wonderful, practical uses of an Evian or other water bottle: cut off the top and use it as a toilet! Because frequently there's no toilet. Every dressing room has all this putrid beer sitting around, so I would urinate into a bottle and leave it in the corner. This is survival, because there's usually no "ladies room!" There are other problems, too: how do you travel on a bus and get sleep? Earplugs and a sleep mask. And take melatonin to adjust sleep patterns in changing time zones. Flip-flops assist in showering in the scummiest of places. I could write a practical guide on how to survive touring shitholes all over the world!

> **I was singing in front of this drunken, drugged mob of boys, and I was pummeled by mushy tomatoes right at my vagina. It left a *stain*, but I didn't even blink.**

On the early Eastern European tours, there was absolutely nothing a vegetarian could eat—forget it. There were no vegetables, no fruits, no drinking water—the whole time I was there I had to drink orange soda pop because you couldn't drink the water; it was too polluted. I got really run-down. I was living on vitamins, but there was little to combine them with so my system could process them. And it seemed like we were there forever: Poland, Czechoslovakia, etc. I got back to New York and started feeling stranger and stranger until finally I just couldn't move. It turned out that I'd caught pneumonia. That was awful. The first doctor's treatment wasn't radical enough, so they put me on a plane to Atlanta and a doctor who cured me with massive doses of antibiotics. As a result of starving on that Eastern European tour, I had destroyed part of my immune system. I

tried all kinds of doctors—New Age, holistic, etc.—and finally it was explained to me: "You have to start eating meat." Slowly I started eating a little chicken, fish, and then the dreaded beef. I have to be careful. Every tour I've been on since then, I get exhausted and a viral infection invariably grips me.

◆ **AJ: My acupuncturist doesn't believe in vegetarianism. Chinese medicine believes in "Moderation in everything—including moderation!"**

◆ J: I was really stubborn in maintaining my vegetarian beliefs on that tour—and I almost died.

◆ **AJ: Did you go to Japan?**

◆ J: When we went to Japan, people were looking at the tattoos on our band members' arms, pointing at them. I wanted to show them my tattoos, too—after all, what's the big deal? So I started to show the snake on my stomach (I wasn't going to take all my clothes off) and everyone started shouting, "No, don't do that!" For women, that was a cultural taboo.

We stayed at a hotel in Tokyo where a lot of music people stay. I had a metallic silver leather sofa and an exotic floral arrangement in my room. Outside the lobby there were hordes of groupies wearing thigh-high boots with 5" spike heels, which made them very tall. Leather right up to the crotch, amazing bras and ultra-flamboyant makeup and hair. Then we found out that the L.A. Guns were staying at our hotel—they were waiting for *them!*

I was in a different wing of the hotel from the rest of the band, and it turned out that next door to me was the guitar player for the L.A. Guns. There were about a hundred little white notes folded up and taped to his door. Early in the morning, he returned to his room with three or four girls and I heard him say, "You can stay if you lay on the floor. *You* get over there!" One girl asked, "Let me get in bed with you," and he said, "Well, you can get in bed with me if you don't move!" Then I heard him pick up an acoustic guitar and play some *Spinal Tap* acoustic-guitar song. [laughs] I was on the other side of the wall grinding my teeth—I couldn't stand hearing him talking to those girls that way. The next morning, I stole one of the notes on his door (I *had* to see what one might say), and it said, "I will wait for you, Room so-and-so on the third floor, and cherish a dream that the Rock God will come see me. I know you have wife and baby—I do not care." [laughs] Can you imagine all this flesh offering itself to you? And those girls were willingly offering themselves to be abused—hoping to get close to the "power"?

There were a few girls there who recognized Michael but they were dressed like students: very conservatively. They started weeping when they saw him, and came up to touch him. Then they followed us for several blocks with tears rolling down their faces. He's perceived really differently over there, I guess. They didn't give a shit about *me*! [laughs]

It really has come full circle: here are people wanting to have sex with me, selling *me* their bodies...in the span of a decade, I've gone from one end of the spectrum to the other.

◆ **AJ: Have things changed? Is there any difference in attitude as to how you're treated?**

◆ J: Initially, we played clubs where hardcore bands would play, and they were filthy, rough places. In Europe, we've been playing intimate theaters—a different kind of environment. On our last U.S. tour we played some rock clubs that were just barbaric. But attitudes—I don't know if attitudes have changed everywhere. In a recording studio, 90% of the engineers and technicians are men. The people you buy equipment from in music stores are still mostly men. In Holland and some places in Norway, though, the stage crew frequently includes females—as does the club 1st Ave in Minneapolis.

During one older recording session we used some outside people, and that was such an intimidating boys' club that I basically gave up. I tried my best, but that situation just killed my creative spirit—everything in me. So that still exists. All those guys are just going to have to *die*, over time, before it's going to be much different. I do get letters from girls who are setting up home studios in their bedrooms—that's good. Just be autonomous.

Once in Lausanne [France], we had some new people helping us with our equipment. I went upstairs and changed, and then came back to see how my gear was being dissembled. There were three guys from the audience in the corner, and they came over to me. I've learned that

I have to be really careful; I have to always be with someone or be prepared, because I seem to attract weird people (I don't know *what* it is) who just want to hurt me or do something to me. This one boy stood there and looked at me and held out his hand. I didn't know what he wanted, but I held out my hand, and he took his other hand and slapped me as hard as he could across my face! His friends started laughing. Again, with this same sacrificial attitude, I leaned over and kissed him on the cheek. And he rubbed it vigorously, like I had "cooties"—then he spit a big gob right in my face. Now would that have happened if I were a man? I don't think so.

♦ **AJ: You were taking on so much, and turning the other cheek; subverting his violence and delivering it back to him, with such restraint. But how did you feel when he spit on you?**

♦ J: Awful. I'm better with that now, but at the time I felt really sad and hurt. He just laughed and thought it was great fun. The fact that I still remember that little scene says something about the impact it had on me.

We played a club in Boston called "The Rat" (Rathskeller). I'd been in the restaurant upstairs (there was no dressing room) and we were about to go onstage, so I went down the stairs and the doorman, a big, beefy guy, denied me entry. I said, "I'm playing tonight, and I'm trying to get to the stage." He said [sarcastically] "Yeah, *sure.*" I said, "You don't understand—I have to get onstage now—will you let me pass?" He said, "No," and then shoved me. I said, "Don't touch me," and I was beginning to panic; I couldn't get through. It was chaotic, crowded and noisy. And there was no one to help me.

Finally I got angry and said, "Fuck you, asshole. Let me through. I'll prove to you that I *am* in the group." Then this guy threw me up against the wall, kicked me down the steps, and came down and began kicking me in the stomach! Another bouncer who had a voicebox (he'd had his larynx removed; you've heard people talk with those things) came up and—I could barely understand him, but he was saying something like, "Stop beating her up!" trying to save me. I was lying there just taking it; it was awful. I literally shit in my pants; I unloaded every ounce of fear from my intestines. It was a nightmare.

♦ **AJ: Then what happened?**

♦ J: I got up, climbed up the stairs to the restaurant, found the promoter (I think her name was Julie) and told her what had happened—I looked like hell. I went into the restroom and cleaned myself up as best I could, then came back down and told her, "This is an outrage. I will never play this place again; I will tell everyone not to play here; this is a terrible place." And she said, "I don't care; no one cares what you think." Amazing! I went onstage and did the set—I don't know how I did it—and when we packed up to leave, the bouncer who had kicked me came up and sneered, "Troublemaker!" And none of the group members tried any macho retaliation (I didn't even let on how much pain I was in). This guy was huge—I don't think he could even fit through the door. It was amazing that I didn't get a hernia or a ruptured spleen from that. Anyway, those are the kinds of experiences I was going to put in my survival guide. Like, this is the kind of mentality you're going to encounter, so always carry something to prove who you are. Now they have

"I didn't join a rock group until around 30—but none of this was due to an early 'crisis'—but more to do with factors falling into place and my choice to exercise tremendous willpower to destroy myself and create another one… ."

Photos (l. to r.): Andrew Catlin, Laura Levine, Hale Coughlin

these laminated IDs, but at the time people didn't have those. And this bouncer just couldn't believe that a woman could be in the group.

◆ **AJ: What year was this?**

◆ **J:** Around '86. I could go on and on telling stories like that. Perhaps because I had multi-colored dreadlocks and was traveling alone to join the group somewhere, I've been strip-searched twice in international airports; those were brutal, horrible experiences. All my bodily cavities were explored—it was agonizing, and I got the feeling this happened not because they thought I had anything illegal on me, but because they just wanted to force me to take off my clothes.

◆ **AJ: Is there a theme here: taking extreme humiliation and turning it around? Is there a strength you've gained from these experiences?**

◆ **J:** Well, I don't feel bitter. I feel a tremendous sense of humility. Any time I start to get a big head or ego about going onstage or getting fan mail, I've always had something knock me down really hard. It's like when you're in school and anticipating the night of your big date, and you get a big pimple on your nose. Symbolically, that has *always* happened to me, and I think it has kept my intentions pure. I'm continuously moved and surprised when I get a nice letter from someone who likes my work and has gotten something from it—that means a great deal to me. I don't take any of that for granted.

Another thing that's happened: I don't cry like I used to. When I was growing up, I was really sensitive. Now, even when something really hideous happens to me, it's interesting to realize: "Hey, I'm not crying. I'm not running and hiding." I guess that just takes years of experience. Someone asked me, "What's the essence of how you feel onstage?" and I replied, "Humility." People who have become really renowned in their field—actors or actresses in particular—often say, "I become someone else. I'm in the role. But if I have a moment of *me* showing through, they're going to find out that I'm this great sham!" Like—they paid money to see *me*? I've had that feeling many times, and you just want to give all the more.

I really value all the experiences I've had, whether there were four hundred people there, or some huge festival where the people were all just little dots. There's no other experience of communication quite like that. And I don't think I was ready to do this earlier; I came into this as

an older person. I moved to New York as a grown woman and started doing this as a grown woman. The idea of being 18 or 20 and starting a rock group and achieving success and recognition by the age of 24—I can't comprehend that. At that age I was still a follower: I wanted to be in the same room with David Lee Roth or Gene Simmons. I never imagined *I'd* be on stage, performing and singing words I wrote.

I could write a practical guide on how to survive touring shitholes all over the world!

It's funny; lately, people I meet have this perception of me as a teetotaling goody-two-shoes. If they had any idea—they haven't a *clue* as to what I did when I was younger, or who I am. And they judge me. They think, "She's polite, she's reserved, she's from the South, she's like a boring little girl."

◆ **AJ: I think you have a dark inner strength. What people are you referring to?**

◆ **J:** People in Europe; people who've met us within the last couple years; and the people who met me when I *first* came to New York. Probably all of Michael's friends dismissed me. They think—I can see it in their eyes: "A good woman. A good girl. She doesn't drink. She doesn't smoke. She hasn't had sex with every guy in town." And of course, it's been said: "the lazy laughing South—with *blood in its mouth*"!

◆ **AJ: There is this notion of bohemianism, that you have to live a self-destructive, wantonly indulgent life—it's so clichéd. Often it's no more than rebellion against mommy and daddy. Some of the wildest, most risk-taking artists have rigorously healthy and responsible lives.**

◆ **J:** When we were affiliated with Mute Records, we were in England a lot; we lived there for a while. I would go into the Mute offices and see Diamanda [Galás] at her desk, doing business and promotion, wearing glasses and just *working*—not in that onstage persona. Then I'd see her at a dinner party, and there'd be this striking difference in her makeup and hair. That always impressed me. I only saw her perform once, at the Cathedral of St. John the Divine, and that was one of the highlights of my life. I was captivated. I loved that show so much I wanted to send her a bunch of roses, but someone said, "Oh, don't do that. That'll be perceived in a weird way." I regret not doing that.

♦ **AJ: She truly is channeling on a shamanistic level; her performances are an exorcism. You can almost see the serpent coming out of her. And yet as a person she is very warm-hearted and giving and polite. To me, that duality enhances her art: not getting caught up in that self-destructive role which is actually *superficial*.**

I remember meeting Lydia Lunch and having dinner with her and Jim Thirwell in Brooklyn when they were living together, and I was so impressed by her beautiful matching designer plates. She made an exquisite gourmet dinner in a gorgeous setting. She's very rigorous and disciplined, and that enhances her work, in my eyes.

♦ J: When I first moved to New York, some people, like Nick Zedd, thought I was a complete geek, like off the fuckin' farm. He came into an apartment we had on 2nd Street and I was scouring the bathtub, which was in the kitchen, wearing my long thermal underwear because it was really cold. Studying me, he was visibly appalled. After that, for some reason, every day I would see him at the post office (zip code 10009). I knew he thought I was a country bumpkin (and I think he hated me for being in Swans), so every time I saw him I'd do this ritual: I'd call across the post office in a faux-hick accent, "Hi there—how y'all doing?" And he would cringe and pretend he didn't know me.

♦ **AJ: In your relationship with Michael, is he supportive?**

♦ J: We've always had this intense relationship—it's never been boring! I'm challenged all the time, and I haven't had any insecurity, inferiority, or hunger for someone else since I've known him. Previously, I was always checking out men. But I haven't done that since 1984, because to

me, Michael is like no one else I've ever met—there are so many sides to him; he's a very detailed person.

Like my father, I started tape-recording Michael when he wasn't aware that I was doing it. I was trying to hold a mirror up to him, because I saw a path of self-destruction that was getting out of hand. One night he was on one of his many, many drinking binges, and we had a real *Who's Afraid of Virginia Woolf?* scene. I never had any problem with New York City or a desire to leave, but I saw it as slowly killing Michael, because he had fallen into a ritual of destruction that I couldn't break, and he wasn't breaking it. My only idea was to physically remove him from this environment. He was going to bars and hanging out with people who really, really drink, and he cannot handle alcohol at that level. He was binging a lot. It was almost like he didn't want to do it, but couldn't stop himself. He'd start at four in the afternoon and continue into the early morning hours. So one time, when he came back late, I taped him.

In that argument, he twisted the issue into one of money: "I can drink because I bought this...I can do what I want." Now, as far as finances go, he's helped me a lot, but I've also worked very hard for him. And like a lot of

Thirteen Masks (1991).

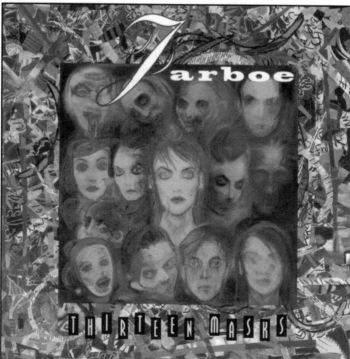

Photo: Masha Calloway

Michael Gira and Jarboe.

to make that person see what they're doing to themselves, but it doesn't work. They have to come to that realization themselves. For years and years Michael had been trying to finish a book, but he just couldn't do it. After he got out of New York, he was able to finish it—a lot of creativity and productivity came to the surface.

♦ **AJ: You don't seem to be sacrificing your life now. You seem very strong—**

♦ **J:** —as long as I travel and keep up with my contacts around the world. We lived in New York for a long time, and my best friends are in New York, so it's still my home. I know New York better than any other place in the world; I know it very intimately. I've intentionally walked almost every single street in this city, trying to learn them, but I always had to get out periodically—go to this cabin in Georgia with no electricity where I could ride horses and get in touch with myself. Because in New York, just going about your daily errands, you're in such an intense *squish* of humanity—*flesh* pressing together—that I need that space, that isolation.

♦ **AJ: As you get older, do you need that interiority more?**

I've come to the conclusion that sometimes you have to be rude, loud, and aggressive— or "bitchy"—to get things done… being a nice girl is just not possible anymore.

♦ **J:** I don't know. It's funny, because I love being onstage and performing; I like facing an audience—I've never felt any stage fright *ever*. I feel a certain sense of command and being strong when I'm onstage; I have confidence. I'm focused. *I become someone else.* But I'd say that, yes, I'm an "interior" person. And I very much enjoy being alone. Even so, as far as my seeming strength is concerned, I feel lonely and de-

artists, I had some family money left to me at one time, so I've had different ways of surviving anyway. But that wasn't the real issue. I said, "Michael, what does money have to do with this destructive pattern? What are you doing? Let's say that I completely support you; are you still going to be self-destructive? Because you're dying." We put this dialogue over a soundtrack on *Drainland*, Michael's solo album. That song gets pretty intense and hairy— a lot of people have trouble getting all the way through it.

♦ **AJ: How did Michael react when he heard the tape?**

♦ **J:** He said that his idea of using that conversation in a song was a tribute to me; it's like a love song, and it's titled "You See Through Me."

♦ **AJ: Was he shocked to see himself?**

♦ **J:** Oh yeah. But I think it took a long time—that tape was made three years ago— for him to detach himself and really hear what was going on. He still drinks, but not in that self-destructive pattern anymore. It's like with a junkie: you can't stop it, you can't understand it, you can try everything in the world

34

feated once in a while, like many others.

♦ **AJ: People make sacrifices in relationships; sometimes a very complex *web* gets formed — especially in creative partnerships between men and women. In your partnership, how do you see your own evolution?**

♦ J: In my work, I'm more interested in symbolic screaming and letting my whole body *go* in a possessed fashion, like a banshee. During this last tour, I began menstruating while performing "Yum Yab" and the blood exploded down my legs — I was screaming with such intensity. I'm not interested in being used only as a soft-voice relief. On the last Swans album, Michael is singing soft, while I'm going full-throttle. It's a reversal of previous roles onstage, where he was screaming and abusing himself every night. Now he's more restrained. Recently he said, "I'm like a retired gentleman now. And you're this unleashed demon!" Maha Kala?

♦ **AJ: Is it hard living together?**

♦ J: I have to have private space. There are times when I'm just thinking, or organizing. I like a sense of order in my life, but Michael lives in creative chaos — just try to find *anything* in his room! Whereas I know where everything is at all times. My mother said that when I was little, at night I'd lay out my clothing neatly on the bed, so in the morning I'd be ready to go to school. That sort of says it all!

♦ **AJ: Have you maintained boundaries for your own needs in life?**

♦ J: There's still a duality. I've decided, "What's so bad about being a bitch? What's so bad about being mean or rude once in a while, if that's what it takes to get what you need?" I was raised with the idea that you have to be nice so people will like you; politeness and "thank you" and "please" were crammed down my throat. And I still, in the back of my mind, follow that code. When people have bad manners I still judge that, and get revolted.

It's important to test personal boundaries. During my college years and beyond I was often following form: "This is what you do. This is what you say" — that's part of the *crap* you carry around with you. I systematically went about deconstructing these restrictions to where they've become just another mask. I'm still sincere and caring to a certain extent, but now I've come to the conclusion that sometimes you have to be "rude," "loud," and aggressive — or "bitchy" — to get things done. You have to demand what you want. The whole idea of being a nice girl is just not possible anymore. ♦ ♦ ♦

discography

♦ JARBOE ♦
Sacrificial Cake (1995)
Drainland, with Michael Gira (1995)
Alphabet City, Beautiful People Ltd., compilation (1994)
Beautiful People Ltd. (1994)
Shrine, compilation (1994)
A Far Cry, compilation (1994)
Thirteen Masks (1993)
Mighty Risen Plea, compilation (1993)
Ten Songs For Another World, World of Skin (1991)
World of Skin (1988)
Shame Humility Revenge, World of Skin (1987)
Blood Women Roses, World of Skin (1986)
Dry Lungs Vols. I & II, compilation (1985)
Walls Are Bleeding, cassette only (1983)
9 U, compilation (1983)

♦ SWANS ♦
The Great Annihilator (1995)
Love of Life (1993)
White Light From the Mouth of Infinity (1992)
The Burning World (1990)
Love Will Tear Us Apart (1989)
Children of God (1987)
Holy Money (1985)
Greed (1985)
Time Is Money, Bastard (1985)

For information/mail-order, send a SASE and $2 (payable to J. Long, Esq.) to: Young God Records, Box 420232, Atlanta, GA, 30342-0232.

equipment list

Akai Sampler, Yamaha digital synthesizer, Hammond Organ (B-3), Ensoniq, Mirage, Mellotron, Steinway grand piano, Mattel toy piano, Alesis midiverb, Electro-Harmonics 16-sec digital delay, Echoplex, Shure SM-58 microphone, RCA ribbon microphone, Boss foot pedal, Crown power amp, JBL speakers, Casio MT-240, Sony Walkman professional recorder, Tibetan hand bells, triangle, doorbells, vibraphone, marimba, zither, kalimba, Calzone cases, Ultimate Support Systems stands

Tribe 8

Tribe 8 is San Francisco's all-dyke punk band. Their stage show often includes the ritualistic castration of a rubber penis. Tribe 8 features Lynn Breedlove on vocals, Leslie Mah on lead guitar, Lynn Flipper on rhythm guitar, Lynn Payne (aka Tantrum) on bass, and Slade Bellum on drums.

◆ ANDREA JUNO: I can't play any instruments.

◆ LYNN BREEDLOVE: Neither can I, except the chainsaw. "*NNNNNNNNNNN!*" [laughs] I had to get an instrument as loud as everybody else's, so I could compete.

◆ **AJ: You sing, and write the lyrics?**

◆ LB: Yeah. I write most of the lyrics. Leslie wrote "Mom Gone Song," about her mom dying of cancer. Lynn Flipper, Tantrum and I all wrote a song called "Wrong Bathroom" that we just recorded. It's about going into truck stops, Denny's, and side-of-the-road America, and being told that the men's room is down the hall! Which is extraneous information—

◆ **AJ: Wait, *you're* being told…**

◆ LB: We're being told that the men's room is down the hall. We have to tell them we're going to the women's room. Little old ladies will come in the women's room behind us and then they'll pop out and look at the sign on the door. Yesterday, this old man followed two of us into the women's room because he thought, "There go those boys, so… " and he *jumped* out. We wrote a song about how silly that is. It's also about how confusing gender is for people who aren't used to living in an atmosphere—like San Francisco—where you have all this gender fluidity.

A lot of my friends are getting sex changes and taking hormones; you can't put them in one of the two or three typical gender boxes. They're making more and more possibilities, all the time.

◆ **AJ: That's exciting. You and the rest of Tribe 8 seem to be the embodiment of "angry women" right now. Some rockers are so *peaceful* nowa-** days: "Oh, *I'm* not angry about anything."

◆ LB: I have a lot of spirituality now, and ways to detach, mellow out and be sane so I can function—I wasn't like that for most of my life. I did as much alcohol, speed and other drugs as I could, to make myself as *insane* as possible. Now I have a lot of things I want to do, and so in order to do them, I have to find ways to chill out and meditate. But I also have a totally dysfunctional, rowdy, out-of-control side of me that has to be released somewhere, somehow. I can do that riding my bike, or skateboarding, or jumping around onstage or—

◆ **AJ: —channeling it creatively.**

◆ LB: Write novels or ridiculous lyrics.

◆ **AJ: We're living in a dysfunctional society, so anybody who's conscious at all has to have *some* sort of anger. Yet I've heard so many women immediately protest, "I'm not angry!"**

◆ LB: Why not? What's wrong with you? [laughs] Did you have a lobotomy? This shit's been going down for four thousand years and you're not pissed yet? There's something wrong with you.

Women have been trained for so many generations not to be angry: it's bad to be angry, it's not feminine to be angry. We must be feminine, we must be loved by men, because we must get married—if we don't then we must die, etc.

That's so ingrained in us, it's practically in our genes by now. It's real hard for women to get angry. You have to go to Bay Area Model Mugging [in San Francisco] and pay $600 to learn how to shout, "No!" and to learn how to

Photo: Chris Toliver

Tribe 8 (clockwise from l.): Lynn Flipper, Lynn Breedlove, Lynn Payne (Tantrum), Slade Bellum, and Leslie Mah.

bite off a guy's dick when he's shoving it down your throat. I'm like, "You can't bite the guy's dick off? Why? Because he's a nice guy? *What*?!" And they're like, "Oh, I couldn't, that would hurt him." Yeah, that *would* hurt him.

◆ **AJ: I thought a lot of women had gotten beyond that—and could start playing with their roles now, and didn't have to be so uptight—worrying that they aren't sexually attractive or they aren't *pleasing* if they are seen as angry. To me, the word "angry" doesn't imply that you're dysfunctional or some raging bitch. But I think a fear of being seen that way is still in the back of women's minds.**

◆ LB: Anger equals insanity.

◆ AJ: Of course, men can take the word "in-sanity" and make it sexy: the angry young man is also the artist or the bohemian. But when it comes to women, "insane" can only describe a raving hysteric.

◆ LB: You think of people like Salvador Dali when you think of insane guys. When you think of crazy women, you think of some poor bitch being forced to have a lobotomy in an institution—forgotten.

I think the only way we can get any respect about our anger is to somehow get into this intellectual realm where men are, and talk "reasonably" about anger. If you theorize about it, that's acceptable. But if you jump around and act out anger, then you're crazy.

◆ **AJ: Historically, there hasn't been much**

37

of a problem with women acting out, raving and committing violent acts in society, (except sometimes towards their children—which is an example of the syndrome where the oppressed act out their frustrations on those who are even more vulnerable). However, I still maintain that you can have a positive kind of anger that isn't about a personal collapse or being out of control and then taking it out violently on society. Healthy anger can be more of a channeling, to move people politically or socially towards an awareness of injustices and inequalities. That's what you seem to be doing with these in-your-face lyrics.

♦ LB: I've always been kind of bitchy, since I was a teenager and I started drinking and using. I had no political consciousness, but I felt all this shit—I was a queer, I was oppressed. That's what my anger was about.

My parents were both very much in control, all the time. They did not believe in my kind of shit, that screaming and yelling—they believed in the silent treatment. My parents got divorced when I was eighteen, and the romantic myth was shattered.

♦ AJ: Are you Catholic, by any chance? Some of your lyrics use Catholic imagery.

♦ LB: My Dad's Catholic. I was baptized, that's about as far as it got. I'm pretty fascinated by Catholicism, though, so it shows up in the lyrics sometimes.

From the family album: A young Lynn Breedlove and her mother (1960).

Photo: Bob Breedlove

I think the reason why I did drugs and alcohol is because I had bought that line about it not being okay to feel angry. I felt like I had to be happy all the time, so I tried to force myself, but what happened is that I got into a lot of violent relationships. The anger just came out even more, at some point, when I was high. It was intensified; it backfired.

I get really resentful when women tell me that stage-diving is a male activity. I'm a woman and I feel aggro, and that means that my aggression is not male. It's coming from me, and I'm definitely all woman... *baby*.

When I was using, I never looked at society as the culprit. Like you said, it was that hierarchical model, where you step on the head of the one below you while you're getting stomped on from above. My girlfriend was the least threatening person to me. If I hit her, she could hit me back and I wouldn't die. If I go up to a cop and hit him, I'm in trouble. I go up to a 250-pound fat boy and hit him, I'm dead. So I had to hit my girlfriend. And she had to hit me. We had to punch each other out, and be totally pissed off at each other and rip each other's faces off—and that, for me, was *nice, non-threatening violence.*

Because we're two girls, we couldn't really hurt each other, and we didn't *want* to hurt each other. I'm not saying that wife-beating or domestic violence in the dyke world doesn't happen, but the kind that I experienced was just like, "Let's roll around on the floor and wrestle, rip each other's hair out, scream at each other and bite."

When I got clean and sober, and read a lot of feminist theory, I started to realize, "Hey wait a minute, there's all kinds of injustice in the world." I started to question a lot of things, started to open my mind, and started to have to actually *feel* every feeling. My usual reaction to any feeling that isn't mad, sad or glad is to just funnel it into one of those three boxes; if it's a negative feeling, like I'm hurt or bummed out or depressed, I usually make that into my mad feeling. I'm *angry*—jump around, scream and yell. I had to work out a lot of bitchiness and rage and anger and jumping around and screaming and yelling during those first years of cleaning up.

♦ AJ: How old were you when you cleaned up?

♦ LB: I was 31. That's five years ago. I was a bike messenger, so I was drinking 6 espressos a day, riding around downtown and screaming at lobby guards. I screamed at lobby guards because they were authority figures, and I was suddenly pissed off at any form of authority.

The Gulf War riots were going on in San Francisco, and I wrote the song "Power Boy" when I was riding around downtown. It was swarming with cops of every stripe on every kind of vehicle. The rage just totally bubbled up inside of me, and as I rode along all day, I wrote down more and more lyrics and pieced them together.

A lot of the early Tribe 8 lyrics are really sarcastic, cutting, and mean—like "Lesbophobia." I was totally dissing straight girls in that song. Now I feel a lot less that way about straight women. I know so many great straight women— it was just this one woman who ticked me off and got me on this tirade.

I don't ever want to let go of my righteous indignation, because I feel like that is what fuels me. I just need to constantly make myself aware of who the real enemy is—as I've gotten older and more sane, I'm not just lashing out at anybody that comes along.

♦ AJ: That kind of blind rage is a problem.

♦ LB: It is. That's not punk rock.

♦ AJ: It's also a problem in the alternative undergrounds—whether we're talking about the dyke, feminist, or punk underground—this sort of narrow us-against-them credo. You know the kind of people that have nothing better to do in their lives than to bitch about who's sold out or—

♦ LB: —nitpick, and divide and conquer. That's what they—the real *they*—want us to do, so that we can't get together and be allies, and find similarities rather than differences. That's what I've been trying to do as Tribe 8 goes along and as I grow. It's like what I said at the Michigan Womyn's Music Festival [in August, 1994]: "Let's quit nitpicking here. Yeah, I have differ-

A more recent photo of Breedlove.

ent sexual practices than you do, but we're all women. Whether we're dykes or not, S/M or not, incest survivors or not, been beaten or not, we've all been oppressed by the same system." *That's* the enemy—not each other. As long as we keep being distracted by that bullshit, which is what *they* have created—*they've* created the divisions among us—then we're going to be controlled by them and killed by them.

Yes, I meditate; yes, I have my spiritual practice; *yes*, I carry a knife and I wear steel toes and I'm ready at all times—to hurt whoever's going to try to hurt me.

♦ AJ: That kind of perspective comes from maturity. I see it happening on the societal level as well. People are starting to say, "No! We don't have to just close ourselves off into this one essentialist point of view."

♦ LB: We were talking earlier about how women aren't allowed to get angry, we're taught not to get angry, we're taught that angry is bad, and all that—we had a lot of discussions about this in Michigan, in two workshops. I was to-

Photo: J. Troute

39

tally shocked to hear these *women* asking *us* why we were angry. I said the same thing as I said earlier: "Why aren't *you* angry?"

When Evelyn McDonell wrote a piece for *Ms.* Magazine last year, about Tribe 8 and the Michigan Womyn's Music Festival, I saw the original version. It was full of all kinds of angry women—women who got angry when they saw the Tribe 8 show, when they saw a rubber dick getting cut off. For them, that was a cathartic ritual, and they suddenly got in touch with their feelings for the first time, and allowed themselves to be angry that they had been raped, that they had been molested, that they had been beaten... whatever. All their lives they had told themselves, "It's my fault, I deserved it. I can't really get mad."

S/M is about power dynamics—even the most *vanilla* kind of sex is about power dynamics. To ignore that, or to deny that, is to not be honest.

That whole part was left out of the final edit in *Ms.* magazine. There had been women saying, "Now, the next time some guy tries to rape me, I'm going to pull a knife on him and I'm going to kill him!" I want to hear about that! I feel empowered by knowing people have pulled knives on their rapists, and cut their throats and got away. Unbelievably, some people aren't comfortable with that. There was a woman who told a story, at Michigan, about killing her rapist, and another woman came up to her after the workshop and said, "You shouldn't have done that."

♦ **AJ: She shouldn't have told the story?**

♦ LB: No—she shouldn't have killed this guy, who was raping her. When she was in the middle of a gang rape, she should not have pulled the knife and slashed the guy's throat.

♦ **AJ: WHAT?!**

♦ LB: When she told that story, so many women had tears streaming down their faces—we were all totally electrified by this story. We all felt like, "That could be me, I could do that. I don't have to lie down and not fight—'if I fight I'm going to die,' and that whole line of bull

they've been handing us forever. I can fight back, and I can get away, and he can get what he deserves while it's possible." But then here was this woman saying, "You shouldn't have done that, that was wrong. It's better to get raped than to kill somebody."

♦ **AJ: Those discussions symbolize the rift between different generations of women. You were the first real punk rock band to play at the Michigan Womyn's Music Festival; not too long ago they wouldn't even let in male children, or transsexuals. Everything had to be serene and non-violent.**

♦ LB: It's changing. There's a whole new generation of women that are dealing with the same issues, but in totally different ways. I think one of the biggest issues at Michigan was about women initially calling us "women haters," misogynists—they had a big banner saying, "Tribe 8 promotes violence against women." One of the members of our band came up to the protesters and said, "You know, I'm a sexual abuse survivor," and reached out her hand—and this woman who was carrying a banner turned her back on her.

I was trying to explain in workshops, and to all these women who were protesting us, "Look, we're all healing differently; some of us are remembering our pain and dealing with it in a different way: 'Fuck you, I'm not going to take it anymore.' Some people want to meditate. I do both."

I don't have to deal with something like incest in my past, but I have been harassed. When I was a two-year-old child in the bathroom on the beach, a guy whipped his dick out and exposed himself to me, and wanted me to touch it. I'm twelve, walking home from the swimming pool with some guy who I was playing with—who's 16—and he grabs me and throws me down and tries to rape me. All these images keep growing on you, and you keep thinking, "I'm a woman; I deserve this."

Every couple of years something else happens. I have to constantly tell myself that just because I'm a woman, this is *not* my normal lot in life. I do not deserve this. And then I need to attack that from all angles, because if I don't, my psyche's going to totally deteriorate. So yes, I meditate; yes, I have my spiritual practice; *yes*, I carry a knife and I wear steel toes and I'm ready at all times—to hurt whoever's going to try to hurt me.

♦ **AJ: The issue of sexuality itself—which you embody on stage, with the S/M references and**

playing with power the way only men used to do—is a whole realm, in and of itself. It isn't just about redressing victims.

♦ LB: Oh, no, not at all. But those women at the festival were acting like they were victims, and we weren't. They saw us as victimizers. We had to explain that we, too, had been through a lot of the same things. But just on its own, S/M is about power dynamics—and so is every other kind of sex. Even the most *vanilla* kind of sex is about power dynamics. To ignore that, or to deny that, is to not be honest.

Photo: Tera Stockton

♦ AJ: The patriarchy tried to define for women what sexuality was supposed to be. That meant, first of all, that we weren't supposed to like sex, or that we had to be passive. Those women who tell you that Tribe 8, or *any* woman who's dealing with sexuality and violence and power, is misogynist are inadvertantly replicating the patriarchy. They are doing exactly what men have always wanted women to do: not really deal with sex, and just be *nice*. Women haven't even been able to own sexuality on their terms until very recently. You're mixing it up with rock'n'roll, which is one of the most phallic bastions of power.

♦ LB: A lot of people say, "You're just trying to be like men," or "You *are* being like men," or "You're being just like the patriarchy and you're ya-ya-ya—you're being like the Dwarves, the Mentors, the Meatmen… "

♦ AJ: Those bands are known for having misogynist record covers and lyrics. What do you say to that kind of accusation?

♦ LB: We *can't* be like them because we're women, so it's a totally different situation. It's all about the source. The source of my experience, my pain, is that I do not come from the oppressor class—they do. So when they try to make a joke about oppression, it's not a joke. It's the same old tired shit that's been going on for four thousand years. *Not funny*. But when I say the same thing that those men are saying, all of a sudden that's a new twist. That *is* funny. That *is* powerful. Women have never had power, so that's new. What they do is old and tired; what we're doing is brand new and exciting.

Women having power are not being like men. Women having power are *women having power*. The fact that men have power, and have been able to jump around, act like eight-year-olds, do rock'n'roll and all kinds of other adventures, does not mean they are being manly—it means that they get power.

I really get resentful when women tell me that stage-diving is a male activity or moshing is a male aggro activity. I'm a woman and I feel aggro, and that means that my aggression is not male. It's coming from me, and I'm definitely all woman… *baby*.

I don't ever want to let go of my righteous indignation, because I feel like that is what fuels me.

♦ AJ: You're not a separatist, though, are you?

♦ LB: No. I do tend to create these enclaves in my life, where I'm surrounded by all women as much as possible. Like Lickety Split, my business back home.

♦ AJ: What is that?

♦ LB: It's an all-women's messenger service. Our clients are women, our messengers are women.

♦ AJ: You run this business?

♦ LB: Yeah. Tribe 8 is also all women. If one

There's a DYKE in the Pit

featuring **Bikini Kill** **Tribe 8**
Lucy Stoners **7 Year Bitch**

There's a Dyke in the Pit, **split 7-inch**
(Outpunk, 1991).

of us were to leave the band, we would not replace that person with anything but a woman. I need to have all women in certain areas of my life. I need to go to those enclaves for security and safety; I can feel my identity there. The rest of the world is full of men.

But I don't want to move to women's land right now; I want to be in the world. I have a lot of straight friends, and I want to interact with them. I don't want to ghettoize myself; I don't want to have to cut myself off from the world. I'd rather change the minds of people in the world to make them conform to *my* standards of morality than have to go grab ten other people who already believe as I do and go live on a mountain somewhere all by ourselves. I'm sacrificing too much to do that. I'd rather change the world.

♦ **AJ: What does S/M mean to you?**

♦ LB: First of all, I would not consider myself a hardcore member of the S/M community—I don't necessarily identify as S/M, I don't walk around dressed in leather from head to toe all the time. The song "Femme Bitch Top" was commissioned by a neighborhood S/M femme bitch top.

♦ **AJ: What do you mean *commissioned?***

♦ LB: She said to me, "All you write about is butches. Why don't you write something about femmes?" I said, "Okay, what do I write?" She said, "Write something about lipstick and fingernails and stuff." So I sat down and wrote the song, because she's big and bad, and I was scared of her.

I don't want to be a spokesperson for the

S/M community. I just want to say, "Look, all kinds of different people do all kinds of different things in bed." Yes, I've done those things; I have done everything that's in the song. I don't do it every day. I can have vanilla sex and be just as happy. I do lots of really rowdy sex that I think is normal, but that other people would think is violent. Sexuality is a giant spectrum, and the main reason I write about it is to let people know there's all different variations of sexuality and levels of intensity, and what we need to do is—just like any other aspect of life—acknowledge diversity.

♦ **AJ: And flexibility.**

♦ LB: Right. I think also that S/M is about adventure, and I'm really into adventure and stretching limits. That's why I did drugs. I want to see what's on the other side. I was scared. So I'd take a bunch of acid or take a bunch of shrooms, or take acid, shrooms and mescaline together—see what happens then! Not using drugs means that I have to go out on other limbs, sexually, and I have to do things like jump out of airplanes.

♦ **AJ: You jump out of airplanes?**

♦ LB: I jumped out of an airplane one time. I want to do it more, but it costs money and I don't have money. That was a rush, and a rush is what I want.

I cut off a rubber dick in the context of talking about gang rape. It's a cathartic ritual; it makes us feel like we are getting some kind of revenge. No, we're not cutting off any real dicks.

♦ **AJ: You jumped with a parachute, right?**

♦ LB: Well, yeah. I'm still here.

♦ **AJ: [laughs] You're Sagittarius. That's a sign of adventure. Of all the twelve signs, that sign would be jumping out of airplanes and wanting to "push the envelope further."**

♦ LB: S/M is a lot about facing fears—looking at your most inner self, your worst fears, the things that creep you out the most, and the things you hate the most, then asking somebody to play out a fantasy with you about that. That's fun. It's like a roller coaster. It's scary to go to the top of a roller coaster and go down at a hundred miles an hour, but people do it; they pay to do it. They go see horror movies. People like to be scared.

♦ AJ: It's a new step for men and women—especially women—to start taking over and playing with the rules and definitions of sexuality. In places like San Francisco or New York, which are in the vanguard of this sexual revolution, people aren't so uptight or specific about sexual identity anymore. Now they can start having fun with it. But people in the suburbs, who aren't exposed to such a free environment, are fed a steady diet on TV and in magazines of very fixed "outlaw" images: rubber and leather. There's bound to be a clash. When you write lyrics about wanting to beat up a girlfriend, I'll bet you get all kinds of criticism.

♦ LB: "Manipulate" was the first song I ever wrote. I was at an AA meeting, and in AA we make fun of ourselves. We make fun of our dysfunction and our character defects. I was really into 12 Steps at that time because I *had* to be—it was my first year of sobriety—and that song was along those lines: "Look how fucked up I am." I wasn't celebrating how fucked up I am, I was laughing at it, stepping outside myself, and witnessing who I am.

♦ AJ: It's hilarious, because it starts off with, "Women's love is so friendly—like herbal tea." [laughs] How many times have I wanted to just go, "Oh, I *hate* that kind of herbal tea and niceness!" Sometimes that makes me feel violent, just the opposite of its intended effect (although I do drink a lot of herbal tea).

♦ LB: The herbal tea section is part of a song written by my friend, Jo; we just picked out an excerpt. That's also spoofing me and who I am. When I first came out, in the late '70s, I listened to Cris Williamson and Theresa Trull, and all the womyn's music, and I'd bring lots of licorice tea on tour for my throat. I drink herbal tea, I'm really into herbs, I'm a goddess worshipper… I'm all those things that I make fun of. Whenever we introduce "Manipulate" we're all like, [sappy voice] "Let's have a healing circle!" People get offended because they think I'm making fun of *the other*, but I'm not. I am all these different paradoxes; we all are.

♦ AJ: Some women seem to misunderstand your intentions. I read that there was this hysterical warning at the Michigan Womyn's Music Festival: "If you're a survivor of any form of sexual abuse, you may not want to attend the Tribe 8 performance at 8 o'clock, as it contains explicit sexual violence."

♦ LB: That's because I cut off a rubber dick in the context of talking about gang rape. It's a cathartic ritual; it makes us feel like we are getting some kind of revenge. No, we're not cutting off any real dicks here, people, so let's just calm down for a second, okay?

The fact that men have power, and have been able to jump around, act like eight-year-olds, do rock'n'roll and all kinds of other adventures, does not mean they are being manly—it means that they get power.

The women who were protesting had never seen Tribe 8 before. Everything they had to go on was hearsay. They were saying that we promoted violence against women and children, because they heard something about "Daddy's girl." That particular phrase is in a song called "All I Can Do," which is about incest; it's about loving a woman who is still dealing with hav-

"Manipulate"

(excerpt)

women's love is so friendly
women's love like herbal tea
women's love it empowers me

i just want to manipulate my girlfriend
i just want to play games with her head
i want her to do some mental pushups
i want her to apologize and beg

it's such a sin
it's so wrong
i feel guilty as fuck
i try to quit
i can't help it
i guess it's just my lousy luck

i just want to objectify my girlfriend
i like her 'cause she's hot between the sheets
i just want to show her off at parties
and dress her up as if she walked the streets

©1995 Tribe 8

ing been raped by her father. It's about how I was dealing with it too, we were dealing with it together—and the horror and trauma of it all.

I think the saddest part of the whole controversy is that 8,000 women of all different sizes, shapes, colors and classes were so busy gossiping, running around, getting little half-assed bits of information, and then making a big hoo-ha out of something that was totally wrong—wasting all this energy—when we could have been *talking* about it. We could have figured out that we're all on the same side a lot sooner.

The protest was actually such a tiny faction of women. It did open up a lot of discussion at the workshops, which a lot of women came to because of the protests. They said, "Oh, there's some kind of hoo-ha going on—we ought to go check it out." We were able to address issues that ordinarily might not have been addressed and explain ourselves more fully, so that was good.

♦ **AJ: It's so ironic, because any number of people who get attracted to S/M and violent sexuality are also replicating sexual abuse. The issue of catharsis is central for those people.**

♦ LB: S/M is a million different things to a million different people, but one of the things that

Lynn Payne's graduation from James Cardinal McGuigan Catholic High School (1989).

it definitely does for people is work as a catharsis. I thought that if I used the phrase "cathartic ritual" for this castration thing, I would be able to communicate effectively to these women who were calling us violent. "Get it? Remember, you do these spiritual practices, and this is *another* spiritual practice."

♦ **The rest of the band arrives** ♦

♦ **AJ: Tribe 8 is one of the few racially mixed bands; most punk rock bands are all white.**
♦ LYNN FLIPPER: Our band is about all our different backgrounds—class, race, whatever—and that's what shapes the whole Tribe 8 experience, rather than having one spokesperson.
♦ **AJ: It can be difficult to conduct an interview with this many people at once. Well, here goes... I'm going to start by going around. What do you play?**
♦ LESLIE MAH: I play guitar now. But when I was 18 years old, I had a crush on a girl who played guitar, and I went out and I bought a bass so I could start a band with her. I didn't know how to play, and I didn't take lessons. I just sort of taught myself, and I ended up being in a band for about five years, with another girl.
♦ **AJ: Where are you from?**
♦ LM: Boulder, Colorado. When I played in that band there, we were really the only women who were playing music at all. The way that it felt to play punk rock then is really different from the way it feels now. I started playing guitar when I joined Tribe 8 because everybody, at that time, was just learning their instruments, and I felt like I wanted to do something different.
♦ **AJ: Did you feel any societal pressures that you couldn't play guitar, or punk rock?**
♦ LM: Oh, yeah.
♦ **AJ: How old are you now?**
♦ LM: I'm 31.
♦ **AJ: Women answer this question about societal pressures differently; younger people are saying "no."**
♦ LM: I definitely got very little support. In those early days, whenever my band got any attention, or if people asked us to do a show, opening for a bigger band, it was like, "It's just because you're girls. That's the only reason—you're a novelty." The Go-Gos were big then, and they were like *the* girl band. People kept saying that they were a novelty. They couldn't just be a band doing a fun thing.

That was the era in which I started to play.

People come to our shows and just stand there and stare with their mouths open. They just couldn't even believe that there were girls on stage. Now it's a lot different. When Tribe 8 plays, all these teenagers, girls and boys, will come up, and they don't have any reservations about just saying, "Hey, that was really great, it was really inspiring!" These boys don't have the same attitude that I encountered even five years ago: [dumb guy voice] "Well, you're pretty good," or, "You're almost as good as I am." Some people still say, "You're the best *girl* band that we've seen," or, "Most girl bands suck, but you guys rock," but younger kids seem different. For them to not be freaked out about the fact that we're dykes, to just say, "You're a good band," is really heartening.

Lynn Payne (Tantrum).

◆ **AJ: That sounds like progress. What about you, Tantrum, where are you from?**

◆ LYNN PAYNE (Tantrum): I'm from Toronto. I'm 24, and I didn't feel that much social pressure about playing music the way that Les did.

◆ **AJ: That's my point, exactly. You're seven years younger. What do you play?**

Some people still say, "You're the best *girl* band that we've seen," but younger kids seem different. For them to not be freaked out about the fact that we're dykes, to just say, "You're a good band," is really heartening.

◆ LP: I play bass. I took music in school when I was nine years old, and I tried to learn to play as many different instruments as I could. My main instrument was tenor saxophone, which I played until I finished high school. I got my first bass when I was 16 years old. Got my first job, got my first check, got my first bass at Sears for $89.99.

◆ LM: *Fist City* was recorded on the Sears bass.

◆ LB: It's little like her. We had to finally force her to get another bass that'd at least sound *bigger*. She was like: "No, I can't swing this one around—my bass is little like me. I want to be able to jump around. This one's heavy and…" We had to argue with her.

◆ LP: I played the Sears bass all the way up until I got this Tune bass, which was just last year.

I learned to play bass on my own, and got into my first band when I was 18. It was an all-women three-piece reggae band called Random Order; I did that for almost three years. Then I played in this seven-piece band that was more funky, jazzy, with some reggae too—there were so many people and so many different influences, the songs just had all different kinds of things thrown into them. That band was all women, too.

◆ **AJ: Are you dyke-identified?**

◆ LP: Oh, yeah. I've been a dyke since sexuality entered my brain. [laughs] I guess I'm one of those ones who was born a dyke.

A friend of mine in Toronto—the lead singer of the band I used to play with, Random Order—had been in San Francisco and had brought back Tribe 8's CD. So I'd heard it once, and that was all I'd ever known about Tribe 8. I went to San Francisco while they were on tour in Europe, and they had been having some

Lynn Payne and her mother (1983): "My mom never discouraged the career choices I made and has always supported who I felt I had to be."

trouble with their bass player. I knew Leslie's roommate, and she suggested to them, "Well, my friend in Toronto's here, and she plays bass—maybe you guys can jam." It just worked very well from there.

◆ **AJ: What about you, Slade? What's your background? And how old are you?**
◆ SLADE BELLUM: I'm going to be 35 in a month. You can call me Gramps.
◆ **AJ: No, I'm the gramps. I'm going to be 40 in a month.**
◆ SB: "The best years of our lives." I've been playing music all my life. I wanted to get into rock, but I didn't get involved in it until I was about 20. It was very hard back then. I was also dyke-oriented and out. I struggled trying to find an all-girl band for many years. We could always find two or three girls, but not a whole band that was girls, at that time. I played in several bands.

When I turned 30, I got burnt out on it. I had really bad carpal tunnel syndrome from drumming and bicycling. I was also really *over* trying to struggle to get some notice and get support from other people. Actually, that was right when things were changing; there were a lot more girls starting to do it, and lots of stuff happening. But I had to quit for three years. I tried getting a career and doing other things.
◆ **AJ: What kind of career?**
◆ SB: I was in the bicycle business.

◆ **AJ: Like Lynn Breedlove's business?**
◆ SB: No, not messengering; working on bikes and selling bikes. I really liked it. I tried different things during those years off. But eventually I decided it didn't matter how old I got; what I really wanted to do was play drums. I let my hands rest for a few years so they were better, and that was when Tribe 8 was having a hard time finding a secure drummer.
◆ **AJ: Did anyone ever tell you that you couldn't play drums—that women have a harder time because of upper-body strength?**
◆ LF: Are you kidding?
◆ **AJ: Do you know how many times people have said that?**
◆ SB: Well, that's why I didn't start drumming until I was 20. I wanted to drum since I was five. Nobody would *allow* it, because I was a girl—that's what they would say. My family didn't help. But I've never heard the upper-body strength thing. I thought it was just more a power deal. It's a powerful instrument, and boys think *they* should do it. [laughs] But in my heart, I feel like drumming is actually a very woman-oriented thing. If you go back to the history of drumming and where it came from, it was very woman-oriented in its origins.

Tribadism is about rubbing against another person, to get off; it's often used to describe dykes, or lesbian sex. One of my friends said that in Victorian England, they used to call lesbians "tribades."

◆ **AJ: Why is that?**
◆ SB: Because it comes from down here.
◆ **AJ: The belly.**
◆ SB: Yeah. What's that line they say—that the beginning of music was the beat? The first instrument was the drum. Just in my intuition, in my genes, and what I've studied, I've concluded that when it was first being done, it was by women. I feel like it was taken over by men in every kind of culture—not just punk or rock'n'roll. Even now, if you look at some of the tribes that try to keep their cultures in a way that isn't saturated by patriarchy, you'll find

more women drummers. If there's any kind of saturation by patriarchy, it's immediately all guy drummers and the women are dancing.

On a personal level, when people would see me drum, I felt like they were really supportive. They knew I was a good drummer; they just didn't know how to put it into the context of society and bands. Sure, I'd get the comment, "Well, you're good for a woman." But basically, I felt like everybody understood that it really comes from my heart and I'm really getting across not just music, but an expression of myself.

Lynn Flipper (rhythm guitar).

It was really more of the question, "Where do I do this? Who do I fit with?" When I heard that Tribe 8 needed a drummer, I asked them if I could audition—and they let me.

♦ **AJ: What about you, Flipper?**

♦ **LF:** My background? Well, unlike all these geniuses, I don't have a musical background. I didn't play guitar before Tribe 8, and I didn't have a punk rock background. I grew up in a working-class Vermont neighborhood, and I listened to everything from metal to reggae. It was a college town, so all kinds of bands came through. I liked all kinds of music, but I wasn't really in the punk scene, growing up.

I met Lynn Breedlove at a point in my life when I was quitting drugs and alcohol, and I had a lot of energy—a *lot* of energy. I played a lot of air guitar in my kitchen, with my girlfriend at the time, Harriet Dodge. She'd play air drums, I'd play air guitar, and we'd go, "We're going to be in a band someday—*yeah*!" But I didn't have an instrument and I only knew like three chords on an acoustic guitar from my childhood—some hippie probably taught me. Lynnie had these really hilarious lyrics, and someone knew that I could play three chords on the guitar, so they were like, "Play my party." We got together and kind of made it up on the spot.

Playing that party was my first experience. For me it was: throw yourself into it, learn as you go, and have a lot of fun doing it. I didn't have any equipment; I tried to get equipment by stealing it. That didn't work. I decided that I'd go the straight and narrow route and try to save my pennies and buy some equipment. It was hard to have the desire to do it, and only gradually be able to accumulate the equipment. It was hard to walk into a guitar store filled with guys. You're some butch dyke—you're already kind of freaky-looking to them—and they're like, "Oh, do you want the blah-blah-blah strings or the dah-dah-dah strings?" And they rattle off five names. I don't know what kind of strings—I just want some strings!

Luckily, this was in San Francisco, where there was a lot of support from the rapidly emerging queer punk scene. Even though we made horrendous noise in the beginning, people were really excited. They loved it, and they were patient with us. Slade was at our first gig, and we were humiliated because she was an actual musician, and we were not—yet. Leslie was there, too, and

Lynn Flipper at age 6.

IN DRAG: Lynn Flipper (with tie) and friends (l. to r.) Tanya Uhlmann, Chloe Sherman, and Harriet Dodge.

we didn't know if she was a musician, but she looked like one. So we were like, "Oh, no! Fear—terror." We played anyway. Years later, Slade wanted to join us, and that was a big deal to me. I moved to San Francisco when I was 19, and I watched Slade play for years. I watched all these women—the few that were there—play for years, and now I get to play with them.

♦ **AJ: How old are you?**

♦ LF: I'm 28.

♦ **AJ: Well, punk rock's all about not necessarily being able to play, but just doing it—not having rules about whether you can or can't. How did you decide on the name Tribe 8?**

♦ LF: It's from the word tribadism.

♦ LM: It's a Latin word, like fellatio or cunnilingus. Tribadism is about rubbing against another person, to get off; it's often used to describe dykes, or lesbian sex. One of my friends said that in Victorian England, they used to call lesbians "tribades."

Lynnie came up with the idea to update the word—to make it Tribe 8 so it had that futuristic connotation, yet the "tribe" thing made it sort of—

♦ LB: —prehistoric.

♦ LM: It emphasized that queer culture does actually have history. She made a great market-

ing point to us about how it included both of these ideas, futuristic culture as well as ancient culture. We said okay, because we'd been arguing about a name for a really long time.

♦ LB: Actually, it was more a *poetic* concept than marketing concept.

♦ **AJ: Do you have certain philosophies that you want to enact with the band?**

♦ LF: There was a statement of purpose when the band first started.

♦ **AJ: Do you still have one?**

♦ LM: No. We needed that statement of purpose to sort of define who we were, because we felt like we were doing something different—although we didn't really set out to do what we're doing now at all. At first it was a joke—it was just about fun. The statement of purpose was necessary to answer people who wondered: "What is this band about? What are these dykes doing up there playing punk rock?" We had to define ourselves before other people did it for us.

♦ LB: It was about how we're talking to other dykes, and to women in general. If other people want to watch—people with penises implied— that's fine. But we're really not addressing this to them. They're totally welcome, but this is between *us*. It's about cultural validation. Our purpose was to say: "There's a bunch of people out there who feel all alone, and this is a way to create community and identity for us."

♦ LF: I also think that sometimes people wonder if there's a political agenda. A lot of our songs are just based on our experiences. Our most recent song, about being mistaken for being a boy in the women's room, is not like: "I need to *represent* myself in this certain way," it's just that this happens to us every day, so we write about it, humorously.

♦ **AJ: Do you care, by the way, if you're mistaken for a boy?**

♦ LF: After a while, when you're 28, and you're mistaken for 15, you get a little over it.

♦ SB: I only care when I'm trying to go to the

bathroom. I don't care if I'm getting a Coke.

♦ LB: Sometimes it's hard. You're sleeping in the van, and you only get a couple hours of sleep at a time. You have to wake up at rest stops, where everybody has to jump out and coordinate their bladders. You're zombieing around, all you want to do is take a fucking leak, and everybody's staring at you like you're some kind of freak! I don't feel like being stared at, or having people tell their kids: "It's okay, he's not going to get you," and all this crap when I'm half asleep. I just feel like: "Accept me. I'm different from you. There's a lot of different people out there who you haven't seen, because you live in fucking Bumfuck, Iowa, so get over it." I get pissed off after a while. "Deal, go travel. Do something, get a life."

> "Accept me. I'm different from you. There's a lot of different people out there who you haven't seen, because you live in fucking Bumfuck, Iowa, so get over it." I get pissed off after a while. "Deal, go travel. Do something, get a life."

♦ LF: People will come up to you and say, "You're in the wrong bathroom," to the point where you really have no other choice but to lift your shirt up and show that you have tits— to say that you can stay in this bathroom. Or managers of restaurants will hold the door open until you leave. It's not just our sensitivity to a particular moment; it gets *extreme*. People actually get downright hostile.

♦ AJ: But I can imagine that it could be fun to be taken for a boy—when it's not a matter of being hassled.

♦ LF: It *can* be fun. Some people don't really have a choice about it. I don't feel good if I look any less butch than this. It's hilarious, but I've been dealing with it for years and years.

♦ AJ: If anyone looks slightly "different" at all, and you go outside of any urban area, let's face it—

♦ LF: That's true.

♦ AJ:—you're going to get shit. It doesn't

even matter if you try really hard to look normal. They look in your eyes and they know— you're not one of them.

♦ LF: This song, "Wrong Bathroom," is also for straight women who look punk, or look weird at all; it's for drag queens, too. The song is for anyone who feels uncomfortable, or is stared at, outside of their own community.

♦ AJ: I try to look "normal," but when I go outside the urban world—it never works. Now I just go, "Thank god!" If they actually accepted me, then—

♦ LP: —you're doing something wrong. Slade, do you like looking like a boy, or being mistaken for one?

♦ SB: Yes, sometimes I do. It makes me feel like I'm dressing myself well, because that's my intention, and it's working.

♦ LF: It has its benefits, definitely.

♦ LB: The thing that's scary is being confusing. If people thought I was a boy all the time, if I totally passed as a man when I needed to, if when I went in the men's room, I wouldn't get my ass kicked for being a queer, a freak, a fag, a dyke—then I would be fine with that. If everybody just agrees that I'm a guy, I'm fine. But the thing that scares me is: "Are you a boy or a girl? Well, if you're not a boy or a girl, then you must be a queer. And if you're a queer I can kill you, because you're a fag or a dyke. You're not human, and I can fag-bash you."

I don't feel safe walking into the men's room, just assuming that everybody in there is going to say, "Okay, you're a boy."

♦ AJ: You're not safe.

♦ LB: I know. I want my other freaky pals around me when I go to the bathroom at a truck stop.

♦ AJ: But if you go in the ladies' room, and they get freaked, *tough*— let 'em run out of the room!

♦ LM: When I grew up in Colorado, I was always really punk, one of the few girls who actually shaved my head and dyed my hair. I got shit all

Leslie Mah (1976).

the time, every day. You start to go to this place in your head where you separate yourself from the outside world—you don't hear what people are saying, because they're always screaming at you from their car windows, and you just tune out so much. It's taken me a long time to try and actually get over that, to listen to other people and be aware of them, instead of completely tuning them out all the time. I still do that to men all the time, which usually is a good thing. But occasionally I meet nice guys on tour, and it just takes me a long time, seeing them over and over again, to think: "Okay, this is a human being, and maybe I can talk to him..."

◆ **AJ: But you can't start off thinking that. When you walk the streets, you have to assume—**

◆ LM: —you put on your armor—

◆ LF: —knowing you can get gay-bashed. I've only been gay-bashed in San Francisco.

◆ **AJ: You have?**

◆ LF: Yeah.

◆ **AJ: What kind of incident?**

◆ LF: I walked into a burrito joint with my lover, and a white guy on speed said, "What are *you* doing here?" He came up and threw food in our faces, and we responded; he gave my lover two black eyes and a bloody lip. Nobody could stop him fast enough. We chased him down, and

Allen's Mom Plus Two CD (1994).

the cops came and got him, but they let him go. If he had stolen a pack of bubble gum, they would've kept him overnight. But because he just hit two dykes, they let him go that same night—and that is right in San Francisco.

◆ **AJ: Did he say anything derogatory about being dykes?**

◆ LF: Did he? Oh, he made it very clear why he was hitting us. "What are *you* doing here, what are *you* doing here, fucking dykes?"

We tried to prosecute. The public defender was really into it because it was a hate crime, and we had witnesses in the burrito place who were really supportive, because they saw the whole thing. They didn't not stop him because they didn't want to, it was just so quick—it kind of blew people away. It was in the daytime, and it's just a restaurant; you don't expect it.

The case never did go anywhere. After a while you think about running into someone like that all the time, and you do feel a change in the way you walk down the street. There really isn't that much you can do in the legal system. There's a victim-assistance program, and they led me on to think they were going to pay for a whole bunch of stuff, and actually accepted bills for years and then wrote me a letter that said: "You responded by fighting back. So actually we're going to turn you down for the money that you're supposed to get"—which was supposed to pay for seeing a therapist for post-traumatic stress. I protested it, and I got the money.

◆ **AJ: Wait a minute. They said the problem was that you responded? You mean, if you'd just rolled over and—**

◆ LF: I threw salsa in the guy's eyes, because he attacked me.

◆ **AJ: So you're going to get punished for that? You weren't a good victim.**

◆ LF: It was typed, it was clear—I didn't even have to read between the lines. It just said: "You fought back. While you didn't instigate it, you encouraged it to continue."

◆ LB: So if you lie down, that's encouraging it to stop?

◆ LF: Yeah. But I called them on it and they did give

me my money.

♦ LM: I was also gay-bashed in San Francisco, in the middle of the day, on the street—really close to the Castro—with my girlfriend, by a guy who was really huge. He started off with verbal stuff about being whores and dykes and whatever you can call women to make them feel bad about themselves—although it doesn't always work, as in my situation. He ended up turning around and coming after us physically, and he fucked up our jaws. It was really, really scary, and people just stood around and watched. We called the cops, and the cops just never even came.

I think a lot of it had to do with the fact that both my girlfriend and I looked punk. Also, the guy was Latino, I'm Eurasian, and she's Native American, so maybe we all looked like— something *else*? Or people assumed something like, "Well, maybe they know each other, it's a drug deal"—I don't know. Nobody would get involved, and it was really scary. There was a lot of people, a lot of fags, just standing there and watching.

♦ AJ: You guys travel around the country, right?

♦ LF: Yeah, and Europe twice.

♦ AJ: What are your audiences like, outside of urban environments? What are some of the reactions you get?

Leslie Mah (r.) and friend Traci (l.), when they were in the band Anti Scrunti Faction in Colorado.

I walked into a burrito joint with my lover, and a white guy on speed said, "What are *you* doing here?" He came up and threw food in our faces, and we responded; he gave my lover two black eyes and a bloody lip.

♦ SB: I've been really surprised by how positive and great the crowds are. Sometimes they're really big; sometimes they're not quite as large a crowd as you would get in a big city. Yet everybody who comes really wants to see us, or really

wants to see a show, and they're so happy they saw us. We always get at least a few dykes in each little area—it just adds so much to their life to have someone like us come through. The rest of the crowd is just whoever is into the punk scene.

♦ AJ: Is it usually a mixed punk audience, gender-wise?

♦ SB: Yeah, it's usually mixed.

♦ LP: Unless we're playing a specifically women's occasion—a festival, or something like that.

Before I started touring with the band, I used to wonder if it would be kind of scary being on the road with Tribe 8. This was when I still had the idea in my head that San Francisco was some kind of mecca for dykes and freaks. I was apprehensive about leaving that safe space and going to, like, Bumfuck, Ohio—how are they going to perceive me out there?

But great people come to our shows. I guess some people think we're kind of freakish, but I also think people can see beyond that and get into the music—not just say, "Oh, there's this freak band." They say, "Hey, there's this really kick-ass band. They may be kind of freakish, but their music rocks."

♦ AJ: I think it's a really positive sign that

Photo: Tera Stockton

Lynn Breedlove.

◆ LF: We just played in Provincetown, at Town Hall. It was a great show. A lot of punk-rock kids, disco fags, dykes and straight people. The cops came in at one point and asked Lynnie to put a shirt on. She did, and she gave a speech about it—

◆ AJ: —you didn't have your shirt on?

◆ LF: *She* didn't have her shirt on.

◆ SB: *Three* of us didn't have our shirts on.

◆ AJ: Is that usual?

◆ LP: Well, you get hot onstage. You get hot and you take off your shirt. Men have been doing that onstage forever. So why is it not okay for us to do? I'm playing, I'm hot, I'm taking off my shirt!

◆ AJ: I love it! [laughs]

◆ LF: But it causes a lot of controversy, that's for sure.

◆ LB: They didn't care about my rubber dick hanging out of my pants the whole show. What they cared about was naked breasts.

◆ SB: But afterwards, it sounded like they *were* offended by that. They bring all of that into the media—what this band brought to their children. "How could we let that happen in our city, our Town Hall? Let's make sure this never happens again." Which they probably will, but we'll just play somewhere else.

◆ AJ: What did they do?

◆ LF: This woman called me from *The Cape Codder*. It was actually more that she wanted the other side of the story. She was an obviously conservative older woman, and she was talking about how she heard there was obscenity, nudity and gyrating pelvic motions with a rubber penis. I had a flashback of Elvis. [laughs] I think she honestly wanted to hear why we did things. I gave her a rundown of what Tantrum said, about taking our shirts off to be comfortable.

It's not always that they want to trash the band itself, but there's this controversy in which the Republican-based part of the community uses something like us as an excuse to shut down all-ages events—to shut down any kind of creative youth project.

◆ LP: All in the name of family values.

you have a mixed punk audience, and it's not a dyke-only crowd, because it's about the music, too. It's good to hear that you have support and encouragement in middle America, because there's this incredibly conservative wave, along with real homophobia, rising right now.

◆ LF: Our shows bring out the people who are really *craving* something alternative. If you look back in history, like in Germany before World War II, all of the arts were exploding all over the place. It seems like something similar is happening right now in this country.

◆ AJ: *Fin de siècle*, the end of an era, the end of the millennium. I wonder whether things are actually positive; do some things just *seem* positive because so much negativity is coming at us hard and fast?

◆ SB: Well, the conservative people definitely do not like us.

◆ LF: No, and they speak up about it. We've had those reactions.

◆ SB: It usually happens after we've played a show, and they find out what our show is like.

◆ LM: It just goes back to all the political controversy over the female body. Men's bodies are their own, whereas women's bodies are regulated.

At the Provincetown show, there were all these boys out in the audience with their shirts off. We told them, "Okay, you guys can't show your tits, either." They actually put their shirts back on! This one boy even borrowed his girlfriend's bra to wear. [laughs] It was very cute.

◆ LB: I think the conservative reaction to us is sadly shallow. The reasons why we do these things they're so upset about are very complex. The reason we cut off those dicks is, we're talking about rape—and we feel about being raped like *you* would feel about having your dick cut off. It's time for you to start putting yourselves in someone else's shoes. You get to walk around completely comfortable in hundred-degree heat—I don't. Why is that? You need to think about that! Why are breasts legal to show in a place where men can masturbate and pay 20 or 50 or 100 bucks, and other men can make money off of those naked breasts being seen—as in *Playboy* or red-light districts—but *I* am not allowed to be comfortable, as a human being? Why, why, *why?*

These are very complex issues, and they're about rights. When conservatives react to them, they don't think about our rights. They think: "That is a rubber penis! Rubber penis equals bad. That is a naked breast! Naked breast equals bad."

You get hot onstage and you take off your shirt. Men have been doing that onstage forever. So why is it not okay for us to do? I'm playing, I'm hot, I'm taking off my shirt!

◆ AJ: The ironic thing is that rock'n'roll had already established the "rights" of male rockers, from Jim Morrison to the Rolling Stones, to be really sexual and lewd onstage. I think that where the new conservative reaction and the real shock comes from is that you have women and queers refusing to be constrained by fixed categories, and starting to create a new gender. The older hippies, who are now yuppies, established that lewd behavior was okay for male rock stars. Oliver Stone makes *The Doors.* Sex, drugs and rock'n'roll!

◆ LM: But it's straight male sexuality that they're talking about—anything deviating from that is going to harm the children. In the '50s, straight male sexuality was menacing, but now the concern is about *women* being up there and being sexual.

Men's bodies are their own, whereas women's bodies are regulated.

We're always viewed through the eyes of male rock journalists, who are writing for a male audience. They're trying to decipher what these women are doing, what these queers are doing. Sometimes they get it, just because they've had some sort of full experience as a human being. But not all of them are getting the idea. You can't look at this women's band and talk about sexuality in the same context. You can't just view us through your male rock glasses.

◆ AJ: Of course these old male rock critics, like Robert Christgau, are pretty geriatric. But you also have some good articles written about you, right?

◆ LF: Yeah. This woman at the *Voice*, Carol Cooper, wrote a great review, putting us in the context of traditional male rock'n'roll. She acknowledged the queer element of our band, but she also was like: "This band has its slot just in rock'n'roll." She placed us in these other traditions—in terms of us being an essential version of true rock'n'roll. That was really cool, because she did both. It's a fine balance to say: "They're perverts, and they're queers, and they do all this stuff—and yet they're right up there, following a lot of rock'n'roll traditions. But it's not traditional, because it's Lynn doing it." I thought it was really well done, but that's a rare article.

I talked to some guy from the *Boston Globe* and he asked: "How do you think of yourself, in terms of being a crossover band?" I think the thing about this band is that we started in San Francisco; we had a queer-punk following. Then we left San Francisco and played to straight, predominantly white punk crowds. That's where we had to get our support, and

Photo: Paul Holtan

Slade Bellum performing at a recital, age 12.

touring, and I do feel a little bit of a different energy, but, it seems like things *are* getting a little scarier as far as conservative stuff.

◆ AJ: Where?

◆ SB: Everywhere in America.

◆ LF: In the world.

◆ **AJ: But, see, I'm reading about it in the media. I want to know if you're actually experiencing it.**

◆ SB: We were talking about going to the bathrooms, going to the truck stops and stuff like that. That's where we're confronted with it the most—otherwise, where do we see all these conservative people? We go right from our van to a club. The conservatives are not hanging out at the punk club in whatever little town we're in. But if we have to go to the gas station, or go get something to eat, or go to the bathroom—that is where we interact with a major part of the population. And in those places, I feel this totally different energy—it's really hostile.

◆ **AJ: That's the problem with looking different. When I had short bright red hair in '79, no one knew what that meant; by 1980, they were shouting, "Devo! Devo!" Once mainstream America knew about the Sex Pistols, they had some way to evaluate these people who looked like freaks to them. It's hostility towards *difference*. Now, punk is mainstream. Now it's selling ads.**

If you don't see yourself represented anywhere in the mainstream culture, you fit into some kind of underground. For example, if there's a butch dyke in a film, she's usually quickly air-brushed out of it.

◆ SB: But there's still an underground. That's what I hold onto, and I think a lot of us in this band do. We don't sell out. We haven't yet.

◆ **AJ: What does "selling out" mean? I've been watching punk rock since '78, and I'm just so confused about a lot of these terms. I want to clarify this, because I'm trying to confirm that some ideals are still being preserved—but I am very leery about the word "underground," at this point.**

they were very supportive. Young kids and older rocker dudes would sing all the words, get up and do all this stuff onstage.

Now we're starting to make a crossover to the gay community. It's just the reverse of how some people would think we got our fans. A lot of gay people are just learning about Tribe 8 now, through the Michigan Festival and through a lot of gay press. It's a new thing, for a lot of lesbians, to come and see a hardcore band—especially one that's singing about them in a real humorous way. The humor is sometimes hard for people to get, because it comes from within our own culture. It's easier for them to grab ahold of the anger, even though a lot of that is *stage anger*, just for show.

There's been a shift, when we're out on the road, of more women coming, being aggressive in the pit, slamming around and having a really good time. Before it was such a male thing that there wasn't really any room, unless you were a hardcore punk rocker, and you were one of four women at the shows. Now it's so mixed at the shows that we play; old biker dudes will come up, 15-year-old girls will come up, lawyers, whatever. That's what's exciting for me about this band, that we get to play to so many people even though—

◆ **AJ: Because it's rock'n'roll.**

◆ SB: It's been really good for Tribe 8 to be

◆ SB: I think the underground is still there. To me, it's a whole community that's not caught up in the rest of those punk politics. The point is to welcome new and different ideas and ways of expression, and to use them for self-empowerment to then make changes for other people.

◆ LF: If you don't see yourself represented anywhere in the mainstream culture, you fit into some kind of underground. For example, I don't see myself in film yet. If there's a butch dyke in a film, she's usually quickly air-brushed out of it.

◆ LM: That's always your fate in the movies: you either die or you grow old lonely.

◆ **AJ: Another stereotype about queers is to be the killer. 85% of the killers in the movies happen to be queer. No one *I* know is represented in the media; kind of like how in the '70s the media depicted hippies in movies like *The Trip*.**

◆ SB: That's why we carefully consider how much national publicity is okay for us to have. Is it okay for us to be in *Rolling Stone* or not? It is important to be out there, and have people see us, yet we're still not "selling out."

◆ **AJ: Defining exactly what "selling out" is seems to be difficult. If we're talking about a supportive underground, we're also talking about these little pockets of community that engage in vicious infighting and mutual accusations of selling out. Do these rules as to what constitutes selling out help or hinder the underground? Some accusers are scared to death of real power, and they're scared to death because you've made a commitment. If you've done something creative and manifested it— whether it's a band, a record, or a book— you've sacrificed a lot for it. Unfortunately, the very people who should be supporting this effort are threatened to death: "Oh, that's selling out."**

◆ SB: I agree; that doesn't accomplish anything. I'm not against selling out as far as getting ahead—getting whatever we've created out to more people, and getting more acknowledgement for that.

◆ **AJ: You can say, maybe, that not selling out is staying true to certain basic nonexploitational ideals.**

◆ LF: What are those?

◆ **AJ: Well, that's a whole can of worms, too.**

◆ LB: They're ideals like artistic freedom and integrity. If they tell us we can't take our shirts off, because if we don't take our shirts off we'll make a lot of money—we'll sell billions of records, just like Michael Jackson—I'll be like, "Nah, sorry. I'd rather not have a billion dollars. I'd rather take my shirt off."

◆ LP: I know why I'm making music and what I want to get out of it. If I start making music for reasons other than those reasons, then I'm selling out. That's the bottom line. If you can't be true to yourself, then you're fucking selling out.

◆ **AJ: And what are some of the reasons?**

◆ LP: I love to play bass. I don't care if I'm doing it in my bedroom or if I'm doing it at Irving Plaza—I'm not interested in fame and popularity and being in the media.

◆ **AJ: But—just to play devil's advocate— what's wrong with playing at Irving Plaza and getting the word out?**

◆ LP: A lot of times you can't get *your* words out and still keep your integrity, because there are other people manipulating the "product."

◆ **AJ: It is possible to sign on a major label without ever having to "sell out." Most of the time it doesn't work that way; given the cyclical pressures of repetitive touring and grinding out new "product," it's a miracle if creativity and vision can survive the process.**

The problem is that the "underground," that very community that should be engaging in this discussion, continues to make simple dismissive statements such as, "Well, they're

Slade Bellum in North Hampton, MA.

on a major label, so they must have sold out." But it's really about, "Can I express my own voice? Can I take off my shirt?" What if you got to the point where major labels saw that they could make money on you without your having to change—which could happen when you get big enough and have that kind of clout, or now, in a climate of "transgression" that sells an illusion of rebellion. Then it's a different discussion.

♦ SB: We're not against the idea of people who manage to accomplish that at all. But that's not the only way. There's still a scene happening where people are putting out their own CDs, or releasing them on a very small label. There is a support network, the whole queercore thing—we are connected with each other and we're trying to help each other out. We're trying to do tours together, we're trying to connect with each other—here's someone that does management; here's someone that's trying to put a record company together—and network on a lower level. If you can keep your respectability and the terms that you want, and move up on a bigger label, and get your message out—hey, that's excellent. I agree, there are people that are doing that.

If we were to do something like that, I think the big problem would be the question of where are the women in those areas? Because, usually, when you get to major labels…

♦ LM: Even at the punk rock level, you still have a lot of straight white boys running the show. Of course they're going to sign their friends to their label and promote their friends' bands. If there were women who wanted to be involved with music but weren't interested in being onstage or didn't know how to play an instrument, I would encourage them to get behind the scenes, on the business side of things— where you actually have real power.

♦ LF: Bands like Fugazi are great, but they're straight white men; I can't overlook that fact. When you have power to give up, it's a lot easier to give it up. If you *haven't* had that power all your life, and you're told that it's selling out to give it up…

♦ AJ: It's true that they're white males—

♦ LF: I love them, by the way. It's not a judgement.

♦ AJ: So it's really more like: "Girls, go and implant in your head that you can do it, too."

♦ LM: Economic power is what talks in this world now. We're not a bunch of teenagers just banging on instruments and screaming any-more. I was in that stage maybe ten years ago— but in ten more years, I'm going to be middle-aged, and I've been doing these wage-slave jobs to get by for my whole life.

Should I have to do that just so I can keep my music pure, and have some kind of special integrity because I've never made a cent off of it? Some people assume that we're making all this money now—

♦ LF: —because we're in *Rolling Stone*.

♦ LM: They say, "God, you're on tour." It's like, "Well, it's better than being at home and having to work my day job." And they're like, "What? You have a day job?"

Being on tour is incredibly hard work. You get 40 minutes of glory when you play; the rest of the time you're driving and schlepping shit, and you don't make money. Sometimes I feel like I'm under a microscope; I have to be charming and nice and considerate—you're staying at people's houses, hoping they'll be aware that you're a human being and you'd like to take a shower and have something to eat.

♦ AJ: A number of women are now running their own record labels.

♦ SB: I think that's the next step. And that's what we need.

♦ LB: But you need money for the publicity and the distribution.

> We don't need men to keep us poor—women will keep each other poor half the time. "Play my benefit, do this and that."

♦ AJ: That's true, but it's really about energy. I know a number of women who have started their own labels with a few singles and EP's—you just have to avoid thinking, "Unless I can make a big-production studio CD, I won't do it."

Women—particularly in lesbian and feminist communities—have a guilt complex about money and success that men don't. There's such shame or defensiveness if they ever get any money.

♦ LF: We don't need men to keep us poor— women will keep each other poor half the time. "Play my benefit, do this and that." I have a small café, Bearded Lady; people helped us out to get us started. As soon as we could pay performers, we always gave them some money—whether it's 10 bucks, 20 bucks—just to get the idea going that we can pay each other.

◆ LB: Economic power is political power. I don't think that success, as far as making a living off your art, is selling out. I think selling out is when you start to say, "It's okay to charge 20 dollars at the door; it's okay to only play clubs." Then you start to become inaccessible to people who have no money, or people who aren't 21. We all value accessibility and distribution. We want to be heard and

Leslie Mah, Tantrum and Lynn Breedlove.

seen by anyone who wants to see and hear us, so I would not allow us to sign with a company, for any amount of money, that would limit that accessibility.

The other thing that I really would want to look into is: what is Warner Brothers investing in with all the money they're making off Tribe 8?

◆ **AJ: Wait, excuse me—is Warner Brothers investing in Tribe 8?**

[laughter]

◆ LF: No, no. She's being hypothetical.

◆ **AJ: Oh, okay.**

◆ LB: They are invested in all kinds of shady activities and global economics. One of the reasons why I started Lickety Split was that I didn't want to deliver packages for Bank of Apartheid. No, thank you. The only way I was able to refuse to do that was to quit my job at Western Messenger—which delivers packages for Bank of Apartheid all day long—and start my own business where I can say, "Sorry, Bank of Apartheid, you cannot have packages delivered by Lickety Split, all-dyke delivery. [raspberry] Eat me."

We want to be really aware of who we are aiding financially, because they're going to make a lot of money off of us. We're not going to get enough to feed our cats, and they're going to go invest their profits in some venture that we

don't agree with. *That's* selling out.

◆ LF: We are such fucking freaks; I just don't see somebody swooping down, put a bunch of makeup on us, and saying, "All right, it's the next Bangles!" I think we're really a circus show for people. So I don't fear success. I do want a little bit of economic power. I also want accessibility. I want to play punk rock shows, and play to the kids, and I also want older dykes to come. On a daily basis, we probably all feel different about this.

◆ SB: At the end of the tour, when we're all tired out, we'd like someone to take care of us. We'd like a nice mobile home, with a shower and a toilet.

◆ LM: We want to go home and have some money so we can take our babes out to dinner, after we haven't seen 'em for over a month.

◆ **AJ: Your babes need to be taken out!**

The underground community has to be careful in looking at what the powers-that-be want right now. Now they actually *want* freakishness.

◆ LF: They want a circus show?

◆ **AJ: They want to flirt with the external gloss of transgression.**

◆ SB: I agree.

◆ LF: My friend's bare chest was in this huge glossy photo in *Spin*. My café was listed in there, too. Aren't we marketable?

Lynn Breedlove (r.) and Anna Joy (l.), her "one and only of three years."

♦ LM: The whole look of piercings and tattoos is totally marketable.

♦ AJ: I did the book *Modern Primitives*, about piercing and tattooing, and then watched the phenomenon become almost mainstream. Capitalism always needs the shock of the new to sell product, lulling people into a false identity of "uniqueness" and rebellion, encouraging them to buy some product and divert their energy from really changing the economic and political system.

♦ LM: I think that's why Tribe 8 is able to get into these magazines. It's not because we're selling so many records. It's because their same old boring stories about Smashing Pumpkins bickering, or the latest Stone Temple Pilots guy going off into rehab, are like yawn, yawn, yawn—then it's like, "Oh, militant lesbian S/M warriors!" We're not making a cent off this, but it helps to spice up their magazine and make them look like they're on the forefront of something. Bisexuality is on the cover of *Newsweek*. All of a sudden, it's a new fad.

We're the real thing, and they couldn't actually swallow this *whole*, but they can sort of—like you said—flirt with the glossy surface of lesbian chic. Howard Stern even said to Phil Donahue, "I've made all my money just talking about lesbians."

♦ LF: Oh ho. Where's *our* money?

♦ LP: C'mon—we live it.

♦ AJ: Well, let's talk about how you live it—let's talk about sex! Do you ever get groupies?

♦ LF: Dykes are learning how to be aggressive, and Tribe 8 has been a big learning lesson for them in this area. [laughs] We're getting more and more groupies.

♦ LP: People get excited; they feel like you've played this great show for them and they just want to be all over you, thankful and grateful. But when you're on the road, you can't be *on* all the time. Sometimes you just want to be left alone. "I'm really tired. I'd just like to have a minute by myself." Sometimes they feel like, "Who's this bitch?"

♦ AJ: What's new is that you're women getting this kind of attention from other women. Rock'n'roll has always been a magnet for sexuality—there you are up onstage with this aura of phallic aggression—guitar in the crotch and all. The older male rocker type kept a scorecard of his groupies, proudly publicizing his 50 trillion fucks... now, how do *women* who are in that position deal with it? Do you believe in monogamy?

♦ LM: None of us believe in monogamy. I've made it my life policy not to be ball-and-chained anymore. But when you go on tour, you go back to these towns and see these women again; you do have to be careful. Safe sex, for me, is a policy. It has been an issue on the road.

♦ AJ: Safe sex?

♦ LM: Sex in general. I think dykes are still really shy. I know I am.

♦ SB: There's definitely a lot of focus on sex at our shows.

♦ AJ: I hope so—it's rock'n'roll.

♦ SB: It *is* rock'n'roll. It's new because we're dykes. It's also new because we talk about butch/femme and transgender issues—it's not just women with women loving each other, lah-di-dah-di-dah. There's a lot of hardcore sex talk. The fact of us doing that is similar to how you said the boys used to be. But it's *our* sexuality.

♦ LM: We're talking about dyke sex, but there are also songs like "Romeo and Julio," which is about having this fantasy about being a fag, and having a fag lover. It's great fantasy material for just about anybody—straight boys, straight girls, dykes. Everyone gets a rush off of sex that they're not necessarily doing.

In this country there's the standard of the heterosexual monogamous marriage. People are put in certain hierarchies according to gender, race and sexuality—all these different things. At the top of this pyramid are straight heterosexuals in monogamous marriages, raising children to be upstanding citizens. But there are *do* many people who are not doing this and that are really good people. They might be heterosexual, they might be bisexual—they might be *anything*—or they might just be freaks in their own way.

All these ads are still focused on this family-values thing. The right is stating that everything else is bad except for this one example. That leaves everybody else out there saying, "Well, this isn't what I want, but what *do* I want?" There aren't any role models for figuring out non-monogamy.

Tribe 8 is able to get into [*Rolling Stone*] not because we're selling so many records, but because their same old boring stories are like yawn, yawn, yawn—then it's like, "Oh, militant lesbian S/M warriors!"

♦ **AJ: What really bugs me is that heterosexual feminists—and sometimes lesbian feminists, too—somehow confuse monogamy with having something to do with feminism. I've never quite understood this.**

♦ LM: There are a lot of heterosexuals who are real purists, but there are a lot of dykes like that, too. They say that if you're a pure dyke, you basically marry another woman, you have a relationship based on heterosexual marriage, you don't fool around—all these things go along with it.

♦ **AJ: I don't think humans are necessarily monogamous, but I do think women are in touch with their emotions enough to know when they're in love and things are going right—to not just have sex indiscriminately. Monogamy, historically, arose as a corollary**

to the ascent of patriarchy—to make sure the inheritance lines would go to the male. People know who the mother is, but establishing a father is difficult unless you have strict prohibitions on female sexuality.

♦ SB: We have a song about it—"Freedom." It's about wanting to be non-monogamous, but not having any role models, so we don't really know how to do it. The concepts are easy to understand, but incorporating it into our lives— it's happening, and certainly people in the band are doing it—but not without a little pain.

Each of us does it in a different way. We ask each other, "How do *you* do it? How does it work for you? What are the rules in your relationship?" It's still a young idea in our little culture and community, but I think it's going to develop.

♦ **AJ: Your point about the lack of role models is a good one. We grow up in this culture, and are still bound by past examples. So I'm not exactly sure how one grows into a different concept of relationships. It's a real struggle. You try, and you look at past mistakes—but it's hard without role models. This is an unknown terrain for humans, especially since it's only been very recent that men and women have had a concept of equality. You may not be forging relationships with men, but we're all trying to figure out the same thing: how can we share ourselves without *merging* ourselves? How can we make emotional and sexual connections without entangling them in security and ego issues?**

♦ SB: That's why it's such a blessing to be in a band of five, where everyone's trying to do this. Since we're driving around on tour, and have all this time in the van to chat—

♦ LB: —we talk about non-monogamy quite a bit. I've fought against monogamy because of its patriarchal origins, as you said. Also, to me, monogamy is about possession, and I'm trying to get away from possession. I'm trying to learn how to detach; how to have some identity and integrity of my own, as a separate person, and not be co-dependent. I feel, as a spiritual being in a human body, that I want to be free to express love on many different levels.

At the same time, we *are* products of our society, and my role models were my parents. They had a monogamous relationship, which, in the end, did not work. So that's confusing. I believe in true love. Well, what is true love? True love is two people possessing each other, and becoming one, becoming a unit. I don't *want*

to be a unit with somebody else—but I do want to give everything to that person. I was raised in a society that puts a lot of value on this romantic love myth, and I'm a poet, so I think it's very *poetic* to have romantic love, to be one, and to totally want to *die* for somebody else.

Again, at the same time, we are creating a new society where we want to be free from those constraints. So it's all confusing and paradoxical, and it's a mess, and there's lots of screaming and crying and pulling of hair and gnashing of teeth. But I think that growth equals pain; you cannot grow without pain. I feel like we're moving forward, and we're learning how to compromise, communicate, and be separate *and* one—how to have passion and commitment at the same time.

I went and got a ten-dollar super ballsy cock—a ten-inch big rubber dick with veins all over it, really gross, and really wobbly.

◆ **AJ: It's hard to try and figure this out if you're also dealing with men, who have held onto the notion that somehow all female sexuality fits either the wife/mother or the whore archetype. I try to present the issue as you're describing it—sexuality as an expression of all different kinds of love and friendship.**

But this is exactly where feminists got confused: for men, "free" sex has been so much about the conquest and not about the mutual pleasure. It served to stroke their egos, and it was marked by hostility to women's bodies. Wilhelm Reich (and afterwards, people like Alexander Lowen) wrote entire tomes about male "armoring" and sexuality. It's difficult for men (as well as women) to completely *feel* their bodies and have fully satisfying orgasms. A lot of men don't have good sex.

◆ LM: They don't have good sex? Is that why they're so mad at us?

◆ LB: I think sexuality is about power. That's why the expression of sexuality has been men's realm. Women can't have sexuality because they're not allowed to have power.

For me to express sexuality in as many different ways as possible means I have power—which is threatening to the patriarchy, because

only people with penises are supposed to have power. That's one reason why they don't like Tribe 8—because we are overtly sexual, which means we're powerful.

◆ LF: The stereotype of queers is that they don't have long relationships, and sometimes that stereotype is true. I wonder why that happens—

◆ **AJ: I know dykes from an older generation who have had extremely long relationships. But then again, I don't think they're particularly sexual. A lot of that generation of women sacrificed sexuality, and just got the—**

◆ LM: —emotional thing.

◆ LF: Right now there's a lot of sexual energy in the dyke community. Everyone's having sex all the time. Maybe their relationships suffer, but this is a whole new world for dykes.

◆ **AJ: Of course, you're talking about younger people, too.**

◆ LF: I think it might be a generational thing.

◆ **AJ: But when people are young, in their twenties, there's usually more sexuality and shorter relationships—**

◆ LM: Well, Flipper's pretty young. And she's in the longest relationship here, out of all of us.

◆ **AJ: Huh! So it's not just about youth—that's good.**

◆ LM: I'm not worried about her. I think she's having enough sex. [laughs]

◆ LF: Yeah. [laughs] I was just thinking in terms of the whole queer community in San Francisco, where I think there's less of this need to grab some partner for five years, go off and be alone. It's like, "Well I have this intense friendship, and we flirt with each other. And I have a fuck buddy here, and I play with this person." There are all these different relationships—instead of either marrying someone or it's a one-night stand, there's an *in-between* thing.

◆ **AJ: The model of a society where you cling to one person is so unbalanced—no one person can do everything for you…**

Lynn, you wanted to clarify some things about the penises, right?

◆ LB: Well, the first reason I got a big rubber dick was because we were lousy and terrible and cacophonous, and we didn't know what we were doing. I thought props would be a good distraction; everybody else had their instruments to wield, so I needed props. I went and got a ten-dollar super ballsy cock—a ten-inch big rubber dick with veins all over it, really gross, and really wobbly.

I got it because we had a song "Power Boy,"

that has this line: "You got your night stick, your surrogate dick." I would strap it on and pull it out to sing "Power Boy," wag it around, and stroke it while we were singing the chorus—which ends in, "Everyone's afraid of you because you're a moral masturbator."

And then, the more songs we wrote, the more it seemed those songs could *also* incorporate penises. Geez, just let it hang out the whole time! I stroked it off to songs like "Romeo and Julio," and started getting people to suck it.

The original public cock-sucking happened in Lexington, Kentucky. I walked out, and there was an all-ages crowd; all these young punks. I wanted a real buff, straight-looking, *scary-looking* guy to suck my dick. I thought that would be the best way to demonstrate that I had power, and that a guy—a

Lynn Breedlove getting her rubber dick sucked.

person who normally has all the power—had *less* power. Because the whole thing about homosexuality, anal penetration and cock-sucking is that if you allow yourself to be penetrated by a penis, you have no power and you are as bad as a woman—therefore, if you are a fag, you are not really a man. So if you are a fag, or a woman, you have no power. I wanted to turn around all these social constructs about the penis as a weapon.

Soon everybody at this show was fighting over who was going to be the most punk rock—who was going to suck my dick. All these little straight boys wanted to prove, by doing that, how punk rock they were.

I started to ask guys to do that all the time. I ask before the show, and I usually have to go around and ask about 20 guys. Most guys will not do it, because they know what it means: If you suck dick you're not a man, and you have no power. You're a whore, and you're this and

that—however many layers of connotations there are.

So it's really hard. Most of the time I can't get fags to do it because they don't want to not be like a man, either; there's this whole new thing in homosexuality about: "I am a *man*. I look straight, and I lift weights, and I wear a lot of leather. Just because I'm a fag doesn't mean I'm not a man." I know what else there is about fags, in particular, not wanting to volunteer to suck my dick. I think there's a lot of fear. If you go up there and suck my dick onstage, what's going to happen to you when you leave the club? I think straight men and gay men alike are worried that they might get gay-bashed if they suck my dick onstage.

One of the guys in this band we played with at Mercury Lounge [in New York] was ready to suck my dick onstage—and then one of them freaked out and said, "No, there's going to be a

Snapshot from the show at the Grog Shop in Cleveland, OH (May 1995).

lot of music-industry people here tonight, and we want to get signed—that would not be good. We might not get signed if you suck a rubber phallus." There's all kind of trips going around about this piece of rubber.

♦ **AJ: What have been some of the audience reactions when you've gotten someone to suck your dick?**

♦ LB: "Oh, my god"—"It's so punk rock"— "It's so shock rock"—"It's so horrible"—"It's so awe-inspiring." Mayoral races in Bloomington, Indiana have revolved around the fact that people have sucked my dick. Some people think it's just the most outlaw and most horrible punk thing possible. But a lot of people think it's really great.

Most of the time, the only fags I can get to come and participate in the act are dykes— dykes who want to be fags, who understand what our song "Romeo and Julio" is about. It's this fantasy that dykes have about being fags— about having total anonymous sex; about the power of two men, who traditionally have power, having sex with each other; and whatever else fag sex means to those kinds of dykes. So I have dykes come up and pretend they're fags with me.

I think that's really powerful, but I also think that the image of a woman sucking dick is not necessarily the image that I want to implant on the minds of straight men who are out there watching. I *really* love to have a big, hunky, straight guy with a five-day beard growth sucking my dick, and have the crowd look at that: me topless with my big rubber dick down that straight guy's throat. I want them to see *that*, because that really freaks them out and turns the whole power thing upside down. It threatens them, and I want them to feel threatened.

For thousands of years they have told us what it is to be a woman. They have identified and defined women—and now, here's a *totally different image*.

♦ **AJ: I understand that aspect of the stage show. But when a guy's getting his dick sucked, it's direct sexual pleasure; is it also pleasurable for you?**

♦ LB: The pleasure comes from the power dynamic in this case. To me, 99% of sex is in your mind.

My cunt just gets to dripping if my girl's sucking my big rubber thing. I know I don't have any nerve endings in it, but to *see* that—all the images that have become part of my sexual psyche are triggered by seeing that image happening. My girlfriend says that she actually feels like she has a dick, and that she can actually feel what's going on, when I'm sucking on her rubber dick—as if she were a man. So a lot of it's mental.

♦ **AJ: Yeah, I can dig that. I love what Diamanda Galás said in *Angry Women*—that fucking a guy in the ass could be really very erotic.**

♦ EVERYONE: It is. [laughter]

♦ LM: Everybody should try it, boys and girls.

♦ LB: There's other symbology for the penis too: "Rock on with your cock on." I introduce the song "Radar Love" by saying, "Rock on with your cock on... cock rock... dress for success, wear a white penis." In this song, rock'n'roll *is* sexuality—everybody light your Bic lighters!

Rock'n'roll was named after a sex act. "Rocking and rolling" means fucking. For men, it's been this big bulge in your spandex—"I'm a sexual icon." So when I whip it out in "Radar Love" and masturbate, and they're wanking on the necks of their guitars—"*wank, wank*"—it's all so phallic. I'm making fun of men, and the narcissistic aspect of rock'n'roll. Picture a man standing there in the spotlight wanking off, glorying in his own wanking—and everybody's watching, all voyeuristic.

♦ LM: It's very homoerotic, just like sports. Sports and music—whenever you have men up there performing, and all these other men watching, getting really excited—really fetishize masculinity. Some guys, when you see them watching sports—do they get this excited when they're having sex?

♦ LB: We're spoofing men, making fun of how the whole focus is on the penis all the time. If you watch heterosexual porn, you'll see that the guy really likes to look at his dick. Even when he's coming on the chick's face or whatever, he wants to see her face and his dick at the same time. He wants to look at his dick squirting stuff. That's the most important thing. That's why you have porn flicks where they pull out and squirt it.

♦ **AJ: Well, how many times have *you* fucked a man?**

♦ LB: About fifteen times. But the fact is, I've talked to plenty of girls—my girlfriends told me,

and they've all had plenty of straight experiences and worked in the sex industry. They've sat in the booth, looking at the guy coming all over himself. He can talk to you for 20 minutes, and watch you turn your butt up in the air and fondle your breasts, and then at the moment of orgasm he's not looking at you, he's looking at his dick. Squirt squirt squirt squirt—woohoo! It's squirting—heeheeheee. They're so excited over that.

My cunt just gets to dripping if my girl's sucking my big rubber thing. I know I don't have any nerve endings in it, but to *see* that—all the images that have become part of my sexual psyche are triggered by seeing that image happening.

The final thing with the dick was the castration aspect. The first time I actually cut off a rubber dick was also at Lexington—after these guys sucked it. We were all so caught up in the *frenzy*—the punk rock, teenage frenzy of it all. They were so excited, screaming the words to "Frat Pig." I had this knife that I had bought at a Wyoming truck stop a couple of weeks earlier. I was just like: "Yeah! And then, I'm going to whack it off!" To myself, I was like: [whispering] "My ten-dollar penis—what am I going to do? I'll have to get another one—Oh, well." All these thoughts were going through my mind at the time. I just whacked it off, and everybody went insane. I threw the balls out in the crowd, and some band we were playing with caught it in the audience, and saw us two weeks later in New York—they still have the balls. All over the country now, there are people with rubber balls nailed to their walls, with red spray paint all over them.

Everybody gets all lathered up over the actual castration, so we just resigned ourselves to the fact that I'm going to have to cut up a lot of dicks. Thank god Good Vibrations [a sex-positive store in San Francisco] was kind enough to donate hundreds of dollars of rubber dicks for our tours. If we had to pay for them, it would be harsh on our budget to chop them up all the time.

◆ **AJ: I can imagine that men might like that part of the show, too.**

◆ LM: The theatrics? Yeah, some of 'em are really into it. Some of 'em will even stand there with their legs crossed, and their hands over their crotches. They're like, "I can't leave—something more intense might happen, and I don't want to miss that." Their girlfriends come up afterwards, saying to us, "Yeah, all these guys think they're so punk rock. They think they're so tough. And you should've seen them *squirm* when you guys were playing! You should've seen the expressions on their faces. It was priceless."

◆ LB: I think the combination of me being topless and having a dick, running around with a knife, a machete and a chainsaw, being in their faces and down their throats, screaming at them, not having to be in tune, and not caring about anything at all—is such a shocking image to them, that it totally turns everything upside down again. That's the most important thing for me, to make them reevaluate what they think is a woman. For thousands of years they have told us what it is to be a woman. They have identified and defined women—and now, here's a *totally different image*.

They're used to seeing women with naked breasts only in a certain context: with their fingers on their pussy saying, "Ooh, baby, fuck me." I'm not saying that. None of us are. I think it's really important for men to see women in that position of power. A penis is a symbol of power in this society, and yes, we're making fun of that. But for them to see the image of a woman with a penis, naked breasts, and weapons—they're going to have to rethink what power is. For a second they might feel like they have less power than that woman. And that's a really good learning tool.

◆ LM: I had a young boy come up and ask, "Do you guys just really hate men?" I started talking to him from the edge of the stage right after we played, explaining the different things that were going on, instead of just sort of writing him off. He was so sweet, I didn't want him to not understand. So I started talking to him, and all of a sudden all these other boys started crowding around and nodding their heads, listening to what I was saying.

The thing that we're constantly fighting about, in moving from the identity politics to the alliance stage, is that the structure that is trying to control us is going to constantly try to drive schisms between us.

◆ **AJ: How'd you respond?**

◆ LM: I said, "No, we don't hate all men. We all have men friends. This is about anger, and this is about rapists. It's about not sitting around and being sad because you're a victim. It's about going out and saying, 'Fuck you, I'm not going to take this anymore.' We're mad at rape, we're mad at rapists, and we want to take revenge." I'm sick of hearing and reading about rape. I'm sick of finding out that every woman I meet has had some horrible experience, like incest or rape.

Part of recovering from rape and incest involves feeling *good* about being angry, feeling like, "This ain't my fault. I'm pissed off. I'm going to maim and mangle *your* body now, and I'm going to fuck *you* up."

◆ **AJ: Do you have to deal with these issues, personally?**

◆ LM: Yes! Most friendships and relationships I've been in have been with people who are incest survivors. It haunts the relationship.

When I was talking to these boys, it was clear that they don't always hear all the words we're saying, and the lyrics we're singing—they just

By the Time We Get to Colorado (1993).

see the big visual picture, and they're seeing it as an attack on men. Because we're not saying great things about men, or loving men, we're seen as *anti-men*.

♦ AJ: **Well, I feel like, "Hey—that's too bad." Why are some men so defensive? Most men I know, the majority of whom are conscious, understand.**

♦ LM: This boy wasn't being defensive, he was just like: "Do you really hate men?"

♦ SB: We have a lot of support from boys. I was pretty much raised by my brother, and my best friends are boys; that's how it's always been. I don't feel negative towards guys—except for the power thing or the rape thing. I think there are so many guys who totally get what we're doing, and love us, all over the world.

Pig Bitch (1991).

♦ LM: But it's frustrating when you realize, "Oh, wow, men *can* be cool human beings." Then it's like: "Okay, but there's no goddamn excuse why it has to be this way then." Why are all these other guys still assholes? I used to feel they were total aliens, and they just didn't even have this potential.

♦ SB: Both our record labels have been run by guys, and they've been really supportive of us. We work well with them—the issue of "Do you hate us?" has never come up between us. That only comes up with people that don't understand us. A lot of guys still might not like the idea of watching a fake penis getting cut off, because they have a penis and it would really hurt to have it cut off.

If I had a penis and watched a penis get cut off, I would grab my balls, too. I think that's totally understandable.

♦ LB: Our biggest fan base, since the beginning, has been guys. In any realm of life, you're going to have mostly guys—because guys go out, guys have adventures, guys have money, guys buy records, guys have money

to go to shows, *guys guys guys guys guys*. Of course, there's always going to be a small but devoted group of dykes and straight women in the front row or in the pit. That faction is growing. But I remember—

♦ AJ: **You're talking about punk rock—not music in general?**

♦ LB: Punk rock is *guys*—white guys. And they love Tribe 8. So for us to say, "All guys are fucked up" would be stupid. They obviously do relate to us, and we relate to them on some level.

♦ AJ: **Right. I think we're on the cusp right now of something new. Because of the scary, horrible things that are brewing in this country, new communities need to form that include men, women, gays, straights, blacks, whites— a whole pantheon. That's absolutely necessary, as opposed to the last 20 years of building up separatist identity politics and factions.**

♦ LM: I was struck by what you just said about men, women, blacks, whites, straights, gays; those are all total opposites, and I think most people fit in between them. A lot of people, for example, fit somewhere in between the strict categories of men and women. Then there's blacks and whites—well, what about Asians and

Leslie Mah performing in New York City.

tity as a political entity. The word "gay" wasn't used in the '50s; people in the common society didn't really know what homosexuality was. It might have been this weird pathology they read about. It didn't exist as a label to the average middle-American—gays were invisible, unthought of, and they certainly didn't have any "rights." In the case of women, and feminism, the pioneers were the women you met at Michigan. Those older women worked to define their identity against what they saw as the patriarchy, and that attempt at self-definition built up a political power base.

Political movements wax and wane in natural cycles; after the early period of definition and separation, a movement has to mature. It doesn't have to be so rigid and predictable. Contemporary feminists are saying: "What is a woman? Hey, it can be herbal tea or punk rock. It can be gentle or violent." You see the same thing happening within other movements. The strictly-defined identities that helped build up political recognition and rights can then be straitjackets; you want a more complex shading—not black and white. It's about shedding the label without shedding the power base.

♦ LM: That's very eloquent.

♦ LB: Just note that *we* said that—that was Lynnie speaking, by the way. [laughs]

♦ AJ: Well, you guys embody that kind of progress and complexity.

♦ LB: Just like there are different stages in mourning, there are different stages in revolution, too. Like you said, the first stage is identity. That means you all have to get together very narrowly and limit yourself to just hanging out with people who are exactly like you. Once you're secure in who you are, and who your friends

Latinos, and all kinds of indigenous people who don't get any kind of recognition? Then there's people like me, who are mixed-race. And as for gays and straights, very few people are purely straight or purely homosexual.

I think this really needs to be acknowledged, because if we keep saying black/white, people are going to keep *thinking* in black and white, instead of acknowledging that it's so much more complex than that.

♦ AJ: Well, in the beginning of a movement, one needs an identity label to say, "I'm gay; I'm black and I'm beautiful; I am woman; etc." Early on, labels are necessary to build up a movement in a society that doesn't acknowledge that iden-

Bitches 'N' Brew, split 7-inch (1992).

are, then you can start reaching out and building alliances. Once you have the *alliances,* you have power. Because there's numbers.

But the thing that we're constantly fighting about, in moving from the identity politics to the alliance stage, is that the structure that is trying to control us is going to constantly try to drive schisms between us. In our case, they're going to do their best through media hype and commodification. The media have a lot of power representing who Tribe 8 is, and that's why we're paranoid. They can manipulate us. Our efforts to ally ourselves with other groups are going to be constantly fucked with by the mainstream media, who are going to try to keep us separated.

♦ **AJ: Another metaphor that works is simply growth. When you're an adolescent, you need to have an identity. You rebel against your parents to find yourself, and you go through different phases. That adolescent phase of identity, of building up an ego, is natural. With it you build up security.**

As you grow up, you realize that you don't have to have this group identity. You can have more flexibility and still be secure. It's just so important for the underground alternative communities to start shedding essentialist identity politics. All these disenfranchised groups have to get together. A perfect example was your decision to play at the Womyn's Festival.

♦ LM: When we're in New York, and we're hanging out with different kinds of people—straight people, whatever, it seems like things might be at that point you're maybe talking

about—it's not an *issue* to have queer friends, or to have interracial relationships.

But there are times on tour, like when we were in the South, when I can't fucking wait to get back to my gay ghetto. I feel like such a fucking goddamn freak. And then again, sometimes I don't want to just preach to the converted; I don't want to be stuck in this gay ghetto. I want to go out there in the world and meet other kinds of people who are doing something similar—with different backgrounds. I think it's important to be inclusive. So having your little ghetto is really important—because it gives you the strength to go out. ♦ ♦ ♦

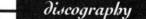

discography

Fist City (1995)
Mother, 7-inch (1994)
Outpunk Dance Party, 7-inch
   compilation (1994)
By the Time We Get to Colorado, EP (1993)
Stars Kill Rock, compilation (1992)
Bitches 'N' Brew, split 7-inch
   with Blatz (1992)
Pig Bitch, 7-inch (1991)
There's a Dyke In the Pit,
   compilation (1991)

equipment list

♦ LYNN BREEDLOVE ♦
Shure 58 microphone, chainsaw, machete, rubber dildos from Good Vibrations

♦ LESLIE MAH ♦
Gibson Flying V guitar, Mesa Boogie Mark III amp, Mesa Boogie pre-amp pedal, wah pedal, crybaby

♦ LYNN FLIPPER ♦
1967 SG Gibson guitar, Fender Strat, orange head 71, Marshall cabinet, DOD metal pedal, delay box

♦ LYNN PAYNE ♦
Tune bass, hollow-body McCarthy bass, Sears bass, Crate bass cabinet, HH head

♦ SLADE BELLUM ♦
1975 Sonar beech wood three-piece jazz drum kit, 1970 Pearl snare, double-bass drum Axis pedal, Paste and Zildjian cymbals

Photo: Chris Buck/Hair: Paige Smitherman/Makeup:Linda Mason/Stylist: Andrea Lee Linet/Satin top by Love NYC.

Joan Jett

Joan Jett has been in the media spotlight since she was a teenager in the Runaways. As a solo artist, backed by the Blackhearts, she released the huge hit album *I Love Rock'n'Roll* in 1980 on her own label, Blackheart records. She has been a fixture in the rock world ever since. She has produced for the Germs and Bikini Kill, and recently she has recorded with L7, Kat from Babes in Toyland, and Kathleen Hanna. After the murder of Mia Zapata, Jett played a number of benefits with Zapata's band, the Gits, and they subsequently released a live album, Evil Stig.

◆ **ANDREA JUNO: You were one of the female rockers who provided the rest of us with brand new role models in the '70s and '80s. You gave a lot of women the inspiration to be stronger.**

◆ JOAN JETT: Well, I'm glad somebody got that message. When I sit here and think back, I wonder how many women actually looked at what we were doing in the Runaways and said, "Hey, that's great." Or, "You make me feel stronger." Because it seemed like the Runaways had a mostly male audience, waiting to see us take our clothes off or something—that's what they expected us to do.

Not many women came to the shows. They felt threatened; I don't know why. Maybe they just couldn't get off on seeing women play music, or they were threatened we were going to steal their boyfriends.

◆ **AJ: So when you reemerged with your own band, the Blackhearts—all men—after the breakup of the Runaways, was there a specific intention to not be another all-female band?**

◆ JJ: Oh, on my part, definitely. I felt that, after the Runaways broke up, people were just laughing and saying, "We told you it wouldn't work. We told you that you guys were no good." You've got to understand the way that felt to me, living right in the middle of the music scene

in Los Angeles; I lived just across the street from the Whiskey.

At first, I didn't know what I was going to do. It was like my life just ended, because I had loved being in the Runaways so much, and thought we were doing something really good—I didn't understand people's reactions, and why they thought it was so strange for women to play music. It just wasn't logical to me. I had grown up with my parents telling me that I could do anything I wanted in life.

If I wanted to be an astronaut, I could be an astronaut. If I wanted to be a doctor, I could do that. I always played kickball and dodgeball with all the neighborhood kids; mostly boys. So it never entered my mind that I couldn't play guitar. There's no *rule* that says girls can't play guitar.

I remember going in for my first guitar lesson, when I wanted to learn how to play rock'n'roll. I was 13 years old. The teacher looked at me with a very strange expression, like he didn't know what I was talking about, and taught me "On Top of Old Smokey."

◆ **AJ: As if you would only be able to do folk singing or something like that?**

◆ JJ: Yeah. So I bought one of those learn-how-to-play-guitar-yourself books, and learned bar chords pretty much by ear. And then, listening to my different records—

◆ **AJ: Like what? What were you into then?**

♦ JJ: Well, let's see. I liked Black Sabbath, because they had nice, big fat chords that I could really follow. There were a lot of other bands I was into, but whose music I just couldn't play. Like Led Zeppelin. Couldn't play it. It seemed too fast. The same with a lot of the glitter music, like Bowie and Sweet.

♦ AJ: During which years were you listening to these records?

♦ JJ: In the early '70s. The Runaways started in '75.

♦ AJ: How did your peers, at that time, think of you playing guitar? Was there any peer pressure in school?

I don't come offstage, blow-dry my hair, go out and start cruising. That's just not me. I'm tired. I've been working my ass off.

♦ JJ: We moved around too much for me to make very good friends. And anyway, I don't recall letting a lot of people know that I played guitar. But I remember that the way I used to dress was a little… *different* from everyone else: platform shoes, glittery stuff, makeup and weird things. I remember people howling at me, saying, "Ah-ooh, Diamond Dogs!" And throwing stones—literally. Now some of those same people ask, "Did you go to so-and-so high school? I think I went there with you."

♦ AJ: When you were a teenager, listening to Led Zeppelin and Black Sabbath and playing along with your records, were you at all uncomfortable with the fact that they were all guys? I used to listen to the same stuff, and yet I would think about them being males. There weren't comparable female roles in the same positions. It was like watching James Bond and identifying along with him, but then realizing that if I were a woman in that world, I'd have to be one of James Bond's disposable creatures.

♦ JJ: You mean that when you thought about rock bands, you'd think about being the people that hang out with them, as opposed to being one of the musicians?

♦ AJ: Well, how did you reconcile that? Did you identify with the men? Or did you actually think about yourself up there onstage?

♦ JJ: I thought about it being *me* up there. I just had no problem with it. I didn't have any problem identifying with those rock bands. Maybe I don't quite understand what you mean…

♦ AJ: Well, there were no females in those roles, so it took a leap of imagination.

♦ JJ: Right. There were hardly any women, except for Janis Joplin. She had real guts and you could look up to her—

♦ AJ: —but she wasn't playing instruments.

♦ JJ: No, that's true. She did not play an instrument.

♦ AJ: And she was kind of victimized by a lot of those guys. They didn't treat her very well, and ultimately they took away her sexuality. So I felt ambivalent. I couldn't really identify with or respect her. I was pissed off that the only woman like that had to be desexualized.

♦ JJ: Right. You couldn't have it all. You couldn't have a great voice and also, if you were a woman, be thought of as sexual and beautiful. It was too threatening. And I think that's what people found threatening—in a totally different way, obviously, from Janis Joplin—in the Runaways. When we did interviews, people were very cynical; they had these smiles on their faces, and they'd sit there and say, "So this is—what? A phase you're going through? A fad?"

We were naive, and *serious*, and we would say, "No, we really mean what we're doing. We want to do this for a career." Or something like that. And then we'd see this change come over them, once they realized that we were serious about what we were doing, and we wanted to talk about the music, not about sexual antics.

They would get very threatened, and then the language would change—they'd start calling us all kinds of names; every name you can call a woman. And, of course, how are you going to react, when you're 16, and you're not seasoned at being taunted? You can only react with "Fuck you, fuck you, fuck you!" And that's what they got. So they would write, "Runaways: Guttermouths." And they got completely around discussing the music.

♦ AJ: It's actually a healthy response, though, to say "Fuck you." A lot of women would just close up.

♦ JJ: Well, when you're asked, "Are you a slut?" or, "You must be a whore or a dyke," the inner response is like, "Wait a minute. How the hell did this conversation just go from talking about music to you all of a sudden accusing us

Photo: Chris Buck/Hair: Paige Smitherman/Makeup:Linda Mason/Stylist: Andrea Lee Linett/Satin top by Love NYC.

of something that we didn't even bring up? We're just sitting here, willing and ready to talk to you, and you're saying this stuff." But instead of responding like that, we just said, "Fuck you, man, blah-blah-blah." And whatever else we all ranted. Sometimes it was me, sometimes it was another of the girls, and sometimes it was all of us. It happened too many times.

There were also some places that gave us a certain amount of respect. In Japan, the Runaways were huge. In Scandinavia, huge. In Europe, we did real well. But in America…

♦ **AJ: Well, America has a lot of ambivalent feelings about women, from extreme P.C. to its opposite. To see women being sexual and powerful at the same time is really a potent combination for most of the public to swallow. You were one of the pioneering women who played in that cock-rock style— I love that stuff.**

♦ JJ: Yeah, I know what you mean. But it just feels funny, being called a pioneer of *anything*. It's just strange.

♦ **AJ: But it's really amazing, because not only *are* you a pioneer—now you're being reclaimed by the next generation of women rockers. You've been working with Kathleen Hanna and L7, collaborating together on different productions. You've stood the test of time, for the last 17 years.**

♦ JJ: There's a certain backlash that sometimes happens along with success. The Blackhearts were a garage band or punk band that happened to have this song "I Love Rock'n'Roll"—which somehow wound up on the radio, and, all of a sudden, was this number-one hit for eight weeks.

When something like that happens, people start to look at you in a different way. They start to think you're mainstream, when, in reality, you haven't changed anything. You're out on the road. You don't even have *time* to change. You're just chugging along and suddenly you stop and realize everybody's looking at you in a different light. So I've got to credit people like L7 and Kathleen Hanna for not saying, "Well, the Run-

Bad Reputation, originally released as *Joan Jett* (1981).

own brains, second-class citizens—so that other women were just competition for the attentions of men. Now, it's such a nice feeling to see this whole network of women growing in music and lots of other fields.

◆ JJ: That's what I mean—nobody feels a sense of competition. And it seems like, for the most part, women are very supportive of each other in the music scene. There might be people who feel otherwise, but, from where I sit, it feels pretty supportive.

◆ **AJ: What about in the music industry itself? You started your own label.**

◆ JJ: Well, it was just a matter of if we wanted anyone to hear the music—which we did—we had to put out our own records. Nobody wanted anything to do with us. It was like, "Well, that Joan Jett from the Runaways has a bad reputation." That's where these album titles come from. You have to get inspired somewhere.

◆ **AJ: "Bad reputation" meaning what?**

◆ JJ: Black leather jacket. Heavy eye makeup. Swears a lot. You know.

◆ **AJ: But every male rock star is—**

◆ JJ: Exactly. But we got 23 rejection letters from the majors *and* indies.

The Runaways' audience was 99 percent male. That was kind of depressing: "Why don't women—our own gender—come out and support us?"

◆ **AJ: What year was this?**

◆ JJ: This was 1980. We had sent them tapes that had "I Love Rock'n'Roll" on it, which eventually was a big hit. And "Do You Want to Touch Me?" was on the tapes; that was a big hit. "Crimson and Clover," was on those tapes too—that song was top ten. So it makes you wonder, does anybody listen? Or do they just throw these tapes into a bin of music, 'cause they don't have enough time to listen? And if they do listen, it's pretty scary that someone could hear three top-ten hits and miss them.

aways weren't cool," or "Joan wasn't cool; so I stopped listening."

They didn't necessarily care. For whatever reasons, they were fans, and they continued to listen. That got back to me, and I'm also a big fan of theirs. So it's a reciprocal sort of thing which has led to us knowing each other and being able to work together. And it's a really good feeling, because I sense a major change in women's attitudes towards watching each other play.

Women can now watch other women, and it doesn't even have to be in any sexual way. You can get off on watching women onstage taking the music and using it to their advantage—instead of being used *by* the music, which has always been the case. Now women can get out these feelings that they have had for so long. And I think that's a real good shift in mental attitude.

◆ **AJ: It's a totally radical shift. You were saying—I felt this, too—that the support structures for women were really not in place back in the early '70s.**

◆ JJ: Well, there *wasn't* any support structure. If the Runaways got shit, we didn't have an L7 or a Bikini Kill to ask, "Hey, we're getting shit. Are you getting the same kind of shit? Or is it just us?" We had nobody to bounce anything off of, in that respect. On a gender level.

◆ **AJ: But you also said that women thought you were going to steal their boyfriends. Only 20 years ago, women were much more, in their**

We got rejection letters saying, "No good songs here, you need a song search." So we scraped together some money and printed up 5,000 copies of what was eventually called *Bad Reputation*. At first, it was just called *Joan Jett*. We were selling them out of the trunk of the car, playing around New York—

♦ **AJ: This is you and the Blackhearts?**

♦ JJ: Yeah. We sold 5,000 of those albums real fast, and there was a buzz starting to happen in the New York tristate area. We printed up another 5,000, and *they* went. The buzz was getting louder; we would play out on Long Island, and freeways would get shut down.

It was just really a fun time; there was such excitement. Finally, we were signed by Neil Bogart, who owned Boardwalk Records; that's the guy who put out *Bad Reputation* and, eventually, *I Love Rock'n'Roll*.

♦ **AJ: Boardwalk is not a major label, right?**

♦ JJ: No, it was a smaller label. And then they went out of business. We have those first four Joan Jett and the Blackhearts albums on Blackheart Records.

♦ **AJ: So you went from Boardwalk to starting your own label?**

♦ JJ: Well, we had started our own label right in the very beginning. So, when we signed to Boardwalk, it was Joan Jett and the Blackhearts, on Blackheart Records, signed to Boardwalk. The albums would come out on both labels. And that's the way we've always done it. When we were on MCA, it was Joan Jett and the Blackhearts on Blackheart through MCA. The same thing with Epic. Now the arrangement is with Warner Brothers.

♦ **AJ: Does that mean that you keep a lot of control?**

♦ JJ: For the most part. It doesn't make me nervous about what I want to do. We were going to do our last album independently, and just put it out on Blackheart. We were half done with it when Warner's came to us and talked about putting out the album. We discussed it, and it sounded like a good thing to do.

♦ **AJ: What do you think of the label Kill Rock Stars, and that whole kind of anti-rock star and anti-major label attitude?**

♦ JJ: Well, I really don't like to judge. To each their own. But actually, I find the title "Kill Rock Stars" really funny. Because a lot of people do act like jerks when they reach that supposed rock star level.

I wasn't really in the scene when it started, and I'm not right in the middle of the scene now.

I just like what a lot of the bands do. You're probably referring to the whole Riot Grrrl thing?

♦ **AJ: Yeah.**

♦ JJ: I just think it's interesting. I think there have to be women out there who are willing to get in people's faces, just to let them know that women *exist*.

If you read some of the zines that those people put out, you see that they're writing about incest and rape and all the other things that don't get talked about with women and teenage girls. These subjects get swept under the rug, and nobody wants to deal with them, because they're "icky." But something like rape or incest is a *heavy* subject for somebody that it happens to. So I think that's a really healthy outlet.

> **There wasn't any support structure. If the Runaways got shit, we didn't have an L7 or Bikini Kill to ask, "Are you getting the same kind of shit? Or is it just us?"**

I wish there had been something like that when we were in the Runaways, just so I could have been in touch with what other teenage girls and older girls in college were thinking. It's an activist, in-your-face kind of thing.

♦ **AJ: It's also about embracing all aspects of women. It used to be that if you were really a feminist, you couldn't be girly or feminine, you couldn't be sexual, you couldn't wear makeup—all these horrible definitions. Now these young women are blowing out a lot of those definitions.**

♦ JJ: Yeah. There was such a stereotype of how you had to be, if you were going to call yourself a feminist. Who's making these rules? That's why everybody in this world hates each other. We're all putting up barriers, all the time. Have we got nothing better to do but make up rules that we each have to follow? It doesn't make sense.

♦ **AJ: How have you been treated by the feminist community, and women in general?**

♦ JJ: I think that women have treated me just great. I'm sure, if you look hard enough, you'll find some who've had negative reactions. But I

don't ever remember seeing feminists come out against the Runaways, or anything like that. I would think that during that time people would have been into it, just because we were trying to break those stereotypes.

◆ **AJ: You have a really strong lesbian fan base, too.**

◆ JJ: Who? The Runaways?

◆ **AJ: Well, with the Runaways, it's a little too early for me to know. I'm talking more about your own fans.**

◆ JJ: Well, they're women, so...

◆ **AJ: So anybody can listen to your songs, no matter what sexual orientation they have.**

ing to do? All of a sudden, sing a song and cut out half the lyrics?

◆ **AJ: Is that the reason that you use interchangeable genders in your songs?**

◆ JJ: In "I Love Rock'n'roll," I say "him." In "Crimson and Clover" I say "her." But usually, I try to use "you" and "me." I think it's important for everyone to be able to apply it. Not all the songs are about sex; some are about relationships that could be friendships. Some aren't about sex *or* a friendship.

◆ **AJ: Right; I want to talk about Mia Zapata of the Gits, and the Home Alive project that you worked on. How did you get involved?**

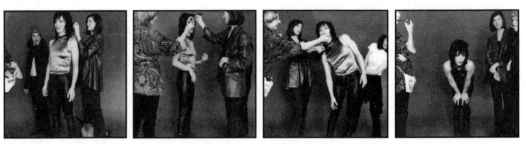

Photo: Chris Buck/Hair: Paige Smitherman/Makeup:Linda Mason/Stylist: Andrea Lee Linett/Satin top by Love NYC.

◆ JJ: Right. Everybody should be able to relate; I don't want people to feel alienated. I can't see cutting out a portion of the audience. And I think that our audience has really grown; we've got this great, democratic coalition of fans. We've got fans who have been fans since the Runaways, or since the early Blackhearts. And we've got new fans that just discovered the band in the last couple of years.

> **I remember the way I used to dress in high school was a little *different* from everyone else: platform shoes, glittery stuff, makeup and weird things.**

Like I said, the Runaways' audience was 99 percent male. That was kind of depressing: "Why don't women—our own gender—come out and support us?" We didn't get it. And now the audience is pretty much 50-50. So what are you go-

◆ JJ: I heard about her murder from a friend, when I was in Seattle writing songs with Kathleen Hanna, and with Kat from Babes In Toyland. I had done some production work with Bikini Kill in March of '93, and we started writing some songs together after that. I was in Seattle from March to August or September. So I was around during the time that Mia was murdered.

It made me realize how I was so unaware, most of the time, about my safety; I didn't really think about it. I always figured somebody else would take care of it so when I was alone, my guard was down more than it should be. I also thought about how many times, when I was in the Runaways, I was out and about when they didn't even know where I was or what I was doing. It all just hit home—it just can't stay the same for me.

When you're on the streets, you've got to be prepared. You've got to have your guard up. You've got to at least have your peripheral vision working. And then you can learn some self-defense, which could just be boundary-setting, like yelling at somebody because it freaks them out, and the attackers aren't used to that—even that is a way to stop somebody. But I'd like to learn things like a little hand-to-hand combat. Basic things like stomping on the instep, or kicking at the side of the knee, or palm to the throat. Little things to just give me that second to get away, which is the point—not to sit there and pummel the person into the ground, saying, "You tried to attacked me, and I'm going to get you back now!"

◆ **AJ: Of course, that would be fun, too. I wouldn't mind doing that if anybody attacked me!**

◆ JJ: Yeah; if you were sure you could get out of there, or get to the point where you could disarm small weapons, like a knife or a gun, should someone be close enough. Those are all intangibles that you don't know about. But at least you can learn. For me, that was what made the connection. I think a lot of people would say, "Well, Mia and Joan, it's like two different things. The Gits are this punk band, and Joan's had all these hits; they're not alike at all." But I say that we're exactly the same, on certain levels.

That was why it was, and is, so moving. Kathleen and I wrote a song called "Go Home" one day, when we were talking about what had happened. It's obviously depressing; we wanted to try and write a song about what you can do. It's not real direct. You'd have to find the message on your own, listening to the song. It's about taking responsibility for yourself.

There's not a cop on the street for every one of us, and it's up to us to learn whatever we can, whatever each woman and guy is comfortable learning to make them feel safe on the street. When I'm even going to the Post Office, I walk with my keys sticking out, so I'm ready to put a hole in someone's face.

When we made the video for the song, my ideas coincided with those of my partner, Kenny Laguna, and the director we decided to work with, Julien Temple (who is an excellent director and filmmaker). The video depicts a woman leaving a bar—much like, I guess, Mia did. In the video she's heading for the train home, and senses someone following her. You see her looking back, and this guy following like 20 or 30 feet behind. But she's not sure; she doesn't want to start running and then feel like a jerk if the guy is just walking behind her.

◆ **AJ: Yeah, but that kills a lot of women: trying to be polite, and not hurt someone else's feelings.**

◆ JJ: Exactly. That's partly the point of screaming at someone; you can't worry about how they're going to think you're nuts, or—

◆ **AJ: But if you're across the street, and some guy takes offense at the way you act to protect yourself, then you have to wonder about the insensitivity of that guy—not realizing that every woman has to suspect every single human on the street.**

◆ JJ: That's why we wanted to make this video, because it shows that indecision. So, the woman gets on the train. She looks around, and doesn't see the guy; she sees a bunch of kids messing around with a passed-out drunk on the train. She's relieved, she sits down, she starts reading a paper.

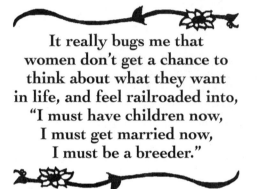

It really bugs me that women don't get a chance to think about what they want in life, and feel railroaded into, "I must have children now, I must get married now, I must be a breeder."

The train keeps going. Stops. The kids get off. But just as the door is shutting, she looks up and realizes the stalker guy just got on. She's alone on the train with the passed-out drunk and this stalker guy, who's now coming, loosening his tie, to get me (I play the woman) in the back of the train. Now it's showdown.

I try to wake up the drunk guy. No response. The stalker gets me in the back, and there's a fight. We really fought in making the video. I mean, we were both bruised and everything. [laughs] He swings me around and smashes me into the wall. And I smash him around. And then the video shows some of the things that you could learn.

Things like chopping at someone's sides; when they've got you up against the wall, their sides are open, so you whack 'em. That's what I did in the video. And then there was some stuff where I was kicking him in the side at the end of the song, and screaming, "No, no, no!" That's something that's taught in self-defense classes. Every time you throw a punch in a fight with an attacker, every time you do *something*, you're supposed to yell, "No!" And not just say it. *Scream* it.

Fake Friends, 7-inch (1983).

So in the video, she runs off the train. At the beginning of the video it says, "For Mia Zapata." And at the end it says, "Mia Zapata was brutally raped and murdered." It gives the date and then fades to black and says, "The killer has not been found."

Steve, from the Gits, wrote to me about the Blackhearts doing a benefit, if we could. I had an idea that was kind of crazy, but I thought it was still a good idea, and I wanted to toss it out to him. I said, "Instead of just doing this benefit the usual way, with the Blackhearts, what if I tried to sing some of the Gits' songs—you figure out the ones that the Gits' fans like, and some ones you guys want to do." I knew that might feel really strange to them. I wanted them to know that my intentions were absolutely pure.

I was doing some songwriting up in Vancouver, and then I was in Seattle, so we met for a drink, and talked about this idea. We didn't know if it would work. I didn't know if I could sing their songs. I didn't know how they were going to feel with me standing in front of them, singing the songs that Mia had sung.

We did a rehearsal, and it sounded great. We didn't have everything together, but we could tell that it could work, so we decided to try it. We put together three benefits, one in Portland and two in Seattle; we wound up recording those shows, and releasing an album under the name

of Evil Stig—"Gits Live" backwards. We only had three or four rehearsals. I had to study the Gits' tapes a lot, and just practice. I had all the lyrics written out on a notepad, on a music stand on the stage. But it worked out great.

It was something that was fun for me to do, and I felt that we were doing some good. Besides raising the money for the investigative fund, I just wanted to see the band relax a little bit and smile. Practically every show they did was a benefit. But when I turned around and looked at them on the stage, in Portland, everybody had grins, ear to ear. It felt really nice.

There were people in the audience singing the songs; I saw people laughing, and I saw somebody crying. It was very cathartic. I noticed it more in Portland. Maybe I was more nervous in Seattle, because that was the Gits' home base. It was extremely, extremely emotional, obviously, for a lot of reasons. I wanted to do the best I could do for the band and for the audience and for myself and for Mia, who, in my view, is looking down on all this. I would think that she'd be into it; if she wasn't, something would have happened to stop this project.

♦ **AJ: You also co-wrote the song "Spinster" with Kathleen Hanna. I've always thought about that word; there's no male equivalent. It must kind of gall you when—**

♦ JJ: People haven't actually called me a spinster. The reason that we wrote it was, first, you've got this word "bachelor." If you're a guy, at any age, 20 to 100, you're a bachelor and you have a swinging lifestyle. But you're right. There's no female equivalent. If a female is out there doing that, she's a slut, instead of just being able to do what she wants to do.

♦ **AJ: Or people think there's something wrong with her.**

♦ JJ: Oh, yeah. Then you've got all that stuff. If a woman is not involved in a serious relationship by the time she's 25, it's like, "What's going on? She can't keep a relationship running? Is there something wrong with her?"

It really bugs me that women don't get a chance to think about what they want in life, and feel railroaded into, "I must have children now, I must get married now, I must be a breeder." If that's what someone wants to do, and it's in her heart, that's beautiful. That's great. But you shouldn't feel pressured to do that. If you look at history, you'll see that in the period before the Industrial Revolution, when women made all the cloth, once you became extremely good at it, very adept at it—you were considered a spinster. You were the breadwinner of the family. That was something that was looked up to. During the Industrial Revolution, somehow along the way, this negative connotation attached itself to the word.

When you walk into a restaurant, you don't know if someone is saying, "Hey, wow, cool, there's Joan," or, "Oh, there's that Joan Jett—who the fuck does she think she is? She's over, man."

♦ **AJ: After the Middle Ages, women had a whole variety of jobs. Spinster. Codwife. Midwife. But then, by the Industrial Revolution, and the scientific revolution, women were reduced to two jobs: prostitute or *husband's* wife.**
♦ JJ: I'm wondering how the word turned from being so positive—you're the breadwinner of the family—to, all of a sudden, meaning something totally different: you're somebody that doesn't want to get married, or can't get married.
♦ **AJ: You're either a lesbian or no man would have you—as if somehow that's still the definition of worth.**
♦ JJ: I've had a lot of women say, "I'm so glad you wrote that song." I think a lot of women probably do feel pressured. Say you've got a lot of female friends, and a lot of them are married; maybe they're having their first kid, or their second kid, and they're doing the family thing. And if *you're* not doing that, you might give yourself a certain amount of pressure about it. Then you get actual peer pressure, where your family or friends are pressuring you. I think a lot of women succumb to it.
♦ **AJ: Well, the press compounds the problem by the way they criticize successful women.**

I never really liked Madonna's music that much, but I felt that all the criticism she got when she was in her twenties was unfair. They said she was sleeping her way to the top. She was in her twenties! What guy has a steady relationship when he's in his twenties?! At that age, you have *tons* of relationships. That used to piss me off so much. I ended up wanting to defend her, thinking, my god, what a double standard.
♦ JJ: It is a double standard—very much so. Madonna's focused. She knows what she wants, and I'm sure she works very hard. It's funny to see the names that she gets called, compared to her male exact equal.
♦ **AJ: In a lot of ways, though, things are radically changing; it's not a big deal to have a woman play guitar now. It's not like when you were in the Runaways: "Oh, aren't they cute?" Or, "What a novelty."**
♦ JJ: There were people who looked at us like we had seven heads. They thought we were crazy. It was surreal. And I really have problems with things that don't make sense, like that. My response was, "If I can throw a football 50 yards, and I can play baseball, and I can do all these other things, you're telling me I can't play guitar?" And there are no *laws* against it. So I would just get myself all worked up and say, "You tell me I can't do it? I'm going to do it that much more, just because you say I can't."

Part of that attitude was just being a teenager, but they really get you by saying, "You're a girl, so you can't do that." It would make me angry when someone would say that. I don't know how much of that resistance comes from

Crimson and Clover, 7-inch (1982).

Photo: Karen Mason

Joan Jett with the Gits (1995).

your own constitution, or how much of that comes from how you're brought up.

♦ **AJ: You seem pretty grounded and healthy. You can tell by people's looks: they're either sallow, or they look like they have life force in them. How have you maintained that kind of centered integrity? It's especially impressive considering that you've been in the public view for a long time.**

It never entered my mind that I couldn't play guitar. There's no *rule* that says girls can't play guitar.

♦ JJ: Man, that's hard to say. I think you partly have to thank your parents for okay genes. But also, throughout the '80s, we were just on the road, touring America, the world. We'd come back. We'd make an album. I exercised a bit, but not that much.

Towards the end of the '80s, I stopped eating red meat. It wasn't a moral thing, at the time. It was more that I can't eat a cheeseburger at two in the morning after I've played. It just wrecks me, and I can't deal with it the next day. So I'll eat breakfast food. And after eight months of eating pancakes and no red meat, I just had no taste for it. Eventually, I stopped eating all meat. I've been a vegetarian for a little over three years.

♦ **AJ: But maintaining your inner health takes more than exercise or eating the right way. A lot of people can't handle fame and being in the public eye for so long. Look at Kurt Cobain.**

♦ JJ: Part of what kept me going and made it easier for me to deal with a lot of that was the fact that we were constantly working throughout the '80s. I didn't stop long enough to sit there and think, "Oh, man, I'm freaking out." I just kept putting more energy into the next thing.

Another thing that's helped me is that I started practicing yoga a little over three years ago. I just love it, and I think that that's what keeps me grounded. People say that yoga keeps you fit. But that's not the main focus for me. The main focus is more a mental and also spiritual thing to keep you really grounded, knowing who you are, and what your relationship to this whole universe really is.

We just did a tour of Australia for six weeks. And on the way back, I stopped in India for a two-week vacation. Man, it was just indescribable. The energy was so different. Here, it just seems like everybody's into everybody else's business; everything is go-go-go and hustle-bustle. Which, I guess, is part of what makes America great. But India's been around way longer than us—ten thousand, eight thousand years. I saw a lot of how people lived there. You see people with nothing. *Nothing*. But they're happy; they're smiling at you. It just gives you a different perspective, when you come back here.

I think it's important to have that different perspective, and practicing yoga helps me too. It's hard when you're on the road, because I really enjoy being in a class where I'm pushed, and I want to get to the level where I can just really practice on my own, and push myself hard enough.

♦ **AJ: You have a purple dot in the middle of your forehead; it looks lovely. Is that from India?**

♦ JJ: It's called a bindi; it's to adorn your third eye. In India, the men and women go to temple every day, to make puja, which is the worship. The priests come out and put a dot on your head. You can buy them, too. So I had to come home with some. I've got my own little altar in my house. Sometimes I do my own puja thing. And there are some days that I like to wear a bindi, just because I'm in the mood.

♦ **AJ: It's really beautiful.**

♦ JJ: Thank you.

♦ **AJ: You said that, in addition to these ways of maintaining inner strength, you also got a lot of support from your family.**

♦ JJ: Oh, yeah. My family's always been great. They never deterred me. I mean, they bought me my first guitar, for Christmas. An electric one. I think maybe they thought it would just be a phase with me. But when I wanted to join a band, I remember specifically going to my mother and saying, "Ma, this is something I really want to do, and I'm going to do it, no matter what—but I'd really rather do it with your blessing."

I'm sure she wasn't crazy about her 15-year-old daughter going to Hollywood all the time, and eventually moving there. But we weren't that far from each other. We were half an hour apart. I was a teenager, out on the road, and I really have to give my parents a lot of credit for not hassling me—they just said, "Go ahead. Just be safe and let us know what you're doing and where you are." They were always just so cool about it. They were always very proud.

♦ **AJ: You survived—whereas a lot of people self-destruct.**

♦ JJ: Well, it's easy to self-destruct, just from everyday pressures. You don't even have to be that well known. It's just dealing with the intricacies of the business, whether you're living in New York, or Los Angeles, or Seattle, or Chicago, or Boston. I'm sure it's all the same, wherever you've got this music scene and everybody talks about everybody else's business.

I sense a major change in women's attitudes in watching each other play. You can get off on watching women onstage taking the music and using it to their advantage—instead of being used *by* the music, which has always been the case.

You can be right in the middle of it, hearing all these things said about yourself—it can make you go crazy. You have to be really strong in what you think, and not give too much credence to other people's criticisms and judgments. Of course, it's easy for me to say that now. Hindsight is always 20/20. But I went through a lot of sadness and crying, after the Runaways broke up—wondering why people didn't get it. Why people didn't like us.

You just have to realize, hey, people are going to say things and do things, and you just can't control it. So why even get uptight about it? Then again, it's easy to say that, and know it's the right thing to do, but getting there is another whole ball game.

♦ **AJ: Because with the price of fame comes not only the false belief that people love you, but also this underbelly of hatred and hostility. It doesn't come without that.**

♦ JJ: For example, you never know what someone's thinking, when you walk into a restaurant. You don't know if someone is saying,

I Hate Myself for Loving You, 7-inch (1988).

"Hey, wow, cool, there's Joan." I've lived in New York for a long time, so a lot of people respond to me like a hometown girl who's done good; a lot of nice people are really cool. But you don't know if there's anybody saying, "Oh, there's that Joan Jett—who the fuck does she think she is? She's over, man."

♦ **AJ: Fame comes with hostility, jealousies, the sense being in a fishbowl and being judged constantly.**

♦ JJ: Yes.

♦ **AJ: Everybody thinks, "Oh, being famous equals being supported and being loved," which is what you want when you're in high school to be popular. When you're famous, and that**

Spinster, 7-inch (1994).

doesn't happen, it's a shock. And that's how so many people who are famous self-destruct.

♦ JJ: An interesting factor is the speed with which people are now able to be well known. A new band will come out, a song will get on the radio, the video will be played, and all of a sudden—they're the hot new band.

Even though they might want to go out and tour and become more well-known, they're sort of ripped from their community and their regular lives, shoved into this limelight, just to wait for the next record of some *other* band to come out. The second you come out with that first good album, you're in trouble. You've got to live up to it and make that second album as good or better, because people are always going to compare, and they have to find something to pick on.

♦ **AJ: Then there's the fact that the band may actually believe their own press clips. So they're in shock when they're no longer the flavor of the month. Well, you've weathered a lot of storms, and now you've grown into icon status.**

The second you come out with that first good album, you're in trouble. You've got to live up to it and make that second album as good or better.

♦ JJ: [laughs] That just sounds so strange to me.

♦ **AJ: I can imagine! [laughs]**

♦ JJ: Because I have these memories of what people said to us when I was in the Runaways. "You'll never make it." I used to wonder, "Is it ever going to be 'normal' for girls to play guitar and drums?"

Here's a major argument that I used to throw at people. "If women can play cellos and violins in symphony orchestras, you're telling me they can't play a guitar? Shot down. Theory gone. So come up with your next question!"

♦ **AJ: You've also been able to keep the kind of onstage sexuality that women used to have to sacrifice. It's very much like the male counterpart, which was called cock-rock. But there seems to be a difference when women embody that kind of sexuality onstage; they generally** don't act out offstage, as opposed to a lot of the male rockers, who can be major assholes.

♦ **JJ:** It's hard for me to even notice that I'm sexual onstage. I mean, I'm just out there playing. The only time I might feel it is: I feel really good if I'm really hot and sweaty. If I'm sopping wet, then I go into another sphere. I totally forget myself. I get really, really loose.

But I'm not really aware of it. I'm not onstage thinking that I've got to do this or that to look sexy. I just do what I do, and make eye contact—which is natural for me.

♦ **AJ: Well, men don't necessarily *try* to act sexy. They're just exhibiting a sexual energy. But the point is more about being the focus of attention, and the way some of these male rockers have made a habit of treating women as objects. That kind of excess is why a lot of young people have that kill-rock-stars attitude. [laughs] It's a reflection of the outsized power that society's placed on the rock star.**

♦ **JJ:** I see what you're saying. It's there onstage with a lot of the guys, and then they carry it with them *offstage*, looking around and cruising. Whereas, with women—I don't come offstage, blow-dry my hair, go out and start cruising. That's just not me. I'm tired. I've been working my ass off. Putting out so much of my own energy and receiving other people's—that transference and communication—can be very draining, but it's a lot of fun.

And you want to keep it fun. That's why, for me, it's not fun to go out after a show. Maybe I've gotten that out of my system—I've definitely had my wilder days, when I was in the Runaways. I would run around and act a little crazy. But I was a teenager; that kind of behavior goes with the territory.

Now, I just focus on what I need to do. I don't really think about the sexual aspect, or how it carries over to my regular daily life. So I'm almost confused by the question—I can't give you a good answer.

♦ **AJ: No, actually, you did; because this is the big difference. As you said, you're not taking the natural sexuality that you express onstage and carrying it offstage to use toward getting more notches on your belt.**

♦ **JJ:** I don't think I play it up. I just dress in jeans and t-shirts, and when I go onstage, I wear a jumpsuit, because that's what's comfortable for me. Granted, it has a slit up the front and the back. But, you know, it gives me some air conditioning. And it's not *that* revealing. It's just sort of fun.

The only place I can see it is in the lyrics. There's definitely sex and sexuality within our lyrics, *for sure*. And that's intentional. I mean—

♦ **AJ: That's rock'n'roll.**

♦ **JJ:** Yeah. And it's part of life, it's part of women's lives, and it's part of my life. Everybody can listen to whatever song it is, and fantasize to their own heart's content about whatever they want to. And that's what's fun for me; when we're playing songs that have anything to do with relationships or sexuality, I want everybody in that audience to think that I'm singing to *them*. ♦ ♦ ♦

discography

♦ JOAN JETT AND THE BLACKHEARTS ♦
Home Alive, compilation (1996)
Evil Stig (1995)
Spirit of '73, compilation with L7 (1995)
Pure and Simple (1994)
Rebel Girl, 7-inch with Bikini Kill (1994)
Flashback (1993)
Notorious (1991)
The Hit List (1990)
Up Your Alley (1988)
Light of Day, soundtrack (1987)
Good Music (1986)
Glorious Results of a Misspent Youth (1984)
Album (1983)
I Love Rock'n'Roll (1981)
Bad Reputation, originally released as *Joan Jett* (1981)

♦ THE RUNAWAYS ♦
Waitin' For the Night (1977)
Queens of Noise (1977)
The Runaways (1976)

equipment list

Gibson Melody Maker guitar, Gibson Epiphone guitar, 1968 Les Paul blond Deluxe guitar (for recording), 1960s white Gibson Melody Maker double-cutaway California-style guitar (for recording), 212 Music Man amp with EV speakers, Music Man bottom with four EV speakers and a Boogie Head that drives the bottom, SM-58 microphone with a cord

Kathleen Hanna
Bikini Kill

Kathleen Hanna is singer for the Olympia, Washington punk band Bikini Kill, which also features Kathi Wilcox on bass, Tobi Vail on drums, and Billy Karren on guitar. Hanna also participates in a number of other projects/bands such as the Fakes; has collaborated with Joan Jett; and writes fanzines. Earlier bands included Amy Carter and Viva Knievel. She is closely associated with the inception of the Riot Grrrl movement.

♦ **ANDREA JUNO: We're going to send you a copy of the interview to make sure that you're quoted accurately—**

♦ KATHLEEN HANNA: Good. In the past we've even gone so far as to write our own articles—like for the *NME* [*New Musical Express*] in England. They made all these promises, but in the end they did the typical thing of taking our writing and twisting it, printing goofy quotations next to photos, and adding mean, catty opinions— it sucked. A lot of times writers have an essay already written, and they just plug you into it. Rather than do an interview, I'll often say, "Why don't you just write what you think of us?" because that's what's going to happen anyway.

♦ **AJ: One of my favorite investigations is the insidious nature of media. It's great that you took the stance of not grabbing at the carrot the media dangles in front of you. Essentially everybody wants to be recognized and loved and be popular; people have this notion that media exposure will facilitate that. Unfortunately, it doesn't work that way at all.**

♦ KH: We were really lucky that we had friends who gained notoriety before we did, so we got to see what happened to them. Because we had access to that information, we were able to make decisions based on personal knowledge.

I used to be involved in a women's cooperative/gallery/event space (which is part of the reason I got involved in music at all). We exhibited feminist photography, painting and comics shows.

We never had enough money to pay the rent, and Nirvana played a couple benefits to help keep our gallery going. I really loved that band, and it was really weird to see them get huge.

After I had seen them play to like thirty people, and then seen them with four thousand people—the whole thing had changed and it was almost like they were factory workers or something. They were playing but it seemed impossible for them to be "present" anymore; they were being forced to play every night; they had computerized set lists. I saw this happen and thought, "I don't want that; that's not why I started playing music. That's not my goal." I watched how they became surrounded by so many music industry types and stuff; it was scary.

♦ **AJ: Despite their own noble efforts to try and stop that from happening; clearly, it was very difficult.**

♦ KH: Personally, I have a history of drug and alcohol addiction, and I don't necessarily trust myself with a lot of money. In the music business there's always been a lot of drugs, and I feel that if people offered them to me I might take them, especially if I was constantly surrounded by suit-guys; you know, I might use drugs as an escape hatch—and, well, I just don't want to die.

♦ **AJ: I always used to rail against drugs, even during early punk rock days, but when Nancy Reagan launched her "Just Say No" campaign I felt cheated; I no longer felt I could** rant against drugs as freely. Yet I've always felt that drugs were the perfect tool to keep a very rebellious, revolutionary force impotent, so that it would self-destruct—it's what the moral guardians of the Republican party would absolutely love! I do believe in the legalization of drugs, but at the same time I think drugs should be dissociated with bohemianism and being cool and chic—they have nothing to do with revolution.

◆ KH: It's a way to keep us thinking about scoring—not thinking about how to fuck this society up. Why not fuck up the government instead of fucking up your body?

◆ AJ: Exactly. What are some of the things your band does to combat that typical image of rock-star laziness and irresponsibility?

Feminism really *is* cool now! ... My mission was to go around the country and tell girls who are not involved in tight feminist communities that it *does* exist, and they need to keep *creating* that. It's not hopeless.

◆ KH: Well, we book our own shows all over the country; we talk on the phone to the person who's going to be paying us, so we have contacts all over the country with actual people who know our voices when we call on the phone. We also try to challenge the idea of *specialization*, where everybody has their own little job and you're not connected to one another. We all switch jobs. One time Tobi will book the tour, then I'll book part of the tour, and later maybe she'll be doing more graphics. In the band, we follow this principle by switching instruments. I have a new respect for Tobi as a drummer, and a new understanding of what she does, because I had to drum on two songs on tour once, and I could barely even do that—it was so difficult for me. Now, to watch her play 45 minutes straight—I know a little bit more about why she paces the show when she writes out the set lists.

◆ AJ: That's a brilliant way to counter the kind of alienation that results from compartmentalization and specialization, mindlessly doing the same job over and over again. What you're do-

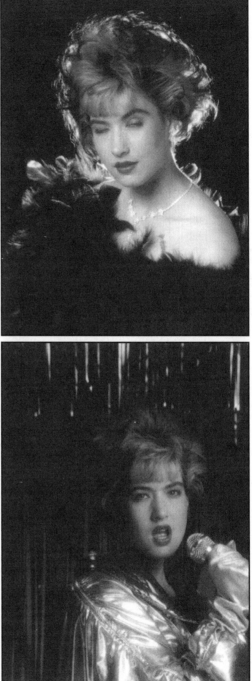

"Now I'm evolving this Las Vegas concept!"

ing is actually harder, but much healthier.

◆ KH: It's like, if you're hungry, you want to be nourished—but nourished for real. What if the only food you have access to is a Twinkie? You'll eat the Twinkie because that's all there is.

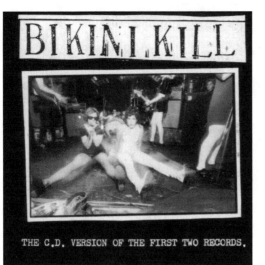

THE C.D. VERSION OF THE FIRST TWO RECORDS.

The CD Version of the First Two Records (1991-92).

What I'm trying to do is look for healthier food; I want to eat a tomato instead of a Twinkie. I'm willing to spend the time to create a garden and grow the vegetables, which seems more labor-intensive, but in the end it's worth it to have the joy of getting something out of your own garden and preparing a meal for your friends, and watching them enjoy it. I know I sound like a hippie or something but the whole fame illusion is a Twinkie! It *seems* like success, but, as happened with my band in particular, the kind of notoriety we got wasn't exactly positive.

◆ **AJ: Or nurturing.**

◆ **KH:** Not at all. Early on, I wrote a piece called "All the Candy's Poison"—looking at fame as a piece of candy. I was really obsessed with personal relationships of abuse and domination in terms of incest, rape, and domestic violence, because I have a history in the domestic violence community. A lot of my thinking came from contemplating the nuclear family, violence and incest.

I wrote about a white middle-class nuclear family. The father buys the daughter a car, and clothes when she wants them, as a payoff for her silence about the fact that she's being raped or beaten (or both), or psychologically terrorized, or a combination of all these factors that are really confusing. And the neighbors go, "That couldn't possibly be happening to Little Cindy—look at how much her father loves her. Look at all these presents he's giving her." In a lot of abuse situations, the men are really nice to absolutely everybody on the surface. People go, "The coach of the football team couldn't possibly have done that!" Or, "The priest couldn't possibly have

done that!" These are men who often have really good alibis, because their surface totally belies their reality. They're totally invested in creating this identity that they're the nicest guys in the world, because that's a way to ensure silence.

You're sitting at a table, and Dad's hand is in your pussy. But above the table, society just sees two smiling people. The media operate with this same sort of sleight-of-hand. "Well, Kathleen, look at all these treats you're getting: all this notoriety." And a part of me thought, "It's like an abusive dad who never pays any attention unless he's hurting me. But at least I'm getting *some* attention. Even though it's not *positive* attention, I'm getting *something*." Just like a lot of survivors of abuse can be tricked into thinking that we liked it, or can have a lot of guilty feelings about having an orgasm when we're being raped. There's a part of me that likes *any* attention at all—especially in a situation where I'm not being touched or loved or held, or nurtured in any real way.

Believe me, I'm not using this analogy lightly—it comes from real experience in both realms. I mean, there's a part of me that *likes* to see my name in a magazine, and I've felt guilty and ashamed about that, because another part of me knows that it's really negative attention. But it's hard to discuss this with anybody in my community—in fact, fame has alienated me from my community because they saw me *getting the treats!* So I experience what I've felt in many abuse situations: total silence. I couldn't *possibly* be abused, because "Look—I've got all this privilege, I've got all this power. I'm in the *Washington Post!*" In reality, I didn't get a new car; the only treats I get are lies being printed about me and my name in *Newsweek*.

◆ **AJ: People cherish this equation: that wealth comes with fame—**

◆ **KH:** It doesn't. I'm lucky I'm able to earn a living doing what I do, without having a side job now. This isn't going to last, and I know it, but this is the first time I've been able to do just my own work, and I consider myself completely blessed. And I've tried to use the access I've been given to open up doors for other women in my community, and other men who are doing important work.

It's amazing how the whole concept of fame changes things—it changes friendships, for example. It's important to actually look at things in context and ask: "Does it really mean you're in a powerful position because you're having things written about you?" Like because I'd written a song about incest, the *Washington Post* reported that I claimed my father raped me. I never said that; I never even *talked* to that reporter. And the *Washington Post* is a big newspaper; I have relatives who live in Washington, D.C., and I had to deal with feeling that I wasn't sure if I could ever *talk* to them again. They don't know that I didn't say that; the *Post* reporter just decided that because I'd written a song called "Daddy's Little Girl," it was about *me*—never thinking, "She's worked at a shelter for two years, and worked with a teenage sexual assault group; maybe she's writing about things she learned there." Maybe that *is* part of my experience, but that's for *me* to know.

This was a very painful event. At the time I was involved in a radical group in D.C., but no one from that community called me to ask if I was okay. I think people assumed I had this imaginary support system which I didn't have—in fact a lot of people in the community resented the fact that I was getting any attention at all and *they* weren't. I thought, "If you want this kind of attention, you can *have* it!" Because it totally ruined my life; it cost me my job.

When we were written about in *Newsweek*, they published a picture which we didn't give them. A woman sold them a private snapshot of us in bikinis on the beach; you could see my tattoos and everything—so a lot of my customers at work (I was a stripper at the time) saw the article and learned my real name and certain other things I didn't want them to know; I think the article

> It's frustrating on tour when these kids come up to me whose biggest preoccupation in life is whether Rancid should join a major label or not. I think, "If that's the worst of your problems, you should consider yourself fuckin' lucky."

called me "a stripper, a feminist and a sexual abuse victim" or something like that. Anyways, this wiped out the separation between my work and my private life that I *needed* in order to function coherently both at work and at home; so, basically, that article created a situation whereby I had to leave my job.

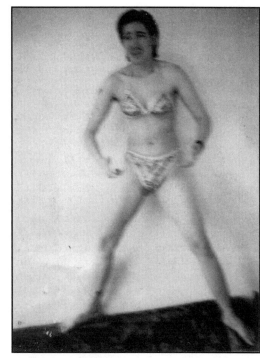

Self-portrait (1994).

◆ **AJ: That's a replication of the kind of violation and abuse that happens within families, but on a *media* level—**

◆ KH: Right, and what if you're a domestic violence survivor who's currently being stalked by a past lover or boyfriend (or whoever), and you're in music? And you need to do interviews as a way to generate income, because publicity really does affect your income—the more people know about you, the more people come to your shows and buy your records. What if (let's just say) you're a woman who's being stalked, and you go into an interview and say, "This is what I want. I don't want my last name used. This is the photograph I want used" (which doesn't look that much like you). And they say, "Okay." But then the interview comes out, and they've printed your last name, they've used another photo—they've lied.

◆ **AJ: Again, being written about does not equate support or community. And the more successful you are, the more jealousy and envy you encounter—these pathological emotions which are endemic to our society.**

◆ KH: I'm 26 now, and I feel a lot different about things than when I was 20. I want to talk about power and privilege in complex ways, recognizing that there is such a thing as privilege that's just given to certain people. There's also

earned privilege. I'm from a scene where I've done a fuck of a lot of shit-work. I was a behind-the-scenes person for years and years; I've set up a lot of shows; I've done a lot of networking with women; I've just done a lot of *work*. And now, seven years later, I'm getting some notoriety, and I'm being resented for that. It's not like some businessman dreamed up the idea of Bikini Kill and we auditioned for the job and got it—we *created* this.

◆ **AJ: There exists a resentment of rewards, a resentment of pleasure. Why? Because we're supposed to be antagonistic toward our bodies. And how we think about sex is really sick; we're never taught how to deal with pleasure. So the simple pleasure of having some success—there's real resentment toward that.**

Also, a lot of members of "the underground" are white, middle- or upper-class people slumming it after art school, and then suddenly imposing their own noblesse-oblige rules: "We should all be poor." Why—because *they* feel guilty about their own backgrounds? At the same time, I don't want to make rules about people with privilege, either; there are some really creative people who can have a trust fund and maintain their creativity. Not many people are capable of taking privilege and doing something progressive with it, but some people are. Some of the most fabulous artists, radical and subversive, come from the upper classes. In "the underground" there are so many status quo notions, like this ideal of the starving artist, that remain unanalyzed.

Playing at the Jabber Jaw (1994).

◆ KH: It's frustrating when we go on tour, and these kids come up to me whose biggest preoccupation in life is whether Rancid should join a major label or not. I think, "If that's the worst of your problems, you should consider yourself fuckin' lucky." I mean, I totally think *how* people get their work out is important—even crucial. It's just that there are a lot of complex issues involved in the whole thing, and getting trapped in little circles of shame and blame isn't going to create serious analysis of the situation—it also isn't going to make corporations or co-optation go away.

This culture thrives on dualistic contrasts. It's glamorous to die; it's glamorous to have your ten minutes of fame and then totally self-destruct.

◆ **AJ: You must have encountered this when you appeared in that Sonic Youth video—how did that come about?**

◆ KH: Somebody called me up and made an offer, "You get a free trip to L.A. and $250." I was actually going to say no because I knew that so many people in my scene would look down on me for doing this and give me shit. But I thought, "I need the money and it might be fun." So I went, and I had enough brains about me that I could look at the situation objectively—I mean, it was interesting and everything, but, ultimately, most videos are complete bullshit anyway—so whatever. It was a job.

Around the same time, the major labels were courting us, and they wanted me to come to L.A. or New York and meet with people. I knew we weren't really interested, because we're really happy with our label, running things the way we want. But I also saw myself getting older, seeing other people of my generation

86

and scene making a lot of money while I didn't, and looking back at my decision and potentially becoming a really bitter person. Because I knew what they were going to do. Riot Grrrl was making a big splash in the media, and I could totally see the New Kids on the Block or the Monkees of Riot Grrrl happening!

♦ **AJ: That kind of appropriation is already going on. Then what happens is that people throw the baby out with the bathwater: "Riot Grrrls—how disgusting!" Or, "Riot Grrrls—how passé!" I think you have to look at the original disseminators who had a vision, and not all the obscuring clutter that came springing up later.**

♦ KH: You're expected to create all this exciting work, and then sit idly by while the powers that be completely rip you off! You're never supposed to step in and say, "I'd like a little bit of that cash; I deserve it." It's like an either/or; like the idea of the illegitimate/legitimate victim in this society. If I allowed myself to be the opposite of the mainstream, then I would be a "legitimate" victim of co-optation. For example, if I never worked with a major label, or if I never worked with a corporation to get funding for a project—if I stayed chaste, poor and suffering, then, when the Riot Grrrl band that was manufactured by Warner Brothers comes along and makes a trillion dollars, people will perhaps feel sorry for me and understand why I'm so bitter.

But if people see me in the Sonic Youth video, this problematizes the situation. And part of the reason I did this was very specific: I'm not interested in being a martyr. I think the martyr thing is a bunch of bullshit. I can't afford to deny myself stupid adventures once in a while, or to turn down money even when what I have to do to make it isn't exactly perfect. And, hey, sometimes I make mistakes. I do things I regret later. I just hate the idea that we're all supposed to suffer all the time. I think it's gross.

Part of the reason I work so hard and do things is that I'm looking for pleasure. I'm a thrill-seeker, and I *also* give a shit about the community I come from, because that's where I get a lot of my pleasure: from seeing things happening for real; seeing things actually changing. And about the major label thing: I could have said, "Fuck you, major label! I hate all you people! You're all assholes; you're destroying our scene! You've done all this bad stuff—blah blah blah." But what I thought was *smarter* was to realize: "They're offering me free plane tickets to New York … " (I have friends who can't afford to

just visit New York City.) "I'm going to say that those friends are my managers and agents, and they need to be flown, too—I'm going to get these people free trips to New York."

So I took friends to New York; I got $5000 financed for a film during this period when the record company thought I might sign. People wanted to show me how much they believed in my artistic vision, or whatever, by throwing a little money my way, and by giving me plane tickets when I needed them. For this six-to-eight-month period, I basically capitalized on this situation and took as much of their money as I possibly could, as many free plane tickets and free hotel rooms as I could get. And I went and listened to what they had to say, so that I could, with a clear head, say, "No, that's not what I want to do." And hanging out with those people wasn't nearly as interesting as hanging out with my friends in our own scene. The shows we go to are ten times more valuable to us than the shows they took us to see in New York or L.A.; the things my friends are doing are much, much more interesting.

♦ **AJ: The idea of the martyr that you referred to is a real problem for the political Left, which has been decimated because of the self-destructiveness of following this antiquated religious stereotype: that to be really pure, you have to be suffering.**

I don't want to just write songs about rape or male domination for the rest of my life. Yet people expect that same thing over and over. And if you stop doing it, you're called a sell-out.

♦ KH: Well, it's not very glamorous to *live* for your cause—it's glamorous to die. And it's not like there's just one cause, anyway.

We were discussing drug addiction earlier, which is so connected to living in an addictive culture with its established behavioral mechanisms of you do the sin, then you repent. You get drunk, you get a hangover, you live through the hangover and maybe you don't drink for a few days, and then you drink again. It's a way to separate leisure time from work time. All these

Kathleen and Laura McDougall (right), creator of the fanzine
Sister Nobody.

different separations are going on: the pure and the impure, up and down. This culture thrives on dualistic contrasts. It's glamorous to die; it's glamorous to have your ten minutes of fame and then totally self-destruct.

♦ **AJ: Life in the fast lane is idealized—**

♦ KH: It's not glamorous when you're around as a musician for twenty years and you keep doing interesting things, and maybe your band turns into a film company—which is something I see happening with us, later, maybe. A lot of people have done interesting work and have maintained it for a long time, even beyond the time when the media shined a spotlight on a certain area of their work and said, "This is the peak." I don't believe in that. Just because the media decided that last year was my peak—fuck that! My peak is yet to come. I think I'm going to have peaks and levelings and more peaks—but all this has to do with the media's polaroid-picture way of dealing with things, that syndrome of instant gratification and commodification.

I feel that in terms of my personal process of growth, the way I dealt with the major label thing was as important as getting up onstage. I tried to be smart about it. I asked myself, "How much money can I get out of these people?" I felt this was okay; it didn't make me any more or less of a victim. I thought, "I'm going to go there and listen to what they have to say; I'm going to make a decision." I wanted to really think it through; not just do the thing I was expected to do.

♦ **AJ: Also, how much money do you really need for a comfortable existence? The do-it-**

yourself lifestyle doesn't necessarily mean a poverty lifestyle—I have faith that the public will buy things that resonate some truth. But what do you really need? You don't *need* a limo. You need a nice apartment, but you don't need a penthouse suite—you need what is truly nurturing. Most people who end up taking the big material carrot give up the real nurturance.

♦ KH: We turn ourselves into machines; we're not really *present* for most of the things that happen to us. There are a lot of interesting aspects of performing that have to do with abuse issues and dissociation. American performance, in general, lends itself to the idea of taking on another personality when you're onstage, and certain punk performers have challenged this. I tried to challenge this for a long time—I tried to be *present* onstage; this was not Memorex, it was *live*. But I had to totally reassess what I wanted to do onstage because of safety issues—I get harassed and sometimes physically assaulted on our tours, and I've had to make decisions as to how much I really want to give to an audience.

I grew up in a family where there weren't many boundaries, I didn't have much privacy, I didn't see a strict separation between who is wife and who is child. If I grew up not really feeling like I was allowed to have my own space at certain times, then of course in a community I'm going to feel myself as being really connected to people, and sometimes not even see that I have a *right* to my own private space. People may applaud me for my intimacy with an audience, but I'm somebody who never learned how to *not* be vulnerable—I know how to be vulnerable, I'm good at that! I'm good at peeling off my skin for lovers and letting it all hang out and being the emotional caretaker—these are traditionally designated places for me to be. Then when I go into a performance situation and act out similar roles, certain people (like men) perceive this as radical, but I think women are *used* to seeing that in each other.

So now what I'm interested in is adding *safety* to that equation: "Maybe I need a certain amount of distance from the audience—especially considering who's mainly in the audiences: men." I don't necessarily *want* to be that vulnerable or open, or expose myself to them. So I'm frustrated by the system of criticism which goes, "The more emotional you are in your music, the more authentically female you are." I'm an artist; I'm strategic in what I do. When I was 19 I was writing songs that were really close to the bone, but I'm not interested in doing that all the time. Now I'm thinking, "I need a little more privacy." So I don't necessarily think that the best thing I can do onstage is to be vulnerable, or be "real"—

♦ **AJ: Also, this idea feeds the stereotypes of how women "should" be.**

♦ KH: A lot of artists in general have accepted the idea that the only way you can create authentic art is if you're suffering, and this helps people stay in the same place. If I write a song about rape and get a lot of attention and applause for that ("Wow, that's really beautiful! She stood up and she told the story about her rape!"), that's all well and good, but I don't want to stay there forever. That is a point in a *process*. And maybe I move on—not necessarily beyond rape or abuse or being female—

♦ **AJ: But beyond being a *victim*. On one level it's really important to acknowledge victimization, but then it's important to cut loose: "Hey— I don't have to remain a victim. I don't have to act out a stereotype." That's one-dimensional.**

One particularly gross dude was trying to grab me, and I beckoned, "C'mon! C'mon!" When he got close I hit him over the head with the microphone, and it made a really loud sound and all the girls went nuts and yelled, "Yeah!"

♦ KH: You create work about being female, and there's a lot to write about—I don't want to just write songs about rape or male domination for the rest of my life. Yet people expect that same thing over and over. And if you stop doing it, you're called a sell-out.

♦ **AJ: Maybe you're growing—you're not stuck. Once you get fame for some little shtick, are you supposed to keep doing that for the next twenty years?**

♦ KH: I began to feel that a lot of people were

coming to see the freak show: "See the victim!" I felt like one of those Keane paintings of a kid with big eyes looking up at the big fist: "Oh, I'm so pathetic." I was doing a lot of spoken-word at our shows about abuse and domination, and the pieces were really personal.

See, I started out being involved in a scene where these boy-bands from all over the country would play at a club I was managing with some women, and these bands were really boring. Here I'm spending a lot of time working at a domestic violence shelter hearing all these women's stories, and I'm seeing the way these teenage girls are supporting each other, and it's one of the most beautiful things in the world. So I start incorporating some of this experience in my performance, and immediately it gets framed as a picture of a victim or a freak show. I'm doing all this stuff on stage, and I feel people are paying money to come in and watch me cry, or freak out.

♦ **AJ: So you were frustrated—**

♦ KH: I was a shitworker at this club where men would come and do boring shows. I did everything from painting the floor to cleaning the grease off the floor to wiping their stupid cock-rock graffiti off the wall after they left, and picking up their cigarette butts, and spending my own long-distance money to book their dumb bands into our club, and then having them yell at me because there's not enough orange juice "backstage," etc. And they were just doing boring work that wasn't interesting. My real life involved working at this domestic violence shelter, and I came from that situation into this club where people were just playing their songs in the same order as on their record, with no engagement between the audience and the performers—even though it's supposed to be punk rock or alterna-whatever, it's still very slick and "I can do this because I'm magic, and you can't." So when I got onstage, my goal was to be really *present*, and pay attention to what was actually happening in the room while we played. Women were getting sexually harassed at these shows— getting fucked with and having to leave. When I'm playing a show, I notice when a woman leaves, and I try to figure out what's going on— is some dude breathing down her neck, making comments in her ear?

♦ **AJ: What do you do about that aggressive, guys-in-the-front mosh pit situation?**

♦ KH: Sometimes we circulate flyers before a show stating that we don't want a mosh pit in front, and how that ruins the show for a lot of

The Anti-Pleasure Dissertation, 7-inch (1995).

people, and, "If you want to mosh, go mosh in the back." At a show, as the person with the microphone I feel like I have a certain responsibility, because I can communicate to everybody in the room. So if I see a woman being fucked with, I might say, "You—outta here now!" and make the community accountable for removing that person.

And sometimes I'm divorced from reality, up there thinking, "We're going to play our twelve songs and then we're going to leave." Maybe I haven't eaten breakfast, or I'm in a town where some relative might show up and I'm freaking out—sometimes I have to dissociate, and that's fine; it's like being a stripper, and I know how to do that. But usually I want to be in my body onstage because it's so awesome to feel the music and have women being really supportive, and to get that energy back. The women who know the words to our songs and are singing along are giving me so much strength to keep going—that's an incredible feeling. And the guy who is yelling, "Take it off!" or, "Slut!" or calling me a whore or a cunt or even a rock star—

♦ AJ: Does that happen a lot?

♦ KH: Yes. I've been spit on, grabbed, and even punched. My friend Laura, who was our roadie, was defending me once and got knocked unconscious by a man who, a few weeks later, murdered a woman named Kristin Lardner in the street with a gun. When he tried to attack me, the audience didn't do anything—they thought it was part of the fuckin' performance! Billy had to take his guitar off, and he and I had to take this guy outside and beat him up. *We* had to do it; no one in the crowd assisted us.

Our friend was lying on the floor unconscious—and people watched and did nothing. Why? Because they thought it was a TV sitcom? Also, I got mace sprayed in my face during this incident, and so I had to sing the rest of the set with mace in my throat; I remember thinking, "Let's just finish this set and get the fuck out of this town." I wasn't one foot off the stage before people were coming up and asking, "Do you have any more lyric sheets? Can I buy a tape from you?" as if they didn't see what had just happened. One of my best friends had just been knocked unconscious, and people were mad because we stopped the show for ten minutes. They were treating us like we worked at Burger King and were just there to fill their order.

♦ AJ: You're perceived as the property of the public.

♦ KH: We just had an experience in Los Angeles where we played two sets; our drummer was sick so other people were sitting in on drums. We'd just driven from Flagstaff, Arizona, and we were really tired. We'd already been touring for maybe a month, and at a lot of the shows we'd gotten fucked with—guys yelling, "Take it off!" or calling us cunts or whatever. Sometimes the girls in the audience would take care of them, but sometimes it ended up being a bad situation.

On our first record, I repeated the same line over and over. We played with shitty P.A. systems and I didn't think anybody could hear me (literally), so I passed out lyric sheets at every show and I'd repeat the same phrase until people "got" it.

It really sucks when you have a "flashback" onstage. Once some guy spat a mouthful of beer in my face—he was *this* close—and it reminded me of when I was 15 and being raped, and the guy came in my face. All of a sudden I had a flashback of this guy coming in my face, and I wondered, "Does Tommy Tutone ever have something like this happen to him? I don't think so."

Anyway, in Los Angeles these crusty punk guys who looked kind of Mad Max-ish started yelling, "Rock star! Rock star!" as soon as I took the stage. They were also telling me my breasts are made of silicone—I think they got me confused with someone else. "You're fake! Your breasts are made of silicone, and you're a fucking cunt rock star bitch!" It was interesting that they were saying cunt and rock star in the same sentence. And every time we stopped playing, during the pause they would chant, "Fuckin' bitch, you fuckin' cunt! Rock star fuckin' cunt!" And they'd also yell, "Girl power is bad! All power is bad!"—I guess their "meaning" was that girl power is just another oppressive institution! These guys were also jumping on women and kicking them in the head with their boots.

I tried to deal with the situation in a number of ways: through humor, through confrontation, and having women who were physically assaulted by these guys come onstage. At this show there was hardly any security; nobody was making the guys leave. And there were too many of them for women to physically remove them; plus, the women weren't organized enough to do that. I knew I had to do *something*, even if it was just a performance art piece for the girls in the front who'd been hit. These guys kept trying to jump onstage and get me, but two security people onstage (they seemed to be the only ones in the house) kept them from grabbing me. I was taunting the harassers back: [sarcastic] "Yeah, I *am* a rock star. Whenever you see a woman with any kind of power, you try to kill it. Well, I'm glad for what I have." I was having fun, reveling in that power.

It was weird; I felt like those guys were planted to show how pervasive these attitudes are. It was almost like a performance piece: just by their presence, they were proving how much what we're doing needs to be done.

♦ **AJ: You weren't capitulating to their harassment?**

♦ KH: At a certain point I felt, "You guys have taken up enough of our time. I'm playing this show for the women in the room—I'm not playing for *you*. I don't give a shit—you can yell all you want." One particularly gross dude was coming up and trying to grab me, and I beckoned, "C'mon! C'mon!" When he got close I hit him over the head with the microphone, and it made a really loud sound (because the mike was on) and all the girls went nuts and yelled, "*Yeah!*" like, totally happy. After the show, the cops came in to arrest me for assault! I thought, "Excuse me—where were you when I was being sexually harassed?" The blow to that dude's head was nothing compared to what happened when I went back to where I was sleep-

ing: I experienced all these traumatic flashbacks; it was totally fucked up.

♦ **AJ: And hadn't this guy physically assaulted other women in the audience?**

♦ **KH: Yes.**

♦ **AJ: So what did the police end up doing?**

♦ KH: I was standing at the back door of the building, and a cop shined a flashlight in my face and went, "You're the singer for the band!" I said, "No I'm not—she went thataway toward that white van!" It was like being in a movie; he immediately raced down the alley after this fictitious girl. I went back into the building and hid until a guy who worked at the theater found me and took me into this locked office. He said he wouldn't tell the police where I was. I was wearing a dress with a picture of a man on the front, and on the back was a picture of the same man seen from the back, and this guy said, "Nice ass." And I said, "What?" and he said, "I mean, that *guy's* ass," but then he reached out and grabbed *my* ass! And I couldn't say anything because this guy was hiding me. It was so weird; I couldn't even believe it was happening.

That night was really awful. But after that happened, I decided to try to write something up saying that if people call us "cunt" and "whore" and basically engage in sexual harassment while we're trying to play, I want them removed immediately. And I want security there who will deal with that so *we* don't have to. Because while I'm trying to sing, I'm sick of always having to be on the lookout for a man approaching the stage with a beer bottle or some other weapon that can be thrown. Those guys

I Like Fucking/I Hate Danger, 7-inch.

Photo: Kathi Wilcox

Queen Kathleen on tour, Fargo, North Dakota (1994).

were throwing bottles and chains at us while we were playing. I had to *duck*, and it's, like, hard to concentrate on what you're singing when… .

♦ **AJ: You're on this ironic trajectory, especially since you're on a label called Kill Rock Stars. At the same time there's nothing you can do about the expansion of your fame in the media; now you *are* a rock star! On one level you can't pretend this isn't happening; on another level, how can you take that power and translate it into something that's healthy for you and acknowledges the situation you're in? Well, didn't you talk about evolving into a film company?**

♦ KH: Right, and opening up access to other people, and continuing to demystify the position we're in. That show I just described—there's always a few of those on every tour. And I wonder how many people come just to see those theatrics?

♦ **AJ: Demolition derby.**

♦ KH: Right, it's a total demolition derby. And people see me getting really upset, because sometimes I internalize it when somebody calls me a bitch or a whore—I actually *feel* it, and it might remind me of something someone in my family once said to me. Because I'm actually *there*, people get to see me react and be in pain. And again, I don't want people to pay money to see me freak out or break down; I want people to come see me totally *shine*. That's why I was questioning the idea of the martyr/female in performance; if a person totally feels it, that can be as much of a pose as anything else. So now I'm evolving this Las Vegas concept!

♦ **AJ: You can't pretend anymore that**

you're in a tiny punk club where you started, surrounded by just your friends. You have to take these heavier challenges as they arise.

♦ KH: We've done one mainstream media interview, because someone told us that unless we were written about in *Melody Maker*, we wouldn't be able to go to England, so we made that decision—it's not like we have rules that are unchangeable. We will make a compromise to get what we need done; we don't ever make a decision on the basis of purity/non-purity. We have made mistakes, and what's more powerful than people in the public eye admitting they've made mistakes? Then people can see themselves in what you're doing.

♦ **AJ: That goes back to the demystification of fame—you're not any different from anybody else. You're not building up some mythology that will also kill you—**

[I want] other women who work in the sex industry to remember that we can be sex-trade workers *and* be philosophers, writers, musicians, artists, or whatever.

♦ KH: —and alienate you from yourself, and make you feel like you're not "real." I live in Olympia again, and am part of the community, and that's a really important place for me to be. I'm putting on shows again, including a recent AIDS benefit, and instead of three bands and a spoken-word performer, I limit each performer to ten minutes—that's how long people's attention spans are these days, anyway! Especially if it's spoken word—I can't deal with two hours straight of spoken word; I fall asleep.

I'm doing a fanzine, too. I interviewed a local musician about heroin and other kinds of addiction. We did a really good interview together.

I'm also including some of my writing about my alcoholism. I feel it's a safe atmosphere to do this, because I've been in the community for a while, and I have an actual (not fictitious) support network; people who actually live in the same house are supportive of me. I feel it's a great time for me to do this work and expose certain things about myself, in order to be more connected with people. Friends of mine are dying, not only from AIDS but from heroin addiction and alcoholism, and I can't just sit by and watch all my friends die without saying anything. I'm trying to talk about this without being condescending or a helping-hand liberal. I'm doing this while still doing the band.

On our first record, a lot of the songs are boring to me now, because I repeat the same line over and over. The reason I did this was: we played with shitty P.A. systems and I didn't think anybody could hear me (literally), so I passed out lyric sheets at every show and I'd repeat the same phrase until people "got" it—I'd repeat "Resist psychic death!" over and over. Now I don't feel the need to repeat words over and over, because people are actually buying our records. And originally I didn't think we'd *ever* be recorded—at that point, all of our material was written for live performance.

Now I'm writing more for recording. I know people are buying our records and memorizing the lyrics, because that's what I see when they come to our shows. Now that people are really listening, I can say things in more complex ways than before. And that's really exciting—I can be more multi-leveled and more poetic. I can talk about dissociation and tokenism—the mainstream media using certain people as tokens for certain ideas, like Tony Randall, for example. He's in there innocuously; my writing is more about subjects like Tank Girl and the marketing of Calvin Klein cologne. I've also written a lot about sex.

Basically, as a band we're now able to be more complex. Now we can afford better recording. Our first album was recorded in like one or two days; all of our singles have been recorded in one day. Now we can afford to spend maybe a week! We can be more experimental musically. The thing about being punk: we did learn how to play in public, and there are people who have seen us from the very beginning and seen us *evolve*. It's stupid to continue playing fake bad, or whatever. There's this idea that if you learn how to play your instrument, then all of a sudden you're not a punk band anymore and you should just give up and quit.

♦ **AJ: Originally, weren't you running a gallery? You started this band as a way to more widely disseminate artistic and philosophic ideas. The band was a wider transmission vehicle—**
♦ KH: Right. I also wanted to make it really cool to be feminist, because this was right when *Time* or *Newsweek* said that feminism was dead, around '89. Now everything was supposedly "post-feminist." I was in college hanging out with photographers who were feminists, like Tammy Rae Carland and Heidi Arbogast, and we started a discussion group outside of school because we weren't getting what we needed in school. My artwork was censored on the campus because it was too "violent" and "pornographic," even though it was totally feminist. So from this discussion group we started a gallery, partly because we needed a place to exhibit our photographs—
♦ **AJ: This is a discussion in itself. Some older feminists are in collusion with conservatives in restricting the ways in which women can even express sexuality.**

> **A lot of artists have accepted the idea that the only way you can create authentic art is if you're suffering, and this helps people stay in the same place.**

♦ KH: If you can't use examples of pornography in your discussion about pornography, how are you supposed to talk about it?
♦ **AJ: Susie Bright talks eloquently about a woman-defined sexuality and pornography; the goal is for women to own sexuality just as men do.**
♦ KH: Andrea Dworkin came to our school and tried to severely limit my definition of what feminism was—basically she told me I didn't fuckin' exist. I had been a sex-trade worker, and to her, feminism and sex-trade work were diametrically-opposed conceptions. She made me cry; it was really depressing. Here she was standing up in front of all these people basically saying that my reality wasn't even there. I totally love certain women, and I totally love myself fiercely. And just because I've been a sex-trade worker does not mean I have no sexuality; that does not mean I'm going to be "paying for it" for the rest of my life—

◆ **AJ: Also, I think you wrote that you'd much rather be making $20 an hour as a sex-trade worker than $5 an hour as a waitress—**

◆ KH: —and being totally shit on. I've been a waitress, and I hated that much more than taking my clothes off for money. This may be really personal, having to do with my individual history, but here's this Dworkin woman trying to erase all these women's lives! And the way she goes about it strategically is so racist and classist. Who are the women most affected by the laws she is helping to enact? Poor women, women of color, women who are already discriminated against in the sex-trade industry itself. Dworkin is saying that women have to register with the police and get fingerprinted and pay a $75 fee to register as a sex-trade worker in the state of Washington—she helped enact that law. That meant I could no longer strip in the state of Washington; I had to go all the way to Oregon (a much longer commute). I'm not willing to go to the police and be fingerprinted—there's no way.

◆ **AJ: The exploitation of women and their sexuality isn't stopped by anti-pornography laws. Women are also exploited when they read *Vogue* magazine or see an anorexic Kate Moss advertisement. But Dworkin's not legislating against *those* forms of exploitation, because advertising is the money base for the right wing that she's working with. Pornography, and the sex trade, are easy targets. Dworkin is just aping the party line that women aren't allowed to own, and deal with, their sexuality.**

◆ KH: It's totally puritanical and totally weird. I think, "Excuse me—you're spending all this time talking about pornography?" Dworkin gets up and gives these really intimate, detailed descriptions of pornography she has studied, and it's obvious she's *fascinated* with pornography. So be fascinated with pornography and *deal* with it!

◆ **AJ: Just like the christian right, who spend all their time talking about pornography—it's obvious how much they're getting off on it.**

◆ KH: I read this essay called "(Male) Desire and (Female) Disgust," having to do with *Hustler* and *Playboy* and class. In it the writer makes an interesting point about a housewife who's obsessed with having everything clean—so basically she devotes her whole life to dirt!

I went to a Feminists Against Censorship Task Force meeting in Seattle, looking to them for some support when my work was censored, and they were totally fucked up, too. They were a group basically in opposition to the Dworkin/

MacKinnon pipeline. This was supposed to be a public discussion, and some man presiding over the meeting gave a long lecture about how *Playboy* could be really revolutionary and radical, and it was so boring. There was a girl present who had worked at one of the same strip clubs I'd worked at, and she was totally tokenized: she was the girl who "loved her job" and "thought everybody was great." And I *know* the kind of shit they do at that club; it's a pay-to-dance situation and they have all these illegal fining systems. And the way the F.A.C. Task Force was using this woman was really gross. Whenever they wanted the voice of the "authentic" person they would ask her, "Don't you like your job?" and she would go, "I love my job." I was sitting there thinking, "I *worked* there, and that place was *fucked up*."

Sometimes even women didn't understand: "Why do you have to have women-only meetings?" We said, "Look, it's only *one* hour a week. *Every* space is male space—what's the problem?"

My friends and I were asking questions like, "We don't want anything censored, but what about the fact that pornography is largely owned and run by men, and they're making most of the money off it? And how is a man jacking off to a static picture of a woman with a staple in her stomach radical? Could you explain that concept to me?" And they were going, "Did Dworkin send you?" They wouldn't answer any of our questions; they thought we'd been sent to ruin their meeting.

We were being problematic; we kept saying, "As a feminist who's also very much against censorship and does not want the government to have any control over blah-blah-blah, I'm just interested in the economic side of things. What do you think about… ?" And they would just completely silence us and call us Dworkin-ites.

◆ **AJ: This is the problem with movements that arise with good intentions, and it's how they self-destruct—they appropriate the very fascism they're against. How do we unravel this pattern so we can create a positive, self-aware, self-questioning movement with momentum? Defen-**

siveness cuts off so much. When you're mainly preoccupied with how your enemies might react, then you're no longer responding to the immediacy of the problems at hand. The community becomes dissociated, and you're led into traps where you start to not listen to true questions.

◆ KH: Oddly enough, at the time we didn't even know who Dworkin was. Then I started reading her. This meeting happened *before* the Dworkin lecture where she treated me condescendingly.

At that lecture of hers, I said that I was a sex worker and a feminist, and she said, "Oh! I appreciate you coming out and saying this in front of all these people. And I just want to tell you that if you think this experience has not affected you, I want you to know that it's going to affect the whole rest of your life. You'll be paying for it forever, blah-blah-blah." And all of my feminism professors were there; I had just

Pyramid Club, NY (1992).

"outed" myself in front of the women I worked with at the domestic violence shelter! And my other friend was silenced too. She stood up and had the guts to say something like, "In the age of AIDS pornography can save lives; what do you think about the fact that queer porn is likely to be the first stuff censored by anti-porn legislation?" And Dworkin replied—I kid you not— "You've been duped by the patriarchy."

I wanted to throw a spitball at her. She was so condescending; I felt like I had been patted on the head. I asked, "What about organizations like Coyote, Whisper, Pony, Puma—all these organizations of sex-trade workers that do not necessarily support you? How dare you stand up there and act like you're speaking for us and for them?" I mean—how does she get off being up there, when actual women who work in the sex industry think she's fucked? And she's getting up in front of all these college-educated women (a lot of whom don't have any first-hand experience with the sex industry) and totally exploiting people, fomenting fear and anger at pornography.

◆ AJ: It's not only patronizing, it *is* the patriarchy, which works by silencing oppressed groups and speaking *for* them. It's perfect that politically she became bedfellows with—

◆ KH: —the *cops*—

◆ AJ: —the fundamentalists, the christian right, Ed Meese, and the Reagan Administration.

◆ KH: At this meeting she was talking about how the cops were going to come in and save us all! I was thinking, "Excuse me, but I live in Green River territory." There was a serial killer who was killing mostly lower-income women, some of whom have been identified as prostitutes (and some of whom haven't been); that's how the media portray them, so you're not supposed to feel sorry for them. The death toll now is supposedly over a hundred! Group burial/ dumping grounds have been found. A lot of women have disappeared over the past decade, and there's enough deviation in the m.o. that police suspect there's more than one killer. And guess what—some of these killings are probably being done by cops; that's why they haven't been

Pussy Whipped (1992).

caught. No duh. You don't have to be a genius to know that if that many *cops* had disappeared, something would have happened by now! And here's Dworkin up there saying the cops are here to help us, and enforce all these pornography laws. I'm thinking, "Are you lobotomized?"

♦ **AJ: I love your desire to reclaim feminism on *your* terms, and make feminism "cool" again.**

♦ KH: It's totally connected with the whole situation. With the Feminists Against Censorship Task Force vs. Andrea Dworkin and the cops, well—where's the third category? For a while, in my performance I saw myself creating a mythic third category, with me as a superhero. Perhaps that's too much of a high-maintenance identity; I don't *really* want to be mythic. But for a while I needed that shield: "I'm a superhero!" I was really into Wonder Woman imagery (now, it seems a bit dumb) and I was really "out" about being a sex-trade worker. I wasn't saying, "This is really cool and everybody should do it," but I wasn't going to hide it, because it was a part of what I did and it had to do with what I thought about.

Whenever we were written about in the press, I wanted my sex-work history to be part of the description, because I wanted other women whom I danced at clubs with (and who never knew my real name) to see themselves reflected in some way. A lot of women who are doing music now have been sex-trade workers, prostitutes, dancers; I thought it was really important that I didn't hide that. But I also didn't want to glamorize that experience as being a super-cool thing in itself. I just wanted other women who

work in the sex industry to remember that we can be sex-trade workers *and* be philosophers, writers, musicians, artists, or whatever.

♦ **AJ: Let's go back to the beginnings of the Riot Grrrl and fanzine movement, which has had a profound impact—**

♦ KH: You really think it did? You know how when you're inside something, you can't really evaluate it.

♦ **AJ: I compare it to *samizdat* in Russia— under that monolithic false-speak totalitarianism, there was an incredible mimeograph/ xerox grass-roots network that disseminated dissent all around the country.**

♦ KH: *Angry Women* might have had a lot to do with this, because that book was being passed around by every woman I knew. I bought a copy and it was expensive—in fact, I don't have that copy anymore because I loaned it to somebody and said, "After you read it, could you give it to somebody else?" That book turned a lot of people on to bell hooks, who in turn influenced a lot of ideas about Riot Grrrl.

I lied and said there were Riot Grrrls all over the country, and named cities. None of them existed at the time—but a year later, there were actual Riot Grrrl chapters in almost all the places I'd mentioned!

♦ **AJ: So how did things start?**

♦ KH: Back around 1990, in Olympia, Bikini Kill started at the same time as Bratmobile. There were a lot of debates about topics like pornography and censorship. Around that time, the girls from Bratmobile came to my apartment and asked me about being a sex-trade worker. Basically, girls started talking to each other, and we put out our first fanzine; Molly Neuman and Allison Wolfe started Bratmobile; Corin Tucker, who's now in Sleater-Kinney, did a short video for one of her classes about different women in bands. It was based on a really sexist record cover: *Blood, Guts and Pussy* by the Dwarves [a photo of naked women smeared with blood]. She showed this cover to different women and got their reactions, talking about sexism in the scene.

Corin later ended up being in Heavens To Betsy, another band which has had a lot to do with everything.

♦ **AJ: What was your first fanzine titled?**

♦ K H : *Fuck Me Blind*. That was before all this, and it was just theoretical; it didn't have anything to do with music—my fanzines don't have much to do with music, usually. I hooked up with Tobi Vail, our drummer, because she did a fanzine called *Jigsaw* which contained some of the most important writing I've ever encountered. The articles were a bit context-oriented and hard to understand for people who weren't living in a certain scene at a certain time, but that's exactly what's so incredible about them: she totally admits her subjectivity. She writes about music and punk rock and feminism and stuff.

This was around '89, just before Bikini Kill started. Tobi was in Go Team, I was in Viva Knievel which was two men and two women, quite short-lived. We did a tour, and on the road I kept meeting women musicians and asking them questions like, "How does rape affect your work? How does being female impact your work?" And everybody was going, "Oh, it doesn't matter that I'm a woman; I'm a musician first." And I was asking, "Okay, I respect the fact that you're a musician, but isn't it weird that the guys in your band insist that you wear a tight dress and lipstick, while they dress totally yucky onstage?" I was meeting women who were telling me stories like this, but in the next breath they'd say that it didn't matter that they were women— they'd *transcended gender*! The other woman in my band also had this weird transcend-gender idea that I found really frustrating. So I wrote to *Jigsaw*....

♦ **AJ: What did you love about *Jigsaw*? What were some of the ideas that turned you on?**

♦ KH: She takes huge risks in what she says, because she's actually living in a scene—she's not living miles from everybody. She's writing about what happens directly around her in terms of going to a show, and what it feels like to be a woman at a show—stuff like that. She writes about major label vs. indie label issues, dualities, and in one breath she'll say, "Oh my god, I love this song so much—it's the raddest thing in the world!" and in the next second she's talking about French feminism. And she does this co-

hesively and beautifully, so you get caught up in it. She's just a really good writer.

I was doing interviews on the road and I thought, "I'll send them to that girl Tobi and try to get her to like me" (she was asking women to write for her fanzine). So I sent her one, and we started corresponding, and then it was like, "I want you to be in a band with me." Then Kathi and Billy joined, and we became this band. Then, partly because of an abusive boyfriend, I had to leave town.

We all decided to move together, so we went to D.C., where The Nation of Ulysses, our sort-of brother band at the time, was—we toured with them. At first we weren't sure if we were going to move to D.C. or to San Francisco. We went to D.C. and stayed for a summer without moving our stuff. I wanted to check out the scene before moving. This was right after these riots in D.C. (in Mt. Pleasant) happened. A lot of people in a neighborhood saw this man get shot in the back by the cops, who then lied and claimed he had been resisting arrest. During that

DORK+cool=COOL=dorky

Being cool in our culture means being cold, stand-offish, uncaring (your too cool to notice a lot of things) and self absorbedYou are attractive in a normal white way but have a little dirt on your chin. You are mysterious and lacking in real friends cuz being cool means being vulnerable with no one. (this increases the value that others place on the rare memories of you sharing anything with them...cool)

For the most part, cool attributes have been claimed by our society as "male". This means that the only way a person brought up GIRL (and thus the opposite of what is cool) can be "truly" cool is to assimulate into male culture via toughness.

By claiming "dork" as cool we can confuse and disrupt this whole process. The idea is that not only have we decided that being a dork (not repressing our supposeofly feminine qualities like niceness and telling people how we feel) iscool and thus, valuable to us BUT also that we are not willing to accept claims that how we are is wrong, undeveloped, bad or.....uncool.

Sure, i can still be sort of removed and aloof sometimes but i'm not gonna get mad at anyone if they ask me whats up....or use my aloofness as a way to avoid confrontations. Being a dork means that the air is clear to talk, even if that means just saying "i can't talk right now cuz i'm too freaked out." Being a dork is about demystifying yourself , not fitting yourself into james dean tv pictureland(cuz it is alienating) and learning about sincerity via true corniness and soul love friendships.

Dorks die when bullets hit them and dorks cry real tears.

Cool+dorky=COOL   dorky=Cool

Page from fanzine "Girl Power" by Kathleen Hanna (1991).

age," pranks to play on cops, etc. Molly worked as a secretary for a Senator or something, and a group of us girls would go to her office late and stay all night, xeroxing *Riot Grrrl* on his copier! I started doing writing that challenged a lot of the men in the scene, and wrote about "coolness," "hip culture," and how that was a really masculine stance. I was really frustrated by notions like "It's cool not to talk," "It's cool to be really stoic and suffer in silence"—all that shit.

♦ **AJ: I like what you wrote about "cool" and gender.**

♦ KH: Right, the whole James Dean idea. I was really frustrated, so I wrote about that. Eventually it was like, "God, if we're thinking of actually moving here, I want to know if there'll be women to do things with—not just our band and Bratmobile. I want to know that there will be a community of women to come to our shows; we can't work in a vacuum." To be a feminist band playing traditionally stupid punk rock venues, you need to have a lot of supporters involved.

We were also talking about starting a widely-distributed fanzine, so I said, "Let's have a meeting about skill-sharing." I wanted to know what people wanted, and if this would be something the D.C. punk scene needed. So in the *Riot Grrrl* fanzine I printed a notice that said something like: "Girls: let's have a meeting about punk rock and feminism! Let's share our skills and put on some rock shows together!" We asked this organization that staged benefits, Positive Force, if we could use their house for a meeting, and they said yes. For the next two weeks I went to

time, Jean Smith, a woman we know who's a writer and musician, said something like, "We need a girl riot, too!" She wasn't trying to posit white women against African-American people; it was more like, "We should *all* be rioting!"

At the same time, Allison and Molly from Bratmobile were also in D.C., and they heard this and said, "We're going to start a fanzine called *Riot Grrrl*." We were all there, sharing ideas, and they produced a one-page fanzine which printed articles like "How to get free post-every show I could and got up onstage and said, "Hi, I'm Kathleen. We're trying to have these, um, women's meetings, and..." We walked around with a clipboard and talked to women. Sometimes it was scary when we walked up to people—guys got really freaked out that they weren't invited.

We had the first meeting and about twenty women showed up. A lot of them had never been in a room with only women before, and were blown away by what it felt like: everybody had so much to say. That felt like an overwhelming response, so we continued our weekly meetings. And out of this bands started, fanzines began, we made necklaces and t-shirts to sell so we could have a project fund.

Anyways, people really freaked out about the meetings, and rumors spread all over the country that we were putting on rock shows and charging men more money than women, etc. I can't tell you how much opposition we experienced, and how much tension there was. It just showed how important what we were doing was, because people really hated it. And sometimes even women didn't understand: "Why do you have to have women-only meetings?" We said, "Look, it's only *one hour* a week. *Every* space is male space—what's the problem?" I didn't understand what the big deal was about—it didn't seem that radical of an idea to me. But people were really offended and called us "separatists." I mean, I was still working with men musically at the time, so whatever.

♦ **AJ: And you have a man in the band—**

♦ KH: Yes, but people conveniently forget that when it doesn't fit into their arguments against us: "You're a separatist!" But I am not nearly as separatist as I *could* be!

♦ **AJ: If you want to be with all women, that should be no big deal. Men go off and drink together or play basketball together; it's actually healthy when men do have real relationships with other men—**

♦ KH: "Go deal with each other!" Anyway, that's how Riot Grrrl started, I guess. Oh yeah, this other interesting thing happened: somebody did an interview with me for the *L.A. Weekly*. At that point, no one else in Bikini Kill was involved in the actual organization of Riot Grrrl; they were doing other activities. So this woman interviewed me. She came to D.C. and interviewed a lot of women who were involved, including our friend Donna Dresch, who's in Team Dresch, and who was involved in *Homocore*.

♦ **AJ: Explain *Homocore*—**

♦ KH: It was a queer fanzine. The content was politics, music, and criticism from a queer perspective. Tom Jennings and G.B. Jones did some really important work with the zine, and Donna was sort of like the *Homocore* poster child; she also did a column about how to play guitar. This woman journalist was researching *Homocore* as part of her article, and by the names she mentioned I knew she knew what was up. People were starting to interview us, and a lot of them wanted to focus on me or the band, whereas I went, "We are not just a band, and I am not the leader of the band. We're members of a community, and without this community, we don't exist. If you're going to do an article on Bikini Kill, you also need to do an article on Bratmobile, on Donna Dresch, on Laura McDougall" (who wrote *Sister Nobody*, a fanzine that really inspired me).

Drugs keep us thinking about scoring—not thinking about how to fuck this society up. Why not fuck up the government instead of fucking up your body?

A lot of people had something to do with this, and none of us were into the idea of being held up as the leaders of any "movement." From the very beginning we wanted a kind of press block; we weren't doing what we did to gain fame, we were just trying to hook up with other freaks. And when the press started calling me the leader, of either Bikini Kill or Riot Grrrl, it was really frustrating—I didn't ask for that. But it's easier for journalists to get their job done when they just do the whole Western, rugged individualist myth-making thing. I did one interview because I thought it was important that other girls have access to what we were doing; I talked to this woman and totally lied. A lot of girls had written me letters from all over the country, saying, "I'm interested in what you're doing, and have some questions." So I lied and said there were Riot Grrrls all over the country, and named six or eight cities where Riot Grrrl chapters were. It was a lie; none of them existed at the time—

♦ **AJ: But so what; it's all about manipulating the press—**

♦ KH: And a year later, there were actual Riot Grrrl chapters in almost all the places I'd mentioned! I guess I figured that girls would go looking for it and wouldn't find it, so because they'd be frustrated, they'd *do* something about it—create it themselves. And a lot of 'em did create stuff for themselves, which is rad.

♦ **AJ: That's a kind of Situationist tactic—**

♦ KH: It's *totally* Situationist!

♦ **AJ: It's also about what's real and what's not real.**

♦ KH: Like maybe we can lie things into existence.

♦ **AJ: And the media product *is* a lie, anyway. To believe that a short interview with anyone is real—it cannot encompass your whole life, your complexity as a human being. It's all reductive and not truly representational.**

♦ KH: People started writing us letters from

Kathleen singing with Cindy from the audience at a show in Las Palmas.

all over the country, and we had to get a P.O. box because we were getting so much mail. I did mailings to hundreds of women, with suggestions like, "Write on your hands with magic marker," because punks used to write words on themselves with magic markers so that when they were photographed, there would be a text or message. Photographs don't have sound, so I felt that if I wrote "slut" or "whore" or "incest victim" on my stomach, then I wouldn't just be silent. I thought a lot of guys might be thinking this anyway when they looked at my picture, so this would be like holding up a mirror to what they were thinking.

In my mailouts I'd list female bands that people could see, plus Bratmobile's tour dates, and what "Riot Grrrl" meant to me—things like that. I wrote, "Go to shows! Write stuff on your hands and arms so that other women will know that you're into feminist stuff too, and they'll come talk to you and then maybe you'll hang out! You'll know who you can discuss things with." This was a way for other women to go, "Oh, she got this mailing, too." And this actually started happening: we'd go to shows and girls would have words written on them—it was working!

Then RGDC [Riot Grrrl D.C. chapter] announced a convention, all these women came, and we had punk rock shows in conjunction with workshops on racism and body image. Things got really big for real! Then the media came in and defined it, and part of the whole idea about Riot Grrrl was that you *couldn't* define it: each person defined it as it happened. So when people would ask what it was, we couldn't say what it was because we didn't know, because it was constantly changing. One week we'd be talking about homophobia, and the next week we'd be planning an action.

Part of the point was to challenge hierarchies of all kinds. We didn't have a "statement" we were all willing to agree with, and we didn't even want to do that, because we didn't want to be a corporation or a corporate identity. We never even called it Riot Grrrl; the media started calling it Riot Grrrl and then I guess we did, too.

♦ **AJ: Labels are like drugs—they're very easy.**

♦ KH: They're catchy.

♦ **AJ: It's interesting to hear how**

things like Riot Grrrl erupt. How do you keep such movements vital, and not let them get stale? They start out with a strong community impetus and a spontaneous, true "underground" feeling. And then more people get involved, which is quite natural. But then bureaucracy evolves, the media start a feedback loop, and concurrent self-consciousness begins—

◆ KH: Also, divisions get exploited and/or ignored instead of being acknowledged and grappled with.

◆ AJ: So what happened?

◆ KH: I don't really know a lot of what happened. I was on tour a lot—I love touring and am addicted to it; I feel like I *have* to tour, no matter how hard it is. I've always tried to find ways to be an activist without having to stay in the same town and have the same job and be "stable," but it's really hard. I can't say what happened to Riot Grrrl, because so many different things happened, and there are so many different groups involved. I do know there was a voluntary media block and certain people respected that: we weren't talking to the media at all.

Roller skating (1995).

Photo: Lisa Darms

> It's important to highlight that a lot of what we do is *humorous*; a lot of our music is really funny. We fuck around with "posing" and "posturing," especially in the way we dress.

◆ AJ: I feel ambivalent on the issue of not talking to the media; you can't put the genie back in the bottle! The media created what I think is a positive thing: now there are high school girls getting turned on to Riot Grrrl ideas, and they'll infuse new life and carry on the struggle. But first they have to get turned on, in all those tiny places all over the country. After your shows, girls share their fanzines with you and talk to each other, and that's very heartening.

◆ KH: Sometimes girls as young as eleven come to our shows. I think it's really cool that they feel included. It's like I achieved my goal; for some of those girls feminism really *is* cool now! And I feel lucky to be a part of that consciousness. I was around all these women, and every time I looked into their eyes I knew that feminism was alive—and here *Time* magazine was proclaiming that it was dead. My mission was to go around the country and tell girls who are not involved in tight feminist communities (like I am) that it *does* exist, and they need to keep *creating* that. It's not hopeless.

◆ AJ: They can marry punk rock to feminism; they don't necessarily have to listen to "womyn's music."

◆ KH: Like Tori Amos or whoever. Things got weird when everybody started having to deal with the media. You couldn't ignore it, but it overtook conversations to such an extent that we weren't doing our *work*. Individually, that happened to me—I became totally obsessed with issues of representation, to the point where I really wasn't doing the work I wanted to do.

◆ AJ: Like anyone who's intelligent and multidimensional, you're involved in a lot of activities. It's very important to see the negative parts of movements, but it's also important not to throw the baby out with the bath water. We need to analyze any underground movement—

◆ KH: —and share that with other people. It's frustrating to see something you really care

about, that's real, turn into a "Flintstones" cartoon, or an episode of "Quincy." Did you ever see the "Quincy" "punk rock" episode? It's like the hippies on "Dragnet." You see something really important to you turned into something totally other than what it was intended to be—turned into a commodity. Then people who should know better go, "Oh, Riot Grrrl—that's all fashion." I'm looking at this man and thinking, "Excuse me—have you ever been to a Riot Grrrl meeting? I don't think so. So shut the fuck up!" People don't understand when it's not their place to make judgments. Magazine writers come out with all these negative judgments: "Riot Grrrl—it's all fashion; it's all fluff; it has nothing to do with substance." And none of them *know* anybody involved. I know they've never been to a meeting in D.C., because they're men. So where are they getting their information? From *Rolling Stone* and *Spin*; from other men who are threatened—

◆ **AJ: And women who are threatened. Just because you're a woman, doesn't mean that you're a "sister."**

◆ KH: I know, and it's totally depressing. I was really naive and idealistic and trusting about that.

◆ **AJ: It's an important lesson: you can't assume that if people are from some "alternative" scene, then they automatically share these noble ideals.**

◆ KH: I've learned so much from this whole experience. How many people have gotten to see how media works on such an immediate

Rebel Girl, 7-inch with Joan Jett (1994).

level? A lot of it was painful, but what an education! How am I going to use this? What's going to happen in the future is really exciting, and I'm definitely not going to remain back in time repeating the same mistakes.

I don't want to create a new novelty product that you can consume and discard. I don't care if I sound like Poly Styrene—I think Poly Styrene is great! I'm not into the novelty of the new.

I want to share information with people so they don't have to re-invent the wheel. Part of the reason the baby *was* thrown out with the bath water is because, in my mind, part of Riot Grrrl *was* fashion, and *is* fashion, and *is* style, and *is* "cool"—although not necessarily in the traditional or commodified sense of the words. It's important to highlight that a lot of what we do is *humorous*; a lot of our music is really funny. A lot of what we do has to do with fucking around with "posing" and "posturing," especially in the way we dress.

We're integrating a lot of different influences and elements. Traditionally, one way women have been able to express themselves has been through clothing and fashion, and I'm not going to throw that out, because I get a great deal of *pleasure* out of dressing myself—I'm not giving that up! Why should I have to? If I want to wear make-up like a mask one day, I'll do it. And if I don't want to do it, I won't. I've had men in the punk scene tell me I was too sexual onstage to be a feminist, and that it was wrong for me to be wearing make-up. I go, "Excuse me, but in terms of what I do in performance, *I'll* make that decision." Kirk Douglas wore make-up onstage—

◆ **AJ: And Alice Cooper!**

◆ KH: And that's part of my history of what I want to do. It was weird: the notion that if you're a feminist you cut your hair short, you wear big pants, you hide your breasts, you don't wear make-up, you wear Birkenstocks or some shit—I'm sorry, that is so boring. I'm not saying women who adopt that dress are wrong or bad in any way—*I* adopt that dress at certain times, and I will continue to. But if sometimes I want to dress up and use what is *feminine drag*—well, *men* use feminine drag, so why can't I?

♦ **AJ: The issue here is flexibility. I love to dress up, and no one's going to tell me I can't. I'm a total feminist, but I've experienced feminine fascism—some of my worst nightmares of being discounted came from women in the feminist movement in the '70s when I was growing up. I love make-up, Las Vegas nails—and artifice in general. Also, I love the freedom to *not* do that. A sense of play is very important.**

♦ KH: I think part of what made people so venomous in their attacks on Riot Grrrl in the underground *and* mainstream press, and to my face, was the fact that it was not cohesive and easily consumable. We didn't have a mission statement we could pass out, we didn't have a sentence that encapsulated it, we didn't have one unified goal, we didn't have one way to dress or look.

Some of the girls did work in the sex industry, but people came from all different backgrounds. Some performers like me went, "I'm sexual onstage, but I'm sexual when I eat a fuckin' tofu burger, too." Actually, I'm sexual in everything I do—I don't see that as disconnected from my friendships, or from taking a shit, or anything. I'm not going to go onstage and just stand there; I want to give people a show! I want to be totally engaged with it in my *body*, and that's just how I do things.

I think that punk boys who hadn't been exposed to that much feminist thought came to our shows and thought, "Feminist performers—they're going to dress really drab and have short hair." So when they were confronted with me and my Valley Girl accent, "Whatever," and then the next minute saying, "Fuck you!" it was totally confusing. I guess I play with notions of macho onstage, or try to.

♦ **AJ: Playing with expectations is always great—**

♦ KH: But that's part of the reason why things got really fucked up, and why there was a lot of opposition from the outside. A lot of men, even those in the scene, didn't comprehend that Riot Grrrl is three-dimensional, not just one thing. A lot of journalistic writing is about pointing out "inconsistencies"—

♦ **AJ: People always try to put you in some little box. Media cynicism is insidious and paralyzing; it fosters impotence. And it's rampant, permeating not only the media but even the artistic underground. People go, "Ho hum, we've seen this before." But what's wrong with enthusiasm?**

♦ KH: People also engage in comparison to cut you down: "Oh, you sing just like Poly Styrene." And I was like, "Yeah! Great!" A lot of girls had never heard of Poly Styrene; maybe they'll hear me and then buy an X-Ray Spex record. I don't care about creating a new sound—everything's been done, anyway. I want to use the tools that are here right now and make something that works; I don't want to create a new novelty product that you can consume and discard. I don't care if I sound like Poly Styrene—I think Poly Styrene is great! I'm not into the *novelty of the new*.

♦ **AJ: Just because something's new doesn't mean it's revolutionary.**

♦ KH: Right—Revlon make-up is supposedly revolutionary, y'know! ♦ ♦ ♦

discography

♦ **BIKINI KILL** ♦

Reject (1996)
The Anti-Pleasure Dissertation,
   7-inch (1995)
I Like Fucking/I Hate Danger,
   7-inch (1995)
Pussy Whipped, split 7-inch (1993)
Rebel Girl, 7-inch with Joan Jett (1994)
Yeah Yeah Yeah Yeah, split album
   with Huggy Bear (1992)
Boy/Girl, split 7-inch
   with Slim Moon (1991)
Bikini Kill, EP (1991)
There's a Dyke in the Pit,
   complilation (1991)
Kill Rock Stars, complilation (1991)
Give Me Back, complilation (1991)
Revoultion Girl Style Now, demo tape
   no longer available (1991)

♦ **OTHER BANDS/PROJECTS** ♦

Suture, Suture, 7-inch (1992)
A Wonderful Treat,
   Wondertwins, (1992)
Real Fiction, Fakes (1994)
Viva Knievel, Viva Knievel (1994)

equipment list

Sure Vocal Master P.A. circa 1960, SM 57 microphone, Green Hagstrom Bass with 2 pick-ups, books

Valerie Agnew is the drummer for the Seattle band 7 Year Bitch (which also includes Elizabeth Davis on bass, Selene Vigil on vocals, and Roisin Dunne on guitar). She co-founded the Home Alive self-defense collective after her friend Mia Zapata of the Gits was raped and murdered in July, 1993. Home Alive subsequently released a double CD *Home Alive: The Art of Self-Defense*, the proceeds of which will go to the Mia Zapata Investigative Fund. For further information contact Home Alive at 1202 E. Pike, Suite 1127, Seattle, WA, 98122; (206) 233-8671.

◆ ANDREA JUNO: Why did you start playing drums?

◆ VALERIE AGNEW: Whenever I listened to music, I always gravitated toward drums—the rhythm section—rather than guitar or vocals; that's just the way I heard music. When I first started playing I was living in a collective, the Rathouse, with some other bands: the Gits, D.C. Beggars, and Alcohol Funny Car. My boyfriend at the time, Steve Moriarty, was the drummer from the Gits and he influenced me a lot. I lived with two other drummers then; the drums were there and it just sort of *happened*—I don't know why! I just decided, "I'm going to play drums." I didn't know anything about music or how I would find a niche or whether it would gel, but I just started and it was fun as hell!

◆ AJ: Were people supportive?

◆ VA: Very much so. The reason we got a chance to play in this town was because we were part of that collective. We got to open for bands who had been playing a long time and were very experienced. We never thought we'd play outside of Seattle; we just thought we would open for our friends. The first time I ever got onstage we had like three songs and I didn't even know how to turn on the snare! But now I can't imagine not playing drums. I don't know why I didn't start in high school; I wish I had.

◆ AJ: But there weren't many women drummers then, that's for sure. In fact, I still hear remarks about the physicality of drumming being better suited to a man than a woman.

◆ VA: When I first started taking lessons at a Seattle drum school, I remember my teacher saying, "You know, a lot of women have problems with their upper arm strength. You have to be very careful about carpal tunnel syndrome and make sure you hold your sticks correctly, because two months down the line, a lot of women drummers find the stress on their muscles is too much." I remember thinking, "That's a complete crock of shit!" I called him on it right away: "Just show me the *right* way to hold the sticks. I'll let you know how I'm doing in a couple months." And I've never had any problems. If you stretch, and you're in reasonably good health and strength, you'll be fine!

Also, there was a contradiction in what he said. After initially giving this warning, a few months later he said, "It's not a matter of strength; it's all in how limber and flexible you are, and how much you let the sticks do the work for you." You don't have to muscle your way into it. There are lots of *Twiggy-ass* punk rock drummers who are coked out, cracked out, or on heroin, but who hit hard as hell; it's *not* in their arm strength—because I can out-wrestle them any time! It's all about technique and how you handle yourself. So that seems like a great rock'n'roll myth to me. I think it's bullshit.

◆ AJ: As you've become more comfortable

drumming, what have you learned about your role in the band?

♦ VA: I never realized how important and instrumental the drummer is until the last year and a half—it's really been sinking in. After seeing tons of bands play and figuring out what I liked about them, I said to myself: "*You* drive the ship. You set the pace for everything. You push the riffs along." There can be a really cool guitar or bass riff, but it won't go anywhere or do anything unless the drums are really thundering behind it. This is something I haven't mastered yet at all; it's still kind of an abstract idea I'm trying to get to.

There are very rare moments when I feel I'm in that element. I'm aware of when I am and when I'm not, but I don't know how to consistently get there.

There are lots of *Twiggy-ass* [male] punk rock drummers who are coked out or on heroin, but who hit hard as hell; it's *not* in their arm strength—because I can out-wrestle them any time! It's all about technique.

♦ AJ: Have you modeled your style on any favorite influences?

♦ VA: I'm mostly influenced by straightforward rock'n'roll, and that's what I play. It's pretty simple and heavy without tons of fills all over the place—like Neil Peart, Rush's drummer does. I have a certain appreciation for that, but I prefer drummers like John Bonham [Led Zeppelin] and Phil Rudd [AC/DC]—people who

7 Year Bitch in 1992 (l. to r.): Selene Vigil, Roisin Dunne, Elizabeth Davis and Valerie Agnew.

are *behind* the beat.

♦ AJ: Your favorite drummers are very macho choices! I happen to love that kind of music myself—

♦ VA: It grabs you. It grabs you in the crotch; it grabs you in the chest; it grabs you everywhere! AC/DC is my all-time favorite band; Phil Rudd is god-like to me. You can compare that kind of music to the Minutemen or No Means No or other bands whose rhythm is really frenetic and changes all the time. They get into a really heavy groove but it's only for three measures; then it switches to something else, then something else, and everything's really frantic. While I can appreciate the level of musicianship it takes to play that kind of music, it's not what I aspire to play. If I could do *both*, that would be great!

I've been focusing more on just hitting really hard and being a really deliberate drummer. If my kick lags for a couple of seconds behind the riff (but it's not off time), the delay makes it sound that much heavier.

♦ AJ: You used the phrase "it grabs you in the crotch." What does it mean when a woman says that?

♦ VA: Have you ever heard Girls Against Boys, from New York? Elizabeth turned me on to them, and their music is very sexual to me—although not in an overt way. The feeling they

Photo : Billy Anderson

Bandmates Elizabeth Davis (l.) and Valerie Agnew (r.).

♦ **AJ: So what was the process that allowed you to finally see yourself as a drummer?**

♦ VA: Sometimes I *still* don't even think of myself as a drummer—especially when I'm trying to fudge my way through something! It might sound kind of cheesy, but just being in this community was so encouraging. Seattle truly is a unique place, despite all the hype about the scene.

♦ **AJ: I spent some time in Seattle when we did the Modern Primitives show here in '89, and I noticed how the very strong women's community was converging with the punk community and the dyke community—**

♦ VA: —right, it's not exclusionary—

♦ **AJ: —they were very integrated with the male punks. It seemed to be a pioneering place.**

♦ VA: The music scene is very diverse; there are a lot of different kinds of bands, and almost every night of the week you can go out and see somebody who'll blow your fuckin' mind. Just being around music all the time, and living in a house with five other musicians who were doing it all the time, was really inspiring. The first time I was onstage, I was sold—it was like being a junkie: "This is *it*; this is what I want to do!" You get *such* a high off it—even if you suck and you screw up every song!

convey is just very *primal*. I think Lori from Babes In Toyland captures that as well. She's never had any formal training; her drive comes from *within*. I asked her if she'd studied drumming and she said, "No, why would I want to learn to play drums the way somebody else does?" I remember being really influenced by that: "Wow—that's such a gutsy way to approach music!" Like I said, I don't feel that I've accomplished, drumwise, what I want to be able to do. Talking about what I like is different from what I've been able to do so far.

♦ **AJ: But there's nothing physical limiting you; it's just a matter of time. Most men have been playing since they were kids—they got drum sets for Christmas when they were 12. You said that when you were growing up, you really liked hard rock—**

♦ VA: When I was a high school stoner in Alaska I listened to AC/DC, Van Halen, Black Sabbath and Motorhead—all the old classics. I was living in *Alaska*, for fuck's sake; nobody there had heard of "alternative music." When I left there and went to school just outside Philadelphia, I started getting into hardcore like Bad Brains, GBH, Gang Green and other pretty straightforward punk bands, because that's what people around me were into.

♦ **AJ: What female role models did you have?**

♦ VA: Chrissie Hynde and Patti Smith were big influences in high school, but I don't remember being influenced by any female rhythm section. I didn't find out about the Runaways and Girl's School until much later, just before I started to play drums. Current bands like the Lunachicks and L7 came *way* later.

The first time I was onstage, I was sold—it was like being a junkie: "This is *it*; this is what I want to do!"

Also, my band inspires me a lot. I feel so lucky, every day, to be able to play music with these people, and to figure out the puzzle: "God, we wrote a song and it's our own. It isn't a cover of somebody else's song; it came from *us*." I don't think it fully hit me until we put out our first single. We got the vinyl back and were looking at a thousand 45s and I thought, "We're never going to sell all of these; they're going to be bookends for the next 10 years."

I can't imagine being in any other band but 7 Year Bitch. I like to jam with other people, but as far as commitment goes, being in a band is like being married. The four of us have been through so much, and we're such good friends and communicate so well; as the rhythm section, Elizabeth and I have developed a whole language. She's a really good drummer—much better than I am—and she teaches me all the time. She'll play a bass line and have an idea for drums ("boom da da doo doo dah"), and now I'll know exactly which part is the kick, which is the snare, and which is the highhat, whereas when we first started, we had no way of communicating about it; it took us forever to write a song.

♦ **AJ: You're all very close, personally—**

♦ **VA:** Very. The way we formed the band, as totally new musicians without past experience (with the exception of Elizabeth being in a Seventh-Day Adventist choir), was with this attitude: "Even if we're not ready, let's just go onstage and do it." I think a lot of guys don't take the same risk; they're much more prone to rehearsing and rehearsing until they feel everything's perfect—*then* they're "ready." Since we were like, "Fuck it! Let's just play for the sake of playing," I think we learned a lot faster—but we've also been open to more criticism.

In general, a lot of women I know take more risks like this, because they're not so worried about what people are going to think: "Is it good enough?" I think this comes from *strength*, not a careless attitude. There's a stigma our band has been dealing with forever, as fallout from the Riot Grrrl thing: "We're just girls, and since we're girls we don't really have to be good, because we're women and we're angry and we're saying what we need to say." But *we've* never had that attitude. It's been pinned on us.

♦ **AJ: What does "Riot Grrrl" mean to you, now that the mass media have hyped the story to the point of overkill? It doesn't seem to mean as much anymore—**

♦ **VA:** —which is unfortunate. Riot Grrrl always was peripheral to us; we didn't go to any Riot Grrrl meetings, although we knew Kathleen Hanna. On our first European tour we were labeled "Riot Grrrls from Seattle."

♦ **AJ: That's the laziness and stereotyping of the media—**

♦ **VA:** But it's really hard to divorce my opinion of what Riot Grrrl is from the media. I don't think Riot Grrrl was a musical movement; it wasn't about women playing music. It was about women speaking their minds and expressing their political ideas or dissatisfaction with their role in the rock world, and on a larger level, women's position in the world. It was the new bratty young women's way of feminism—which I don't relate to.

When it started out, it seemed kind of cool: girls writing back and forth to each other, across the country, "networking" and being able to tap into what somebody was doing in Tallahassee when you're in the Northwest. Or you're living in a suburb of Chicago and can find out what somebody's doing in Gainesville, Florida—that's a really powerful thing, in and of itself. But I think the media have spoiled that. Actually, I don't know how much of that is the fault of the media, and how much is the fault of people who were trying to speak for the movement.

I feel that if you're going to be in the mosh pit, you're *going to be in the pit*, and you'd better be ready to kick somebody's ass!

I'm taking a leap here, but since Mia Zapata, the singer from the Gits, was killed two years ago, I co-founded a collective here in Seattle called Home Alive. We raise money through the arts community: music, art, film, photography and theater, to teach self-defense classes. I noticed some parallels between how people viewed this endeavor and how they viewed Riot Grrrl. The only thing that's helped us is that our project hasn't been exclusively a women's or all-girls' thing; it's everyone who's been affected by what happened. Nevertheless, we did get some of the same kind of criticism that Riot Grrrl got: "Here are these girls just spouting off, using music to feed their fire!" We're putting out a double CD on Epic Records and I'm thinking, "Are we going to get the same kind of bullshit that the Riot Grrrls got?" I want to make sure that everybody in the collective is very careful when speaking to the press. You can't come up with some three-word descriptive sentence, and you don't want to—because it waters down what you do.

♦ **AJ: The media have a vicious life of their own, which is to support the status quo and trivialize as girly, banal, and stupid anything**

that might have an impact.

◆ VA: So what can you do? I think Riot Grrrl's attempt at media blackout backfired—

◆ **AJ: And yet it was a noble effort.**

◆ VA: Definitely. In one way I totally support them and want them to continue doing their thing despite the criticism they get, because if *one* girl in Gainesville, Florida stands up to an abusive relationship or gets the *cojones* ["balls"] to do what she really wants to do—that's worth it, to me. I still have very idealistic feelings about Riot Grrrl.

But I don't necessarily stand behind their ways of doing things—for example, they would hand out literature at shows and it was girls-only—they wouldn't give the fanzines to guys. Or guys had to pay a higher cover price to get into their shows. Or if there was a guy slam-dancing, the band would stop the show and make a big deal out of throwing the guy out. I'm very opposed to that; I think it's reactionary and takes you back ten steps. I feel that if you're going to be in the mosh pit, you're *going to be in the pit*, and you'd better be ready to kick somebody's ass!

Womyn's music my ass—you'd better put some Motorhead in that section, because as far as I'm concerned, that's women's music!

◆ **AJ: Were you ever in the pit?**

◆ VA: Yes.

◆ **AJ: And do you like that atmosphere?**

◆ VA: Sometimes. It's not my thing; to me that's more of a youth culture thing. When I was first getting into hardcore, I thought, "I've got to be out there and *prove* myself." Then I realized I would much rather stand back and absorb the band and what they're doing, and suck everybody else's energy. I don't have to be in the middle—

◆ **AJ: —getting bruised and kicked around!**

◆ VA: Liz and I went to a Metallica concert and busted our way up to the front. We got fucked with for half an hour. One guy put his hand down my shirt and grabbed my tit; Liz got her bra strap wrapped around some guy's hand. But once we stayed and established that we weren't there to be picked up (we just wanted to see the show), then people mellowed out.

But it was definitely weird to do that. We were an anomaly.

◆ **AJ: Women feel that energy in the crotch, too, just like men, and you do want to physicalize it. Sometimes I look at the mosh pit and think, "I'd love to go in there!"**

◆ VA: You get that rush and just want to act out what you're feeling, because the music affects you that much. When I was in college, I went on an International Women's Studies Program with ten other women. I was always talking about music, and going to see Metallica if we were in a city they were playing. Some of the women were really into "womyn's music" like Cris Williamson, Holly Near—to me it's *gag-reflex* music. I said to them, "Womyn's music my ass—you'd better put some Motorhead in that section, because as far as I'm concerned *that's* women's music!"

Yet I'm always excited to see women up there playing—I can't deny that. We saw a band the other day, Lord High Fixers, and this woman was an *amazing* drummer—across the board, no gender involved. But part of what was so exciting to me was the fact that she *was* a woman. She was totally comfortable onstage, and had mastered all the elements of the kind of drummer I want to be. I have to admit I was much more excited watching her than if it had been a guy, although I still would have thought, "Wow, he's a fuckin' great drummer." But that novelty element is still there, even though everyone's trying to integrate it and go [blasé voice], "Yeah, it's not a big thing anymore that women are playing music." Well—it *still* is!

◆ **AJ: When I was a teenager I listened to—and identified with—Blue Oyster Cult and Led Zeppelin, but that kind of identification gets complicated for women because it requires shutting off parts of yourself. And I couldn't have been accepted by them anyway. As a woman, I could only have been fucked by, or been the girlfriend—how horrible—of one of these guys. Their lyrics are totally oppressive to women ("Wait a minute—this is against me!"), yet I still wanted to identify with their power. It's really mind-bending.**

◆ VA: AC/DC is a classic example of that—their lyric "I'm just givin' the dog a bone" is totally about fucking some girl you don't give a shit about. And Motorhead's "Jailbait" is about sleeping with underage girls; Metallica also has lyrics like that. People would constantly ask me, "How can you be a feminist and be into these bands?" To me, that's reality—it's just the way society is. And to deny myself the enjoyment I get out of the music because ideologically I don't like their lyrics...if you weigh the pro's and con's, the pro's are on the music side. It's not that I *excuse* what's going on lyrically; if I could talk to them face-to-face I'd ask, "So what's up with this? Do you really think this way, and treat people like that?"

◆ **AJ: And the answer would probably be, "Yes!"**

◆ VA: Yeah. But there are tons of other bands who might not be so overtly sexist, with whom I might have some other kind of ideological disagreement—I still like those bands for what they are. I think this comes with maturity; after going through many different phases, you realize that

7 Year Bitch in 1992 (l. to r.): Selene Vigil, Elizabeth Davis, Stefanie Sargent (who died that year) and Valerie Agnew.

Photo: Tina Canellas

you don't have to be so nitpicky and hard-line about everything. That doesn't make you inconsistent or not true to your ideals; you're just more easy-going about things.

◆ **AJ: I also think music expresses a language that is outside rationality, politics and ideology. I remember in the early '80s thinking that punk had "sold out" (a naive stance, and one that I don't have now) when I saw this conservative suburban jock singing along with the Dead Kennedys' "California Uber Alles"—he could have been singing some fraternity song, or a commercial jingle that was stuck in his head, because the politics of that song were completely meaningless to him.**

◆ VA: I noticed a modern-day comparison to that when we did a tour with Rage Against The Machine and Cypress Hill. Talk about stepping off the deep end—we're playing to Cypress Hill's crowd?! We were four punk-rock chicks onstage who weren't quite sure what we were doing and had never played that big a venue. Rage Against The Machine were singing, "Fuck you, I won't do what you tell me"—that's a very political song, and they're a very overtly political band. Most of the crowd was made up of college fratboys

who were just *singing along* with rebellion—but they did *not* get the message at all. This happened in the '60s, the '70s, the '80s, and it will always happen. You can't discredit that kind of music or lyric just because it doesn't always sink in...

◆ **AJ: I think that to even have this expectation that music can change people's politics is completely unrealistic. Look at the hippies; look at the Grateful Dead—**

◆ VA: When the Deadheads leave, there's ten million tons of trash left behind. They're supposedly espousing this "Take care of Mother Earth," Jah Love thing, but we're talking about a bunch of drug addicts finding an excuse to eat tofu.

◆ **AJ: Yet there is something undeniably powerful and incredibly radical to see you four onstage taking over what used to be a masculine province, and not only playing powerful, driving music but also singing lyrics that don't make me cringe.**

◆ VA: One of the most common questions we're asked is, "What is it like being women playing rock'n'roll?" Or, "Do you see yourselves as a feminist band and are you using the band to educate people about feminism?" And we go, "No! We're musicians trying to play just like

anybody else." Individually we may have those ideas, but we're not using the band as a soapbox. It may come across that way because Selene writes about things that happened to us, or things that are very personal, but a lot of her lyrics have nothing to do with guys or with gender issues. Some are relationship-oriented, and some are about friends who have died; there's not a preconceived political agenda. We'll write music, and Selene will sit and listen and get a "feeling" and then come up with lyrics. That's the way we've always worked. If we like something, and it makes sense to us, and we enjoy playing the song—that's all that matters. We're not worried about whether somebody else is going to understand or get it. Our attitude is, "We'll just do it."

Doing the Cypress Hill tour, for example, was a huge leap for us. We were *way* out of our element. It was entirely intimidating. We got there the first day and they rolled my drums onto the drum riser; I'm talking to this sound guy in a black hole and he's telling me that my drums sound like a bucket of shit. I'm going, "Fuck—how do I tune them?" At this point I take a humble standpoint. I asked the nearest sound person, "Do you have any idea how to tune drums? I don't. Go for it." Not pretending: "I know *exactly* what I'm doing, and don't get in my way—I'm a woman drummer!" Instead I said, "You're right, I'm clueless. Help me out!"

♦ AJ: That illustrates perfectly what you said about women taking risks—a lot of men won't admit they don't know how to do something, because their ego is always on the line.

♦ VA: Right—rather than getting help to have

Lorna, 7-inch (1991).

Lorna
No Fuckin' War
You Smell Lonely

it sound better, they make it sound like shit and then act stoic: "This is *my* sound." Whereas I'm much more relaxed about something like that, and it's benefited me: I've learned a lot. Now I can tune my drums; people say, "Wow, your drums sound really good!" But it's not because I was holed up in a closet figuring it out by myself.

I called a friend's house looking for Mia and they only told me that she had been strangled—but I knew right away she had been raped. I just *knew*, because those two crimes go hand in hand.

I don't have this need to be a pioneer steamrolling my way through everything. In my relationship with Liz, she writes a lot of the drum parts for our songs, and at first I thought, "I'm the drummer—*I* should be figuring this out." Then I realized, "No, she has a gift for this that I don't have." Maybe that kind of flexibility *is* more of a woman's thing.

♦ AJ: Maybe women have more of a community sense—

♦ VA: —and *communication*, and *trust* that's not ego-oriented.

♦ AJ: A lot of men believe in the mythology of the lone "self-reliant" cowboy out on the frontier...

♦ VA: "I don't need any help."

♦ AJ: And they don't have real friendships...

♦ VA: Dee from L7 just called me; we've been friends with them for a long time. In articles all over our press kit, we're always constantly compared to L7 or Babes In Toyland. When we go on the road, we always get ridiculous questions. Once some guy asked: "Who would win in a fistfight between you and L7?" I just looked at him and said, "That is the stupidest question. I have no desire to punch out anybody in L7; they're our friends. We don't have a competition with them; they play an entirely different kind of music from us. We've done shows with them; they're awesome; I respect them immensely, so don't even try to belittle us with stupid shit like that." We refuse to answer that kind of question.

♦ AJ: Journalists love to promote that cat-fight mentality in the press—

♦ VA: People really have this idea that we're fighting other women bands.

♦ AJ: When women were powerless, they would fight with each other—for what? Usually it was for a man who had power, and other women were just competition for that power. Now, women have power too.

Tell us more about Home Alive and Mia Zapata—

♦ VA: Mia was a huge influence on me and on our band. I went to school with the Gits at Antioch College, in Ohio. I moved to Seattle with them and then met Elizabeth, Selene and Stefanie; actually, I met Stefanie through Mia.

We went to the Gits' shows all the time. They were a cult-status band and their shows were very energetic—we'd all be up front and there was a lot of exchange between the band and the audience. The Gits' way of playing music was so inspiring—it was mesmerizing. Mia was an amazing performer. She sang a lot of punk rock with the Gits, but she also sang acoustic material and was very blues-influenced—she'd do solo performances by herself and sing songs by Patti Smith and Bonnie Raitt, and some really old blues tunes. She had an incredible whiskey voice: very passionate and very much from her crotch and her gut.

> I'm very much an advocate of women becoming familiar and comfortable with guns. They have every right to carry a gun and blow the motherfuckin' head off some guy who climbs in your window or fucks with you in any way.

Mia lived in the bedroom above the practice space at the Rathouse. Whenever we were practicing, she had to hear all our fumblings through everything. And she was always immensely supportive of us: "What you guys are doing is so unique; it's so awesome." We had a really close friendship with the Gits; they got us our first shows.

The album cover of *¡Viva Zapata!* (1994), a portrait of Mia Zapata by Scott Musgrove.

Right before Mia died, both of our bands were in L.A. talking to labels. Things happened for us before they happened for the Gits, even though they were the reason we were able to be where we were. That was weird, but it never interfered with our friendship. The night Mia was killed, Selene and I were hanging out with her at the Comet drinking. In two weeks, we were supposed to go on a one-month tour with the Gits. We had just been with them in L.A. on the anniversary of the death of our first guitarist, Stefanie, and Mia really helped us through that: "You have to go on; you have to play—that's the most important thing. Music is what you live—that's what you do, and you'll go crazy if you don't do it. Stefanie's gone, but she would want you to keep going." When Stefanie died, we didn't know if we could ever play any of those songs again, or even keep the name—we were devastated.

That night at the Comet, we were talking about things and how great it would be to tour together. She left early, and—not the next day, but the day after—we found out that she had been killed. I called a friend's house looking for Mia and they only told me that she had been strangled—but I knew right away she had been raped. I just *knew*, because those two crimes go hand in hand. And I was freaking out! That stuff happens all the time; I've been attacked; tons of women I know have been attacked; people are raped all the time—it's not like it was a *new thing*. But for some reason, because of who Mia was and how strong she was, and how invincible

she seemed to be, I was scared shitless that she had died like that—that somebody had been able to take her life like that. I was fuckin' livid.

At first the cops didn't say publicly that she had been raped. But I went to people who had gone and seen her body at the coroner's office: "You *have* to tell me what happened, because I know it's horrible—I need to know; I can't fuckin' sleep until I know the truth." I forced it out of people. The way the police were handling it was: we weren't supposed to talk about it amongst ourselves, because they thought the killer was somebody who had been stalking her—somebody who knew her, and probably knew *us*, and was probably hanging out at the local bar—yet we were still not supposed to talk about it! I just rebelled: "No—that's fuckin' bullshit!"

Women our age who don't give any lip service to feminism make me angry. I give props to the feminist movement 24-7!

I told everybody I knew, and we did an interview in a local paper in which I said, "Despite popular belief, Mia was *raped* and murdered," because the press was trying to pawn off her death as a drug-related crime, and saying she left the bar drunk—something which had nothing to do with the fact that what happened to her was a very brutal crime. It was a brutal rape and a brutal murder and the killer left her on the side of the fuckin' road—he threw her out of the car.

I just could not reconcile that. Our band left a week later to do part of the tour with the Gits, and while I was on the East coast driving around I kept thinking, "I can't go back there and just *accept* this. I have to *do* something—I don't know what, but if I don't, I'm going to lose my mind." When I got back I called Gretta Harley and other friends and we started having meetings at my house. Originally there were about twenty people involved, men and women, but it ended up just being women—which is interesting. Now there's a solid nine women who are in the Home Alive collective.

We thought, "What's the most viable, valuable resource in Seattle through which we could

most quickly raise money?" Obviously, the answer was the music community, because it's so strong. But we also wanted to embrace the rest of the arts community (spoken word, visual art, etc.) so over time we were able to incorporate that. What makes our efforts powerful, and what makes it all happen, is that we're not espousing any traditional idea about self-defense.

I'm very much an advocate of women becoming familiar with, and comfortable with, guns and other weapons, and feeling that they have every right to carry a gun and blow the motherfuckin' head off some guy who climbs in your window or fucks with you in any way—I'm *very* pro-weapon.

◆ **AJ: I am too. I used to have an arsenal.**

◆ **VA: Oh, good—I'm surprised. Most of the women in the collective are not into guns. My whole thing is education; if guns are a reality, you have to know them, understand them, and not panic when they're in your face, because your chances of survival are that much better.

◆ **AJ: Also, a gun is a true equalizer—**

◆ **VA: Totally!**

◆ **AJ: And you don't use a gun unless you're willing to kill somebody. You don't shoot to wound; you shoot to kill!**

◆ VA: That's what we get from male self-defense instructors: "You really need to be sure that you can go through with this." I think, "There's no question in *my* mind. Don't even *patronize* me with that kind of talk, because I'm not here paying all this money and going through this if I'm not ready to blow somebody away." That's my take on it, but the collective tries to offer everything: any kind of self-defense, even if it's just teaching women how to yell. So many women who come to us have never raised their voice or said, "No—get away from me!" It's really been a learning process for me to accept that.

I think another thing that makes us powerful is: we're very locally focused. Even though we're going international with this record [*Home Alive: The Art of Self-Defense*], this is still a local, collective, community-based organization. The reason it works so well is that we're not trying to take on the entire nation; we're not taking on domestic violence or rape throughout the United States. We're talking about right here in Seattle, and what is viable and available to people here. I'm not sure how it's going to go; we haven't done any major press yet. Already I can anticipate misrepresentation… .

Organizing this collective was the only thing I could do to *digest* the anger I felt. If I hadn't gotten involved in doing this, I don't know what I would have done.

♦ **AJ: I've talked to a number of women who say, "Oh, the feminist revolution is won already!" That's in their own subculture, and on one level I respect that you can't constantly be raging against sexism in the larger world— especially if you have an insular community, so you're not constantly encountering sexism. But you do come up against the fact that yes, you can be raped. This possibility just isn't part of a man's daily reality.**

♦ VA: I read this article about rape in a magazine, and one quotation struck me: "If all men aren't rapists, then all women aren't victims." With Home Alive especially, this is the main point we're trying to make: you don't have to accept these roles. You don't have to fit into a victimization status. You don't have to rely on somebody else: the cops, your boyfriend, whoever, to keep you safe from these threats. It's unrealistic to do that. Look at the way the cops handled Mia's murder: if we had gone along with what they had said, and not talked about it, none of this would have happened. None of this dialogue would have continued, and there would have been a dismissal of what happened to Mia—which is absolutely fuckin' outrageous and absolutely fuckin' unacceptable.

♦ **AJ: You mean the idea that the police were trying to "protect" you? If they thought there was a stalker involved, why would they keep it secret?**

Take the Bosnian rape camps— what was the solution? [Counseling the] rape victims. They don't need counseling! Fuckin' send them AK-47s!

♦ VA: Their whole reasoning was: "You can't say anything, because it's going to jeopardize the case."

♦ **AJ: So their "advice" was to wait until you got killed, too?!**

♦ VA: Exactly, like I'm going to wait for two more of my friends to turn up dead! *Then* maybe I'd finally realize, "Wait a minute—this police force *can't* protect me." That's a radical stance, because you're taught all your life to trust "Big

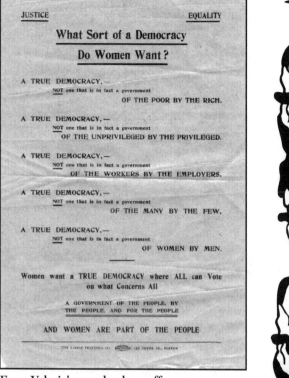

From Valerie's scrapbook: a suffragette manifesto (circa 1910).

Brother," to believe that *men* take care of everything. But in reality, women need to learn self-defense tactics—actually, *anybody* should. There's been a lot of gay-bashing here; a lot of my non-gay friends have been bashed because somebody thought they were gay. Other friends have been mugged. The concept of self-defense comes down to *believing that your life is worth defending*. It's amazing how many people won't take that stance: "Fuck you—I will kill you before you kill me, because my life is worth more than yours."

This is a fundamental self-esteem issue—and I'm amazed by how many people of our generation lack that simple belief. It's sick. And I'm scared shitless, too; it's not like I've "overcome" all my fears or am "beyond" it. But I do believe I have the right to self-defense, and I don't apologize for this or think it's some "man-hating feminist theory." It's just belief in yourself as a human being, whether you're male or female. Violence does happen to *women* 90% of the time, so you don't want to belittle that fact. But at the same time, the average person hasn't thought about these issues enough—

♦ **AJ: The average white person. Blacks al-**

7 year bitch

MEET YOU AT THE BAR!

The first band sticker.

ready know that the authority figures are out to kill them!

You still have male friends, right?

◆ VA: Fuck, yeah! I have a lot of guy friends and men in my family who I also think are totally sexist, racist, and more—they say things that offend me all the time! But there are still other things about them that I realize are good. I believe in them as human beings and still trust them as friends. I learn from men every day. I'm going out with a guy right now; I don't feel the need to be a separatist. The more I know men and the more I interact with them, the stronger my convictions become.

But I have to say that when it comes down to counting on people and trusting them implicitly—it's women in my life. I play in a band with all women; I work in a collective with all women; I'm very close to my mother. Most of the people I really open up to and respond to, in a truly vulnerable sense, are women.

◆ AJ: I think that the majority of women are more open emotionally, more complex, smarter—

◆ VA: I agree!

◆ AJ: For deeper emotional relations, the people who actually have the capacity to relate on many multiple levels tend to be women, with very rare exceptions. [laughs] And I do like men—especially in bed…

◆ VA: Yeah, exactly: give me a stiff cock any day! I'm down for it totally; I can get all over that.

◆ AJ: That's the best part of a guy. [laughs]

◆ VA: Don't fuck that up; we can use that to our advantage! I often feel sorry for men. A lot of my guy friends are really unhappy. I can see right through them; they think that it's "weak" to admit certain things. A lot of guys I know totally respect women, even though they may do things that are fucked-up, or behave really fucked-up in a relationship, or say things with a locker-room mentality. A lot of these guys, when it comes down to it, also rely on women as well—

their mothers, their sisters, their friends.

Guys always say to me, "I can *talk* to you. You're like a guy." Just as women "fraternize" with each other—well, men do the same thing. A boy's club isn't necessarily bad.

◆ AJ: I think it's actually a positive thing for men to have male friends. Unfortunately, too often they can't let down their guard; it's the alpha wolf syndrome.

◆ VA: Maybe that's just the way it is; I'm not on a mission to change that. If guys talk about things with guy friends, hopefully they'll emerge a little wiser and more clued-in to the world. It helps me to just be with women friends; I don't want any male energy in the room—not because I don't like it, but because I really get high off of just being around women. It's a contradiction, though, and I usually don't like to talk about this in interviews, because it's so easily misconstrued.

◆ AJ: Especially if it's not considered in its full context—because it's not a soundbite.

You're in a band that plays rock music "from the crotch," so to speak. For men, that sexuality is unfettered; a lot of male rock musicians, like Kiss or Aerosmith, have a consuming desire for anonymous sex encounters. How do men view you? What are your encounters like on a sexual level, where you're the "phallic object" like Mick Jagger would be?

◆ VA: From the audience standpoint? Or a fan standpoint? Or even my friends, or boyfriends?

I'm just not modest about sex. I'll say, "Yeah, I like to suck cock, I like to suck clit— whatever. Sex—fuck yes! It feeds me, it keeps me alive; it's part of what I do."

◆ AJ: Being a woman, how do you deal with your own sexuality and channel it as a rock performer onstage? Is it different from what Aerosmith does?

◆ VA: When Elizabeth and I started in the band, we were both in long-term relationships with guys who were also musicians, and there was a lot of jealousy and competition about our band's success, or about us having other commitments like, "We need to go practice right now," or, "We're taking off on tour." It was really, really hard. I believe those relationships ended partly because of our involvement with the band, even though these two particular men were fairly advanced, competent and aware of gender issues. They weren't your stoic, stereotypical, beefy macho guys. Nevertheless, it still was hard for them to accept that we had our own sources of power, creativity and interests.

I especially noticed this on the road. I'm very sexual; I like to have sex every day. I have a conflict about non-monogamy: wanting a monogamous relationship and then *not* wanting one. When I go on tour, I don't know what's going to happen or who I'm going to meet, and that's the way it is. That's a very reversed role for a woman—one that I don't apologize for. But I don't just go out and *fuck* people; I don't pick somebody up and fuck them in the van and then leave them. It's more that I get involved with people with whom we're on the road for an extended amount of time; I end up having a tour relationship with somebody for a month or two. And I get a lot of criticism—not only from men, but from women: "You seem so callous, or so cold about people's feelings." I say, "No, not at all—I'm very upfront with people and very honest with them: 'This is where I'm coming from; this is what I'm doing; we're here right now and we can enjoy each other's company; we can have *rad sex*, and it doesn't need to be more complicated than that.'" Of course, it always is.

I think that in our band, I'm the most casual about this. I'm involved in a monogamous relationship now; he's in a band that tours; he lives in New York and I live here and we don't see each other that much but I've stuck to just being with him—which is really unusual for me.

◆ **AJ: Why have you stuck with him? [laughs]**
◆ **VA:** I don't know. Some people come along and you really feel something for them that's *way stronger…* you adapt to whatever your feelings are. But I think that women should be as free on the road as men—just so long as they're honest.

◆ **AJ: But that's not how a lot of men are!**
◆ **VA:** They're just the opposite. Instead of saying, "Hey, I'm on tour and this is what I'm doing," and being comfortable with that, they feel that they're being assholes or sexist jerks, so they try to validate what they're doing with some other lie. They get the stigma the *other* way: if they're free sexually, then they're sexist pigs. And that's not the case. I think women need to

Men, Money, and Moonshine, split single with Thatcher on Acid (1992).

take responsibility here and stop whining: "Oh, I slept with this rock'n'roll guy a couple times and he led me to believe… and then he left me." I think, "Fuck you! You knew exactly what you were getting into. Take responsibility for it and quit giving *us* a bad name."

The same thing in rape cases; I know a lot of women who have claimed to have been abused at times when they really weren't—and that pisses me off more than anything. I will fuckin' rip your head off if I believe that you've manipulated that! One of my best friends from high school is involved in a case now where he's been accused of rape, and it's really hard for me… the whole "cry wolf!" thing is really insidious and damaging.

◆ **AJ: People have to remember that "crying wolf" instances are actually quite rare, compared to real rapes. But when it does happen, it's reflective of a system where women feel somewhat victimized and powerless—so they don't take responsibility for their own sexuality. These few instances leave the rest of us reeling, because real rape exists all around us, and to "cry wolf" is about the most irresponsible act a woman can commit…**

Another thing related to this is that feminism seems to be linked to some incredibly puerile nuclear-family monogamy.
◆ VA: I hope not!
◆ **AJ: You hear this constantly: "That man was bad, because he was with somebody else, or left a relationship to be with someone else." That's life—the vagaries of love—and women**

do it too. It has nothing to do with feminism. Now, lying and the fear of emotional commitments is another story—one that's simply unfortunate, and more about a lack of maturity.

♦ VA: But that's a human issue, not a gender issue.

♦ AJ: Exactly. Don't put this off on feminism.

♦ VA: Because that's taking us twenty steps back.

♦ AJ: As if a woman is so fragile that she needs to be taken care of by this one man! And as if women don't have diverse sexual feelings.

♦ VA: Like, you can't speak up for yourself and say, "Sorry, this isn't working for me. The way you go about a relationship makes me feel like shit. I'm out of here!" Instead of that, everybody's going, "I want to draw you in more; you need to give me more of this and more of that." I've got *no* time for that!

♦ AJ: Yet there are still these powerless women buying into the system of neediness, equating men's love with security because they don't have a sense of worth derived independent of men. And men allow that, too. They love that kind of ego boost!

♦ VA: It feeds right in. I believe—hopefully—that the feminist movement will go on from there. I went for a pap smear the other day at a feminist collective clinic, and filled out a form that asked how you found out about the clinic. One of the questions was, "Is the label 'feminist' positive, negative, or other?"

♦ AJ: Interesting question—

♦ VA: Yeah. I wrote "positive," but all day long I was thinking about it. Women our age who don't give any lip service to feminism ("I'm not a feminist! I do what I do because I'm a woman!") make me angry, because we would not be able to do and say a lot of things we do and say without the history of the feminist movement having happened. Emma Goldman was a huge influence on me; I read her autobiography and it changed my fuckin' life! She was a total free thinker, and there were others I read along the way—how can you discredit that? Why is it that women are so ashamed and afraid of claiming feminism as part of who they are now?

There's something really fucked up there that I don't understand, and I don't know how to change that, except that I give props to the feminist movement 24-7—twenty-four hours a day, seven days a week!

♦ AJ: Your view on feminism reflects the strength you already have: about your sexuality, and the fact that you are a woman and don't necessarily follow rules about what some feminists call "feminism." For example, the Andrea Dworkins of the world would like to think that women don't have sexuality.

♦ VA: But I really respect Andrea Dworkin; I've read a lot by her. I disagree with her philosophies a lot, but I think she and Catherine MacKinnon went out on such a limb. There are tons of holes in their theories which I can't get behind. The same for Camille Paglia; she's *out there*. But these women are saying things that have never been said before; they're futuristic thinkers. They're presenting something to chew on, and just the fact that it's there (whether I agree with it or not)—I would rather it *be* there than it not be there.

♦ AJ: That's a good point… . It's important to give homage to the sacrifices of an older generation. None of us were *born* with all this knowledge—women only got the right to vote within our grandmothers' lifetimes! Women couldn't even get credit cards in their own names, and not their husbands', as recently as the '60s.

♦ VA: Freedom does not exist in a vacuum. If you compare women's history to black, Hispanic, Asian, or any other history, you can't deny the work your foremothers or forefathers did to get you where you are now—that's ludicrous. I don't understand the whole backlash against feminism.

♦ AJ: A lot of the backlash was orchestrated by the right-wing media. There are always certain women who betray other women (and themselves, in the process)—male-identified women who are all too ready to—

♦ VA: Phyllis Schlafley?

♦ AJ: Or Katie Roiphe, who wrote a book claiming that the date-rape crisis was fictitious. Even though her statistics were wrong, she was the darling of the *New York Times* and other status-quo media for a long time. The *Baffler #6* published an article critiquing Roiphe, showing how the *New York Times* promoted her to major stardom despite the irrelevance and bankruptcy of her argument (and, oddly, her book was made out to have sold better than it actually did). In a sense she was saying, "Whiney women—you're all victims." And yes, there is a grain of truth there. But that has nothing to do with the reality that women are raped all the time. So she threw the baby (women themselves) out with the bath-water—which is all too often a role the oppressed will enact, because they identify with what they perceive as the power, and then stab in the back (of course) other oppressed people they should be supporting.

◆ VA: A lot of times when women are talking about feminism or different movements (say, anti-rape or domestic violence) or issues like unequal pay, they're still trying to speak outside of the reality that *we live in a patriarchal society*. It doesn't matter which culture you're talking about; women are oppressed in every single one, yet there's this fear from women now (especially our age) to be bold and outspoken about it. I find that so frustrating. I can back this shit up. I know what I'm talking about. I can list tons of examples. Why am I still trying to prove this is true? It is a fucking fact. It is reality.

We're always constantly compared to L7 or Babes In Toyland. Some guy asked: "Who would win in a fistfight between you and L7?" I just looked at him and said, "That is the stupidest question. They're our friends."

◆ AJ: *Time* magazine's feature on domestic violence claimed that "Men get beat up, too"—yet if you look at the actual comparative statistics—

◆ VA: There is *no* comparison. It's juvenile. I was reading in the paper today about how the Japanese government, now on the 50th anniversary of World War II, was trying to ex-

7 Year Bitch (l. to r.): Elizabeth Davis, Selene Vigil, Roisin Dunne and Valerie Agnew.

tend apologies to the 250,000 women who were used as sex slaves. They're making some lame-ass attempt to give restitution for these women's lives—only about 25,000 of them are still alive, and they're really old. Most of them won't even step forward to admit they were part of this, because they've tried to put it behind them. The government is trying to put a band-aid on their wounds: have them go through counseling, or give them money for their current living situation. One of these women was 13 years old and gang-raped by a group of Japanese soldiers, and then taken as a sex slave and forced to sleep with twenty to thirty men a day as a "comfort woman"—that's what they were called. And people didn't even bat an eye at this report: "Oh yeah, those 'comfort women'... " I thought, "*What*?!"

Take the Bosnian rape camps—what was the solution? They sent over counselors to the rape victims. They don't need counseling! Fuckin' send them AK-47s! It's a done deal; they've been violated, they've been fucked with; what they need is to learn how to fuckin' fight. So when a soldier busts into house #1, the women can protect themselves. The whole idea that if the men are gone, therefore the women are helpless is just archaic.

◆ AJ: Women are starting to "own" sexuality in a way that isn't about being *against* men, yet no longer with this constant reference to men—

◆ VA: But for a lot of women, sexuality still revolves around men. How many women my age

Photo: Stacey Wescott

Valerie's tattoo of Lilith.

at the point where I offend people because I'm too crass about sex. I'll make references to it all the time; I'm really open about it—I'm just not modest about sex. I'll say, "Yeah, I like to suck cock, I like to suck clit—whatever. Sex—fuck yes! It feeds me, it keeps me alive; it's part of what I do." Not everybody's like that. It's not that other people who aren't like that are repressed or behind the times; it just may not be in their nature to be like that. But if it is—go with it! There's no one standard that's right or wrong.

♦ **AJ: But there is a degree of discomfort about sex which reaches down to a lot of people's deepest foundations. It's very refreshing to hear someone like Susie Bright talk so openly about sex. The Good Vibrations store in San Francisco is a pioneering landmark, openly offering all kinds of information and access to sexual aids—**

♦ **VA:** There's a store like that in Seattle called Toys in Babeland. It's great. They have a little vibrator tryout room; they have everything.

♦ **AJ: That's a great name. How did the name "7 Year Bitch" come about?**

♦ **VA:** Actually, a friend thought of it—Ben London from the band Alcohol Funny Car. We were sitting around the Comet before our first show, a Books To Prisoners benefit, which Left Bank, an anarchist bookstore here, was putting on. A bunch of other bands were involved; we only had three songs and were going to play for 10 minutes. But we had to have a name for the flyer, and we thought, "This will just be temporary, for this one show." When Ben suggested "7 Year Bitch," I liked it instantly; I laughed and thought, "That's fuckin' great!" It was hilarious; a take-off on the Marilyn Monroe movie *Seven Year Itch*. (Elizabeth and Selene really didn't like it at first; Stefanie and I liked it.) And then it ended up being on a t-shirt they made for that show (which we didn't know they were going to do). Once you start playing under a name, it's really hard to change it. Everybody just grew to like it.

♦ **AJ: It's a classic name; it works.**

have still never had an orgasm with a man. It's un-fuckin'-believable! It's astounding. Friends of mine have said they just don't *get off* having sex with men. Maybe before, after, or through masturbation or whatever—yes. But in actual sex acts, they're not aggressive enough to go for it the way men do. And that baffles me.

♦ **AJ: For decades it has been drilled into women that "sex is bad," and if a woman enjoys sex she's not a "good woman." Now women are able to ask for what they want. Most people in general want communication; they *want* to know more about sex and what their partners want. But too often, unfortunately, women are ashamed to talk frankly about sex and their bodies.**

♦ **VA:** That whole christian morality has been inbred into people's minds, especially in the United States. I'm like the opposite of that. I'm

◆ VA: It's good. But to come back to music — this is the way we view *life* and how we approach every aspect of it. Our life fits in with the way we play music or the way we take on the supposed obstacles we're supposed to face as "women in rock." I always laugh at that question: "What's it like to be a woman in rock?" I don't really have any memory of being a *man* in rock, so I have nothing to compare it to! It's a silly question, like asking, "What's it like to be a woman in the world?" Fuck — if you really want to sit down with me for a couple hours, I can tell you all kinds of things I think —

◆ AJ: —and lots of contradictions.

> I always laugh at that question: "What's it like to be a woman in rock?" I don't have any memory of being a *man* in rock, so I have nothing to compare it to!

◆ VA: I'm proud of our band, proud of us not being intimidated by stigmas, coming up with our own thing and standing behind it: "This is our music, this is how we write." This may seem juvenile to some people: we were on "Beavis and Butthead." It was in the context of Women's History Month at the high school, and they cut to our video and made some joke, "If your name is Bitch, you don't have to know how to play your instrument." I was thinking about this: "Yeah, there are so many bands out there with really good musicians in them, but they *suck*!" Because it doesn't come down to just musical ability; it comes down to an *aesthetic*.

We write all our own material. Everything's derivative, and you can't deny the influences you have — we write songs about which we can directly say, "That was influenced by the Jesus Lizard," or "That was influenced by Girls Against Boys," or "That was influenced by Neurosis." But we're still taking that inspiration and putting it in our *own* language; that's infinitely exciting to me.

◆ AJ: Tell me about your tattoos.

◆ VA: I used to manage a medicinal herb shop in Pike's Place Market; if I wasn't in a band right now I'd be studying Chinese herbal medicine. When I saw the poisonous herbal borders in *Angry Women*, I thought, "This is so cool —

those borders are great tattoo ideas, too!" They tied into the whole midwife/witch mythology that has always fascinated me.

I have Barbara Coultin's *Book of Lilith*, which I scrutinized looking for images for a tattoo. Most of the representations of Lilith were from old Egyptian or Sumerian stone carvings, but I didn't want that look on my arm. I went to a Seattle tattoo artist, Vyvyn Lazonga, and she had a *Femme Fatale* book which contained a lot of paintings and old medieval goddess drawings. This one painting was simply titled "Bat Woman" and when I saw it I went, "That looks totally cool! *That's* what I want!" The wings were there, but the moon and the flames weren't (it was just her body with the wings and her hands hanging suspended, not grabbing onto anything). She was often known as a screech owl, so I want to put owls on either side and her name down the middle. But she was also known to be in half-flames or half-owl, so I couldn't decide whether I wanted her to have claw feet or flaming feet. It will all be worked out in the end. ◆ ◆ ◆

discography

Gato Negro (1996)
Notes From the Underground, compilation (1995)
Mad Love, soundtrack (1995)
¡Viva Zapata! (1994)
Rock-A-Bye, 7-inch (1994)
Sick 'Em (1992)
10-inch Picture Disc (1992)
Men, Money and Moonshine, split single with Thatcher On Acid with "Can We Laugh Now" (1992)
Powerflush, compilation (1992)
Antidisestablishmentarianism, 7-inch (1992)
There's a Dyke in the Pit, compilation (1991)
Lorna, 7-inch (1991)

equipment list

14" brass snare by Tama, Camco chain drive, kick pedal, Sabien cymbals, Vic Firth wood tip drum sticks, all hardware by Mapex

Lois Maffeo

Lois Maffeo went to Evergreen State College in Olympia, Washington. She had an influential all-girl radio show in Olympia for two years in the early 80's. She began playing guitar and singing in the mid-'80s, forming an all-girl band called the Lumihoops. She then had a band called Courtney Love, and now calls her band simply "Lois."

◆ LOIS MAFFEO: I've been *waiting* for people to start caring about women in rock'n'roll. I originally thought this would become an academic subject; I never thought there would be "Foxcore" or "Riot Grrrl." I thought it would eventually enter the common consciousness as people noticed, "Oh—there are all these women playing rock'n'roll now."

◆ **ANDREA JUNO: Well, how did you develop musically?**

◆ LM: When I was a child, I sang in my chorus class, surrounded by girls who would just be belting out: "If I had a hammer... ." And the boys would just be mouthing the words, *pretending* to sing—they had such shame! I looked at my sister's and brother's record collections and saw the Beatles, Iron Butterfly, even Burt Bacharach... everything was boys, boys, boys. I could not understand this: "These guys who hate to sing, who are so ashamed of performing even just among their classmates—how do they become the Beatles? Girls *love* doing this; *I* love doing this—why aren't there more records by women?" At school dances boys would never be flamboyant, while girls would be doing the Hustle! But as the girls became more sexual beings, they felt, "Oh, I have to be cool so I can impress this boy."

I lived in Phoenix and wasn't that aware of contemporary music. I saw the Talking Heads on "American Bandstand" doing "Take Me To The River," and I thought, "That's weird—I like it!" At that point I didn't realize that you could go to a record store and buy a Talking Heads

record; I just didn't know what was happening.

At school I started asking people: "Have you heard of Devo?" and finally hooked up with some girls who weren't considered "nice." We all started figuring out how to hear more music like this, and found a record shop near the local university called Dangerous Rhythms. Once there, we uncovered the nascent punk scene in Phoenix; JFA (Jodie Foster's Army) was getting started, Meat Puppets were getting started. We discovered the world of indie music shows and I just forgot about high school. That was when I realized: "It's *music* that makes me really happy!" But again, girls watched while boys played.

◆ **AJ: When was this?**

◆ LM: 1980, when I was 16. In the early days of my punk experience in Phoenix, a lot of the women thought the boys in bands were cute; musicians had—and still have—a cachet. But I wasn't drawn to punk rock because the boys were cute. I had grown up feeling I was missing something; I read a lot of books and magazines and always thought, "*This* doesn't happen here, and *that* doesn't happen here." So when I discovered punk rock, I felt it was a *ticket out...* to another culture or awareness.

Back then I didn't question gender differences so much, because I felt they were the price I had to pay for being part of this scene. All I knew was: there was this *thing* happening, and I could pay my $3 and watch it and be a part of it.

◆ **AJ: But you did feel a sense of compromise while being part of this "subversive scene"?**

◆ LM: Definitely.

By my senior year of high school, I had been going to clubs for some time. The main punk club was a great place called Madison Square Garden. It was a boxing ring which had turned into a wrestling ring with a cage around it. No beer was served, so there was no age restriction, whereas if you went to a bar, somebody might card you. Later on, the concept of all-ages shows as a knocking-down of *privilege of age* became widely known, but back then this concept did not exist. I remember my resentment at not being able to get into certain shows, and that resentment still fuels

people like Calvin Johnson [musician; partner in K Records]; that kind of *elitism* makes him, and other musicians, chafe.

♦ **AJ: I think the concept of all-ages shows, which enable subversion to be experienced by all ages, is wonderful. But unfortunately the concept has been tied to this bizarre American Puritanism in the form of the straight-edge movement, where no alcohol, tobacco or drugs (and often even sex and meat/dairy-consumption) are allowed. America seems to always veer toward extreme polarities: either shit-faced alcoholism or teetotaling quasi-fascistic repression. I like the European attitudes of moderation.**

♦ LM: I think ageism is a drag—it's very important for me to perform in front of all ages. When I moved to Olympia in 1981, I discovered that almost all music was performed in bars where the minimum drinking age is 21. It's like there was a rule: *music goes with alcohol*.

Personally, I don't like playing in bars, or for drunk people. Music and alcohol is not my favorite combination. When I play in bars, I have to try a lot harder to entertain these people who are talking and hoisting beers; it makes me feel that I'm *secondary* to what's happening. But at an all-ages show, I know that everybody wanted to pay five dollars to basically watch music. I do agree with you that there is a Puritanical element involved, but I don't think the all-ages concept should *necessarily* be equated with straight-edge militancy.

When I discovered punk rock, I felt it was a *ticket out*... to another culture or awareness.

However, I think the start of all-ages shows and the start of the straight-edge movement developed concurrently. I loved Southern California hardcore: Black Flag, Circle Jerks, the Bags. But when I heard about straight-edge, I thought, "If we're part of this whole movement that's trying to subvert the rules, why do you want to make a bunch more rules? So you can have more power structure in your life?"

Lois at age 2 (1965).

I went to the Evergreen State College in Olympia, Washington, because their catalog said they didn't have grades or even majors— you just studied what you wanted to. My parents said, "Well, we wish you'd stay in Arizona, but if that's what you want… " I thought, "No way am I going to stay *here*!"

I got to Evergreen College, moved into the dorm, and took the bus downtown. In retrospect it felt like the bus doors opened, the clouds parted and the sun shone—immediately I could sense that girls ran the town! Walking around downtown, I saw all these girl artists (many of whom still live here) in Louise Brooks haircuts dyed black, in Catholic schoolgirl skirts and cowboy boots and ripped t-shirts and crazy eyeliner just walking around looking great.

As I started meeting people, I realized there was a very strong arts community among these really young women, most of whom were attending Evergreen. I met Stella Marrs, an amazing artist who does these great postcards; at the time she was making paintings with bras and slips. Her art has always been very feminine, subverting the idea of women's fashions; high heels, bikinis and Barbie dolls were always her subject matter. Another woman named Jan Loftness (whose band, Twin Diet, sang only commercial jingles) was going out with Bruce Pavitt long

Ginnie Daugherty, Lois and Julie Fay (l. to r., 1984).

before he started Subpop records; at the time Bruce was just doing a fanzine called *Subpop*. An enormous woman named Debbie Rohrbach was the punkest person I'd ever seen, with chains, a huge trenchcoat, crazed hair and tattoos—which I'd never seen be-

fore on a woman; this was 1981. She had a female symbol with her social security number tattooed next to it. When I finally summoned up the nerve to ask her about it, she said, "Oh— that's my identity."

Obviously, there were boy artists and boy punks doing stuff, too. There was a great amount of art in the air. Again, I felt I had stumbled onto something that was "happening," just as when I had first discovered Madison Square Garden in Phoenix. And again, my first impulse was to just watch. But the difference was: here people were saying, "You can do this too." Or, "Help me—I'm making these postcards to sell, 'cause I'm broke."

When I got to Evergreen College, it felt like the bus doors opened, the clouds parted and immediately I could sense that girls ran the town!

◆ **AJ: You felt you could actually *participate*, instead of just watching—**
◆ **LM:** Definitely. There was a hierarchy, where they were cool and I was uncool, but suddenly I could do anything I want—it didn't matter if I was a girl. I think the presence of Evergreen College had a lot to do with this. It was an experimental college out in the woods, supporting all this radical thought. The faculty was pretty amazing, including feminists, lesbians—brilliant women who had a real effect on people. Also, the teaching style was "seminar": small classes where everyone was *expected* to talk. The Riot Grrrl idea of the cell, the operative and the meeting definitely used the Evergreen model; the arts community, Subpop, and *OP* magazine were also influenced. The idea of group ownership, or democratic/socialist models of shared responsibility within the Olympia punk scene, also came from Evergreen.

Stella Marrs and her friends rented a storefront for $150 a month and started a space called Girl City, to sell girls' art cheaply. Girl City was oriented around clothing, earrings, jewelry— wearable art. Occasionally paintings were exhibited, but mainly decorative art was shown. It could be clothes; girls would drink coffee and stay up all night sewing fur onto the necks of t-shirts. Stella made postcards using pictures from

National Geographic (purchased at garage sales). She scalloped the edges, stamped a little red arrow on them and they became Stella Marrs postcards. Girl City also had fashion shows. It was run collectively; there was no boss; you signed up for when you wanted to sit in the shop and work, and everyone shared the rent. And it was for girls only, although this was never written anywhere. All this was amazing to me—that they were even *doing* this.

About three years prior to my coming to Evergreen a group of friends—John Foster, David Rauh, and Toni Holm—who were interested in music, but not really that sure about what punk or new music *was*, decided they hated the Evergreen jazz station, KAOS, which played crappy music. They said, "Why don't we get the jobs of General Manager, Program Director and Music Director?" and they planned and executed a coup d'etat. They had heard about independent music, and implemented a policy of playing 85% independent records—they could be any genre: blues, punk—anything *not* from the seven major labels, which at that time controlled 95% of the music in the United States (I think the statistic is worse now, probably 99%).

♦ **AJ: Most of the larger independents were bought by majors—**
♦ **LM:** That's the nature of capitalism! Anyway, they implemented this "green line" policy (all the records were marked with green or red stickers; green line signified independent records; red line meant major-label records) and you had to play 85% green line records. KAOS is still known as a good station for independent music. Once they began receiving records from everywhere, John Foster said, "Let's start a magazine; I never read about this music anywhere." So they started *OP*. Originally they started the Lost Music Network, which was supposed to be a clearinghouse for information as to how one could locate independent records for the station, and disseminate information about independent music.

♦ **AJ: Why did they choose the name *OP*?**
♦ **LM:** Lost Music Network's initials was LMN, and since the next letters in the alphabet are OP, that's what they named the magazine. *OP* started in '81. The covers featured Willie Dixon, the Raincoats—anything they thought was interesting. It had tons of record reviews. They paid a lot of attention to cassette-only releases, music by people of color, and punk rock, which at the time wasn't well-covered, although punk zines were starting up. In Olympia there was never a big leather-jacket punk rock scene.

They had decided there would be 24 issues of *OP*, one for each letter of the alphabet. At the end of the "Z" issue, the staff had a convention in the summer of 1984. They invited everybody who had ever contributed to come to Olympia: "We'll have bands play, we'll

Lois in a solo acoustic show in Austin, Texas (1995).

talk about music, and at the end we'll give away the magazine. So whoever wants it—come to Olympia." They planned to give away all their advertising and subscriber information to whoever wanted to take it over.

Two people took them up on their offer. There was a magazine called *Sound Choice* from the Bay Area, and a magazine which became *Option* from Los Angeles, and both people took all the information. It was an interesting convention; lots of bands and people came. I think that was the first time people had an inkling that bands from other places would come to Olympia for an event— something which was definitely exploited by Calvin [Johnson] for the International Pop Underground Convention in 1991. Last year the Yo Yo A Go Go took place here. There have been

Strumpet (1993).

Riot Grrrl conventions that used the same model—like a music festival, although the Riot Grrrl organizers were trying to make it not be like a music convention or a CMJ event but more a situation where people could sit around and talk and *also* hear great bands.

♦ **AJ: During this time what were women doing, besides making objects at Stella Marrs' studio?**

♦ LM: Women were also involved in *OP* magazine. It was published by John Foster but designed by his partner Dana Lee Squires, and this woman Toni Holm was the business manager.

♦ **AJ: Women are traditionally involved in publishing as designers—**

♦ LM: Right. I'm sure that *OP* was generally perceived as John's magazine, but I think Dana and Toni really did a lot just to keep it going—which is another completely "normal" way of doing things: women do most of the work, and men get all the credit!

Also, women were busy encouraging other young women who were coming to Evergreen: "You can do whatever you want!" Stella started Satellite Kitchens, a big studio space for people to work in—mainly visual arts. She also threw parties where you either brought something to eat, sang a song, or performed a musical piece—you had to contribute *something*. That's how I became interested in performing—at these parties. Another great thing about Olympia is that everybody will clap for *anything*. You could get up and sing some godawful song and everybody would be like, "Yeah! Good for you, that's so excellent!" Some people have criticized this: "Oh, you guys just love everything! You have no aesthetics at all!"

♦ **AJ: But that can be such a refreshing antidote to the cynicism that keeps people bottled up and all their creativity under a lid because,**

"Oh god, that's not cool." "Cool" is probably *the* most insidious disease—it kills creativity and any kind of risk-taking in life.

♦ LM: "Cool" has come to bear in Olympia, too—it's everywhere now.

There were lots of musical events and bands starting up then, with all ages involved. When I was at Evergreen, there was a core group of about six or seven strong girls that were my age, almost like a gang; they were highly intellectual, very feisty and really tough. They were having reading groups: "Okay, everybody, pull out a mirror. We're looking at our vaginas!"—that kind of thing, like a feminist consciousness-raising group.

> **Another thing great about Olympia is that everybody will clap for *anything*. You could get up and sing some godawful song and everybody would be like, "Yeah! Good for you, that's so excellent!"**

♦ **AJ: But this was different from feminism in the '60s or '70s. Wasn't there more of a punk edge?**

♦ LM: Yes, I think they were rejecting traditional feminism of the time, which was not yet at the point documented in Susan Faludi's *Backlash*. Seventies feminism still existed, but it was losing speed. Personally, I hated fighting about issues; I've always been more of a practical person, and I felt, "Here they are, always blabbing, blabbing, blabbing about women and Virginia Woolf in their reading groups—and it never amounts to anything!"

There was a local radio show which played womyn's music like Holly Near, and these girls' response was against that kind of formalized feminism which they regarded as awful and boring—I felt the same way. So when one of them, Ginnie Daugherty, was talking about how there should be an all-girl radio show, I decided to just *do* it.

The Trouble with Me, 7-inch (1993).

♦ **AJ: Describe this group—**

♦ **LM:** They were punk intellectuals. There were some formidable college-age women thinkers involved. It didn't matter what they said because nobody was going to "call" them on anything; they didn't have an audience other than themselves. This core group was trying to make a punk experience. Everyone seemed to be forming bands; a club called the Tropicana started up which again was run collectively; the people who put out the *Sub Pop* fanzine started putting out cassettes of interesting music; Calvin was starting to release cassettes on K Records; everybody seemed to be involved in music. This group of girls was saying, "We're going to be part of this too, but we're not going to be about music (although that's what we like); we're going to be the intellectual component to your punk activities."

♦ **AJ: I'm confused as to what you thought about them—**

♦ **LM:** I thought what

<table>
<tr><td>"Dominatrix Sleeps Tonight," Dominatrix (Streetwise)</td></tr>
<tr><td>"Black Sheep," Vice Squad (Anagram)</td></tr>
<tr><td>"Last Request," Red Scare (Upstart)</td></tr>
<tr><td>"Catholic Boy," Dangerous Birds (Propellor)</td></tr>
<tr><td>"Cum Again," Au Pairs (AK/X)</td></tr>
<tr><td>"Spooky Cooties," Jr. Chemistry (Sub)</td></tr>
<tr><td>"Malhabile," Calamities (Posh Boy)</td></tr>
<tr><td>"Town Without Pity," Lori Green (Propellor)</td></tr>
<tr><td>"Riboflavin," Forty Five Grave (Enigma)</td></tr>
<tr><td>"Lesbian Connection," Sister Candy & Purple Man (Enterprise)</td></tr>
<tr><td>"Problem? What Problem?" Mechanical Servants (Mystery Toast)</td></tr>
<tr><td>"Pow Wow," Legal Weapon (Invasion)</td></tr>
<tr><td>"Francine's List," Pink Section (MR)</td></tr>
<tr><td>"From the Morning Glories," Trypes (Coyote)</td></tr>
<tr><td>"Restless," Bangles (Columbia)</td></tr>
<tr><td>"Paranoia Reception," Dadistics (Bomp)</td></tr>
<tr><td>"Final Day," Young Marble Giants (Rough Trade)</td></tr>
<tr><td>"Another Bridge," Everything But the Girl (Sire)</td></tr>
<tr><td>"Man Next Door," The Slits (Rough Trade)</td></tr>
<tr><td>"Eye of the Hurricane," Drongos (Proteus)</td></tr>
<tr><td>"Getting Nowhere Fast," Girls at Our Best (Record)</td></tr>
<tr><td>"Others," Judy Nylon (On-U)</td></tr>
<tr><td>"I Wanna Be You," Your Funeral (Local Anesthetic)</td></tr>
<tr><td>"Lilting/Brother" OH OK (DB)</td></tr>
<tr><td>"Caucasian Guilt," Noh Mercy (Fast)</td></tr>
<tr><td>"Oh Ricky," Beverly Sisters (Cowboy Carl)</td></tr>
<tr><td>"Fester," Conflict (Unjust)</td></tr>
<tr><td>"Music is Your Body," Moral Lepers (Modamu)</td></tr>
<tr><td>"Beyond and Back," Rumbounds (Bogus)</td></tr>
<tr><td>"Pussy X," Kas Product (Cachalot)</td></tr>
<tr><td>"Vegas," Nico (Flicknife)</td></tr>
<tr><td>"Cool," Pylon (DB)</td></tr>
<tr><td>"Drumbeat for Baby," Weekend (Rough Trade)</td></tr>
<tr><td>"What Is It?" Lydia Lunch (Giorno Poetry Systems)</td></tr>
<tr><td>"Poseur," X-Ray Specs (EMI)</td></tr>
</table>

Selections from Lois' playlist for a women's rock radio show on a listener sponsored community radio station in Olympia, WA. The show was entitled "Your Dream Girl" (Novermber 19, 1984).

they did was great—except that I didn't want to sit around with a group of girls and talk about *Orlando* and look at my vagina; I wanted to be a punk rocker. I'm not anti-intellectual, and I don't want to sound like Milquetoast, but I don't really have the breadth of mind to make all these jumps between: "Here's punk, and here's Jacques Derrida, and here's Michel Foucault... ." I might read some essay making all these connections and think, "Yeah, I get it," but at the end I still feel, "*Now* what?!"

So regarding this core group of girls, I was acutely interested in what they did; at the same time I felt no desire to be a part of their group, which was kind of a precursor to the Riot Grrrl movement. They were pressuring boys to be feminists; when this club Tropicana was opening, they applied pressure to make sure women were in-

volved in it. They wanted all of the first recordings that came out on K Records to have women on them—even though there was a feeling that it didn't matter if you were a boy or a girl. These were basically artists, students and people on the fringes just enjoying themselves and all working together to create this whole scene.

♦ **AJ: So how did you start your radio show?**

♦ **LM:** At Evergreen, I already had a noon-time talk radio show; I'd drag anybody in and we'd talk about *Star Trek* or traveling or whatever. In Arizona I'd heard some punk rock and liked reggae and rockabilly a lot, but when I got to Olympia, the gods were the Modern Lovers, which was Jonathan Richman's punk band—their music was anti-elitist. It was all about "Going to the Stop-and-Shop; I got my radio on," with

Lois, Donna Dresch of Team Dresch, and Molly Neuman of Bratmobile (l. to r.) practicing in a laundry room in Olympia for the Lois album, *Strumpet* (1992).

experiential lyrics descriptive of the people who were making it. A band from the Midwest called the Embarrassment were very popular, as well as bands like the Slits and the Raincoats and other British post-punk bands like Young Marble Giants and Scritti Politti. Also, Southern California hardcore like Black Flag was very popular. So I suddenly heard music that was a broad spectrum of more styles and was homemade.

I started substituting on a night-time radio show. The greatest thing about doing radio was having access to this huge roomful of records and being able to play anything I wanted. A DJ was going away for a few days and asked me to do his show; I thought, "I'm going to take Ginnie Daugherty up on her suggestion to do an all-girl rock'n'roll radio show." It was simple to fill up two hours.

I had heard about punk rock a long time before I ever heard it, because you'd read about it in *Rolling Stone*. When I was 15 or 16 and heard about the Sex Pistols, I had no opportunity whatsoever to hear the music itself, because I didn't know where to go. I didn't know where there was a punk rock record shop. I thought punk rock was going to physically hurt my ears; they

made it sound so evil and weird and crazy—they have safety pins and they spit and all that stuff—I thought it was going to be a totally different physical sensation than turning on the radio and hearing, say, the Doors. When I finally heard the Sex Pistols I was like, "This is the Sex Pistols? This is just rock'n'roll." I was shocked. I thought it was going to be *radical*. But then when I heard the Raincoats and their screeching violins, or Young Marble Giants with practically only a bass and woman's voice, I really felt like *that* was radical music.

◆ **AJ: It's amazing how quickly we get habituated to a certain sound. You listen to the Sex Pistols now and you can't even believe that was ever a radical sound; they sound so melodic.**

◆ LM: I've watched our culture gobble up "alternative" or "underground music." Well, there's nothing underground about it anymore. I try and retain some kind of feeling for it, but it's really hard to not feel ripped off personally, as a community and as a culture.

At the time I was describing, the Northwest was still isolated; touring bands never came here. Bands never came to Seattle. I know it's hard to imagine, now that Seattle's the rock'n'roll capital of everything; but then, bands from the United Kingdom, especially, would only fly to New York or San Francisco. Even bands touring the United States would just go as far north as San Francisco. Which always seemed crazy to me, because between San Francisco and Vancouver, British Columbia, there were so many places you could play. We would travel to Vancouver to see the Jam, or go to San Francisco to see the Cocteau Twins.

On the radio show, I was inspired by what was happening musically, to actually feel something that I'd never felt in watching live hardcore bands or rock'n'roll bands: *to play music myself.*

The printed word was the means of communication for music that was happening outside of this area, and that's why *OP*, *SubPop*, and other

Fanzines from Lois' archives (l. to r.): *Meat Joy Songbook, Sister Nobody, Chainsaw* and *Dresch-84*.

fanzines were created. Since you couldn't see the bands, you had to send for the music by mail order or read about it somewhere.

◆ **AJ: Your radio show also must have been a magnet for the local girls and women. You talked about the female punk intellectuals; what were the female musicians like?**

◆ LM: I started interviewing girl bands, and I'd run into all these women that were like, "*We don't want to be known as a girl band; we just want to be thought of as a band*." I'd ask, "Why? You just want to be part of this morass of rock'n'roll?" I just could never understand that. Why would you want to be judged using a system that's totally outdated? Why would you want to have the technical gear-headed macho sound-guy life, rather than, "Fuck all of you. We've got our own thing. You raise your consciousness to deal with us. We don't want to lower our consciousness to deal with you."

A lot of the Riot Grrrl bands I saw were very confrontational to sound men; they were like, "You stupid guy with a perm. We need to fucking put the monitors right, we're getting too much feedback!" I played *acoustic*, and all these guys would be like, "Yeah, I know where to put the microphone so it'll sound the best." And I would say, "Go ahead. Put the microphone where you want." Then they walk to the back to their sound place, the show starts, I put the microphone where I know it sounds best—'cause I've done this a million times. I don't want to be in charge of educating this *ape* about feminism. I don't have time! He's not listening to me anyway and I don't want to fight with anybody. If he happens to be standing back there and goes, "Hey, it does sound better there," great for me.

But it's not my responsibility.

◆ **AJ: Was it your work on that radio show that made you want to actually play music?**

◆ LM: I was inspired by what was happening, musically, on the radio show to actually feel something that I'd never felt in watching live hardcore bands or rock'n'roll bands: *to play music myself*. I was particularly influenced by a British band called the Marine Girls. A woman named Tracey Thorn was in it; she's now in Everything But the Girl. The Marine Girls just had

From Lois' archives: an inspirational issue of *Who Put the Bomp!* (Spring 1976).

From Lois' punk rock window in Olympia, WA: The Smithfield Cafe (left), site of her first public performance singing "Hit the Road to Dreamland" (1984) and only public performance of her first band Lumihoops (1987); Seagull Books & Crafts (right) is the original site of the art store Girl City.

suddenly, the high school kids from Olympia, many of them the sons and daughters of Evergreen faculty, started to become involved. Tobi Vail from Bikini Kill was one of those kids.

This was a group of people that was truly influenced by only Olympia. They'd grown up here and they were 14- or 15-year-olds that were into music because it was accessible to them, because there was this all-ages place downtown where they could actually go and see music. They started fanzines and bands; Donna Dresch created *Dresch*

one guitar and some percussion; it was simplistic. They sang these really beautiful songs which had a kind of samba mood. And hearing that made me feel like, "You know, I really wish I could actually play, because I would like to sing some songs like that."

Meanwhile, because of this collectively-run club, the Tropicana, that had started downtown, bands were finally starting to come up here. There'd be shows by bands like Butthole Surfers and 45 Grave. Bands from California or other places were coming to Olympia and having these great fun shows because everyone here is so enthusiastic—maybe they wouldn't make tons of money, but they'd be feted by all these kids. And

Patrick Maley and Lois Maffeo of the band Courtney Love (1989).

'84, her fanzine that she printed on the mimeograph machine at high school. So here I am, doing the radio show, thinking rock'n'roll's great, and suddenly all these kids are starting to buy guitars. I'm maybe 20 and they're like 16, but that's a big difference after you're in college vs. being in high school. I felt this pressure coming from the younger kids: if they could rock out, buy guitars, and actually start to get radio shows too, because KAOS was so accessible (you didn't have to go to Evergreen to get a radio show there)… I felt like, "I'm painting myself into a corner here, I've got to do this."

So I bought a crappy $40 guitar. It was on a whim, because I missed Olympia, and I felt that having a guitar would connect me in a way. I had moved to Portland to work at the film studies center there, and I had also taken my radio show to the community radio station in Portland called KBOO. At that time in Portland there was a really druggy Goth scene. I lived in this house where everyone took Valium all the time and complained and drank a lot. I'd come from Olympia, this town that was so active and vigorous—you'd see a kid at a copy shop running off their fanzine, you'd walk down the street and one person would say, "We're going to have a show in the alley tonight," and another kid would say, "There's going to be a film tomorrow night!" And then to land in this place that was so Gothic, and *stoned*!

128

I decided I missed Olympia so much that I quit a really great job and came back. I was just starting to play guitar. And that's the period when a lot of stuff was happening in Olympia that could be considered performance-esque.

There's a series of apartments on top of a florist's shop here. Kill Rock Stars is in one of them now. I lived in one, this guy Randall Hunting lived in one. We'd have these thematic parties where each person would open up their house for a different part of the party. There was a Berlin 1919 party; everybody sang Brecht-Weill songs and dressed up in that Marlene Dietrich style. We had a Swinging '60s London party with paper dresses, strobe lights, and decorations like huge stencils. People were encouraged to perform in the style of whatever the party was.

> **For women, you can't just wear black jeans and black Converse sneakers and still maintain that mystique of being 16, so they go back to a more adolescent model, the baby-doll look.**

♦ AJ: What were these performances like?
♦ LM: My friend Margaret Doherty and I planned a whole performance after we saw this Frankie Avalon film called *The Million Eyes of Sumaru*. It's an awful, stupid movie but we were totally consumed with the plot: an evil genius woman had these minions of women; they were all totally sexy and they planned to become the girlfriends or wives of world leaders—they were going to bump off all the world leaders at the same time and then Sumaru, the evil genius woman, was going to gain world control! We got so into this movie: "Yeah, that's the greatest idea ever!" There's a scene in the movie where one of the bikini-clad girls has actually fallen in love with her world leader and doesn't want to kill him; so when she's swimming one day these two amazon, buxom, beautiful women—bezombified minions of the evil genius—come swimming out into the water with knives to kill her.

So we made up a song and performance. We made punk cave-girl costumes out of fake fur, and summarized the plot of the movie into this song: "Two bikini girls kill one bikini girl, glug glug

glug she's dead. And her tan still looks great, and her bikini hasn't lost its shape, but… " It was a surfy a cappella song we did dressed in black wigs and fur suits, and the whole performance was called "Bikini Kill."

A couple years later I got a letter from Tobi Vail that said, "I'm playing music with this girl Kathleen and this girl Kathi, and we were tossing around band names, and I recall there was this band… ." She might still be

Fanzine *Koo Koo* created by Lois Maffeo.

confused to this day, because she didn't see this performance. I think she had heard this name in the lore of Olympia and thought it was a band name that Rebecca Gates from the Spinanes and I had discarded; we were in a band called the Cradle Robbers. I never bothered to tell her what it was actually about, because she didn't say, "We're thinking about it," she said, "I seem to recall that you discarded the name Bikini Kill and opted for Cradle Robbers, so *we're* going to be Bikini Kill." It's a free world, I don't care, do what you want! It's interesting, though, to look back and see that what was basically a feminist girl takeover performance became, down the line, the name of a *band* that was a feminist girl takeover project. There is bit of poetic justice in that!

♦ AJ: Go back to what you think is the genesis of Riot Grrrl, and what happened to it.
♦ LM: I moved back to Olympia in '86 and a lot of stuff was happening here. Young people were starting to feel incredibly empowered because there were places to put on shows; in a lot of towns there's no place for kids to play music or gather or

Lois playing at a Riot Grrrl Convention in Los Angeles (1995).

♦ **AJ: But that stuff is so provincial. I care about ideas.**

♦ **LM:** Olympia went kind of quickly from being the kind of place where punk rock kids got beat up by local rednecks to a place where "underground music" became acceptable via its "discovery" by MTV and other forms of major media. Some bands got a bit caught up in the hoopla. There was a sense of entitlement created by the sudden attention and money.

Once I saw a Riot Grrrl band hassle a promoter to pay them more than their guarantee. They had received their guarantee, but they were like, "Man, there was a ton of people here, and you're ripping us off!" They were using what they thought was their personal power as performers and feminists to really take it to this guy who had been really nice—he'd fed everybody. I felt like, "Okay, you've learned the lesson that you've got to be aggressive and fight for what's right—but here's a situation where it is completely inappropriate."

♦ **AJ: In '73 I was in college, and while I was there some pseudo-radical students took over the classroom of the only liberal Marxist teacher. Of course, they wouldn't have done that to the authoritarian teachers who would have been more like the real status quo, and who the students would have been more intimidated by; no, they did it to the person who was like a lamb, who was a great teacher. They announced that they wanted to participate in the direction of the class—so they gave these really boring lectures. I was so pissed, because I wanted to hear what this teacher had to say—not these obnoxious young students.**

They couldn't see that this teacher was not the enemy, and that they were actually replicating the power structure in silencing him. And this happens so often in these underground situations where there's no analysis of real power; of who has power, who doesn't, and that this does not mean a license—

♦ **LM:** —to attack. The situation I was describing took place in Worcester, Mass, a working class town. If that promoter didn't put on shows there, nobody else would. Recently I heard how all these kids protested a Fugazi show in New York because they played at a big hall instead of ABC No Rio [a small punk club]. The

do anything. Here was this setup that all these people had worked to achieve: there was a club, a place you could record, a place you could dub off all your cassettes (K was trying to be as open as possible about letting people use their equipment). I was starting to play music; my friend Pat Maley and I had a band called Courtney Love, and we put out three singles on K.

I lived in Olympia and I lived in Washington D.C.—the polar points of Riot Grrrl—so I get asked a lot about Riot Grrrl, and I repeat a lot about Riot Grrrl, but there's this great suspicion among these younger girls that were actually in the Riot Grrrl groups: who am *I* to talk about this thing? Well, I feel that I, more than a lot of people, was intensely scrutinizing what happened because I felt it was the fruition of everything I had hoped would happen, and that I *expected* to happen, as far as my own commitment to women in music through my radio show, and in general trying to encourage young girls here in Olympia, "Sure, do it! Put on a show! Be in a band!"

What I've learned over the last 5 years of being a performer and being very accessible to fanzine people and other people, is that self-censoring fear that you'll say something that'll be read as: "Oh, so-and-so's a flake." I've learned to try and make sense of why if I thought someone had a chip on their shoulder about K Records, how that made sense within the topic we're talking about, and how Bratmobile and Heavens to Betsy—Riot Grrrl bands—put out a single on K, and the first Bikini Kill tape was distributed on K, and then suddenly there was a big to-do because of *personal* things that people felt and different experiences people had on a *personal* level.

Artwork from a page of Lois' fanzine *Koo Koo*.

people in Fugazi take advantage of no one. Their shows are $5 to get into; anybody can get five dollars. They let anyone into their shows, and they try so hard to find a place that isn't run by these huge promoters like Ron Delsener. You want to say to these kids, these self-righteous vegan Riot Grrrl and Riot Boy types, "Don't you have a better enemy than the people who are actually looking out for you?"

In fact, there is somewhat of a backlash to all this self-righteousness. Some of us have joked to each other, "Did you get zined?" Being "zined" happened most often to boys; their "white male privileges" were exposed in these Riot Grrrl zines, like: "I thought he was sympathetic to our cause, but it turned out that he just wanted to have sex." I remember this young man coming to me and saying, "I don't want to judge, but I don't understand. I had great sex with this girl, and then afterward we're just lying there in this postcoital daze, and she starts talking about how all sex is essentially rape. I just felt awful!" I had sympathy for this young man—I'd feel pretty shitty too!

♦ AJ: Poor guy! That's an example of the typical degeneration of liberatory ideas into dogma and mass media fodder. Some aspects of Riot Grrrl need to be critiqued; sometimes I wonder why there's so much of an emphasis on *girlhood*—to me it's like, "Wait a minute, let's be *women*. Let's break the hymen." There's already such an over-emphasis on youth in our culture.

♦ LM: A lot of people continue to refer to themselves as girls, even though they're well past adolescence and into their 30s. I still sometimes refer to myself as a girl; I'm 31 years old, and there's no reason why that should be how I characterize myself.

I think a lot of this imagery of girls and baby

doll dresses and stuff like that is because so much of punk rock culture came from being the misfit, the one who was beaten up, the weaker, the smaller. In the world of rock'n'roll, there's also the icon of the eternal teenager, wanting to stay at that arrested state of, "I'm 16" and, "rock'n'roll forever." For women, you can't just wear black jeans and black Converse sneakers and still maintain that mystique of being 16 forever, so they go back to a slightly more adolescent model, the baby-doll look.

You see it in Courtney Love a little bit: the frilly, baton-twirling, "cutest baby" or "cutest little Miss Fashion," that imagery of the beauty

Inside Lois' fanzine *Koo Koo*.

Butterfly Kiss (1992).

pageant and the child being the prettiest girl. It's completely valid as a self-esteem issue. Stella Marrs' postcards, with their '50s and '60s imagery, have a lot to do with not only the subversion of those images, but extracting whatever was actually good about the feminine.

Lois and Heather Dunn, a member of Lois (1995).

♦ **AJ: But on that older model of the Donna Reed promise—**
♦ **LM: It's** definitely very Donna Reed.
♦ **AJ: Let's talk more about the whole baby doll thing. It's the part I have a problem with, and it's probably because of my own personal experience; I don't look back with fondness to my own childhood or adolescence—there was such a feeling of powerlessness. So I never had much nostalgia for the trappings of girlhood. But again,**

that's me, personally.
♦ LM: I also have to critique this from an outside position. I never wore short skirts and knee socks and pinafores. The first person I remember who was an influence on my thinking, in regard to frilly baby-doll fashion, was one of my housemates when I lived in Portland in 1985. I lived with a butch/femme lesbian couple, two women who were both small and blonde; neither of them was particularly stereotypically "dykey." So their butch/femme roles were defined by Mary wearing the very frilly diaphanous lingerie and baby-doll nighties. She created a fashion style that grew out of the clothes she could wear out in the world that were closely akin to that "nightie" style; it was the first time I realized that in a fashion sense it was like doll clothes. And that had a radical component for me, as much as seeing the bright hair of the punks: "Wow, I can't believe you're going *outside* in that!"

You can go on and on about what the possible primary meanings are for dressing this way. The adult criteria for beauty are very severe, but more pliable for young girls. Cute is defined in more ways than glamorous or beautiful is, and a lot of adolescent girls who are searching for their own sense of allure don't necessarily define themselves as beautiful or glamorous; cute is a closer possibility for them.

Men think that if you can do a really flawless guitar solo, you're a great musician! To me that's bogus. My own career is based on the eradication of the guitar solo.

♦ **AJ: It's also important to remember that so often, with women rockers and particularly with the Riot Grrrls, more is made of the clothes and the look than the songs and music.**
♦ LM: An issue we haven't even touched upon is virtuosity and whether or not women can play as good as men. Men think that if you can do a really flawless guitar solo, you're a great musician! To me that's bogus. My own career is based on the eradication of the guitar solo. I think that is just complete wanking, and I don't want anything to do with it! People talk about hooks and

bridges within songs and I'm like, "Call 'em whatever you want, I can only write a song as it comes out, and my songs don't have to have a structure that's already well-defined in male-dominated music."

♦ AJ: **Right now there's this wonderful period of creativity which punk rock was founded on: not knowing your instrument, so therefore you can create an entirely new, innovative and creative sound, because you're subverting the whole technique and tradition.**

But it's not going to last, because this is the first generation in which young women will start playing earlier, and they're going to be really good musicians by the time they're in high school. If they want to be musicians, they'll do it, and they'll learn their guitars or their drums at the age when guys do, and they spend all their lonely time practicing in their rooms...

♦ LM: I don't want that to happen! I look at some of the men I know who are particularly talented on guitar, and they spent their entire adolescence in their rooms practicing note-for-note Van Halen or Led Zeppelin *IV* until they could completely mimic it. It's not virtuosity, it's mimicry in a lot of these people who are supposedly great musicians.

♦ AJ: **I wouldn't say, "Don't learn," and in fact I've talked to a lot of women who started off not knowing their instruments at all, and who experienced that freedom from musical rules and standards. But then there's another stage when you *do* start to know your instrument; it's just another process.**

♦ LM: You're right. I don't think that *not* knowing your instrument makes you a more virtuous performer. I have been handed tape after tape of people who are trying to find their voices, and who aren't very good musicians—I don't give them extra credit for being crappy musicians. You can't ride on the fact that you're raw, unless there's something really thrillingly original about it.

♦ AJ: **It's a lot of work to be an artist.**

♦ LM: I think that if you take rawness and then continue working on communicating what your ideal is, maybe you'll never be so articulate with music as to reach a status of literacy, in a musical context, but you'll still have this enthusiasm that translates. Your music will always seem somehow fresh because you've engaged in this experiment.

♦ AJ: **This is the dilemma of all the arts that have a beginning, middle and end. Once the cycle is played out, it's a matter of reinvention.**

♦ LM: My hope, and I feel kind of chagrined in a sense to feel this way, is that the Nirvanas and Pearl Jams and Soundgardens for the kids now, are going to be bands like Boston and Styx were for me: the logy, tired, '70s behemoths that were overproduced and had no connection to what my life experience was. I was just so happy to see punk rock puncturing holes in their importance so they would deflate. ♦ ♦ ♦

♦ discography ♦

♦ LOIS ♦
Bet the Sky (1995)
Shy Town, EP (1995)
Lowrider, cassette (1994)
Indie, 7-inch split single (1994)
Strumpet (1993)
The Trouble With Me, 7-inch (1993)
International Hip Swing, compilation (1993)
Unnecessary Niceness, compilation (1993)
Press Play & Record, 7-inch (1992)
Butterfly Kiss (1992)

♦ COURTNEY LOVE (THE BAND) ♦
Teenbeat 50, compilation (1993)
International Pop Underground, compilation (1992)
One Last Kiss, compilation (1992)
Kill Rock Stars, compilation (1991)
Highlights, 7-inch (1990)
Hey! Antoinette, 7-inch (1990)
Uncrushworthy, EP (1989)

♦ LUMIHOOPS ♦
Throw, compilation (1994)

♦ LOIS WITH GO-TEAM ♦
Archer Come Sparrow, compilation (1988)

♦ LOIS MAFFEO (SOLO) ♦
Dangerous Business International, compilation (1985)

equipment list

1975 Guild acoustic guitar, Fender acoustic guitar, Gretsch practice amp, D'Armond pick-up, stage tuner, lots of extra strings, Built By Wendy guitar strap.

Naomi Yang

Naomi Yang has been playing bass since 1987, first with Galaxie 500 and then with Damon & Naomi and Magic Hour. She and her partner, Damon Krukowski (drummer in Galaxie 500 and Magic Hour), have collaborated on songs for Galaxie 500 and, since 1991, for their folk-rock duo Damon & Naomi. They also run Exact Change, a Boston press that specializes in reprinting lost classics of experimental literature. Yang designs all the books and has also done all of the artwork for her bands. She is also a painter, and had her first one-person show in 1994. She can be reached at Exact Change, P.O. Box 1917, Boston, MA, 02205.

♦ **ANDREA JUNO: You mentioned that** *Guitar Player* **magazine always prints musicians' equipment lists. Women don't usually get asked questions about their equipment; has anybody asked you?**

♦ **NAOMI YANG:** No. Most interviewers don't talk much about music, except in general terms. And there aren't that many women in *Guitar Player* magazine to begin with. But if you were going to be in *Guitar Player*, it always seemed to me that the equipment lists were the best thing about the publication! On a practical and aesthetic level, as a musician, your equipment is an important issue to you—your choices define your aesthetic statement.

But listing equipment is kind of a macho thing. You probably haven't gone to many music stores, right?

♦ **AJ: No. [laughs]**

♦ **NY:** There's a whole mentality that prevails there, and guys do it to other guys—it's not completely sexist. In any big music store, the sales help tend to treat you like a jerk unless they recognize you from your Grammy award ceremony. There's a "who knows more about equipment" game that's played.

When I went shopping for a bass, I had no idea how to play—so I used purely visual criteria. I chose the most beautiful bass in the store.

I didn't have a hero or heroine in mind; I wasn't thinking, "So-and-so plays a Fender; I have to play one too." In fact, I didn't even know enough then to have *noticed* who was playing what. But I was lucky; in choosing one that was unique-looking, I also ended up with one that had a very warm, natural, *old* sound. It's not an L.A. studio sound; it's a sound that drives sound-engineers crazy because it's kind of out-of-control; not so *limited*. Of course, I could have just as easily wound up with a really great-looking bass that sounded horrible—and I probably would have stopped right there!

For me, getting involved in music meant learning about it, asking myself, "What should *I* do? How can I make it sound different?" Music is about making sounds, and, for me, it's always been about making a *beautiful* sound.

You also have to learn the technicalities; it's like knowing the code words of a secret society. If you're able to confidently discuss your amplifer with the sound-man, this doesn't necessarily make him treat you better, but it cuts out a potential amount of: [patronizing guy's voice] "Oh, do I have to tell you where to plug it in?"

♦ **AJ: Men, for the most part, have grown up with role models of other men who play in rock bands. Women did not have that. The earliest example of a woman-in-a-band role**

Self-portrait, Japan (1995).

model I can think of was Patti Smith.

♦ NY: She played guitar—

♦ AJ: —but she was known more for being a singer; she wasn't like Keith Richards. She, Joan Jett, Chrissie Hynde, Fanny and maybe a handful of others were *the* role models for so many women—and they're late in rock'n'roll history. It's only in the '90s, that women-in-rock role models can finally be considered "natural" or "ordinary".

♦ NY: Right. A few years ago, I probably would have said about women role models, "What's the point? Why can't you have a male role model just as easily?" And I think a woman *can* have a male role model in terms of one's art. I think you can learn from any art that anyone

has done; you can appreciate the craft and the artistry, and just be really moved by how fantastic something is.

But it's definitely true that a role model for me was Kendra Smith, who I first listened to when she played in the Dream Syndicate. She sang in a way that I'd never heard a woman sing before.

♦ AJ: Meaning what?

♦ NY: It didn't sound compromised to me. Her style wasn't taking the position of a vulnerable little-girl voice, like the Bangles' Susanna Hoffs, or earlier weepy girl groups from the '60s. She sounded very strong and self-confident. It was like *pure art* to me; not a gender or a sex thing. It wasn't about attraction or

Photo: David Corio

Naomi Yang and Damon Krukowski of Damon and Naomi.

the "glamour of rock'n'roll," or about the singer as sex siren. It was about singing as expressing art and making something beautiful or real. Obviously, she's not the only woman who ever did that. But for me, Kendra Smith changed my whole outlook, because I could see myself in her position. And once you can *imagine* yourself in another circumstance, it gives you the courage to try something you might otherwise never have tried.

I was thinking about all the bass players I love, and I realized that they're all these big macho-looking guys with handlebar mustaches!

Years ago, when I first started playing, I was listening to Peter Hook a lot. I was listening to Joy Division and New Order, and I realized that

what I was *really* listening to, and singing along with in my mind, was the bass player, Peter Hook. I had never thought about the bass as an instrument before; I guess a lot of people regard the bass as something "below" that you never listen to. Peter Hook took the instrument away from being a workhorse and was playing these incredibly heartbreaking, melodic bass lines. I realized, "Oh my god, this is just as expressive as a voice."

I took two lessons from a Berklee-style teacher and was completely turned off.

◆ **AJ: What does Berklee-style mean?**

◆ NY: Berklee is a music school in Boston; but what I meant is an emphasis on technique—worrying about how fast you can play scales, not playing by intuition. At the end of the first lesson, my teacher said, "Next lesson, bring me some bass lines you like and I'll teach you how to play them." I said, "Great." I went home and taped a Joy Division song, "Atmosphere." I brought it in and played it for him and he asked, "Do you know what he's playing?" I said, "No." He said, "He's playing a fifth, and then sliding up one octave." This was a very basic, simple move—the easiest thing in the world to play, and if you have trained ears, like that teacher, it's easy to pick out. He said, really sarcastically, "What a genius, huh?" And I thought, "That's *all* he's playing?"

That teacher had just handed me a miracle! This was one of the most beautiful and elegant things I'd ever heard, and it was so simple. Peter Hook wasn't doing something magical that I couldn't do; he was doing something very simple which I learned in Bass Lesson Number Two. I thought, "I don't need this teacher anymore!" It was a leap: "You don't have to be a virtuoso to play bass. You can play incredibly simple themes but they can still be melodic and from the heart."

A woman artist doesn't necessarily have to paste her tampons on the wall; her art does not have to be so explicit or simplistic.

♦ **AJ: But not everybody can do that. There's some soul that goes into it. And isn't talent a factor?**

♦ **NY:** That's a question I've always wondered: "If I can make things look or sound beautiful, does that mean I'm talented, or just that sometimes I have some good taste?" So I suppose there's a need for facility, but of course there's also a need for soul. The important thing is having an aesthetic for crystalline melody. That's what Peter Hook had, and that's what I'm always striving for: a bass line that's a counter-melody within the song.

I also like Holger Czukay from Can, a '70s experimental band, and Hugh Hopper from Soft Machine, and Jah Wobble from Public Image, Ltd. A new discovery for me is the vintage Lemmy—not in Motorhead, but in Hawkwind, this insane number one act in England in the '70s. They had a theme: every song was about outer space! The albums are called things like *Space Ritual*, and the lyrics are so bad, like: "Space is big and you're so small." But beyond these ridiculous lyrics are these amazingly plaintive bass lines that are so beautiful; they circle around and around your head. Meanwhile, the rest of the band is making these awful space sounds on an early synthesizer, and reciting poems between

songs like "In the 10th Second to Infinity" (*all* space-related); Lemmy seems like he's just minding his own business and propelling the music along with these riveting bass lines.

I was thinking about all the bass players I love, and I realized that they're all these big macho-looking guys with handlebar mustaches! Every single one has a mustache, and I don't know what that means. The bass is a big instrument; physically, bass players tend to be big hulking guys who stand in back; they have these huge ugly Fenders! The bass isn't seen like the guitar, which is considered a more delicate instrument.

Many bass players leave all the delicacy up to the guitars, but when the bass is used as a melodic instrument, as another voice, that's when it becomes interesting. The range of the bass is where I sing, too, because I'm not a soprano, I'm an alto. So I play high on the bass, pretty much on the G and D strings—I don't play the low strings (the ones you think of as "bass"). Also, playing the bass higher cuts through the overall sound better. The lower notes have no definition; they're rumbling down there and you can't really follow them. But the higher notes are clear and you can follow the melodic line.

I started playing when we were a trio: just bass, drums and guitar. In the studio, you can record as many tracks as you need to fill out a song and make it sound very layered and rich, but live, we had just that one guitar and bass. So when the guitar went to a lead, I preferred to

The Wondrous World of Damon and Naomi, **Damon and Naomi's latest album (1995).**

Galaxie 500 (l. to r.): *Today* (1988), *On Fire* (1989) and *This is Our Music* (1990).

play a counter-melody rather than booms or thumps. The bass players whom I love play very beautiful, elegant bass lines floating throughout the piece.

That subtle structure really has to be there in the rhythm section—I think Damon [Krukowski—also Yang's partner in book publishing company Exact Change] has a similar "melodic" approach to his drum kit. All the fancy guitar work and "hook-laden" melodies in the world can't make up for a bad rhythm section! The bass became truly interesting when I realized I could turn it into something more than just the background-filler for the guitar. Suddenly it was this aesthetic challenge: how can you make this song sound more beautiful?

♦ AJ: So why didn't you want to take further lessons from that teacher?

♦ NY: Because he was making fun of simplicity: "This is the simplest thing in the world, therefore it's not worthy. This is not *enough* for a bass line." But to me, it was the opposite. I felt he had handed me a *key*, a secret ability. I knew that I was able to figure out something like that. There was no way I was going to learn all the fancy techniques, or even necessarily which note was which on the bass, or any of the theory, or how to slap the strings with my thumb (which always sounded awful to me—and looked rather idiotic).

The ability to take the simplest technique and the simplest musical relationships was beautiful enough. Originally, I had dreaded the possibility of the teacher saying, "Oh, that's very difficult and takes *years* of practice to master. Maybe fifteen years from now you'll be able to play something like that." But the fact that he just laughed: "*That*? That guy's a genius, huh? He just plays a fifth and an octave." But I thought, "Yes, he *is* a genius."

♦ AJ: When was this?

♦ NY: Around 1987. I was in architecture school and feeling miserable. They expected you to give your entire life over to architecture, and work from 9 a.m. till 4 a.m. in the studio and have no other life. I've always hated being in situations where I feel like a number, one of five hundred people, a drone. And that's what architecture school was, especially the Harvard Graduate School of Design, where I was enrolled. I always felt, "I can't be doing this—what everyone else is doing." It made me feel utterly demoralized.

You should be able to have your differences. Male artists can express themselves without their "maleness" continually spotlighted; your feminine qualities are just one aspect of a greater complexity.

♦ AJ: What was the connection between Kendra Smith, Peter Hook, and those bass lessons?

♦ NY: I love this quote from Lucy Lippard, in 1967: "It is time that the word *intuitive* regain its dignity and rejoined the word *conceptual* as a necessary aesthetic ingredient." Thinking about the whole question of being a woman in rock, I note that I wasn't afraid to take the intuitive route, the one that says, "It's *fine* to just know how to play the octave and the fifth." I basically play just on the two top strings; after all, all the notes are there. You lose the big, booming, macho, thudding notes, but the notes you play are much clearer. Maybe it's just my natural temperament to take the intuitive route that said, "I want to create bass lines with my own ears; I don't want to *have to* master the technique that the world says you must in order to play something expressive and beautiful."

As for Kendra Smith: I considered her a fantastic singer and a fantastic musical presence. She wasn't some girl up front, doing a ditsy routine. But frankly, it wasn't her bass playing that was a motivation to me. I think it was just her *presence* in the band that made me think, "That looks like something interesting to do" and enabled me to project myself into that situation. Artistically, I projected myself more into what *men* bass players were doing. As of yet, there's no woman bass player that I sit around and listen to.

♦ **AJ: There's not much of an established history, *yet*. It's only in the most recent generation that women in any numbers have started to create distinct styles. So when did you think it was a possibility for you to be in a band?**

♦ NY: In college, Damon had been in a punk band called Speedy and the Castanets with our friends Dean and Marc (all four of us had gone to high school together). They were pretty bad, but they had soul. They were in a "battle of the bands" contest and came in last in all categories, including "looks"! I painted them a backdrop, and always sat and listened and drew while they rehearsed, but I never thought of participating musically. After listening to Peter Hook, I became very interested in the bass as an instrument, but I actually finally bought my bass for a stupid reason.

Damon and I had gone to graduate school, and Marc, who had become a born-again christian and stopped playing bass (his church told him, "You can't play the devil's music!"), became deprogrammed and started working for his father, who owns a gallery. He started hanging out with all these '80s artists. Damon and Dean were trying to put another band together, and were looking for another bass player. One

day Marc said that he had been hanging out with Julian Schnabel, and he had decided that he was going to start painting. He said he thought he had the theoretical side down; all that remained was the extra part: actually making the painting. I had been painting for years and I was so pissed off at that—it was so obnoxious. I said, "Then I'm going to play bass! If *he* can paint, *I'm* going to play bass!" Damon and Dean had been auditioning bass players for ages and hadn't found anyone, and I came in and announced, "I'm playing bass." Then I went out and bought a bass! Once I get interested in something, I can't help trying to make something meaningful of it— or I wouldn't be able to sustain it for long.

♦ **AJ: You read that quote of Lucy Lippard's about intuition, and that obviously had a lot to do with how you originally approached**

Magic Hour (clockwise from l.): Damon Krukowski, Kate Biggar, Naomi Yang and Wayne Rogers (1995).

Photo: David Corio

No Excess is Absurd, **Magic Hour** (1993).

music. **What made you start reading Lucy Lippard now?**

♦ N Y: I've been thinking: What does "art from a woman's point of view" mean? And so I've been going back and reading some "early" feminist writings to see what was happening in the '60s and '70s, when so much changed. Also, that era of feminism is so attacked now—I wanted to see what it was about. Until recently, I probably would have felt it had nothing to do with me. I always wanted to be taken very seriously on purely aesthetic terms in my painting and in my music: "I made this painting and I want you to judge it purely on its artistic merit"—which I think is still valid. I would have said there was no way you could say that my gender had anything to do with what I created, because I wasn't thinking about that when I worked.

♦ **AJ: You didn't feel any connection with your gender, in terms of experiences or role models?**

♦ N Y: Women who put *issues* in their art do so much more explicitly than I choose to—

♦ **AJ: —like Judy Chicago?**

♦ N Y: Right.

♦ **AJ: She was a product of a different world than the one we were privileged enough to grow up in. For centuries, a whole system literally—and legally—excluded women from the art world and art marketplace (and the broader social realm). So when women finally forced the art world to include them, they often make a very self-conscious entrance, which leads to a reputation for stultifyingly narrow "women's" art.**

♦ N Y: Exactly, and I always felt very distanced from that. But my painting work, right now, includes images of Victorian children who are somehow, strangely, all pre-adolescent little girls; my work has never contained anything representational before in this way. So I'm wondering, "What is this? It has to mean something." I'm not sure why that connection has led me back to '60s and '70s feminist writing. Lucy Lippard notes that in 1971 she used the pronoun "he" whenever she referred to "the artist," and she also referred to "the critic" as "he." But by 1975, her consciousness had changed, and she could look back on her writing in 1971 and ask herself, "Oh my god, how could I have *done* that?"

Your whole self goes into creating any work of art, including the fact that you're a woman in society. And because society's the way it is, there are certain pressures or events that have formed you—that's the political truth. But a woman artist doesn't necessarily have to paste her tampons on the wall; the outcome of her art does not have to be so explicit or simplistic.

♦ **AJ: Of course not. But why do you even consider that part of the equation?**

♦ N Y: I don't know. I always felt like that had to be the expression of *any* kind of feminism, or any kind of aspect of being a woman in art. Whenever critics discuss Georgia O'Keefe, they talk about the sexuality in her paintings. Maybe for her that wasn't inherently there, but that's the *only* way it gets read. This happens to men's art too: "The *phallic* nature of so-and-so's work . . . "

> **It's sad when women coming into [rock] behave just as stupidly as the men. I don't think that counts as any great achievement: a band of all women acting like idiots.**

♦ **AJ: Yes, but men's art has encompassed every style and hue. Since men basically comprised *all* of art that was allowed to be shown and represented until recently, there was a huge range of diversity within their work. I've been trying hard to get people to not back off from feminism and critiques of sexism, because the tragedy is that "women's art" was**

given such a narrowed scope by economics, society and very early feminist role models. In reaction, and because of their greater freedoms, female artists want to proclaim, "My art has nothing to do with gender!"—because that seems to echo male freedom.

♦ N Y: Women artists hadn't been allowed to say anything for so long, so maybe that's what came out first: the expression of their differences from maleness. Then the reaction sets in: "Wait a minute. I don't want to have to put myself in that *camp*, and limit myself to just talking about femaleness. I want to have access to all the issues that *men* have access to. I want to be able to list my equipment and have that be taken seriously." You should be able to have your differences; they're just part of you. Male artists can express themselves without their "maleness" being continually spotlighted; your feminine qualities are just *one* aspect of a greater complexity. You can escape a lot of influences, but there are certain influences you can't escape, such as: you happen to have been born a woman in 1964 in a certain country—all these facts affect your art and your choices. For years, I denied the feminine aspect of my art because I would think: "No, I don't want any of that; I just want what the men have."

But now I think that I *am* integrating the feminine aspect more, because I'm dealing with it in my painting. With music it's different, because it's more abstract; it's when you get to representation that you're revealing all this. Now, instead of having to deny my feminine side in order to incorporate any masculine advantage, liberties or privileges, I'm integrating the feminine and accepting it as being just as *normal* as anything else—as nothing you have to hide or apologize for when you're doing art.

That's what was so fantastic about meeting the artist Nancy Spero. It's not like I've been around so many artists, but I realized that I had never before met a successful woman artist. She's in her sixties and was a groundbreaker doing art with feminist topics since the '60s. She had enormous trouble for years, and still faces difficulty in terms of recognition. She always openly incorporated women's imagery, feminist imagery, and ancient symbolic issues in her art in a very unapologetic way. I think that's what my understanding of being a woman in an art field is coming to: that unapologetic-ness. You don't have to be ashamed of feminine aspects; you don't have to want to be exactly like the male artists and deny any issues you might have.

You don't have to start smoking cigars and take on all the rotten male attitudes.

I was talking to Damon about this and he said, "The thing is, you don't want to just say that you're going to incorporate the feminine and not critique the masculine stereotypes, because that's part of it too. You can't say, 'I'm going to embrace the feminine *and* I'm going to embrace the masculine stereotypes, attitudes and privileges—you still have to be able to critique the masculine and the feminine and *anything* dishonest, or anything involving people treating each other badly."

I was always able to reap the benefits of [earlier] feminists having done all the screaming, yelling and picketing. It was easy for me to say, "What's the problem? I'm equal to any guy here."

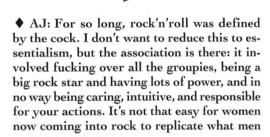

♦ AJ: For so long, rock'n'roll was defined by the cock. I don't want to reduce this to essentialism, but the association is there: it involved fucking over all the groupies, being a big rock star and having lots of power, and in no way being caring, intuitive, and responsible for your actions. It's not that easy for women now coming into rock to replicate what men

Will They Turn You On Or Will They Turn On You, Magic Hour (1995).

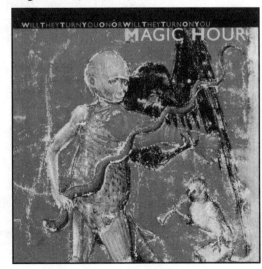

have always done. Both the masculine and the feminine have to be realigned.

♦ NY: It's sad when women coming into this want to behave just as stupidly as the men. I don't think that counts as any great achievement: a band of all women acting like idiots.

At the beginning of any movement, people are always really loud. I guess the suffrage movement of the '20s was just as strident. But nobody's complaining about the suffragettes!

♦ AJ: That kind of behavior just maintains the status quo. You can see this reflected in some movies where they invert the gender roles while still using the same power equations and a world that's based on the same

Photograph of Naomi done by her father, John Yang (1996).

hierarchies. They allow a few women to be seen as powerful protagonists—anti-heroines who act like assholes. *The Last Seduction* recycled the same old film-noir stereotypes, featuring a woman who's homicidal, psychopathic, tough, and fucks men casually—and this is touted as a feminist movie! As if this "heroine" has anything to do with liberation—

♦ NY: "Liberation" to behave as stupidly as men have.

♦ AJ: And this serves the power structure—

♦ NY: —and is an example of "ideal" behavior. Simone de Beauvoir makes the point that in this society, it's not these two equal poles; the man is the neutral, the normal, the what's-supposed-to-be, and the woman is the Other. I thought this was a great distinction: it's not two aspects of one unit; there's *one* unit, and there's the other thing as well that's the "not"—the not-male. So when you see *The Last Seduction*, the heroine is presented as "great—isn't she powerful?" This is how I think of Madonna: everyone applauds her for being this great feminist. Oh, wow, she can act like just as much of a jerk as any record company executive. Congratulations!

♦ AJ: To play devil's advocate in her defense, I think that, like a Trojan horse or a mutating virus, women or minorities coming into power *will* change things. And in a lot of ways she isn't like other male rock stars around her.

♦ NY: But is she really trying to change anything, or just promoting herself? Does she really care about changing the status quo?

♦ AJ: Madonna is a complicated topic. She's obviously part of the status quo and the corporate structure. At the same time, unlike many male rockers, she tries to tackle controversial subjects in an age of censorship personified by Jesse Helms: sexuality, homosexuality—she has many gay friends and co-workers—and the reality of AIDS. I don't see Billy Joel or Keith Richards taking on controversial causes like AIDS.

◆ NY: I feel cynical about Madonna; I think it's all self-promotion. That's pop culture, and I feel very alienated from that; it seems like something I have nothing to do with.

◆ AJ: Yes, on the other hand, I agree that she's part of a corporate pop structure that's about selling bland product and selling desire which is not about sex at all, even though she's promoting a semi-liberatory atmosphere. It's about selling records. Major record labels are—

◆ NY: —dens of evil. They're about mediocrity, not music.

Personally, a big change came when I was able to integrate music into my other art, and to feel like it was an artistic pursuit, because it had started out as a dare! It got more and more serious, but the whole time it felt *ironic*. Damon and I were supposed to be in Harvard graduate school, but instead we were playing in a band. So music never lost that irony for us, and any success we obtained always seemed so bizarre— it was hard to take our musical success seriously.

I was talking about incorporating the feminine side as another element in my work; not pretending it didn't exist. I think I have a compulsion to keep things separate in my life: this is this, and that is that. I have to strive toward incorporation and rectifying things. I remember feeling enormously depressed at times, even when Galaxie 500 was successful, because I felt I was being rewarded for doing the wrong thing. I was supposed to be painting and doing "real" art, and here I was in a band. I felt I was getting recognition for the wrong work.

> ## AJ: Major record labels are— NY: —dens of evil. They're about mediocrity, not music.

◆ AJ: Did you feel the band was just a product?

◆ NY: We never let it be that. Damon and I were always so scrupulous about keeping our artistic intentions very clear. We never let our own artistic direction be polluted by a record company, or outside pressures to do something to make ourselves more popular. It's not like I felt we had compromised, but I felt that what I

More Sad Hits, **Damon & Naomi (1992).**

was doing was just entertainment, a sort of "lower" form of art. Painting was what I was *really* supposed to be devoting my energy and my thinking to, and I wasn't doing that because I was on tour all the time.

After the band broke up and I thought we had retired, I went back to painting and running our press. I still felt the same way about music: I had taken it pretty far, because I had taken it seriously and I could learn from it and understand certain principles that were abstract. Thinking about music was not that dissimilar from thinking about painting or art. Now that I'm playing music again, I feel that how I think about the music is so much more integrated into the rest of my art—with both Magic Hour and our Damon & Naomi records.

◆ AJ: Magic Hour plays songs that are a half-hour each! [laughs]

◆ NY: Right; Magic Hour is not necessarily doing something that's easy to connect with. It will never be like my favorite pop song was to me growing up, but it's still of enormous interest in that there's something very *real* to it, especially playing live. It's an organic art form in motion. But of course we also have our Damon & Naomi soft-rock duo, where we're writing the songs. That satisfies our need to really wallow in our love of the melancholy.

◆ AJ: What is the definition of "feminine" which you're coming to grips with? Does it have to do with what you mentioned before about intuition?

◆ NY: I still don't know. I'm making these paintings and I wish I could figure it out. It's

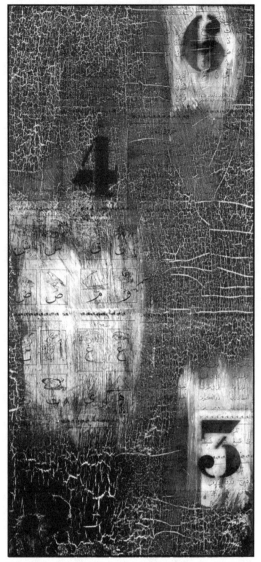

Work from Naomi's solo gallery show at the Gallery Mourlot in Boston (1994).

me to say, "What's the *problem*? I'm equal to any guy here. Why do you have to beat me over the head with that?" When I was in architecture school and postmodernism was the big craze, our teachers said: "You know what? Those old iconic spaces—the church, the schoolyard, the courtyard, the town green—are valid. They mean something to people; they carry a memory; they carry associations; they're powerful spaces." I thought, "Yeah—what's the problem? *Obviously* they're valid." But these teachers had, when they were young, rebelled against the canons of modernism, which said: "You got urban problems? We're going to knock down these old cities and put up cement slab buildings that go on for miles. You got problems in the streets? We'll cover everything with cement and build people shopping malls and everything will be fine."

My teachers' generation was fighting these battles: "No, no, no—don't tear down all the buildings! Leave us our town center, our main street, our little church that *looks* like a church." They were fighting an older generation that was saying, "There should be no ornament. Form follows function," and dictating very rigid rules. A lot of terrifying urban destruction came out of this, as well as some great architecture. Our teachers had been taught by teachers who said, "You're not allowed to put any ornament on your buildings. A school should look the same as a factory should look the same as a church should look the same as a housing project"—you know what those concrete bunkers look like.

Similarly, feminists had to say, "Wait a minute—this is completely unfair. We have something valid to say which might be different from what you men have to say."

In terms of changing the structure of the music industry, more women means just another type of music to exploit!

♦ **AJ: You're talking about the older generation of feminists?**

♦ NY: Right. They had to write books on women artists: "Isn't it amazing that women artists do exist?" They had to fight to even say this was possible. But now, I'm the next genera-

funny to be reading all this old-fashioned feminist writing and feel like it's *not* just people getting all worked up—they really do have something to say. For a long time I thought, "Feminists are so loud—what's their problem?"

♦ **AJ: That's what pop culture does: it takes the seeds of underground or grass-roots movements and creates manipulated propaganda to sell back to people as if it were the truth. And then people go, "Fuck that!" because at that point what they see *is* a cartoon.**

♦ NY: I grew up at a time when I was able to reap the benefits of feminists having done all the screaming, yelling and picketing. It was easy for

tion, and I *don't* have to fight that battle, so I can be like, "What's your problem? I'm equal to any man. I don't have to say 'I'm a woman' in my art to make it valid. In fact, I'm not going to mention that at all, because I see *you* mentioning it a lot, and to me there are *other* issues." To the earlier generation, it had been unspoken, so it was the *main* issue.

Now I'm finding that I have to be able to go back and incorporate it, and be more mature about it—not just say, "Oh, that's not at all of interest to me."

♦ AJ: The right wing used that sense of discomfort in their backlash, charging that feminists were ugly, hag-like shrewish women who weren't real women, and they burned bras!—some cartoon image of Andrea Dworkin who hates sex, or the image of a Judy Chicago-like artist who just does endless vaginal paintings. This younger generation was raised with the fruits that the earlier generation had won: not being in immediate slavery—

♦ NY: —just a subtle one.

♦ AJ: But the problem is: because it's not immediately tangible to certain white middle-class women's lives, they forget that *every* woman still has to contend with inequities and restrictions of freedom such as rape, and that women *still* make less than 70 cents on the dollar. There are still an enormous number of issues that get swept under the rug while some women are proclaiming, "Oh, we've won our battles!"—even as the right wing is trying to dismantle abortion rights.

On the other hand, there is also progress. A lot of the men you choose to surround yourself with treat you as an equal. So the next step is not about polarization between men and women, but about the enormous problems men and women have to work on *together*. For the past several hundred years we've been on a very masculine trajectory, but now women can, with this hard-won freedom, work with men. It's no longer "women against men," which then leads to more polarization, which happens with all initial identity-politics groupings.

♦ NY: I guess at first women had to do that, because there was no way to say it subtly.

♦ AJ: People forget, but only thirty years ago women couldn't get credit! It's only been thirty years—talk to any older woman.

♦ NY: I remember looking, as a child, at my mother's charge cards, and they all said "Mrs. John Yang." My mother never called herself that, so I asked her, "Why don't they have *your*

name on them?" She said, "Well, that's how Bloomingdale's gives it to you."

At the beginning of any movement, people are always really loud. I guess the suffrage movement of the '20s was just as strident. But nobody's complaining about the suffragettes!

♦ AJ: I think it's very important to always remember the feedback loop of the media. A lot of the figures who are held up by media are self-destructive cartoons. Who is allowed to get famous? Katie Roiphe, Camille Paglia. In music, think of all the influences you love whom nobody's heard of. Yet when you survey music history, you know that a power structure dictated who got famous—

♦ NY: It's not purely the power structure, it's also the temperament of the times—

Anthropologists say that art happens when you finally have the leisure to stop toiling all day in your fields. Art isn't done by people who are worried about survival.

♦ AJ: But let's just consider the music industry. You know, because you complain about it—who gets the major-label contracts? Who gets the promotion? It's usually people like Barry Manilow, Billy Joel or Weezer who fit a risk-free mediocrity. If you look back in history, there's a long uncelebrated parade of musicians and bands who never get talked about—

♦ NY: —at least not on a mass media level. But that's true for every subject. There are about five people in every field who the general public knows: the five most famous ice-skaters, runners, bands or feminists. In any topic of interest, you can do just a little bit of investigation and find an entire world of people who are not the ones getting famous, but who are toiling away doing interesting work. Obviously there are people who are household names; everybody knows Picasso, but not many people outside of the art world know Tàpies. So the cartoon feminists who everybody knows are on the top, and down below are a lot of women writing and living the life.

♦ AJ: You've seen a wave of women coming

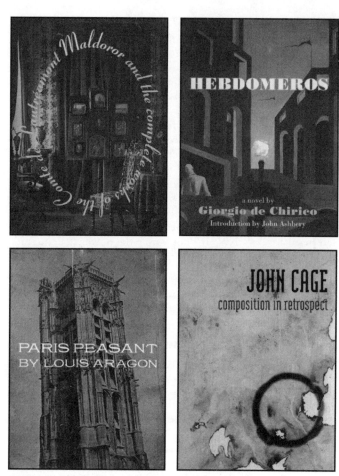

Bookjackets from Exact Change Press (designs by Naomi).

into rock music; have you observed any changes?

♦ NY: The more women get involved, the more it seems like this influx of new sensibilities might change the traditional thrust of rock. Other girls will see them and become interested, and think *they* might have a place in that field as well. If there are fewer women involved, it takes more of a leap of faith and confidence to put yourself in that situation. *I* didn't mind, because I was always happy to do something I wasn't *supposed* to be doing. Maybe now I wouldn't join a band; maybe I'd think, "That's what all the women are doing—I have to find something else!"

In terms of changing the structure of the music industry, more women means just another type of music to exploit! Maybe musically, women's bands will say something interesting, but that happens all the time anyway; every generation thinks of something that's

their own to say. But the music industry structure is just this huge, scary monster that stomps on everything, so I don't think women are going to make a difference—though I do wonder.

♦ AJ: A lot of younger women are saying, "Gender? There's no issue of gender!" What's your view?

♦ NY: If we had talked about this a year ago, I would've said, "I don't even know why I'm talking to you about this; the fact that you're making this an issue is bringing me backwards. I am so free and equal that I can't say this is an issue for me." So it's weird to find myself reading early feminist writing and using Victorian girls in my painting and thinking, "Maybe this *is* an issue. Maybe it's not a liability or something I have to apologize for."

♦ AJ: I always think that younger generations have many things to teach an older generation. Older generations always have such blind arrogance, and dismiss younger generations, entirely forgetting their *own* youth and how they rejected *their* parents. They say, "These kids of today, these slackers, are so stupid and lazy." Whereas I see things in the younger generation that are really healthy.

Alternative music is a white upper/middle-class preoccupation; it has nothing to do with minority culture.

♦ NY: In a way it's not necessary anymore to write a book about women in rock, because these women are *not* the women who fought the feminist battles; they're much younger. You don't *need* to be saying, "Hey, women can play rock music"—because they already are!

I have a book from the '50s, *The Artist in His*

Studio, [laughs] and the cover has about fifty names on it. And the only woman artist included is Corita—who's a nun!—she's the *only one* the writer could find to include. And this is from the late '50s. At some point, people had to write books that said, "Hello! Jackie Winsor exists! Agnes Martin exists! Nancy Spero exists! And they're all doing art!" But I bet that women in rock now feel like they don't need a spokesperson to say that they exist at all, and that they can fully exist in the real world of ambition and careers.

That's why I was saying that you should include equipment lists, because the next step is absolutely equal treatment, not just acknowledging women's presence. If you do a book on male rock guitarists, you list their equipment. If it's of interest to men, then it's only fair to give women the same consideration. I'm a musician, I'm doing something musical, and *that's* what's of interest to me.

◆ **AJ: It's going to take a little while before the female Miles Davises and Jimi Hendrixes show up—virtuosi who influence entire generations of other musicians. That comes from having a pool of thousands of male musicians. With any art form, there is a mentorship, and since women have only recently come into rock music en masse, it's just a matter of time.**

But I still think there's an enormous amount of sexism in the music industry. Let's face it: who are the executives? Who are the A&R scouts? Who holds most of the power? Men.

◆ **N Y: I wonder if female bands get smaller advances than male bands?**

◆ **AJ: I wouldn't be surprised. Also, tokenism is just as insulting—*so what* if you herald a few women bands? "The Year of Women in Rock"—how cute!**

◆ N Y: Yes—"That was the year that women were in rock!" [laughs] "Soon we'll be back to normal, folks—don't worry!"

I'm sure every single woman you've interviewed has experienced sexism. But when you asked me about being in this book, I thought, "I feel ambivalent about this project; should I be doing this? Do I have anything to say? Is this even an issue for me?" But my attributes as a woman, and my place in society because of that, have clearly affected and formed me; I can't say they're completely irrelevant.

◆ **AJ: To completely dismiss gender as a factor is untenable. At the same time, there has to be acknowledgment of the enormous gains that feminists and other progressives have**

made; it *is* a very different world. It's unbelievable how different the depictions of women in the media have become in just the past five years. On the TV show "The X-Files," a woman FBI agent no longer has to be a sexpot to be the star; ironically, it's the male character who's been sexualized. Five years ago we would have had—

◆ N Y: Loni Anderson!

I want my work to be liked, but so much that is venerated is really bad. It makes me distrust popularity.

◆ **AJ: And the Loni Andersons are still with us; both types of women are still here. But at the same time there has been an enormous leap, so you can't keep flogging the same wound. There now are far more varied options, psychologically, for women. Certain roads have been paved. At this point it's normal to have a woman drummer or a woman guitarist in a rock band. It's no longer a joke or a big deal.**

◆ N Y: That used to be much rarer. When we were in Galaxie 500, we once played a show where we got to choose the rest of the bill. We chose Crystalized Movements (Kate Biggar and Wayne Rogers' old band) and Antietam, whose guitarist is Tara Key. They were just bands that we happened to like, but when we got to the show that night, we realized, "Hey, all three bands have these very strong women—" it was amazing. Tara Key gets down on her knees while she plays her heart out on guitar in a completely unselfconscious way. At that time, it was more unusual than it is now.

◆ **AJ: Within a certain avant-garde population, there's now a lot more freedom for women your age. But many women my age are struggling with this issue involving male peers, because the women of my generation are so much more advanced than the men (who weren't raised in a post-feminist environment like your peers)—there's a lag time in consciousness. I get patronized all the time, even though I'm successful.**

Also, it's hard to find women of my age who

aren't male-identified.

♦ NY: What is a male-identified woman like?

♦ AJ: A woman who is very competitive with other women, who doesn't view other women as particularly interesting. They internalize the dominant society's view of women as inferior. For instance, if a man walks into the room—all her energy goes toward that man.

♦ NY: Lucy Lippard writes about that. She says that five years before writing her book, she would only talk to male artists. Their wives would be in the kitchen, and she felt she had to ignore them in order to reinforce her role as a journalist, and to maintain the respect she was trying to earn in this role and in the structure of the relationship with the man being interviewed. Then her consciousness was raised, because she realized the wife was in the kitchen making this amazing painting! Yet at the time, she had to ignore the wife in order to maintain the place that she had clawed her way to.

♦ AJ: I don't think women musicians in rock bands have been given too many chances to talk much about the *art* of making music. You're exploring the intricacies of the actual music and developing your unique aesthetic, and this is quite new. You might take this for granted, but for a woman to be talking unselfconsciously about the musical process is a freedom that's only recently been claimed.

♦ NY: Because before you had to be talking just about the fact that you were there at all! *Politically*, the discussion is now about the music itself. When you told me the title was *Angry Women In Rock*, I immediately thought, "But I'm not angry!"

♦ AJ: I know. But no man ever backs away from the word "angry." If you say "Angry Young Men," they go, "All right! I'm cool!" No male goes, "Oh no, I'm not angry. I swear to god I'm a nice guy!"

Naomi for Galaxie 500 in Manchester, U.K. (1989).

Photo: Ian Tilton

♦ NY: That's a great point. I did an interview with a journalist on the subject of "Minorities in Alternative Rock." He was desperately trying to get me to say, "Yes, it was so much harder for me because my father is Chinese and my mother is Jewish and I was trying to be an alternative rocker." But I said, "No! It was absolutely never an issue that I was Chinese-Jewish in a band! But the fact that I'm a *woman* was an issue." I immediately thought, "I can't believe I just said that! Why did I say that?" The journalist was terribly disappointed.

He was asking why there aren't more minorities in alternative rock. I said, "It's purely a class thing, and this type of music is a luxury. It's not going to support your family. If your parents worked hard as immigrants, being in a band isn't going to pull you up; it's not going to be the responsible thing to do. The children of first-generation immigrants all go to law school or medical school."

Alternative music is a white upper/middle-class preoccupation; it has nothing to do with minority culture. My family's been here long enough so that I can be doing this, and being a member of a minority is not an issue. If I had grown up in a household that spoke Chinese or Yiddish, I'm sure it would be a much bigger deal that I was playing in a rock band rather than going to law school or getting a job on Wall Street.

This journalist asked, "Was it very difficult for you? Did your parents get upset?" I replied, "No, my parents are *artists*! It was not a big deal to them. They don't want to have day jobs either!" But had the situation involved my father and grandfather, it would have been a much bigger deal. For him to be in a band and have that unsure lifestyle—that would be an issue.

> I was always happy to do something I wasn't supposed to be doing. Maybe now I wouldn't join a band; "That's what all the women are doing— I have to find something else."

Anthropologists say that art happens when you finally have the leisure to stop toiling all day in your fields. Then you can worry about decorating your hatchet or whatever. Art isn't done by people who are worried about survival. Although most musicians are struggling, and many have horrible day jobs at the same time—but that's not what anthropologists meant.

◆ AJ: Your band, Magic Hour, has a "luxury" aesthetic—

◆ NY: It's totally useless!

◆ AJ: It's not feeding the "product" machinery—

◆ NY: And if it were feeding the product machinery, would it still be worthwhile? Does that automatically disqualify it? I feel ambivalent about this; I want my work to be liked, but so much that is venerated is really bad. It makes me distrust popularity. I'm wondering if people are saying this to you now: "My ambition is to be musically meaningful to people, but it doesn't have to be very many people." I have a feeling that this attitude isn't around anymore.

When we started playing, we were on bills with Evan Dando, Juliana Hatfield and other people whom we didn't exactly admire, musically. It's just so weird that they revealed their pure ambition. I mean—ambition's fine, but you can't forget that the point to begin with was making music.

◆ AJ: But ambition to just be part of the media machinery is so boring.

◆ NY: Which would *you* prefer: being rich or famous?

◆ AJ: Rich, of course. I've seen in other people how devastating fame can be. We all want to be loved, and if fame gave you that, it would be great. But I've seen how much hate and envy and competition fame inspires.

◆ NY: So if you were a musician, you'd like to be successful purely for the money?

◆ AJ: A music career? Totally for power and money. [laughs] The books I create are different; I try to keep them unsullied. The only thing about fame that's appealing is revenge against your enemies! That can fuel a lot of hard work. ◆ ◆ ◆

discography

◆ DAMON & NAOMI ◆
The Wondrous World of Damon & Naomi (1995)
More Sad Hits (1992)
Pierre Etoile, EP (1991)

◆ MAGIC HOUR ◆
Secession '96 (1996)
Will They Turn You On or Will They Turn On You (1995)
I Had a Thought, 7-inch (1995)
After Tomorrow, EP (1994)
No Excess is Absurd (1993)
Heads Down, 7-inch (1993)

◆ GALAXIE 500 ◆
This is Our Music (1990)
Fourth of July, EP (1990)
On Fire (1989)
Blue Thunder, EP (1989)
Today (1988)
Tugboat, 7-inch (1988)

equipment list

Cherry red 1968 Gibson EB-2DC bass (semi-hollow-bodied bass, shaped like a 335 Gibson guitar), Trace Eliot AH200 amp head and a single 15" EV speaker for playing live, old Ampeg B-18 Portaflex amp for recording, Boss Super-Overdrive pedal (used rarely)

Kendra Smith

Kendra Smith played bass in the early-'80s neo-psychedelic band the Dream Syndicate. She departed the band just before they signed to a major label. Her next band was Opal, and Smith also left that band; it turned into Mazzy Star. Since the late '80s Smith has lived self-sufficiently in rural Northern California, emerging only to record an EP with friends in 1993 and a solo album in 1995.

♦ **ANDREA JUNO: You've moved to the country; what made you decide to leave L.A.?**
♦ KENDRA SMITH: I wanted to be away from the urban environment. I see that it has a certain purpose; I see that a lot of things come together in the city. But I'm a pretty sensitive person, and I needed to get where there would be a little less stimuli. I realized that I knew almost nothing except music and typing, and I really wanted to get some hands-on experience: find out about nature, and find out what was actually required to survive. Necessity versus created desires.

I've noticed that some physical activities can trigger things in your brain that might not get triggered otherwise—you can do certain kinds of work to meditate. But our whole culture is oriented towards the avoidance of physical labor. We've been given this myth: "We're going to relieve you of your work, and create more leisure for you." I think there's a conspiracy behind that. I wanted to find out for myself what we were being deprived of.

♦ **AJ: You don't have electricity, right?**
♦ KS: Right. I'm not netted in by the magnetic field that's created by electricity—which I suspect is bad for the human organism. I have solar panels, so I do have a little bit of direct DC power. The first time I went back to Los Angeles after I moved up here, I stayed with some friends and was trying to sleep in their apartment—I could hear the whole building humming. If you extrapolate, I could feel the whole

city humming. And when you drive into the city and see the whole thing lit up...I know from study and experience that AC electricity can cause a lot of illness, or mutation. I would prefer self-induced mutations to those imposed by the environment.

♦ **AJ: I love technology and computers. But the electromagnetic fields of these electrical appliances that we're surrounded by are so enervating. And these innovations have caused the exact opposite of leisure. Not only are we working more, but we're also being sapped of vital energy and connection with ourselves and others.**
♦ KS: This is true, but can't be reduced to the notion that all technology is evil, and Nature all beneficent. Some friends of mine who were working up here lived near a beautiful big creek, and the whole area was surrounded by redwoods. From appearances, it looked like it would be a very healthful area, but they found that they were getting ill. Every time another friend of mine went there, he got really bad headaches. They found out that there were actually water lines under the earth that created the same energy patterns as bad electromagnetic lines. A Buddhist monk came to check out the property; and his reaction was, "If you were ill, this would be a good place to come and heal. But if you are healthy, it will make you sick."

The redwoods *are* that way. You aren't supposed to live under the redwoods; the Indians wouldn't live under them. I think something's too strong there.

♦ **AJ: Also, homes in the redwoods are so damp that mold grows everywhere.**

♦ KS: Yeah. It's dinosaur country. [laughs]

♦ **AJ: How long have you lived in the country?**

♦ KS: In '88 I started coming up on and off, and I've been here solidly since 1989. It's been a while.

♦ **AJ: What are the changes you see in yourself and in your art? Has it been a matter of detoxing?**

♦ KS: The changes have come through detoxing. They were apparent in myself, first, because I had decided to not think about art for a while; I could do that by not having to interact with other people and other influences. I became more focused, and aware of what my own thought patterns were and what was driving me. I gained so much immediate knowledge 6 *cycles*—natural cycles. I realized that humans have natural cycles, too—and that our whole society is built up on ignoring them.

Photo: A. Phillip Uberman

You can see evidence of that in how we're made to work on the "work schedule." The way I work now, there's a right time for everything. In winter, you feel a natural need for hibernation—especially if you don't have artificial light. When you plant something, you could plant it at one time, and it won't do anything; at another time, it'll completely shoot out of the ground. There's always a right time. I started to apply that more to my own organization and how I approached work.

Work should be something you love; some-thing that you don't want to avoid. Part of that has to do, I think, with having the right time and space to do it in. It's important to recognize that you're not always putting out, either—sometimes you're drawing in. It was educational to see that everything was alive, and everything *did* have a consciousness. When I started to put that together with my ideas about music, I felt as if I had a giant opportunity to prove a number of things that had not been articulated—like my feeling that music, since it's funneled through an industry, isn't usually done for integral reasons. I wanted to see whether music was just an

Photo: Rita Gonzalez

The Guild of the Temporal Adventurers (1992).

arbitrary interest for me, or whether it was something I was really drawn to.

♦ **AJ: The worst thing that happened to the arts was when glamour and money got involved. A hundred years ago, art was something you had to absolutely, deeply feel and get out — like the birth of a child. An unstoppable force.**

♦ KS: It wasn't seen as a career either.

♦ **AJ: Exactly. Often artists were vilified; you had to be dedicated. The material rewards were slim.**

♦ KS: Now it's considered a career option. A lot of people are drawn to it thinking, "I want a job where I can drink beer and be glamorous." Like you say, the glamorization of our arts culture is a really weird thing. Another thing I really didn't dig was seeing a lot of people becoming even more infantile with success and recognition, instead of more responsible. It was actually encouraged.

♦ **AJ: That goes back to your point about cycles. Our culture is so linear and frozen in isolated moments; we aren't encouraged to grow and have cycles. If you're an artist, once you have a hit record, or hit *something*, you're then encouraged to keep replicating it — you aren't encouraged to change or mature. You're**

certainly not encouraged to draw in and be reflective.

♦ KS: That's only for the ease of the industry, to make their jobs easier. That's also where the idea of putting out a record every year or every two years comes from. Some people say that I'm not very prolific — but at the same time, *I'd* say that some people are recording when they shouldn't! It's not right to put art on that kind of schedule. Obviously, you churn out a lot at certain points, and at others you don't. Must it all be publicly consumed in order to call oneself an "artist"?

♦ **AJ: It's courageous — I think it should be normal, but our society considers it courageous — that you walked away from some bands that could have become much bigger.**

♦ KS: Well, that probably has a lot to do with my nature. Even though I couldn't have said so at the time, I could always see where things were going. I could already see that being-stuck-in-time syndrome you described. I shied away from big contracts; if I don't feel like I could respect such an arrangement, then I shouldn't get into it. I had so much change in my younger days that it seems like I've lived many lives — and I don't mind starting over. I really kind of get off on it. I think some people's cycles are larger, and some are smaller, as if a spiral were loosely or more tightly wound.

I complete phases pretty quickly, and I couldn't see myself doing one thing for my entire life. But change or no change, it doesn't matter. The inward direction can be unaffected. At each time of change I was a little nervous, and didn't know what was ahead, but I could already see that there wasn't enough room for growth. And since growth and a certain amount of personal freedom are more important things to me, I had to respond to those needs. Everyone says, "Well, you could get in that situation [with a big recording contract] and then you would have more freedom to do what you want," but I've never seen that proved. I've always been leery of those things.

♦ **AJ: This is so healthy to hear — especially your response to those carrots of fame and media — particularly because you're in the music industry, where so often artists are in the situation of being served. Money's always nice, because it affords a certain freedom. But you don't just get the money. You also get this huge grab bag of negative things, as well.**

♦ KS: There's a certain enslavement involved. If you get into one of those arrangements, it's because of certain desires you have, and the expectation that you'd be more financially comfortable. But I've seen that financial freedom comes more from simply not *believing* that you have to spend money on certain things. Not buying into consumer myths gives you a lot more financial freedom than becoming wealthy—which usually binds you in some other way.

♦ **AJ: And once you have money, you have the fear of loss, too.**

♦ KS: Exactly. You have to have a guard dog.

I realized that humans have natural cycles, too—and that our whole society is built up on ignoring them.

♦ **AJ: You're pretty self-sufficient, right?**

♦ KS: I try to be. I grow about fifty percent of my food; the power of the food and the pleasure and solitude of the work keep me away from doctors. I cut fallen trees for heat and mill them for lumber. All with help, barter and exchange with a few friends and neighbors. Around my property, I dress for work in clothes that are... [clears throat] pretty amusing. I'd wear them when I go out, except they're so filthy. I love to get dirty as much as costuming up. It's liberating if you don't have to go out and *purchase* entertainment, since you're entertained by your own world. In my work here, I've spent a long time just being amused, because it was new and I was learning. The creatures were entertaining, and so was looking at all the different plants. Chickens replaced television. [laughs] You realize you've lost it when you're standing around talking to people at a party and end up talking about chickens. You know you've gone country.

I've never been a really big telephone or TV person. I've always been a big reader. So I get to read a lot, more than I ever did before. And as opposed to university assignments, I can study what I want.

♦ **AJ: What are some of the things you study?**

♦ KS: Have you heard of the *Journal of Borderland Research*? It's a magazine that's been around since the '40s. They've been doing work, for a

long time, on where occult and science meet. Their contributors write about suppressed science: free energy, Nikola Tesla, Wilhelm Reich, weather and earth changes. There are also articles about the planets, metals, agriculture and anthroposophy (from Rudolf Steiner).

At present I'm reading *Agriculture for Tomorrow*, by Eugene and Lily Kolisko, two of Steiner's pupils. Lily continued working long after her partner/husband's death. Basically they tested various organic and inorganic substances with litmus paper dipped in gold or silver nitrate. The images clearly show patterns of life force in subtle variations of color, and they change under different conditions (during planetary alignments, at night or day, underground or at solstice). Stag's urine creates a fiery image of stag's horns. The picture of honey is full of tendrillic branches; saccharine is flat, with no movement. The patterns can reveal disorder or disease. This book could provoke investigation in many different fields.

♦ **AJ: Have you applied these ideas?**

♦ KS: As far as agriculture goes, I'm interested in biodynamics, which come out of Steiner's studies. They're connected somewhat to organics, but go further. They use these medicines for the earth that are prepared astrologically. They do things like packing steer manure into a cow horn, and then bury it at a certain time of the moon's cycle. When you bring it back up, you've got this really potent stuff that you stir in water to create a homeopathic medicine, which you spray on the earth. They've got many different applications, ones that use different planetary forces to build either the body of the plant, the soil or the roots.

I've applied the biodynamics ideas to my garden, and I've definitely seen results. Again, it's one step further than organics. When they first started doing it in the early 1900s, they could already see that the soil was losing its vitality. The idea is that you don't just feed plants nutrients, you feed the life and spirit of the earth, plants and people. Steiner's anthroposophy is called "spiritual science" and covers so much I hate to categorize it. I've also been studying homeopathy, but I only use it on myself and my animals.

♦ **AJ: Do you actually make homeopathic treatments?**

♦ KS: No, I don't make the remedies. I could; I make my own herbs for just herbal cures. But the remedies are so inexpensive and so accessible. To have every remedy I wanted, I'd have to grow a lot of plants—and crush some bees, too.

♦ **AJ: Crush bees?**

**Biodynamic leek from
Kendra's garden (1993).**

♦ KS: Yeah, there are remedies, one called "Apis," made from bee venom or crushed bee. You use that for bee stings. Homeopathy is really amazing medicine.

♦ **AJ: I believe in it. I take a few things, and they're absolutely perfect.**

♦ KS: It's pretty phenomenal. A lot of people that say it's power of suggestion, but I've used it on animals. A cat of mine was having paralysis, and I gave him a remedy; he's fine now. Animals don't know what you're doing, so it *can't* be power of suggestion.

♦ **AJ: That's what the scientific belief system always says when it comes up against alternative medicine. I got turned on to homeopathic treatments because of a doctor who's an actual M.D., and who also teaches acupuncture to other doctors. He gave me remedies, which he sometimes makes himself. He also cured me of asthma. It took about nine months.**

♦ KS: That's fast.

♦ **AJ: It was getting pretty bad. I haven't had it since. I'll go every once in a while for an acupuncture tune-up.**

♦ KS: That's great. My homeopathist is also an M.D. He was ready to be a traditional doctor, and then he discovered homeopathy—it's great to have someone who knows both. Homeopathy works on such a deep level that it's really good for mental problems as well. Supposedly the story is that the AMA formed, in part, because homeopathy was so prevalent. At about the time of the Civil War, it was the main medicine. So the AMA formed to drive homeopathic practitioners out, and called them quacks.

♦ **AJ: That makes sense. The rise of the Royal Academy of Sciences, in the 16th and 17th centuries, was largely to consolidate the power base of male doctors, because at that point the** midwives and women healers were really strong. Of course, this was in conjunction with the genocide of all those women through the witch trials.

♦ KS: From what I understand, the midwives then were really adept, and capable of performing Caesareans. But then the doctors invented the forceps, and said they had the magical tool—

♦ **AJ: —which was brutal.**

♦ KS: Right. As far as my other work, I've also been studying music in a more spiritual context. I've been thinking more and more that the original functions of music in society were either magical—for healing, driving out demons, or calling in beneficial forces—or they were social and communal. Everyone could participate in these unglamorized musical events; you didn't have to be a virtuoso, and anybody could at least bang on a drum. There were songs for communal experiences: working songs, coffee-grinding songs, shepherding songs. They are passed on in the sharing of work or community. The magical lineage is more protected, but has also to do with the well-being of the community.

♦ **AJ: That's far from the role music has in society today. How have you tried to apply those magical functions to the music you're making now?**

♦ KS: Well, I first got opened up to this when I met the two other members of The Guild of Temporal Adventurers. I was just about to leave the band Opal. I had a lot of undefined dissatisfaction with what I was doing, and where I was going.

You realize you've lost it when you're standing around talking to people at a party and end up talking about chickens. You know you've gone country.

♦ **AJ: What year is this?**

♦ KS: This is about '87. Jonah Corey and A. Phillip Uberman, who were from the Venice, California area, were doing ambient music at that time, under the name Ejaculating Buddhas. I heard some of their tapes and talked to them a bit. They were the first people I had met who were really not into the rock scene—and not just saying it. They were solely devotees of Shiva and the Goddess; their whole orientation was that music is an amazing psychic tool. You can do all these things with it: you can make someone's heart beat faster, you can make them weep, you can cause great change—you can do a lot of things. That is what music's real function is. It's a very high art.

It was the first time I talked to anybody who identified with music apart from its being a product—or some sort of personal trip. They triggered me to start in a new direction, and I ended up recording with them later. *The Guild of Temporal Adventurers* is the EP we did around '91.

I was up here at that time, and I was still "not doing music." But a young woman named Sunshine got ahold of me, due to great persistence. She put out 10-inch vinyl on her small label, Fiasco, and she said, "I'd really like to put out a record by you." I had just been thinking that maybe I'd like to record again, so I got together with Jonah Corey and Alex Uberman in L.A. and said, "If we like her and we can do this as a cooperative venture, we'll do it." The EP was recorded in two weeks. Our intent was to do devotional music in the form of pop songs. Jonah Corey, besides being into this ambient stuff, is one of the greatest pop writers and singers I've ever heard. He's totally unknown, but he had a few songs that I thought were beautiful, and that I really wanted to record ("Wheel of the Law," "Stars Are In Your Eyes," "Waiting In the Rain").

We recorded these three and wrote three more, adding several vibrational interludes. The whole point was to be really single-minded, to think of the record not for what it was going to get us, or do for us—but as strictly devotional music. Obviously they had worked like that before, but it was my first experience with just trying to go beyond our individual purposes, get out of the way of the music and let it really *do itself*. We were united and had one thought in mind.

It's probably the purest of all the recordings I've done; I was really happy with it. *Five Ways* has more different energies in it, but *The Guild of Temporal Adventurers* is really, sonically, just one flow. That was very encouraging to me. It also provoked other people to say, "Oh, she's recording again. Let's see if she wants to do another record." But the whole point of it was just to send a certain kind of energy out into the world.

As far as I'm concerned, most of the music being made now is what you could call *black magic*. You're sending out this energy, and what's it really about? Even some of the most so-called altruistic lyrics—what lies behind them? It's scary. I'm not attacking bands that are dealing aggro energy; some of the most supposedly soothing music is demonic in this way. Musically and lyrically it seems to reinforce the most restrictive patterns.

♦ **AJ: I know what you're talking about: the deeper energy level that exists beneath the surface. TV, for example, is so enervating that it doesn't even matter what's on it. Another thing that comes to mind is how a CD's digital music is recorded and played. It operates on the same principle as computer language—either a byte is on or off. Digital music sharpens and flattens the sonic wave; it doesn't have the same pulsations as an old '78, which has a psychic, almost physical resonance that's much deeper—more like live music. The subtle effect this has on a person isn't consciously registered—like how homeopathy works.**

> **Music is an amazing psychic tool. You can make someone's heart beat faster, you can make them weep, you can cause great change. That is music's real function. It's a very high art.**

♦ KS: That's the effect of analog versus digital, definitely. Sound waves go in a curve—a natural, undulating curve—and analog reproduces that. But digital breaks it up into little bits. Although you don't hear it, here's silence between each bit; so you're not really getting a true sound wave. CDs actually are inferior, sonically, to anything that's analog, even though all the sound buffs really like them.

♦ **AJ: Along the same lines, I think most top 40 music leaves you feeling hungry—like junk food or saccharine. Obviously you've thought about this a lot more. Can you give an example of what you mean when you say something like "demonic music"?**

♦ KS: Well, a lot of the effect of art reflects the intent of the artist's will, right? So, what is the artist's intention when he or she is actually doing the piece? I think that has a lot to do with it.

For example, on the *Guild* record we put our intentions in a certain place. But when you put

The Guild of Temporal Adventurers (1992).

your average band in the studio, what's in the back of their minds? They're usually doing it to glorify themselves in a certain way, or to make money, get more beer, get chicks—whatever. There are all these things they want to get out of it. And *that's* what gets transmitted—no matter what the words are saying, that's what the actual transmission is.

◆ **AJ: You're talking about the magical use of will, which is important. What kind of preparation or intentions did you have for doing that record?**

◆ KS: With the Guild, we're basically like a musical lodge, and we're just starting to put that out more in the physical world. Between just the three of us, we don't have to do much externally; we don't light candles or anything. But I think that whatever it takes to help you focus your energy is good. I can't even really say what we did; it's more in what we *didn't* do. And that's usually how it is. Even in more secular forms of music, I still think that the idea is to get my preconceptions out of the way and let the music come *through* me—how can I possibly decide in advance what the results should be? Usually in the random factor, in accidents, you find the things that really work.

The Guild record was done so quickly and so simply. We used the harmonium, guitars, percussion and the pump organ. The idea was to use what was at hand. You don't say, "Oh, we need a hot lead guitarist—we've got to go out and get somebody." There's three of us here, and we know what we're about. Certain musicians appeared fortuitously, and each of their contri-

butions was perfect.

◆ **AJ: Are you three also on *Five Ways of Disappearing*?**

◆ KS: Uberman is. He co-wrote a lot of the songs with me, and helped me produce it. I work with him a lot because I really don't have to explain a thing to him. I mean, he explained a lot to me, when we first began to work together, and answered a lot of my questions. The two of them are the only people I presently feel comfortable working with. Uberman is closer to where I live.

◆ **AJ: Do they live in your area?**

◆ KS: No, Jonah Corey lives in Los Angeles. He's still doing other stuff. The Guild will probably record again, and we're thinking of possibly doing some performances—but not the nightclub type. They would be more involved with theater, more symbolic kinds of musical experience. I'm not that hot about the nightclub environment; it's just another repetitive social gathering.

I've had a lot of different thoughts about performing. I love to perform. I'm not shy in that way, but—as you've probably heard—I just don't like going on the road and doing something over and over. I think it's really unmusical. It doesn't address cycles, as we said.

Most of the music being made now is what you could call *black magic*. Even some of the most so-called altruistic lyrics—what lies behind them? It's scary.

It's weird. I'm pretty out of touch with certain things, by choice, and it doesn't seem to matter; normally I feel like a freak, but that's okay. And that's why even up here, I don't collaborate with too many musicians—because I just end up finding that there's a huge barrier. You could say, "Oh, we like the same bands." But then you find out you like them for totally different reasons. Or you have a totally different understanding of what's happening.

◆ **AJ: You're concentrating on making the sacred in everyday life.**

◆ KS: That's what I hope to do. As far as I see,

there shouldn't be a division. We put the so-called sacred in buildings: in temples and churches. But it should be *integrated*, part of your everyday life. There shouldn't be this dressed-up-for-Sunday type of experience, where it's really alien. I was raised in your basic Protestant scene, and I got turned off to it when I was pretty young, just knowing that it couldn't possibly be correct. If you have any spiritual inclinations at all, you can immediately see the problems with it.

◆ **AJ: It's so life-denying. It's like a death cult.**

◆ KS: It's even death-denying. I think fear of death and suppression of the idea of death lies behind most of the damage in our culture, most of the illness and crime.

◆ **AJ: And the correlates of death are sex, and the earth, and women. It's hard to find the words to talk about this critically—it sounds so hokey.**

◆ KS: Especially in the "New Age" when all these things have been cornified.

◆ **AJ: It would be wonderful to wrest those great concepts away from the New Age people—it's sad.**

◆ KS: I know.

◆ **AJ: As an astrologer, and having an Eastern and Western magical background, I'm going back to look at a lot of myths and how they've changed as the patriarchy and christianity took over older religions, mostly for purely economic concerns.**

◆ KS: We have no proper mythology anymore. In a way, that's something else that's happened to rock'n'roll. We've mythologized a lot of the musicians; but that's only for a lack of—

◆ **AJ: —I always feel that the arts especially hold purpose in such a dysfunctional, bankrupt society. They've played a sort of shamanistic role, and now even *that's* been taken away by all this glamour and money.**

◆ KS: [affected voice] "My previous incarnation was Cleopatra." [laughs]

◆ **AJ: It's like, "Get in line."**

◆ KS: Shaman for bucks. [laughs]

◆ **AJ: Well, even the pure sense of what shamanism is—channeling energy for the community—has been lost, because now the word "shaman" is weakened from overuse.**

◆ KS: It's been watered down.

◆ **AJ: We no longer have a language that hasn't been appropriated by products and crass consumerism.**

◆ KS: Well, the Guild members really showed me these things that are beyond words—im-

mediately. I feel really lucky that I made contact with them. It's funny that they're men, too, because they're the best goddess-worshipper sect I've ever met. I'm really glad to see it, especially with the male sex as a whole getting dissed these days—and not unjustly! Seeing that there *are* some living examples of guys who know what's going on really inspired me a lot. Especially in rock'n'roll, because it's so guy-damaged; everything is viewed from a guy's perspective.

> We put the "sacred" in temples and churches. But it should be *integrated*, part of your everyday life.

Rock'n'roll—if you believe it—came from Moroccan music, or from different African sources and traditions that were shamanistic; it's interesting to see what it's come through, and where it's gone. I'm really interested in Moroccan joujouka music; I've been studying Middle Eastern music and dance for about four years now. It was a boost for me to start hearing rhythms and other time signatures besides 4/4, to see what could be done with really potent music—and to see how it affected *me*.

When I started Middle Eastern dance, it was the music that drew me in. It can lift me up or make me weep. The physical movements of the dance—which really do open up all your chakras as well as make your body incredibly strong—have such a strong effect on the psyche.

Dance is probably the whole reason that rock'n'roll exists. And dance is a cool thing, but I wish we would reserve it for proper festival occasions, instead of it being this kind of random event. A whole bunch of people dancing at once sends out powerful energy, and is a recharge to be done at specific times and with purpose. It has a real function. But now it's become more narcissistic.

◆ **AJ: You've got a really good tap on that aspect of the music scene. Producing this book was the first time I've really had to deal with the "music industry," and I've never found anything more evil and life-denying in my entire life than the major labels and a lot of the phony narrow-minded people working in them.**

◆ KS: Some of it's that blatant; some of it's more

Photo from The Dream Syndicate's album *The Day of Wine and Roses* (1982).

subtle. For all my opinions, I'm not terribly well-informed—and not sure I need to know more of the details. I'm still, right now, testing the water. But what I could see right away is that it would be very uncomfortable having someone else represent me and my interests. Especially the larger entities; with a small label like 4AD, if there's a difference or a misunderstanding, I can correct it pretty easily. I spoke to a couple of larger labels before I signed to 4AD for this one record, and I just couldn't bring myself to do it. From what I know, half the people are suits. They don't know anything about music—they're just number crunchers.

I had an argument with one woman who was a critic and a big fan. She said our culture idolizes musicians. I said, no, it actually degrades them. It's kind of a toss-up however you look at it. People do idolize musicians, but only for the sheer pleasure of feeling like they have the power to create them and bring them down.

♦ **AJ: The monetary side of things in the music industry is shocking. The actual profit margins are just astronomical.**

♦ KS: But not much of it's going to the artist. It's going to all the various jobs that are created supposedly *for* the artist. The legal fees, the accounting, the caterers—when you look around, it just goes on and on. It disturbs me because a lot of it is just for the sake of promotion. It's a bunch of garbage, a bunch of doodads. To my mind, if you have to promote something, then it's not *worth* anything.

No one has to sell me on what I eat. Like those coupons for stuff that you can get a deal on at the market—I never buy any of that. It's not even real food. I'm always suspicious. The more something is hyped, the more I think it must *need* to be hyped. In the music industry, all of the artists are equally promoted. It takes a lot of muscle for an artist to try and get anything done differently. It's a profoundly unfair financial arrangement, especially considering what you said about mark-up. CDs cost so much more than LPs or cassettes, when they actually cost less to manufacture.

♦ **AJ: Most musicians have no idea of the business side of things—especially when they first start out... How did you come to think of yourself as a musician?**

♦ KS: When I was a kid, I studied a couple of instruments and I sang in church. But I didn't like *studying* music. I didn't want to learn to read it, because I liked to play by ear. So, I always kind of goofed away from music. Although it was the '70s, I was never one of those girls who sang along to Fleetwood Mac albums or anything. [laughs] I never thought that I would be a musician because I studied literature, and I was more oriented towards writing. I was going to U.C. Davis, and working at the radio station there. Because punk rock made music more accessible and fun again, I started to play a little bit.

> **To my mind, if you have to promote something, it's not worth anything. No one has to sell me on what I *eat*.**

♦ **AJ: With punk, you didn't have to know how to play. You didn't have to have formal training.**

♦ KS: Right. With all the emphasis on people being technical virtuosos, they can still leave you, as you said, hungry. Technical virtuosity is obviously not the only key. That realization opened the door for me, and I saw and heard different women performing who inspired me. I saw Tina Weymouth on the first Talking Heads tour, and I heard Patti Smith, Nico and Lydia Lunch's stuff. There weren't too many women around then, but when I heard male rock'n'roll I just made the translation in my head. I never worried, "Oh, because

I'm not a guy I can't do that." I just picked what I liked.

♦ **AJ: What did you play?**

♦ KS: I started playing bass. And that's what I played in the Dream Syndicate. I had done a little bit of singing with a really bad garage band when I was about 17 or 18. I didn't like being the girl singer in a band where I wasn't even writing the music or anything. That really bugged me.

♦ **AJ: You felt you were just an appendage?**

♦ KS: Yeah. But when I discovered the bass, I felt an immediate sense of power. I had never thought the bass was a great instrument, but once I started

Kendra Smith performing live, 1987.

playing I realized it was, because it combines percussion and melody. It's very much a *root* instrument in rock'n'roll music. The minute I picked up the bass I was very excited. And then the Dream Syndicate came together pretty naturally without much planning.

♦ **AJ: Was this your band?**

♦ KS: Steve Wynn was the main songwriter in the group. We were pretty good friends. He had another friend, Karl Precoda, who played with a real fluid feedback style. We were playing together with no big plans. Then we picked up Dennis Duck from the Human Hands. I had been a big fan of that band—I used to go see Monitor, another one of my favorite groups, and the Human Hands—so Dennis was like a rock god to me. The minute he started playing with us, it was like, "Oh, we're a real band." [laughs]

The Dream Syndicate was fun because the bass and drums did this really simple—but repetitive and powerful—locomotive drone; I could really trance out. That was very satisfying. Part of the formula was that we felt free to extend the songs as long as we wanted to in improvisation. There was darkness and humor;

if people wanted them short and fast, we played them long and slow. We just had fun. We didn't belong to any hip scene. It was that classic outsider thing that always makes a rock band work. [laughs]

♦ **AJ: You never felt inhibited, playing the bass, because you were a woman?**

♦ KS: No, not all. Maybe it was just the context I was in at the time, with friends. I've never let being a woman stop me from pursuit of an interest, intellectual or physical. I was even once a slalom racer.

♦ **AJ: You mean skiing.**

♦ KS: Yeah. When I was young I lived in Germany, and I used to race. I'm kind of a thrill-seeker buried underneath this contained surface. I rode horses for a long time. I've done a lot of different things. So, when I was growing up— even though I was in a family with classic mother-father roles—my parents always encouraged me to try things and not feel hung up about being a girl. Obviously, all around me I saw examples of girls getting hung up about it. But I always hoped to try and break that from myself.

I never felt that there was no entree. I felt

that it was something to really think about—for example, I was aware that I didn't want to use the sex-kitten role to my personal benefit.

◆ **AJ: And when you did Opal, wasn't it more under your control?**

◆ **KS:** I had more opportunities with Opal. I was learning to play guitar, and writing my first songs. I'd say the band was equally shared between David Roback and myself. At that time he knew more about production than I did; I was still learning. But it was always just the two of us as the songwriters. I wrote "Fell From the Sun," which was my first song. At that time I was writing songs without really knowing what I was doing on guitar at all. I avoided taking lessons till much later because I didn't want to be shaped in any way, and I would only study under people I fully liked and respected.

Opal was more of a studio thing; we did a lot of recording. We didn't play live too much. For me, it was a chance to develop and learn more about what I could do as a songwriter, and learn more about singing.

◆ **AJ: That sounds like a good situation. How did your departures from these bands occur?**

◆ **KS:** What happened both times is that the bands wanted to get in a more stable—i.e., label—situation. When each of them got to that point, I had to ask myself if I really wanted to get locked in. With the Dream Syndicate the question was, "Do I really want to be a bass player?" I could see it wouldn't leave me time for much else—especially since I wasn't even a songwriter, which is where you might actually get some income. I could also see that things would be

required of me that I didn't really want to do—when you're on tour, you're basically a lackey out there promoting—and there wouldn't be much room left for growth.

With Opal it was the same thing. They really wanted to sign to a label. And even though I had been enjoying the opportunity to learn about recording and my own singing and writing—I could just tell that it wasn't going to work as a long-term collaboration. I was incredibly dissatisfied.

If anybody knew me during that period, I was nasty. I was unhappy. Part of that was being in Los Angeles. For my first few years there, I thought L.A. was fascinating, because it was my first city. I went and saw bands, and I was working straight jobs and going to school, running around. But after a few years, I was longing for something that wasn't covered in concrete. I think I was near my Saturn return actually. All this stuff was changing, and I hadn't quite put it into words. As I said, when I met the Guild, I realized that for me music was this really heavy thing. It made me really miserable to compromise it. And it was making everyone else around me miserable.

Right now being way out is being "way in." There's almost no shock value left.

I'm not saying there's no point in compromise ever. But in terms of the big plan in your life, it's not good to put yourself in a place where there's no *happy* compromise. If things can't be worked out, I always feel like I'm doing myself and everybody else a favor if I bolt. [laughs]

◆ **AJ: Even though the bohemianism of the past was full of flaws, at least there was an acknowledgment—in the '50s and '60s—of the**

need to walk away from the encrustations of power and money. The notion, in the '60s, of leaving your high-stress job and "finding yourself" was romantic and naive, but now it seems almost refreshing. Today, all the trappings of faux transgression, from the beatniks to the hippies, are championed *without* that critique of the power structure, of why you're working a meaningless, empty job just for money.

♦ KS: Yeah. Right now, being "way out" is being way in. There's almost no shock value left. Anything "shocking" is done more to participate in the game than to reject it.

♦ AJ: Right. There's no analysis that looks beyond those externals; it's not about shock at all.

♦ KS: In the Hindu Cycles, there's the Golden Age, this and that. But the value for this time is supposed to be an Era Preceding Dissolution of the Universe—a very, very poor time.

♦ AJ: I thought we were supposedly in the Kala Uga already.

♦ KS: I think we are. Supposedly it's the worst of all times, but it's also the time when you can advance more quickly—because everything's just out there, out in the open.

♦ AJ: A favorite author of mine, Demetra George, did a lot of work on cycles. She's the feminist astrologer who made asteroids popular, and she wrote this book I really love: *The Mysteries of the Dark Moon.* According to her we're at the end of a 40,000 year cycle; the Ugas match this. She also did a lot of work that looks at how mythical goddesses—such as the Greek ones—changed over the years as a consequence of changes in white male rule.

♦ KS: It's really hard to talk about this, because I've seen so much goddess worship that's so goofy.

♦ AJ: I know, and it's embarrassing. It makes it difficult to talk about significant parts of our history that are reflections of the shifts of gender power.

♦ KS: But this is relevant; we're talking now about doing art, or how you live your life. A lot of it has to do with being *submissive* to your life, and accepting everything that comes at you. That's like accepting the goddess, because the world that manifests around you is She. To make discriminations against this or that—to bemoan a certain curse in your life—is a ridiculous approach.

♦ AJ: You mean having sort of polarized hatred.

♦ KS: Saying, "I want only good to happen to me." Or even to think that good exists without

also that which appears to you to be bad. That's the whole kind of Christian Science thing our society wants—all flowery and light. We don't want to acknowledge the dark, yet we're continually going that way. It gives the other side a power that's beyond our control to process.

♦ AJ: And there's this heavy "victim" kind of polarity, like the dogma: "All men are *evil!*"

♦ KS: It's all attachment. Either it goes through you, or you attach to one side or the other side. People are encouraged to think in polarities—but most of your dilemmas can be solved by *not* thinking in polarities.

♦ AJ: By going into that middle borderland where your brain fuses a little. ♦ ♦ ♦

◊iscography

♦ **THE DREAM SYNDICATE** ♦
The Day Before Wine and Roses, live at KPFK, 9/5/82 (1995)
Tell Me When It's Over, EP (1983)
The Days of Wine and Roses (1982)
The Dream Syndicate, EP (1982)

♦ **OPAL** ♦
Early Recordings (1989)
Happy Nightmare Baby (1987)
Northern Line, 12-inch (1986)

♦ **SOLO/OTHER PROJECTS** ♦
Five Ways of Disappearing (1995)
Savage Republic: Recordings from Live Performances 1981-83, compilation (1995)
The Guild of Temporal Adventurers (1992)
Fell From the Sun, EP with David Roback and Keith Mitchell (1984)
Fell From the Sun b/w All Souls, 7-inch with Clay Allison (1984)
Rainy Day, compilation (1984)

equipment list

1940s Estey field organ (portable, foot-pumped), 1963 Gibson Acoustic guitar, 1972 Fender, Telecaster guitar, 1970s Ibanez Iceman, Harmonium (hand-pumped, made in India), 1980s Aria ¾-scale bass, Fender bass, Guild bass, darbukka (clay hand drum), miscellaneous percussive instruments, tube amps, pre-digital synthesizers

Phranc

Phranc began her career in the late '70s with the San Francisco punk bands Nervous Gender and Catholic Discipline (featured in the punk documentary *The Decline of Western Civilization* by Penelope Spheeris). In 1981 she went solo, evolving into "The All-American Jewish Lesbian Folksinger," and in 1992 she introduced Hot August Phranc, a sometime alter-ego and spoof of Neil Diamond.

♦ **ANDREA JUNO: You've started recording again, after taking a break for a few years. What's it like to go from a major label to an independent?**

♦ P: It's good to be back in the indie world again. I'm absolutely thrilled to be on a label where they really want me. They're real people. The office of this record company [Kill Rock Stars] looks like an apartment I lived in when I was in Nervous Gender. It makes me want to make records again.

It seems like music right now is a lot the way it was 15 years ago. There's a whole new scene starting up that reminds me of how it used to be.

♦ **AJ: What strikes you as particularly reminiscent of those days?**

♦ P: I went up to Portland to do a show with Team Dresch. It was a "Free to Fight" show: all about self-defense for women. Jody [Bleyle] set it up. There were about fifteen performers, almost all of them women. Everybody played for about fifteen minutes. Team Dresch, Bikini Kill, Rebecca from the Spinanes, Lois, Misery, 151, and I all played. The audience was packed, and it was a really young crowd: 13-to-20 years old, bright and shining eyes, mostly young women. Part of the show was a thirty-minute self-defense demonstration. It was just so amazing, with role playing and everything—and you could've heard a pin drop. The audience was completely responsive. I went out and saw everybody do a little bit; I'd go walk around and then stand in the back of the room behind the sound gal.

It was so exciting to me. I thought, "This is *it*. Where have I been? Where am I trying to go? This is where I belong, this is where I fit in. This is rock 'n' roll, and it's *real*." There was so much energy in the room. There was nothing fake, nothing businesslike about it at all. It was a completely impassioned evening. And *that* is the essence of it all to me: you don't have to know how to play your instrument perfectly, or have this amazing skill—you just have to have this passion that makes you want to sing or play music so much, you're willing to do anything to get that chance.

I hadn't felt that great in 10 years, because I'd stopped going out. It just wasn't fun to go out any more. But now there's a new energy. The true indie labels have a completely hands-on approach, which means that the bands are better off; they're really controlling their own destiny—at least while they're deciding *if* they want to be on a major label, *what* they want to give up, whether they do or don't want to compromise. They can make that decision in their own good time, and not just eat the first piece of candy that somebody gives them.

♦ **AJ: I've had a similar reaction. I also had dropped out of the music scene for a good decade. But I just recently went to Portland, Olympia, and Seattle—and it was so refreshing! I thought, like you did, "God, these kids just seem to be healthier."**

Phranc at age 2.

♦ P: The audience was *conscious* when I played. That's what was so wild. I looked out and the little eyes were firing back at me. I'm sure there were some people in the audience who were wasted, but it was nothing like it was back then: that *glaze*. I was just like, "My God, they're alive, and—I think they're absorbing this!" It was really cool.

I went to a party in Portland at somebody's house. Everybody paid a couple bucks, they had some beer, and a bunch of bands played in the basement. And everything—the furniture, everybody's outfits, and the music—was just like San Francisco in 1976. I thought, "This is so cool! I had that shirt! We had that couch!" And then down in the basement, a band was playing, and it reminded me of when the Avengers played our loft party. I thought, "Hmm, this is strange. Could I possibly be old enough to be remembering another time?" I have all these memories, so I guess that does mean I'm older, but… it's wild to me.

♦ **AJ: I have mixed memories; as fun, and wonderful, and exciting as that original scene was, I grew very critical of it, starting around '81 and '82. I was particularly critical of the kind of energy that I felt. There was a sense of male dominance—an unbalanced energy that**

Phranc with Nervous Gender (circa 1977).

I didn't like at all.

♦ P: That *was* always there. Somebody asked me the other day, "Who else was out then?" And, "What was the sexual politics back then?" I said that it had been very sexually ambiguous. There was a lot going on, but it was all in the closet, and nobody was out. Everybody was pretty wasted on drugs and alcohol.

I went solo in '81, which is when I became more political and more outspoken. That's when I started organizing the folk shows, a handful of which I produced at the Whiskey that same year.

♦ **AJ: So that's when you left punk behind, and got into folk?**

♦ P: Right. But I was a folkie even before the punk rock stuff. I grew up on folk music, and that was the music I really liked: acoustic music. I didn't get into rock'n'roll until Patti Smith. So, for me, it was just a return to what I knew and loved. I wasn't doing something that was new for me. And the same audience that had been there for my punk bands stayed with me. I was still playing with the Dead Kennedys and the Circle Jerks. But I was playing acoustic guitar instead of screaming with Nervous Gender, playing the synthesizer.

A lot of that change was because of politics. It started because I wrote this song, "Take Off Your Swastika," and I wanted people to actually *hear* the words. It had become so politically frustrating within that scene.

♦ **AJ: You were in Nervous Gender—**

♦ P: Gerardo Velasquez was the genius behind Nervous Gender; he died about two years ago. It was just me and these three boys, and we'd go on stage with a quart bottle each of our favorite liquor, just get pounded, and play these pretty contrived shows, because—especially for Gerardo and Edward—their idols were the Screamers.

I screamed all these really wonderful misogynist songs at the top of my lungs. [laughs] I can remember standing on stage, screaming—"Jesus was a cocksucking Jew from Galilee, Jesus was just like me, a homosexual nymphomaniac, a homosexual nymphomaniac"—insane stuff!

♦ **AJ: You, singing misogynistic lyrics?**

♦ P: It kind of challenged *everything*. I came out at 17, moved out of my parents' house, and dove headfirst into the lesbian separatist community. For about three years, before I moved to San Francisco, I was very involved with that community. I went to the feminist studio workshop. And I worked on a couple of political magazines: *Lesbian Tide*, *Sister Newspaper*. I was just this junior dyke.

Phranc in 1976: "I dropped out of high school to be a lesbian."

◆ **AJ: Does that mean you were listening to "womyn's music," with a "y"?**

◆ P: Oh, yeah. I was listening to womyn's music. Margie Adam and Cris Williamson; stuff like that.

◆ **AJ: Holly Near?**

◆ P: No, I never really listened to Holly Near. But I do have to say I was a Margie Adam and Cris Williamson fan.

◆ **AJ: [laughs]**

I'm not the junior dyke anymore; I'm becoming more like the *sea hag*.

◆ P: I used to play my guitar in the bathroom of the women's building, and I used to play at Dorothy Baker's coffeehouse at the women's building, when it was at the Chouinard Art Building before it moved to Spring Street. I was politically active in the West L.A. lesbian scene, and there was a very separate distinction at that time between the East Side and the West Side. Within the scene, that tension was a big class issue.

◆ **AJ: What were the distinctions between the East Side and West Side lesbian scenes?**

◆ P: The "women's building," on the East Side, was all arty; the "women's center" and the magazines, on the West Side, were more political. There wasn't a very strong meld at the time; there was some dissension in the community. But I was a part of both of these worlds. And I was the baby, which is what's so weird now: I'm not the junior dyke anymore, I'm becoming more like the *sea hag*. I don't really mind, it's just different.

◆ **AJ: What led you to San Francisco?**

◆ P: I finished with the lesbian community in L.A. I thought, "I've done everything I can do here, so I'm moving to San Francisco, the *mecca* for lesbians." So I moved up to San Francisco, and I tell you, there wasn't one lesbian that was friendly to me in San Francisco; it was just not a very warm scene. I went to visit a friend who lived on Howard, and when I walked in the door I met Judy, who was in the Blowdryers—she lived there too. A neighbor of hers, Joanne, had just come over. She was dressed from head to toe in leather, and had this huge white dog; she lived across the street in this loft and they needed

Photo: Melanie Nissen

Phranc in Nervous Gender with Gerardo Velasquez.

a roommate. There I am, this tough little separatist junior dyke, whose idol is Jill Johnston. I hadn't really spoken to a man in three or four years. I was only listening to Alix Dobkin, and then I came to San Francisco, and saw this vision in leather. I was just like, "Wow!" I went over and looked at this place, and then I went back to L.A. and packed up all my stuff and moved to San Francisco.

◆ **AJ: What year is this?**
◆ P: This is like '76. I moved in with quite an eclectic bunch. There was Scott, who was a gay actor; Joanne, who was into leather and fire-

Part of a flyer from Phranc's first lesbian concert, held at the L.A. Women's Saloon (1977).

phranc

men; Amy, who was a B-movie queen; Brian, who was a speed dealer; and me—the man-hater from L.A! It was really wild for me: a completely new world. It was the first time that I ever felt I had a peer group, because I had never been around anyone my own age; everyone in the lesbian community was at least 10 years older than me. But everyone I met in San Francisco was like 18, 19, 20.

There was no work in San Francisco. I had been trained as an offset printer, and a silkscreen printer, but the only work I could get was nude modeling at the Art Institute, which is where all our friends went to school. Scott and I would wake up really early in the morning and we'd sneak into Joanne's room, where she had a big bag of leather toys, and we'd take stuff from her bag and go to the Art Institute. We'd pull out all this junk to model with for the art classes. That was really a fun time. I never made very much money out there, but I made a lot of really good friends.

◆ **AJ: What was the philosophical leap required to go to punk from "gentle" womyn's music? Wasn't that the exact opposite of the violent imagery that punks had? To me, they're just like night and day.**

◆ P: They *were* night and day. It all happened as a surprise to me. The punk rockers I met were a lot friendlier than any of the lesbians I met in San Francisco at the time. Nobody really welcomed me with open arms. In my mind I had this vision that there were going to be lots of lovable lesbians in San Francisco, it was going to be this mecca; instead, it was really disappointing. The only people that were nice to me were the punk rockers. I hung out for a few minutes and I thought, "Whoa, I'm kind of more like *you* than I am like *them*, and . . . this is pretty cool!"

There was something really exciting about all the big leaps that I made. It was just like, "Okay. When you leave home at 17 you just pack all your stuff in your box and you go—you're out of there." That's the way I did it. My parents went away for Thanksgiving, and I couldn't be a dyke in their house, so I moved. But you're wondering how I went from being with the dykes in L.A. to being with the punk rockers in San Francisco...

◆ **AJ: Well, some people have philosophical things that lead up to it. Like dissatisfaction—**
◆ P: I was *dissatisfied*, that's why I left L.A. I was frustrated in the women's community, because we spent a lot of time sitting in a circle, talking. Very little of what we talked about ever

got outside the brick walls. I was taught, as a junior dyke, that the personal is political, and I still believe that today; I take my politics with me wherever I go. So, then, "why aren't we taking them outside?" That's still my belief today: that I'm accountable for myself, and I exhibit the politics that I believe in. It's a challenge from time to time, but part of the reason I left and moved to San Francisco was that I just felt that I

Phranc (1980).

needed to take what I'd learned, and go *outside*. I guess you could call that philosophical.

♦ **AJ: How was the political manifested in punk rock back then; how did you do this in Nervous Gender?**

♦ P: All I wanted to do was be in a band. I wasn't playing my acoustic guitar at the time. I had gotten an electric guitar, and I would go to all the shows—I tried to dress real cool—and stand there and look cool enough for someone to ask me to be in a band. One day Edward from Nervous Gender walked up to me and asked me to be in his band, 'cause I looked cool enough! That's how it happened.

I surf almost every day, 'cause when I'm in the water, nothing can make me feel bad.

♦ **AJ: [laughs] Describe your outfits!**

♦ P: [laughs] My hair was—I didn't have a flat-top then, but it was short, kind of like a young Bobby Kennedy look; that's kind of what I sported at the time. My hair was always pretty short from the time I was 17 on. I would wear a skinny little suit look: a jacket, a tie, a tab-collared shirt, black pants and boy scout shoes that

I got at the Salvation Army. I still have them: original punk rock clothes. I would get all dressed up, and I probably looked like a 12-year-old boy. And one night at Baces Hall on Vermont—I think it was an Avengers/Mutants show—Edward came up to me and asked me if I would be in his band. And that's how I got to be in Nervous Gender.

Now, where were my ethics at that time? I just wanted to be in a band! Was I trying to be politically correct? No. Did it push every button that said "*aaannnnnh!*"? Yes. Every misogynist thing they did was like, "*aaannnnnh!*" But I thought, "I'm going to let this slide right now, 'cause I really want to be in a band!" Can I say I'm proud about that now? So what. I just went for it. I just went for the gusto, and I had a great time with those guys, and I learned a lot. And we were really, really different from each other. But we were the same, in a way—we wanted a lot of the same things. And, from the shows, I got to know Claude from Slash [Records]—

♦ **AJ: Claude Bessy?**

♦ P: Yeah. I haven't talked to him in a couple years. And Craig Lee, who I was really close to, and Alice from the Bags—

♦ **AJ: Craig Lee worked at Slash too, right?**

♦ P: Yeah. He was the guitarist for the Bags. And I *worshipped* Alice Bag. I just would stand at the base of the stage when Alice was on; I was madly in love with her. She was such an inspiration. I just aspired to be that *cool*.

Photo: Edward C. Colver

Phranc playing at Vinyl Fetish (1981).

Gradually I became friends with everybody. We went out every night, and everybody I knew was in a band; we hung out, and partied, and people played, and we talked, and made fliers, and saw each other at the xerox shop—just like it is now! There are a lot of the same hands-on elements. There were the little labels, like Danger House, and other people who were into putting out records themselves, and figuring out all that stuff. Slash at that time was a magazine, and not even a record label. There were lots of parties on the roof at Slash, and I met Craig there, and got close to him. All of the bands were going on at the same time, so I was in Nervous Gender at the same time I was in Catholic Discipline—although Catholic Discipline only lasted a couple

months, because everybody was in another band, or two, or three. And I went solo soon after that. That's how it all evolved for me.

♦ **AJ: Even though there were things I was critical of, there really were so many exciting things going on, and it was so much fun; there was a kind of healthy politic that sought to just tweak every button. In a certain sense you do need to zig, and zag—**

♦ P: Right.

♦ **AJ: It's good to let go and give in to the total opposite. I wouldn't do, let's say, *The Industrial Culture Handbook* again, but I'm glad I did it then (in '82).**

♦ P: Well, Nervous Gender worshipped Throbbing Gristle. So we're talking about the same period of time. Genesis P-Orridge was Gerardo's idol. I was just like, *"Hello?"* I was not really into anything that they were into. Would I do a Nervous Gender again right now? Probably not! I did what I did, and I did it then. It was very much a boys' club. A lot of it was just shock value: "This is going to give that old lady on the street a heart attack, and it's going to piss my parents off."

The one thing about punk rock that I identified with was the anger. Going to high school in the '70s—which I hated and never graduated from—was such a disappointing experience, because I wanted to have these radical teenage years, and everyone was completely apathetic. No one wanted to do anything. No one wanted to get into trouble.

♦ **AJ: This was in the early '70s?**

♦ P: Yeah. I would have graduated in, I think, '75.

♦ **AJ: You dropped out of high school?**

"Take off your Swastika"

Take off your swastika
It's making me angry
Take off your swastika
It really nauseates me
You say "Phranc it's just a symbol
It's just an emblem, it's just a
  righteous decoration"
Well it means a little more to me

'Cuz fascism isn't anarchy
Fascism isn't anarchy
Fascism is not anarchy

Sure I've got Jewish damage
What the hell do you expect
Thirteen years of Hebrew school
And all the slides that they'd project

Of all the burning bodies
Of all the concentration camps

All the concerts that I go to
And on many TV shows
I see little Hitlers
Everywhere I go

Take off your swastika
It's making me angry
Take off your swastika
It really nauseates me
You say "Phranc it's just
  a symbol
It's just an emblem, it's just a
  righteous decoration"
Well it means a little more to me

'Cuz I'm a Jewish lesbian
You see fascism isn't anarchy

Fascism isn't anarchy
Fascism isn't anarchy
Fascism isn't anarchy

And if it was you in those ovens
You wouldn't think it was so cool
If it was you in those ovens you
  wouldn't
think it was so cool
If it was you in those ovens you
  wouldn't think
It was so god damned cool

® 1981 Folkswim Music (BMI)

◆ P: Yeah. To be a lesbian.

I carried my giant, hardback copy of *Lesbian Nation* around school for as long as I could, and then I just had to leave. I've got pictures of myself walking around high school with long hair, mirrored sunglasses, a tie, walking shorts, boots, and my copy of *Lesbian Nation*—with Jill Johnston on the cover, my *idol*! That's why I wear my boots today.

So the anger of punk rockers was what I identified with. They were my own age, they were mad at a lot of the stuff I was mad at—they wanted to raise some hell, and shoot their mouths off, and just be who they were. The first time I walked into a lesbian drop-in rap, I felt like, "I can fit in here. I am not alone." And that was the way I felt about punk rock. For the first time in my life, I fit in with people my own age. That had never happened before, and this happened when I was like, 19.

I can remember standing on stage with Nervous Gender, screaming—"Jesus was a cocksucking Jew from Galilee, Jesus was just like me, a homosexual nymphomaniac"— insane stuff!

I identified with the anger, but on the other hand there was all this nasty crap that I didn't like at all. Swastikas were the big deal for me. Being pretty strongly identified as a Jew, and being pretty strongly identified as a dyke, I really didn't feel that anybody else was being too responsible for what they were doing, and it made me really angry. That song "Take Off Your Swastika" is a really literal song that I wrote at that time, and it was a major turning point in my career. That's when I really decided to go solo, because I just felt like you couldn't hear the words in punk rock.

◆ AJ: Right.

◆ P: So much of the stuff was so brilliant, the lyrics were so great—but you could barely hear them. I still love that Avengers 7-inch, *I Believe In Me, I Make My Dreams Real*; it's just so cool. When I put out the single "Bulldagger Swagger" last summer, I wanted it to be clear red vinyl,

Postcard from the Morrissey tour (l. to r.): Phranc, Morrissey, Gary Day and Alain Whyte (1991).

just like the Avengers single. And it is! There are things that are really symbolic in my life; I don't like them to change. I like things to stay the same, and if I can recreate them, or keep them somehow, it's meaningful to me.

So that's how I came to do what I do now; you can hear the words. I talk about some stuff that people don't want to listen to, and I believe that it's really important for me to be out as a lesbian—on stage, in my life, every day. In the market, in the bank, wherever I go, all the time, that's my job. That's the feeling I got when I was in the back of that room in Portland. I thought, "I have to keep doing my job. My job isn't over, there's nobody that really does my job but me. *I* do my job. I go on stage, and I'm out, and I talk about—

◆ AJ: It seems that playing that show in Portland was so important for you. Why hadn't you played in so long?

◆ P: For the past four years I really took a break from my music. I had a lot of stuff happen in my life…

In '91, when I was on Island Records, I was out touring with Morrissey. Those were the biggest places that I've ever played. When I had played with the Smiths, earlier, I played some big places; but when I played with him in '91, I played the L.A. Forum—

Ticket for Vinyl Fetish concert. The tickets cost $2.00 at the door and $1.50 in advance (1981).

HOT AUGUST PHRANC: "Neil Diamond kind of gave me my career back."

♦ **AJ: Wow.**

♦ P: There were houses of ten and twenty thousand people where it was just me with my acoustic guitar. That was pretty wild to me. My record *Positively Phranc* had come out and things were starting to move up to one more level, and then I think it was about six days before I was supposed to play Madison Square Garden—

♦ **AJ: Ha!**

♦ P: My brother was murdered.

♦ **AJ: Oh.**

♦ P: And once again, my life changed.

♦ **AJ: How did that happen?**

♦ P: He lived in San Diego; he owned a little gun shop. These gangbangers—Crips—straight out of Compton [in L.A.], came and shot him and his dog; they stole all his guns. I was on a radio station in Boston, live. We were spinning the record, and the phone rang in the back room, and they said it was for me. I went back in the back room and took the call, and my father told

me my brother had been murdered. In two hours I was on the plane home.

♦ **AJ: So you didn't go to Madison Square Garden?**

♦ P: No. I came off that tour. And the record label dropped me because... for whatever reasons, in show business the show must go on; it has very little to do with real life. I couldn't work. I needed to be at home; I had to take care of all my brother's stuff. He was my only sibling, and I felt like I needed to be with my family. Morrissey kept calling to get me back on the tour, and I would say, "I can't come yet," and then in September (this had happened July 2nd) I went back to do some dates with him in London. And on stage, it went fine; but it felt completely hollow. I didn't know whether I wanted to be on stage again. I didn't know what I wanted to do, so I went home and...went surfing a lot.

♦ **AJ: You surf?**

♦ P: I surf almost every day, 'cause when I'm in the water, nothing can make me feel bad. And I'm just perfectly the right size when I'm in the ocean; it's so much bigger than me. I'm not in charge. It's really beautiful, and it was the only place where I could go where I didn't cry. It gave me some kind of comfort. I had surfed before, and so I returned and recommitted to surfing, and to swimming—I swim on a Master's team. I spend a lot of time in the water.

♦ **AJ: What made you want to start performing again?**

♦ P: About two and half years ago, I decided I needed to get back on stage, and to do that I'd have to do something pretty ridiculous and have a pretty good time. That's how Hot August Phranc came to be, which was my Neil Diamond full drag show. A big part of the reason I could go on stage last night [in New York] was because of Neil Diamond; I really have to hand it to him. Neil Diamond kind of gave me my career back. It's so weird: I grew up hating Neil Diamond—I was *never* a fan of Neil Diamond.

I did a folk festival in '89 or '90 in Mariposa up in Canada, and there was a workshop called "The Worst Song You Ever Learned." I played "Solitary Man," a song of his, and they went *nuts*. I was telling the story to someone a couple years later, and they said, "You should do that! You should do Neil Diamond." I was like, "No, you're kidding." But I was at a point in my life when I just decided, "You know what? I'm just going to do something that is completely—" I put a band together (I hadn't had a band in a really long time), and I learned all these *Neil Diamond* songs (I hardly ever do covers). Once I started learning them, I was like, "Oh, my God, these songs are so completely bizarre!" He's just, well... you could say a *genius*, in a way.

♦ **AJ: A twisted genius.**

♦ P: It's amazing. The first time I did the show, Phranc was the opening act: the All-American Jewish Lesbian Folksinger. Then there was an intermission, and then I'd come back as Hot August Phranc. My hair would be parted on the other side, or I'd flatten it down, and I'd change my outfit. That evolved into Phranc always being the opening act, and then Hot August Phranc with full band, costumes, chest hair, wig, the replica guitar; everything.

Phranc at a G.I. Joe convention (1994).

That was a lot of fun. And *that* got me back on stage, got me thinking about going back and working again. And then the shows up in Portland showed me: "Yes, the political work you do is so important. It's important to be political on

I decided to go solo, because I felt like you couldn't hear the words in punk rock.

stage, it's important to write the songs you always wrote." The thing that was a little scary about the Hot August Phranc shows was that they were some of the most successful shows I ever did. And to get this acknowledgment as a drag king, and really not as Phranc...I didn't want to take it any further, because I don't want to be seen as a drag king. I'm not a drag king, I'm a dyke.

It's fun to dress up, and it was really fun to do that show, and I'll do it again, but I'll only do it in a context where it can help Phranc. It's not my intention to go on and make a career of doing Neil Diamond. It was something that really helped me, and it was a lot of fun to do. And I'll do it again. I think he's great now—I'm a *huge* fan. I went to see him at the L.A. Forum. He played five nights, sold out. And... I have to say that I cried. I'm a sucker. He is one of the most fantastic performers I have ever seen in my life. Have you ever seen him live?

♦ **AJ: No, I'd love to.**

♦ P: You must go. I am such a huge fan. It's weird, I know, but it's the truth; I'm not lying. I was transformed by the experience. What can I say? [laughs]

♦ **AJ: I've never seen you do Neil Diamond, although I've heard about it, and loved the idea; I love Neil Diamond. I've seen you do a Phranc show, in San Francisco—**

♦ P: Oh, yeah. You saw the show with Team

Dresch, right?

◆ **AJ: Yeah. It was amazing what you did with that audience—there really was this sense of leadership, from songs like "Bulldagger Swagger": that Lesbian-Jew empowerment. There was something so positive, that even some of the stuff that could have been corny, wasn't. It was real!**

◆ P: There *is* some corniness in my stuff.

◆ **AJ: But I don't mind corniness. It almost helps, because we're in an age where—**

◆ P: —we can use a little corniness.

◆ **AJ: I was looking, with my friend, at this audience—it was so positive and genuine. It was so endearing, and so lovely.**

P: That night in San Francisco was an amazing experience for me. Q-TIP (Queers Together in Punkness), with Miriam and her friends from Epicenter, put that show together; $6 at the door, soda pop sold in the back room. They brought in Cheesecake (a band from Boston), Team Dresch, me and the Bucktooth Varmints. They brought us all together, put us in this wonderful space, charged six bucks at the door, and had all the people that work there have gaffer's tape stickers on them (they'd taken tape and made signs that said, "We're volunteering"). Everybody volunteered. Nobody made any money, the bands only got paid a little bit, and—what a great time people had. That was the first time I'd seen Team Dresch play. I was just so moved; the tears were running down my jaw. I was just blown away. Had you seen them before that?

◆ **AJ: No, that was the first time for me. I** was blown away, too.

◆ P: Donna was just a blur on the side of the stage. It was just like those old punk rock days. I hadn't been that motivated—

◆ **AJ: Yeah!**

◆ P: I was there with my friend Gail. We were standing there together watching the show and we were looking at each other, going, "My God, can you believe this?"

◆ **AJ: I was with my friend Margaret, who I also knew in '79—**

◆ P: And weren't you punching each other and going "Aaah! This is it, This is *it*!"

> **The thing that was scary about the Hot August Phranc shows was that they were some of the most successful shows I ever did. I got this acknowledgement as a drag king [but] I don't want to be seen as a drag king, I'm a dyke.**

◆ **AJ: The energy! It was it—but it wasn't the same.**

◆ P: Yeah, it was different. It seems like it's so much smarter now. And it was all girls!

◆ **AJ: Well, there were guys there, too.**

◆ P: Yeah, but there was only one man on stage, and he was part of the Bucktooth Varmints.

◆ **AJ: Oh, on stage, yeah! The interesting thing was that the audience was, let's say, maybe three-quarters women; it was a nice proportion.**

◆ P: It was a mish-mash—it was the young ones *and* the old-time punk rockers; It was a good blend of every kind, which is the best crowd you can hope for.

◆ **AJ: It was like the original energy, but without a lot of the hard-edged male bent to it. Back then, I really**

FROM BUTCH TO BARBIE
The April Fool's Cover of *Paper* magazine (1991): "Phranc loves being a girl, but her heart belongs to G.I. Joe."

felt that aspect; and when I was so young, I didn't even really have my own identity, anyway. I wanted to fit in, and even the women who were in the scene had a kind of male, cool attitude. Especially in a place like San Francisco, which has always had more attitude per square inch than any other place.

♦ P: Right.

♦ AJ: I don't really have that; I tend to be more enthusiastic, and maybe femme-y [laughs]. I tried really hard to fit in, and it never quite worked. What I see in this new generation is the same feeling you get from something vital, something politically liberating, something—

♦ P: —fun—

♦ AJ: —really artistic, nice, and totally fun—

♦ P: That's a big element. If you don't have a sense of humor, then what's it all worth? What's the point?

♦ AJ: At that show, I felt like, "Ahh!" I could be accepted—now that I'm 40. [laughs]

♦ P: It feels right. You wonder why all this stuff would happen in someone's life; maybe I just needed to get slowed down enough so I could get to do this right now. Who knows what would have happened. Maybe I was supposed to go on a tour with Morrissey all the way around the world, and...

♦ AJ: You played with the Smiths, and then just Morrissey, at shows in such big, major venues. Did you ever feel alienated?

♦ P: I'm just so committed to doing my job. I feel like my job is to reach as many people as possible, to be out on stage as a lesbian and show that I have a sense of humor; ultimately, my job is to show that you can be who you are. People have asked me why I didn't wait until I was more successful and made more money before I came out as a dyke. But for me, part of the reason that I am so committed to doing what I do is because I had such a hard time coming out and growing up. I tried to kill myself a couple of times because I was queer—

♦ AJ: As a teenager?

♦ P: Yes; because I thought nobody would ever love me, and I thought I was the only one in the world. But, thank God, someone gave me Jill Johnston. And a few years later I got Alix Dobkin. These were people who gave me hope and inspiration, and made me feel like I wasn't the only one. I came out to save my life. It was not even a political choice at that time for me; it was a life or death choice for me.

I feel that I need to give that inspiration to

Record company Kill Rock Stars postcard (1995).

Photo: Ken Seino

others, I owe it to them, because *I* lived. It's my job to go out and be *out*, to say, if nothing else, that you can grow up and be whoever you are. Whether you're straight, or gay, or lesbian—you can grow up and be who you are. You can go to a rock show, when you least expect it, and see somebody that's a dyke on stage, who has a sense of humor, is having a good time, and is making a living, and is *out there*—you are not the only one in the world. That's my job. And if I can do it at the L.A. Forum for twenty thousand people at the same time—if I can reach just one person in that crowd, then it's my job to do it.

Of course, I prefer playing to a room of 100; I prefer playing a room like Fez [in New York], where I played last night. You have that intimate feeling: you can see almost everybody in the room. You don't have that in those huge places. You can only see the first two rows. It's all black when the lights come on; you're playing to, like, a big black piece of construction paper, and you can kind of hear where the people are clapping, or listening, or laughing, but it's like playing blind. Those big venues have no soul.

Phranc in concert with the Smiths at the The Pier, NYC (1986).

didn't heckle sometimes, or kids didn't get freaked out; but if you're ever going to be out in front of an audience, how nice for it to be *his* audience. They're young and smart. A lot of them (like a lot of young audiences), are trying to figure out their sexual identities, and who they are and what they want to be. It's a great audience to play to.

Most of my experiences on stage have been really positive. In all the years, I can only count maybe a couple that were really stinkers. I've been challenged many times, but only a couple times was it really aggressive. And even then, I feel like I have been victorious. 'Cause I'm still here.

♦ **AJ: All right!**

♦ P: To get to play the show I played last night, with Elliott Smith, who I love, and Mary Lou Lord, and Emily XYZ, and Slim Moon; to get to play with Team Dresch, and Bikini Kill, and have them play on my record, just for me—wow! I'm so honored and thrilled to get to play with these people now, and hang out with them, and talk. It's really motivating and inspiring.

♦ **AJ: What was it like being with Morrissey?**

♦ P: He's a wonderful guy, and he's always been really supportive of me. We had a lot of fun on the tour.

♦ **AJ: Is he gay?**

♦ P: Who knows? I think he's still celibate. I can't say. I'm only out for myself. [laughs]

If I had stayed on that tour with him, I would've done Japan, and Australia and finished the world with him. We started out in Europe, played all through Europe and came over to the U.S. We were almost done with the shows here—

♦ **AJ: And you were doing Phranc?**

♦ P: I was Phranc. The All-American Jewish Lesbian folksinger, onstage, in front of all those children—it was wonderful.

♦ **AJ: How was that received?**

♦ P: They loved it. Send a lesbian on stage, the crowd goes wild. That's not to say that people

It's a good time for me. Maybe I just needed to get slowed down. It's weird. Right around the time when my brother died, all my friends started dying of AIDS, too; it has been about four years of almost straight loss. Craig Lee died not too long after my brother died, and I was very, very close with him. I still feel really close to him, I feel a strong connection, and I know that he is just loving all these girls, 'cause he was such a champion of girl rockers. I can just feel him smirking, in his own special way. Losing him and Gerardo and many friends—and the rest of my grandparents—everyone just started dropping like flies.

♦ **AJ: Right now, I feel that on one hand there is this healthy rise of wonderful new "underground" rockers; but also, in the mainstream politic, it's becoming scarier and scarier—**

♦ P: The country's turning right, and the christians are taking over—

♦ **AJ: When you're on tour—or just in your everyday life—do you see evidence of this? Have you encountered increased homophobia?**

♦ P: When I was in Portland just recently, I didn't see anything like that. But the last time I was in Portland, a couple of years ago, was when

I'm Not Romantic, 7-inch (1991) and *Goofyfoot* (1995).

they were in the process of trying to defeating Proposition 9, the anti-gay initiative.

♦ **AJ: It won in Colorado, which is scary.**

I feel that my job is to be out on stage as a lesbian and show that I have a sense of humor. I am so committed because I had a hard time coming out and growing up. I tried to kill myself a couple of times because I was queer.

♦ P: This was a couple of years earlier, before Colorado. I did a show in Portland, and it was a women-produced, lesbian show; it wasn't a rock show. There was a death threat. It was just like, "We hear that Jewish dyke is playing, and we're going to kill her." The promoter of the show freaked out; we were doing the show in a church, and this promoter got a couple of phone calls. That was really scary.

That's direct personal evidence that I have of that kind of hatred or violence. I've dealt with quite a bit of homophobia on stage; I deal with that wonderful, invisible...*sheet* of homophobia in the music industry. "Things are all better now, 'cause a couple of people came out." [laughs] "There really isn't homophobia anymore, things are all better for women, and queers, and... hey, there's no problems, it's 1995!"

But you know what? It's almost exactly the way it was in 1985, and pretty close to the way it was in 1975; things have really not changed very much at all. Which is all the more reason to

shoot your mouth off, and raise some hell, and be who you are. And yeah, that *is* getting a little riskier, because the christian right is really scary.

♦ **AJ: Very scary.**

♦ P: What's going on in Bosnia right now is also very scary, because it's exactly what happened with Hitler and the Jews. *It's exactly the same.* I ended my set last night with "Take Off Your Swastika," which is a song that should be so fucking obsolete by now. I wrote that song in 1980? '81? Come on, is this song 15 years old? Am I still playing the exact same song with the exact same lyrics? Things have not changed. People say, "It's never going to happen again." Well, it's happening right now, and everybody's pretending that it's *not* happening, exactly the same way they pretended it wasn't happening before. How can that be? What can one person do? What can *I* do? Try to raise some hell. ♦ ♦ ♦

♦ discography

Goofyfoot, EP (1995)
Phranc, 7-inch featuring "Bulldagger Swagger" and "Hillary's Eyebrows" (1994)
Phranc (1991)
I Enjoy Being a Girl (1989)
The Lonesome Death of Hattie Carroll, 7-inch (1986)
Amazons, 7-inch and 12-inch (1986)
Folksinger (1985)

♦ equipment list

'66 Martin 0018 guitar

Candice Pedersen
K Records

Candice Pedersen is co-owner, along with Calvin Johnson, of K Records in Olympia, Washington—ground zero for a number of music-related movements including Riot Grrrls. K Records was started in 1983; Candice began an internship in 1986 that turned into a full-time job, and eventually a partnership. K Records has released numerous cassettes, singles, and albums/CDs. For a catalog send a SASE to P.O. Box 7154, Olympia, WA, 98507.

♦ ANDREA JUNO: Tell me about life in Olympia—

♦ CANDICE PEDERSEN: The thing about Olympia, Washington is: people are "nice" and they do things like bake somebody a pie. I don't think there's anything wrong or "uncool" about that. People here are enthusiastic.

In Olympia, it's easy to be a "woman in rock." I've had the same experiences any woman has, of some guy being a jerk at a show. But in general, no one has ever stopped me from doing what I wanted. I thought every punk rock community was like Olympia's. Then I discovered this was not so.

♦ AJ: There seems to be a history of strong women in Olympia. That's unique.

♦ CP: I've lived here all my life. I grew up on a farm and didn't get into town more than once a month. But I would go regularly to this store called Girl City where all these women were creating different kinds of art. At performances, more than half the people would be women. That's where it all began, with people like the artist Stella Marrs, or Julie Fay who did performances, or a painter named Dana Squires who helped start Girl City.

When I graduated from high school in '83, I attended Evergreen College. Now I'm 30.

♦ AJ: What was the genesis of K Records?

♦ CP: K Records' first release was a cassette titled *Supreme Cool Beings*. It included Heather Lewis from Beat Happening, plus Doug Monahan and Gary Allen May. That was in 1982. K Records was started by Calvin Johnson; in 1986 I did an internship with him and was hired. By then, the first Beat Happening album and single had been released, plus some cassettes. K was just beginning to release a series of singles titled *International Pop Underground*—now we're up to number 70!

♦ AJ: Are you now a co-owner?

♦ CP: Yes. I do a lot of the straight-ahead business; I'm pretty organized. I can look at a page of numbers and figure them out. I bring bands or projects to the label and basically do managerial tasks.

♦ AJ: And this supports you?

♦ CP: Calvin and I have both been living off K Records since 1990. We have six employees. None of us get paid a lot, but Olympia is a very inexpensive place to live.

♦ AJ: What's the philosophy of K Records?

♦ CP: *Independence.* We like to work with really independent people who have a vision of what they want. People call us out of the blue: "Will you put out our record?" I say, "Put it out yourself and we'll distribute it." Almost everybody we work with has done something for *themselves.* They feel strongly about what they're doing, and I can respect that. I want to—not exactly *help* people like that, but enable them to do their thing. That benefits the community, punk rock, us and them. A Lois record could exist because she can make the music, but can one person release their own album and get it out there? That's what we're there for: as a *conduit.*

I like to work with strong-minded individuals—interesting, creative people—and amazingly enough (to some people, but not to us) they're often women. Today I was thinking about vocals by Rebecca Gates or Lois or P.J. Harvey, and I realized that men don't play with their vocals as much as women, so it's not as interesting. Take Dolly Parton—no voice in the world is like that. That's why regular rock'n'roll doesn't interest me. You know what the music is going to sound like, you know what the boy's voice is going to sound like… it's all so boring. That doesn't mean it's *bad*—technically that music is often very good—but it's not very interesting.

 *Photo: Scott Plouf*

♦ **AJ: You saw the groundswell of what is now labeled Riot Grrrl. Can you talk about the beginning, middle and end—**

♦ **CP:** I'm *sure* it's not over! Riot Grrrl is so important to so many people—especially young girls, of course. It provides them with a network that prevents them from thinking they're insane. I hope the concept never goes away, because it saves them so much time and agony!

> **Maybe what happens after a riot is what's most important to look at. Because a riot blows everything up—but who's there picking up all the pieces?**

When I was a young girl I didn't know I liked punk rock music; I just knew I didn't like "regular" music. I can't really be a spokesperson for Riot Grrrl because I wasn't directly involved, but I know the people involved and what sparked them. The two halves of Riot Grrrl started in Olympia and in D.C. In each place, there was a community where you could be a woman and be involved in music and do what you wanted. At the same time, things weren't as open as they were for men—women *still* don't own recording studios; they don't own sound equipment to be sound technicians… so women don't yet *own* the right to have things exactly as we want them.

Riot Grrrl wasn't just about music, it was also about style: creating all *kinds* of different worlds and personas that weren't determined by a male community. They put on concerts in their own way: "Hey, for our sound let's find that one woman who does sound. Maybe she's not considered to be as good as somebody else, but there's only one way she's going to get better!" That attitude was really important to women like Kathleen Hanna and Molly Neuman and Allison Wolfe, who did the first *Riot Grrrl* fanzine. They had a vision, and it was a *powerful* one. It was self-created by people who were really hard workers.

I think a lot of things got mixed up because the Information Age goes by so fast now. Suddenly everybody was on to them, and that could scare anybody—especially people who *themselves* hadn't yet figured out what "Riot Grrrl" means—they didn't have a chance to breathe! So now there's a lot of backlash: "Oh, it didn't do any good." That is *so* not true! That disparagement is wishful thinking on the part of status-quo-loving people, but it's false.

People also said, "Everyone looks the same!" Or, "All the girl bands sound the same!" They missed the crux of the point, which is: "We don't

 177

The Softies, 7-inch (K Records).

care what you think! We're having fun!" And it *was* about fun. It was an art scene, and people were having a good time.

♦ AJ: If I were a kid, hearing about something like Riot Grrrl would have given me a window onto so many more possibilities. It would have taken away some doubt and confusion.

♦ CP: Exactly, especially on self-esteem issues. I have a computer and I'm on-line now, so sometimes I check into what the girls are saying to each other in the America Online Riot Grrrl folder. And they pass on so much great information. If I could have asked just *one* question when I was fifteen (perhaps about an issue like being gay), I'd probably be an amazingly different person today. *If only* there had been somebody to talk to, back in 1980… .

Now my high school has an organization to deal with questions like that. Once people decide to create their own organization, that organization then propels people into being more active, because they no longer have to deal with self-esteem issues like, "Am I the only one? Am I a freak? Why doesn't anyone understand me? Even though I dress like most people, somehow they can still figure out that I'm a freak!"

♦ AJ: Aside from Riot Grrrl, have there been other fundamental changes in the world of indie rock?

♦ CP: There was a time when people never talked about money or major labels. Punk rock seemed to exist in its own vacuum. In the past three years, the biggest change I've noticed is that people talk about money, fame, and the "major vs. indie" issue

a lot more. Someone like Patti Smith was always on a major label, although back then there wasn't any indie scene. She was still very "punk" and independent; the majors were all that were available to her, and didn't seem to put constraints on her goals. But now (even though I don't think *anybody* in Olympia is on a major label) I see this change: people seem more savvy about the industry; not exactly more bitter, but…

♦ AJ: Isn't that the natural process of an underground which starts out fresh and local, and then, when the media spotlights come on…

♦ CP: I'm such a pessimist and cynic, yet I'm the biggest idealist you could ever imagine. So even though that media process may be "natural," I'm still disappointed!

♦ AJ: But there's a natural cycle of growth and change; people have to let go and create new forms of expression. I've been comparing some of these more recent movements to the ones that I experienced almost 20 years ago. Early punk rock happened in London, New York, Los Angeles and San Francisco—

♦ CP: —and everyone still knew each other, even though they were 3,000 miles apart!

♦ AJ: There were only a handful of punk rock clubs in the whole country.

♦ CP: That's how I feel. I know the D.C. scene, New York, San Francisco, Olympia, Seattle—I don't know L.A. I do think it's natural to mature. We all want to do things like buy a house.

The thing about Olympia, WA is: people are "nice" and they do things like bake somebody a pie. I don't think there's anything "uncool" about that.

♦ AJ: I wouldn't necessarily equate buying a house with the process of maturing (although I don't think it's a bad thing either.) Maturity doesn't necessarily mean materialism or losing your vision and creativity. It doesn't have to mean that to be responsible means you'll turn into your parents, or become conservative.

♦ CP: And maturity doesn't mean you're not punk. I always hear people dichotomizing: "Either you're punk or you're not punk."

♦ AJ: It's a wonderful, heady feeling when you're in a small, seemingly liberatory, creative group uprising. But group identity has its dangers, especially when you get stuck in one and can't grow.

◆ CP: I remember how I felt when I finally found people who thought like me. When I went to high school, basic things didn't make sense to me, like being mean to the girl who looked a little different. But nobody said, "That doesn't seem right." So when I finally met some people who thought sexism and racism and all forms of hatred were wrong, I had this incredible sense of *relief*! Because I grew up so isolated, I've always been very much a loner and perhaps have been spared some of the immaturity that comes from staying in any one group. So if someone writes a book 20 years from now about Riot Grrrl, I'll know that I was there. But like I said, I wasn't really part of Riot Grrrl; I am independent in many ways.

◆ AJ: Can you envision another phase of feminism in the near future?

◆ CP: I don't think there'll be another phase yet, actually, because I don't feel this phase is over. I feel that this time around, feminism is really intrinsic to the way people think about music—maybe that's just my idealism! I think it's just going to be considered part of what's music, punk rock, indie rock—whatever people choose to call it. There are too many Loises and Kim Gordons and Kathleen Hannas out there, and they're too strong for it to go away. They make up too strong a composite role model for people *not* to want to copy them, and not see them as an inspiration!

People like Kathleen and Lois take what they're doing very seriously. I think they see themselves as responsible for cultivating an atmosphere where creativity is encouraged. That's part of their being involved in rock. I really don't feel it's a *phase*. All those 12-year-old girls involved in Riot Grrrl are not all going to do music or art—maybe they'll just work in a library, but *how* they work in that library will be significantly different than 10 or 15 years ago. People are beginning to realize that all the decisions they make are very political, like deciding to be a punk rocker—even *that* is a political choice.

◆ AJ: How is that "political"—besides just listening to punk rock lyrics?

◆ CP: It implies this sense of independence: I'm going to do whatever I want, in the way I want.

◆ AJ: But it's not just about doing *anything* you want! There are a lot of irresponsible people out there. I think in a lot of cases "punk" has become a lazy form of credentials;

you don't have to actually do anything radical, you can just call yourself "punk." Punk rock originally implied a critique of the so-called normal capitalist, materialistic, corporate world, etc.—

If a punk rocker from 1977 jumped ahead via a time capsule to 1995, he would think, "You guys are a bunch of squares! This isn't punk rock." But to me it's not about style.

◆ CP: For me this is still true, although for some people it might not be true. When I look at a listing of the top "indie" bands—well, that word doesn't mean "independent" anymore! It refers to a certain kind of music, according to somebody—but I don't know who that somebody is!

◆ AJ: Punk rock now means Green Day and Offspring—a *style*. It doesn't mean what it used to. When I talk about the ability to give up the external form while keeping the internal meaning, I'm not talking about style but about deeper values as to what truly constitutes "community."

◆ CP: If those values are in your core, you'll be

Godzilla, Nikki McClure, 7-inch (K Records, 1995).

Photo: Scott Plouf

Some of Candice's favorite K Records releases.

sustenance. I would not necessarily leave the punk rock world or even Olympia, because I now consider certain conditions "normal"—and if I leave, I'm going to discover very quickly that's no longer true! I'm referring to conditions like "being nice to people," and living in an atmosphere where you aren't derided for doing something risky, performance-wise; it's more like: "Well, maybe I didn't like that particular performance, but it's really great that you did it, anyway!" I choose to stay in a community that encourages that.

♦ **AJ: Punk rock is now a meaningless term to me; it's unmoored from the original context in which I experienced it. What's so refreshing about your community is that you've redefined punk rock to include the original principle of revolution in everyday life. It comes down to things as simple as this unabashed "niceness" that I sense in Olympia—and which is not exactly an original punk rock concept.**

♦ CP: Well, I define punk rock as "Making decisions—that may be contrary to what is publicly considered normal—within a community that encourages those choices." Say I decide to make t-shirts in my bedroom for a living. I consider that punk rock, because I'll be making a choice whereby, perhaps financially my world's going to suck, but it's *what I want to do*. I may throw the term "punk rock" around very cavalierly, but that's how I define it for myself and my community. If a punk rocker from 1977 jumped ahead via a time capsule to 1995, he would think, "You guys are a bunch of squares! This isn't punk rock." But to me it's not about style, it's about doing what you want. And if you're diligent, you *can* be really successful.

I never thought I'd be this successful: living off what I like to do. It just seemed like something interesting—far more interesting than going to school and becoming a lawyer. Now I read lots of books about music and art and theory, and maybe I'm not the most successful or financially stable person, but I bet I'm one of the happiest people around.

♦ **AJ: Do you think the Riot Grrrl concept**

able to make changes and meet the people you need to meet and propel forward. Maybe I'm being too basic, but I think that if you can get it together to figure out what you really want, then it's going to be there—whether the form is punk rock or hippie or beat or Bloomsbury group. I think there will always be a place for people with a similar mindset to go.

I don't think [Riot Grrrl's] something you "grow out of." I think we're going to be strong Riot Women.

♦ **AJ: By "independent," I know you don't mean the lone cowboy out on the frontier: that kind of self-centeredness. You have a real community spirit—**

♦ CP: I mean "independent" from general, accepted opinions. I certainly don't think I stand alone in the world at all—when I *did* think that, I was very unhappy. Now, even though I have a community (and extended, it's quite large—thousands of people), I am still very independent. Any arts community can have 10,000 people in it, but considering the population of the world, that's not many people—you're still standing alone and taking a lot of risks.

People search out community so they can get

can mature into a "Riot Woman" concept: a rowdy feminism for an older generation?

♦ CP: I would guess that will happen, but I'm not sure. I'm not in a position to know what the future holds for my generation.

♦ AJ: What about the *present*? You're no longer a girl—

♦ CP: —and I haven't been one for quite some time! Now I'm surrounded by women who are very smart, very strong, very determined, very politically-oriented and very successful in the world of art. That stems, somewhat, from Riot Grrrl, and I don't think it's something you "grow out of." I don't think Kathleen Hanna is suddenly going to grow out of being a strong person! I think we're going to be strong Riot Women...

Actually, maybe what happens *after* a riot is what's most important to look at. Because a riot blows everything up—but who's there picking up all the pieces? I don't see that any of those women have abandoned the concept of picking up the pieces and carrying them forward.

♦ AJ: Good point. Are there more women involved in the *structure* of the music world? Are there more women who are sound engineers, managers—

Sometimes I just want to *shake* somebody who sounds pretentious about what they've done and tell them, "Make a great record and maybe even get rich off it, but then take that money and do something really great—like put it into your community!"

♦ CP: There definitely are more women managers, women lawyers and women booking agents. I haven't seen that much increase in women sound-engineers, but I think it's coming. The Spinanes really wanted a female to produce their record, but the only women available either weren't very experienced, or were in another realm—like they'd produced a Prince album. I think it'll be a while until a middle ground of women engineers and producers is available.

♦ AJ: You often hear people say that women

Tiger Trap LP (K Records).

can't play their instruments "good enough." But you have to start somewhere—

♦ CP: That's definitely one of the things Riot Grrrl was all about: "Who cares? If they can't play their instruments, they're going to learn." The same is true in business. Lots of major labels think women shouldn't be A&R scouts, because "What do *they* know about music?" But those companies are slowly learning that some women know an awful lot about music; they can determine what the world wants just as well as men can. People think it's "reverse sexism" to hire a woman just because she's a woman, but I believe that has to be done until hiring a woman becomes "normal," and enough women get experience in every field of expertise. Maybe it is a bit risky—but what's wrong with that?! I'd rather take a risk than hire somebody and think, "Well, he obviously knows what he's doing, but he doesn't seem to have any *love* for this."

I think women have an interesting perspective on things, whether it's business or music—*especially* in the music industry. You could go to a meeting at Warner Brothers and just be surrounded by middle-aged white men; if you throw any different element in there (a woman, a black man, a Cambodian) there's going to be a different perspective present. A lot of people are afraid of that. I don't think the punk rock community is afraid of that; we encourage difference—that's what we *look* for. We seek out other perspectives.

But all this sounds so *serious*. Mostly, I just think this is so much fun—even the tedious parts; I wouldn't trade them for anything! I have fun

working in rock'n'roll, I love to go to shows, I love that spark of, "Oh my god—that was a great band!" I love meeting all the people I've met. Ten years ago, none of this existed for me. So many incredible opportunities are available to me because I reached out and did work. That's why I would encourage any woman to do something like this. It's hard work and it can be frustrating, and sometimes you *do* feel like you're a "woman in rock," but the trade-off is worth it. When you asked who had inspired me, I thought, "Until I'd met those Riot Grrrl people, I had never *been* inspired!" They caused an amazing change in my life. And the part of me that's egotistical hopes that I can inspire others, too.

♦ **AJ: I think the lack of fun is what destroys so much earnest, political work. When there isn't that glowing ember—libido, excitement, spontaneity, whatever it is that makes something alive—then mind-numbing dogmatism takes over.**

I'd be inspired by Ian MacKaye before I'd be inspired by Liz Phair, regardless of gender.

♦ CP: It's obvious that, psychologically and socially, music has always been important in all cultures. But in our culture, where the music itself isn't even intrinsic to our souls—we've taken bits and pieces from all over the place—if you make a great record and that's all you do, what have you *really* done?

Sometimes I just want to *shake* somebody who sounds pretentious about what they've done and tell them, "It's not important! You're not changing the world! Make a great record and maybe even get rich off it, but then take that money and do something really great—like put it into your community!" I know there are bands who do that—Pearl Jam and Fugazi do that very discreetly. But most musicians think that if they've made a "great record," that's enough. Whereas I think, "You could do so much more—and you *should*. That's *just* a record. If you go into a used record store, you see all these records. And someday, your record will be there, too, regardless of whether it's a great Beatles or Sonic Youth or Lois record."

♦ **AJ: Ultimately, it's just music. *Then* what do you do?**
♦ CP: Exactly. One of the things that's great about Olympia is: people are doing other things, like Lois with the "Free to Fight" tour [accompanied by a booklet and CD, emphasizing self-defense]. But people get lazy and think they've done enough. Kathleen Hanna has worked at women's health clinics. You could say you dislike her music, or disparagingly call her a "radical feminist," but disregarding everything she's done musically, there is this other work she's done. By her example she has proven she is *not* a selfish person. The same with Lois's choices, and those of other artists…

♦ **AJ: 7 Year Bitch created Home Alive, the self-defense collective in Seattle—**
♦ CP: Right. If they take that extra step, you can really respect them. You could dislike one of these bands' music, but you could never deride the fact that members of that band are doing something for their immediate community.

♦ **AJ: Music is important and fun, but it is not politics and is not a substitute for deeds. You can't say, "Well, I listen to Fugazi, and that's how I show my solidarity; I don't have to do anything in the real world."**
♦ CP: And if all the band chose to do was be Fugazi, that wouldn't be respectable. What's respectable is: in D.C., they'll only play free shows. They play to prisons. They do things they think are important; they stand by their ideals and don't make a big brouhaha about them, either. Those are the kinds of people you want to be inspired by—I'd be inspired by Ian MacKaye before I'd be inspired by Liz Phair, regardless of gender.

♦ **AJ: This is the way in which artists can make their work matter socially. L7 started the Rock for Choice benefits—that's *conscious*, and that's how they can influence the people who already like their music.**
♦ CP: It's a lot of work, especially for people who are so busy. 7 Year Bitch is busy, Bikini Kill is busy, Lois is busy. But what they manage to do proves they're not as selfish as other artists might be. What's important is really thinking about your world, and making choices that don't only affect *you*. ♦ ♦ ♦

equipment list

computer, telephone, Sharpies (pens), *rolodex*

Bettina Richards
Thrill Jockey Records

Bettina Richards learned about the music industry first-hand with jobs at major labels and the Pier Platters record store in Hoboken, New Jersey. She started her own independent record label, Thrill Jockey, in 1992, with the release of H.P. Zinker's *Perserverance*, and in 1994 she moved Thrill Jockey to Chicago. She distributes through Touch and Go. For a Thrill Jockey catalogue, send a SASE to: Thrill Jockey, P.O. Box 476794, Chicago, IL, 60647.

♦ **ANDREA JUNO: How did you start the Thrill Jockey label?**
♦ BETTINA RICHARDS: I started Thrill Jockey three years ago. I had worked at a couple of major labels and really hated it, and I also knew a lot of people who worked at indie labels. So I had access to all this information — that, plus money, is all you need. I had some savings, and I borrowed money from my grandmother to get going.

A friend runs the Drag City label, and he told me where to get records and CDs manufactured. If you're a small label, the plant tends to charge you a high per-copy price because your volume is low. There are smaller plants that will give you a good price — you just have to know who they are.

♦ **AJ: You worked at a major label previously. I'm curious about what it's like behind the scenes. What kind of job did you have?**
♦ BR: I got a job doing A&R [artist & repertoire] research at Atlantic, which involved going through playlists and finding bands to check out. I worked for what they called the "Progressive" department — only a few years ago, they didn't think "alternative" music would make them any money. I picked out a number of bands, and my job turned into an A&R position. At first, there were four other women doing A&R, but within a year I was the only one left. It was definitely a boy's club.

My greatest dissatisfaction involved the way musicians were treated as commodities. They were no longer artists, they were "product." The system was completely inflexible; if something didn't "fit," it was chucked. Fine — except that what was being shoved through the system was *people*.

A lot of bands are blinded by the advance money, and they don't have the tools to work the system. They don't have a lawyer who's well-versed in music-biz legalese; they have a manager who's a friend, but who doesn't know how to manipulate the system. A major label is like a huge octopus: every department is its own world, and the different departments don't talk to each other or interact. One band's record would get squashed while their promotion guy was pushing another record he knew his boss liked — because he wanted a bigger office. People were making decisions based on reasons like *that*, not: "This record is great; let's work really hard for it." I never *once* heard anybody say that!

♦ **AJ: In my brief experiences with major labels, I've heard the same hypocrisy over and over — that because it's rock'n'roll, there are some kind of transgressive underpinnings. But it's just the opposite. They're extremely conservative and exploit most of the musicians.**
♦ BR: That's not all. I can't tell you how many times I was told that maybe if I changed what I wore to work, or took the right guy to an ice hockey game, I would be more "effective." I thought, "I'm not going to take some *asshole* out to a hockey game just to get him to do his job!" In

thing they get is *recoupable*. They think, "We're flying around on this promo tour; isn't this great?" not realizing that *they're* paying for it, not the record company. It's not that they're stupid; a lot of bands just don't have the savvy to understand the system, or to ask, "I just paid for 80 radio people to each have a $15 lunch. Do I really need to do this to sell my record?"

I do a 50/50 profit split. That means that if any of my bands sell 2000 records, they get *paid*. You can sell 100,000 records on a major label and not get paid a cent — other than your mechanical royalties.

A mechanical royalty is a form of publishing royalty. You get so many cents per song per record manufactured — that's fixed. The only way many of these bands make any money at all is through publishing. They *don't* make money off record sales. But here's another problem: a lot of bands sign away their publishing rights when they sign to a major label deal, because they think, "Wow, I'm getting this big advance!" *Big* mistake.

♦ **AJ: When you started your label, how did you set out to conduct business differently?**

♦ BR: I wanted to make sure that this was a band's label as much as mine; that it was a kind of *partnership* in which a band was able to do whatever they wanted — within my pretty severe financial limitations, of course! Any decision they want to make — to send out *no* freebies, to send out 100, to have a certain kind of artwork, to have a record that's two minutes long or seventy minutes long — is fine, as long as I can afford it.

I don't have any contracts. Again, I do a 50/50 profit split, and when I license a record to Europe, the band gets 50% upfront, which can be a couple grand to buy a van with, or whatever. Since I don't have contracts, if I don't do a good job, or if they're not happy with the situation, there's no

that environment, you have to go through the appropriate political system and pat all the right people on the back.

I was never so happy as after I quit that job.
♦ **AJ: I read Steve Albini's article in *The Baffler #5*, detailing the finances involved in a typical major-label signing. After a $250,000 advance, the band ends up $14,000 in debt!**

♦ BR: A lot of people who are used to making a record for $4,000 sign with a major label and find they can't *possibly* record for under $80,000. All of a sudden it's somebody else's decision as to what the sequence of songs is —

♦ **AJ: —or somebody else decides that the record doesn't sound "good enough," and it needs another $50,000 in studio time. There is this mythology that if you sign to a major label, you will be rich. Isn't that rare?**

♦ BR: *Extremely* rare. Upon getting an advance, some bands purchase a bunch of new gear; suddenly they require more tour support, and maybe they'll start touring in a bigger vehicle than they can afford. After they finish the tour, they've made *no* money because their expenses were so high. Maybe they end up with their new gear, but that's about it. They don't realize that every-

bickering—the bands are free to leave.

◆ AJ: What's a major-label contract like?

◆ BR: A standard major-label deal specifies two to three records, firm, with an option for five to seven more. Conceivably, a company could keep optioning a band for the next 10-12 years; they *own* the rights to that band! A large number of independent labels have contracts—although Dischord, Touch and Go, Simple Machines and Teenbeat don't. I think all those labels also do 50/50 profit splits.

◆ AJ: Is your company profitable yet?

◆ BR: I'm not profitable yet, but finally, after three years, the company is paying for itself. I'm not losing money anymore.

◆ AJ: Are you able to support yourself?

◆ BR: No, I bartend.

◆ AJ: Oh no! I was hoping you would be an example for more young women to emulate. People are understandably leery of starting businesses that won't pay the rent.

◆ BR: I'm too paranoid to take money from my label yet. Profit isn't a yardstick by which I measure success, anyway. To me, success means paying the bands and having them be happy with the way their record turned out. Last night, two of my bands played in Philadelphia, and the club was full. None of that audience would have known about my bands if I hadn't done what I did—*that's* more satisfying to me than being able to pay myself. But someday... I bartend at two bars, and it would be nice not to have to do that.

> A lot of bands sign away their publishing rights when they sign to a major label deal, because they think, "Wow, I'm getting this big advance!" *Big* mistake.

◆ AJ: Do you think that eventually you can live off your label?

◆ BR: Oh, yeah! It can be done, although the climate is different from when labels like Dischord and Touch and Go started; they now have several employees and make a living off what they do. It's a lot more difficult for an independent label to start up now, because it's hard to compete in the distribution system when you

Thrill Jockey releases (clockwise from top left): *Trans Am*, Trans Am (1996); *Perseverance*, H.P. Zinker (1992); *Millions Now Living Will Never Die*, Tortoise (1996) and *Gaunt*, Gaunt (1995).

have "one nation/one label" corporations like WEA, [Warner Brothers/ Elektra/Atlantic] that own ADA [Alternative Distribution Alliance] and their "independent" distribution arms, shoving money at the same stores I'm trying to get into.

◆ AJ: Distribution is the key for an independent label. Has that dried up?

◆ BR: There just aren't that many fully independent distributors left. There's Touch and Go, Revolver, and regional ones like Cargo, Ajax, and Dutch East. It's extremely hard for them to compete with Caroline [owned by Virgin/EMI] or ADA [owned by WEA].

◆ AJ: Couldn't you get distributed by Caroline?

◆ BR: My first two records were distributed by Caroline, but I felt like I was working back at my old job! I gave them exclusive distribution—because I had a friend who worked there at the time—and it was a total nightmare. They were doing co-op ad deals; at my level, you can't give away 200 free records for a co-op ad. It doesn't make any sense. Plus, what's the point of shoving that many records of an independent band into a chain store? If my records are sitting in a Sam Goody chain store, they're going to be returned, because the people who know about my records don't usually shop at Sam Goody. I had other problems with Caroline, too. When I released a record by a West Coast band, they forgot to solicit West Coast orders, so there were no records for sale in the band's home town!

The band was very upset.

After the first two records, I started distributing on my own, using no one exclusively, and getting no financial aid. Recently Touch and Go started distributing my records, because my sales had increased to the point where I had to re-press my back catalog, and that took all my money. If a record sells incredibly fast, that can bankrupt you as well, because you have to keep re-pressing that one record and you don't have money to get out your new recordings. In this case, there was demand for my back catalog, which I had to re-press, but the bands I had just recorded needed *their* records pressed. I made a deal with Touch and Go whereby we both pick the records that merit larger distribution, and they pay all manufacturing costs and get a percentage of the profit.

♦ AJ: Is there a support and information network with other independent labels?

♦ BR: Yes. When I was starting out, even if someone didn't know me, they'd tell me where their extra-thick album covers were manufactured. The fact that you want to operate outside the established system creates a definite bond with other people from independent labels. But the notion of "independence" as a virtue is dying, compared to what it used to be. So many independent labels are willing to sell themselves to bigger labels.

♦ AJ: Yet you're still determined to try and create a non-exploitative framework—

♦ BR: —a new system that doesn't take advantage of either bands *or* consumers. You don't have to sell a CD for $15; it costs $1.25 to manufacture. They cost less than vinyl!

Old Paint, Freakwater (Thrill Jockey, 1995).

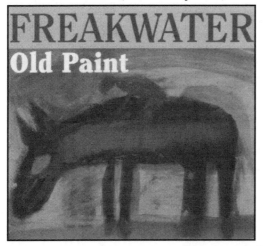

An interesting thing happened in the switch from LPs to CDs. It took the major labels quite some time to restructure their royalty systems when they reissued all those records on CD. I've heard that whoever reissued all the James Brown material made a way bigger profit margin because they went by the old contracts' royalty rate. Hmm—who's making out on that one?

I had to sit in marketing meetings and watch these videos showing babes strutting around that just made me totally ill.

♦ AJ: People have no idea of the extent of these profit margins; the major labels are just usurious. When CDs were first introduced, they were considered "riskier" than LPs, and recording contracts included a 25% withholding of royalties to cover greater anticipated returns. I think some contracts still include this antiquated ripoff clause.

♦ BR: People think, "CDs are high-tech—they must cost more to make." But they cost considerably less! Major labels didn't stop making vinyl because records weren't selling; they calculated all their costs and realized that the film cost for 12-inch album artwork was quadruple the cost of the same artwork for a CD booklet. You can fit a couple sheets of a CD booklet on one sheet of film; you can't do that with an LP. With an LP, after your mastering cost, you need to have lacquers made, plates made, test pressings and initial pressings. There's a lot more room for error—at any stage of the process, something can get damaged. With CDs, you get your glass master made and then you make your CDs.

If I use a regular jewel box, my CDs cost— not counting the costs of the booklet, shrink-wrap, and insertion of the booklet—about $1.15 each. That's at my volume of manufacturing, 2,000 at a time. So Warner Brothers, at their volume of 100,000 at a time, is paying 35 cents! Yet their CDs retail for 30% higher to the public. It doesn't have to be that way. I wholesale my CDs for $7.50 and LPs for $4.50 (I don't make cassettes at all). My CDs usually end up selling in stores from $10.99 to $12.99, and the LPs retail from $7.99 to $9.99. This is hard to control, because different distributors and stores have different markups. I sell my CDs through mail order for $9 each, and that includes postage; I still make my money back. My objective is to make enough money to keep going; greed is not a motivator.

♦ AJ: You don't seem to have a set agenda for the kind of music you release. Are there other women who run their own labels, and do they have a deliberate goal to release "women's music" only?

♦ BR: I think Lisa Fancher, who's been running Frontier Records for ten years, has been doing this the longest. Her label was never

men's music.

♦ BR: Exactly. To me it's almost the same thing as the obscenity of "Black Music Departments" at major labels. Why, when R&B is the biggest income generator for many labels, do they have to be segregated to some department? It doesn't necessarily mean they're any *less* of a department, but the perception is that they're seperate from the whole.

♦ AJ: It sounds like you also saw a lot of sexism at major labels.

♦ BR: What I noticed the most was the size of my paycheck. I knew this guy who started at another label doing the same job as me, and he

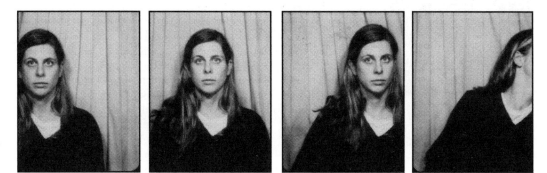

women-oriented at all. Simple Machines, which is run by two women, isn't otherwise women-oriented, other than they release recordings of their own band. I know another woman, Tinuviel, who used to work at Kill Rock Stars. She runs her own label now, Villa Villakula, and is extremely into women-only bands—which I think is perfectly fine.

I think it's great to see women setting up networks for themselves, and putting out fanzines oriented toward themselves. Women can call me up and ask, "Where do you get your singles manufactured?" That's half the battle: once you get the $1000 together to press your single, you need to know where to have it done. There's a place in California called Punks With Presses that prints up 45 sleeves, CD booklets and tray cards extremely cheaply. That can make a big difference to someone who's starting out and couldn't afford a regular printer. I'm happy to share what I've learned.

As for the music itself, lots of people ask me why I don't just release women-only recordings. I think that would almost be taking a step backwards, personally. I don't feel I should have to make that distinction.

♦ AJ: Men don't feel they should only release

had signed no bands, yet he was earning about two-and-a-half times my salary. That is not uncommon. I was one of the only women doing my job for two companies, and I found that most of the women employees were in the publicity department. Sylvia Rhone is head of EastWest Records (a subsidiary of Elektra), but how many heads of companies are women? How many heads of A&R departments are women? Not more than one or two. Even though they may have been kidding, more than once A&R men whispered to me, "Be *very* nice to that band, because we want them." That's not funny! A lot of this business is a boys' club where you have to hang out at a bar or a hockey game or some other crap I don't want to do; just by nature of that you're excluded.

I had to sit in marketing meetings and watch these videos showing babes strutting around that just made me totally ill. And nobody seemed very sensitive to that. Atlantic made a "Women of Video" compilation, and it was all these Aerosmith-type video clips of women in bikinis. I was in an elevator with product-manager guys who were talking about how great it was, and I said, "Man, I think that's totally sick." It hadn't even *occurred* to them that people

The Biz, The Sea and the Cake (top) and *Dolomite*, Dolomite (bottom) both from Thrill Jockey (1995).

they work with wouldn't find this "cool."

♦ **AJ: Did you encounter any gender problems from more "alternative" types when you started your label?**

♦ BR: No. I got nothing but help, even from people I didn't know and just called up to ask, "I bought your record, and your vinyl is really thick—who manufactured it?" In direct business dealings, I've never had any manufacturers or distributors treat me like a silly girl. The only thing I've felt is, "I'm being treated this way because I'm a small label." And that's usually from major label people who call me up and want me to send them free CDs and don't understand why I won't! But with manufacturers or distributors, the people I work with day to day, I've never had a problem. All this has only strengthened my feeling of independence.

♦ **AJ: Now there's a lot of *psychological* empowerment to do things that didn't exist twenty years ago. Women who are running record labels or playing in bands are no longer unique.**

♦ BR: There *are* a lot of women running their own businesses or being recognized as artists, but it's still unusual. Female actors still don't get the same pay or recognition as male actors. Female painters have more hurdles to overcome than male painters. I think this is all a matter of time, because as more women of our generation do things, they'll establish a new network that's hopefully more equitable and in which female participants aren't so unusual. However, plenty of obstacles remain to be overcome.

♦ **AJ: For women, anger has such a narrow definition: it denotes a PMS hag; a shrewish bitch who is not sexy or libidinal. Whereas with male artists—do you think Michael Stipe**

would say that he wasn't angry?

♦ BR: He's angry about certain inequities he sees, that motivate him to write certain lyrics or have Greenpeace booths at his shows, and that certainly isn't seen as negative. But a woman isn't assertive, she's "pushy." If you know people who work for a woman who is professionally exacting and demanding, you're probably not surprised when she's called a "bitch." This would not be the case if she were a man; people would just say, "Oh, he demands a lot."

When I talk to people on the phone, I don't compromise on what my bands want or what I want. There was a big clothing store chain that wanted to put one of my band's records in all their stores. I asked the band, and they didn't want to be a "clothing accessory"—I don't blame them! If the store had wanted to *buy* the records, there wouldn't have been a problem, but the band didn't want to *give* them 50 free records just to provide "atmosphere" for their stores. The store representative said, "Don't you see? We're a national chain, and this is going to help you." But I told him, "I'm not interested. I don't shop in your store; none of my bands do. You don't matter to our world." If I were a man, he probably would have thought, "Well, he was a real hard-ass, but he knows what he wants." But I'm sure that after he hung up the phone he went, "What a bitch!"

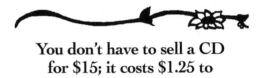

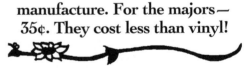

You don't have to sell a CD for $15; it costs $1.25 to manufacture. For the majors— 35¢. They cost less than vinyl!

A rock writer for a trade magazine, *Album Network*, called me and asked for free CDs so he could review them. I said, "No, I'm not going to send you free review copies." He asked, "Don't you know what *Album Network* is?" (he didn't know that I used to work at a major label; I know exactly what it is). I said, "Yeah, it's a trade magazine. I'm not interested in having the music industry know about my records—other than people who are fans and *want* to hear them. I'm not interested in working the industry." As he hung up the phone I heard him say, "*What a bitch!*"

I think it's fair to think of myself as angry; I'm doing what I'm doing because I didn't like the system I saw.

It blew my mind when Liz Phair became so popular, and mostly male writers were saying she was a spokeswoman for women of her age—because she used phrases like "fuck and run" and posed lying in beds with a guitar between her legs, squeezing her cleavage. I thought, "These rock writers are so dumb!" It woke me up again to realize that there are so many people who *still* just don't get it!

◆ AJ: Although many people, including some women, discount the idea that women have anything to be angry about at this point, there are clearly still problems of inequity and blatant sexism that exist at both the mainstream *and* alternative or underground level.

The reason major labels have started to make vinyl again is because it's "cool." Well, who told them it was cool? The kids and small labels who refused to buy into their CD-only propaganda.

◆ BR: That's true. It's very rare to see a woman live-sound engineer or road manager. It's rare to see a woman engineer or producer in a recording studio; women are extremely in the minority on the technical and business sides of things. If I know a woman who's a sound person, I feel I should make efforts to help her or at least be supportive. You have to be aware of what other women are trying to do, and if you can be supportive in some way, you should be.

I know this woman in Chicago, Sheila Cronin, who's a sound engineer. When she shows up at a club, nobody ever expects her to go behind the mixing board. I know she gets untold amounts of crap from some of these bands: "*She's* doing our sound?!" I think to myself: *I* select the people I work with, whereas she can't.

Everyone I work with I *choose* to work with. I have the power of decision to use a certain manufacturer or distributor, to put out a record or not, but a lot of women aren't in that position. The majority of club promoters are men, and if you're a female road manager and you have to collect the band's money at the end of the night, I'm sure your picture is much less rosy than mine. The percentage of male club owners trying to rip you off or just give you a hard time because you're a woman tour manager is high—no doubt about it.

◆ AJ: I think the political goals of those who are trying to oppose mainstream big business are laudable, but I'm concerned with the issue of how we make alternative economic structures. Aside from the rhetoric, do you see this happening in the independent network you're trying to cultivate?

◆ BR: I think that what keeps a lot of independents going is the knowledge that you are empowered to determine your own path. There are no "you-have-to's." Plenty of people still make vinyl-only releases, even though it's been said that vinyl is dead. The reason major labels have started to make vinyl again is because it's "cool." Well, who told them it was cool? The kids and small labels who refused to buy into their CD-only propaganda. In cases like this, the independent system and its supporters had enough clout to affect what was happening throughout the industry.

Thank god Fugazi sells 100,000 records and is still independent, because independent distributors need that kind of volume to survive in business. If every independent band that starts selling that many records leaves for a big label, the independent system will remain stuck at a certain level of growth. If more bands take Fugazi's example and turn down that carrot, and more labels don't sell themselves off and stay in the independent network, that network will be viable to change the system. Independent labels originally built up because to the bands, they were as important as profits; there was a balance. Unfortunately, that sense of ethics isn't as strong as it used to be. Sure, this is difficult—financially, it's really hard—but it *can* be done.

◆ AJ: And people cannot live by bread alone! ◆ ◆ ◆

◆ **equipment list** ◆

Musicians who I admire musically and who I personally respect, computer, telephone, cash, patience, and "the fear of God" to scare distributors who may have fallen behind in payments

Chrissie Hynde
Pretenders

Chrissie Hynde, singer and guitarist for The Pretenders, has led the band to a number of international top-ten hits since their first album in 1980. She has lived in London since the mid-'70s, has two daughters, and is an outspoken member of the animal rights group PETA.

♦ **ANDREA JUNO: When did you learn how to play guitar?**
♦ CHRISSIE HYNDE: When I was a teenager. I learned on my own, with books of chords. I didn't learn by jamming with people.
♦ **AJ: You never felt, internally, that you couldn't do it?**
♦ CH: No, I never felt that. But at the time— we're talking about the '60s—the rock bands that I aspired to didn't feature women; so I felt like I could never really achieve my goal. Luckily, I wasn't thinking too much in terms of goals. I just carried on and did it.

It all seemed renegade and anti-establishment, and I never really related too much to gender roles anyway. I didn't feel like I couldn't do it; I just felt that there might not be a place for me.
♦ **AJ: But you obviously made a place for yourself.**
♦ CH: Well, yeah. But at that time, I wasn't thinking about it too much yet. I was sitting in my room, with my little guitar, just goofing around. I didn't pursue music for a few years after that; I hadn't thought, "I'd like to be in a rock band." I started going to university when I was 17.
♦ **AJ: Oh, that's early.**
♦ CH: Well, I graduated from high school when I was 17, and then I started going to Kent State University two weeks later.
♦ **AJ: Were you there during the shooting?**
♦ CH: Oh, yeah.
♦ **AJ: Oh, my god. Did you know any of the people?**
♦ CH: I did know one of the guys.
♦ **AJ: Did that affect you, politically?**

♦ CH: I can't really say I was disillusioned. I didn't have very many illusions, even then, about the ways that the powers-that-be operated. It was shocking, but at the same time it wasn't.
♦ **AJ: You never had faith in government or establishment?**
♦ CH: No.
♦ **AJ: How did you end up in London?**
♦ CH: Kent State University was evacuated when the shooting happened. I never finished university. I didn't want to live in the States, so I got a job, saved about $500, and came to London.
♦ **AJ: Why didn't you want to live in the States?**
♦ CH: I didn't want to have to buy a car, just so I could get to work to *pay* for my car. [laughs] From an early age, I felt there was something drawing me away. I was attracted to England because of the music scene, and when I was younger, I associated it with horses, and other things that I *thought* were English.

There was always a strong pull. I wasn't an Anglophile yet; I didn't know anything about England. I just knew I wanted to go *somewhere*. I'd read my Jack Kerouac books, and from the age of about 16 I was ready to jump on a freight train and go. I used to cry in homeroom when the train passed my school.
♦ **AJ: So the political climate in America and the shootings at Kent State didn't influence that decision?**
♦ CH: No. It didn't make me *more* compelled to stay, but that's not why I left. I've never been very politically motivated.
♦ **AJ: Which is probably good, because you've avoided any of the dogma or PC rheto-**

ric that comes with that terrain. And yet, in a certain sense, your whole career has been a really positive model for others. You're very independent, and you were one of the first women rockers who could really play, too.

♦ CH: I see that all as just a matter of timing. I don't think I was a pioneer.

♦ AJ: Why not?

♦ CH: Well, if I hadn't been there, I don't think it would have changed anything. I was probably attracted to the same aspects of "rockness" that Patti Smith was—I don't know her, so I'm just guessing—the genderless sexuality of it all.

♦ AJ: It was pioneering when women like Patti Smith and you started to embrace that Kerouac-style, beat-generation rebellion.

♦ CH: It was very much a part of the time that we were in. We grew up in the '60s, when there was a huge shift in consciousness; you certainly saw that in the youth culture, where there was a lot of experimentation and searching for other value systems. People explored different religions, mysticism and everything that went with the whole psychedelic period.

When I say that I don't think I was a pioneer, I mean that if we were talking about the '50s, I might have been. But it seemed, in the '60s, that the lid had blown off everything. You could do anything you wanted. There was nothing holding me back. There were no restrictions imposed upon me, other than self-imposed ones. I freed myself up from feeling attached to anything, and felt like I could be what, in England, are called "the travelers." I could be a vagabond. I lived a hand-to-mouth existence for years.

I've been asked endlessly about being a female in a man's field, blah-blah-blah, and it's tedious because I didn't think it was a man's field; *I* was in it, for a start.

I went to England for a while, and met people in the music scene, and some people that wrote for a music paper [*New Musical Express*]. I dabbled in writing for the *NME* a bit, but merely as an extension of that hand-to-mouth existence, not because I was at all interested in being a

Chrissie Hynde (circa 1976).

Photo: Kate Simon

writer. I never felt that I could write. When I tumbled into the job, I saw it as comparable to making picture frames or modeling in an art college. I didn't know what I was doing; it wasn't rock journalism. I thought people had to be qualified to do that—what was I doing there? I didn't realize that you just made it up.

♦ AJ: Right.

♦ CH: Then someone asked me to sing in a band, in France. I went over there with about 40 quid, and stayed about six months. I got very frustrated, because I didn't have any roots there, and the problems of putting a band together in France—not speaking the language, people who didn't have my sort of background in music—were hard to overcome.

I moved back to Cleveland, for another six months, and there I did get in a band. At that point, I was very driven: being in a band is what I wanted to do. I had met Malcolm McClaren, and all these characters, in London. Malcolm wrote to me, and said he would give me a ticket back to England, to be in a band he was putting together. I think this was just prior to the Sex Pistols. I declined, because I was learning how to sing in the Cleveland band. But that was short-lived.

I drove with a couple of girlfriends out west, because I had nothing else to do. I went to Tucson and tried to find work as a cocktail waitress. I was very depressed there, because everyone was into country music. I felt very displaced, and didn't know what the hell I was doing out in the heat.

I felt that something was happening in England; I had an instinct. I got back to England—this was about 1976. The punk scene was starting to happen. I thought, at the age of about 24, that it might be too late for me to get in a band; I was too old. Things were really different back then. You were kind of over the hill at 24.

♦ AJ: Rock was actually confined to youth back then.

♦ CH: It was a teenager thing. But when punk exploded, suddenly there were chicks in bands. What characterized the whole punk scene for me, in that first six months of 1977 when it was really going strong and there were tons of bands, was that the tone of it was non-discriminatory. There was no racism or sexism. It was an anarchy of -isms, a matter of abolishing them all. So it was unthinkable to go see a band and even consider that they were just "good for girls." You didn't have that kind of restriction or judgment.

Chrissie at approximately age 8, Cleveland, OH (1959).

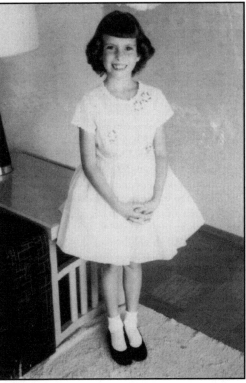

You just took the music for what it was, and that was fantastic for someone like me. I felt I could start throwing some stakes in there. I didn't want to be a novelty act. My timing is just luck, isn't it? I grew up and the time was right, and I kept banging away and trying to play with different people.

What characterized the whole punk scene for me in 1977 was there was no racism or sexism. It was an anarchy of -isms, a matter of abolishing them all.

There were a lot of people in London looking for bands, and running clothing stores—Malcolm [McLaren] sort of pioneered that, going from the clothing store to putting a band together, and making an extension of the whole thing.

♦ AJ: Did you know Vivienne Westwood?

♦ CH: Oh, yeah. I worked for them before I went on my crusade to get a band together.

♦ AJ: I'm trying to get a feel for what it was like in London back then. I came into the punk scene here, in America, around '79. There was the same freedom that you described, between women and men, and there was also the same feeling of anarchy. But I saw a lot of hypocrisy, too.

♦ CH: By 1979 there was no longer any punk scene here. It really only lasted from the beginning of 1977 until about the middle of 1977. The English experience and the American one are so different that I might as well have been in Germany or France or anywhere else; I can't compare them. By the time I got into the music scene in London, the punk scene was kind of gone. My first record came out in 1979.

♦ AJ: Did you have a support system with other women in the London scene?

♦ CH: No, there wasn't a support system. It felt very evenly distributed. I tried to work with a lot of different guys around town, because they were the ones who were putting bands together. There was only one guy I tried to work with who didn't treat me the same as if I were just another guy. He said to me, "Look, I just don't think women can sing rock." I was like, "Oh, well, okay." I think that's a good point. As far as I'm concerned, if you don't like the sound of the female voice singing rock, that's just because it's a different instrument—it's a matter of taste.

But I never thought there was anything to distinguish a female guitar player or a male guitar player, any more than you can distinguish a male cellist or a female cellist. Other than the fact that chicks never seemed to be nearly as good at guitar.

♦ **AJ: Why do you think that is?**

♦ CH: I think that, inherently, they don't have the aptitude for it, like men do.

♦ **AJ: Do you think that inability might be self-imposed—that women just think they can't do it?**

♦ CH: Yeah, I think it is self-imposed. When I say aptitude, I don't know if it's the way our brains are wired up, if it's biological, or what it is. All I know is that since I got interested in rock'n'roll music, and up to this present day, I've never heard a woman be an innovator on the guitar, like Jimi Hendrix, Jeff Beck, or any of the great guitar players. I'm not concluding anything from that other than what's obvious: they're not as good at it. I'm not saying why, or for what reason. It's just that so far, no girls have done it.

♦ **AJ: Do you know June Millington from Fanny?**

♦ CH: I remember her. There's always the exception to the rule. You might be able to name one obscure name that a few people would know, someone who was great at the time. I never said women *couldn't* do it. I mean, *I* was doing it. But, for some reason, they *didn't* do it.

There are a lot of reasons why chicks probably don't get into playing, or haven't gotten into playing. Let's just be clinical about it. Up until the advent of birth control, women who were sexually active and heterosexual were having children. We don't need to go any further into that particular scenario.

> **The whole idea of being in a rock band, in the first place, was to say, "Hey, I'm an ugly duckling, fuck you."**

♦ **AJ: But you have two children.**

♦ CH: I got my band together before I had them. I'm talking about before the advent of birth control. Most women, by the time they were 24, would likely have a kid. They're looking after the kid, not thinking about getting in a rock band.

Photo: Gavin Evans

A rock band is an adolescent thing. That's why women weren't rockers. And then it busted open in the '60s, because people were free to do what they wanted. They weren't restricted by what they considered the traditional restrictions.

It did puzzle me that, from the '60s through the '80s, there still wasn't some awesome babe who came out and just blew everyone's mind. I don't mean someone who's just really, really good, but someone who's invented an entire new genre.

I've been asked endlessly about being a female in a man's field, blah-blah-blah, and it's tedious to be asked those questions, because I didn't think it was a man's field; *I* was in it, for a start. I never felt discriminated against. I never felt that I had to work harder than a man. I never thought I had anything to prove, and I'm not competitive.

I never gave the answers that these so-called feminists wanted. They would ask me the same question over and over within the same interview, trying to get me to say, "Yes, it's been harder because I'm a woman. I've had to prove myself. Men have given me a hard time. Men haven't

Chrissie at age 15 holding her first guitar, the Rolling Stones' *December's Children* and Bob Dylan's *Subterranean Home-Sick Blues* (1966).

taken me seriously." But it just wasn't the case. I always imagine these interviewers walking away with their hands in the air, pissed off.

♦ **AJ: I've done a lot of interviews for this book. Hardly any of the women say they've had *that* hard of a time in the rock world. In this day and age, I think that assertion would be a sign of self-imposed victimization.**

♦ CH: I would have to conclude that, too— because I'm not anything so special. I'm *not* a great guitar player. I'm fair at being a band leader, and I know the ropes, as far as what I want to do in a rock band. But I'd say my skills are pretty average. I was never technical. I've never known the names of the chords; I go by the dots on the guitar. When the bass player comes in, I'd say, "Can you now play above the third dot, please?" I never saw anyone roll their eyes, like I was an idiot—people could see I might not know how to say it, but I know what I'm trying to get out. I've never pretended to have any technical knowledge, or be interested in engineering.

I've never tried to act like any kind of hotshot guitar player. I'd get the guys to help me. As soon as I started tuning my guitar, guys would always grab it and start tuning it for me. I'd just let them do it; if I don't have to tune my guitar, it gives me more time to write a song. That was never a problem for me. I'd be bummed if a guy didn't offer to carry my guitar. I hate carrying shit.

There's no point in shooting yourself in the foot. You just have to accept things the way they are, and get on with it. None of the women I know who are at the top of their respective fields have ever claimed that they were feminists, or felt like they were discriminated against. I'm not talking so much about executives, although I am talking about the music industry, and people in record companies; people who have made it and sustained themselves and are respected, like my manager. I know, because I've asked them.

♦ **AJ: Well, what does feminism mean to you? I think there's a confusion as to what the word actually means. There are many different kinds of feminism.**

♦ CH: About twenty years ago, when I was writing at the *NME*, I met this feminist, who might be a famous writer. I never remembered her name. She confronted me with this, "Are you a feminist?" I said, "I don't know. What's a feminist?" And she was obviously a bit put out that I even asked her to qualify it.

She said, "Let me ask you this. Do you expect that you should be able to do the same job as a man?" I said, "I *do*." She goes, "Well, do you think you should be paid the same?" I said, "I *am*." She said, "Well, what if you want to get a credit card, for example, from a department store?" I said, "I don't want one." She says, "Okay, let's say you're going to buy a car, and you want to pay the down payment." I said, "I don't want a car."

Finally she said, "All right, let me put it this way, what about some women that *do* want these things?" I said, "Well, they have to sort it out." And she said, "You're not a feminist." For the next 20 years, if anyone asked me, I'd just say, "No, I'm not a feminist." She seemed to know what they were, because she was one of these leading feminists, and she told me I wasn't. Who was I to dispute it?

♦ **AJ: That's a good story.**

♦ CH: Throughout the '70s and the '80s, I was still trying to answer the question of why I think women can't play the guitar. One aspect of that question has to do with the growing process from adolescence into adulthood. Girls are great communicators. They easily talk to each other, and they certainly talk about their emotions. They'll talk on the phone for hours. If they have a problem, or if they fancy a boy, or if they're into a band, or if they're listening to records they love on the radio, they'll get their girlfriends on the phone, sit down in front of the stereo, and actually listen to the radio together, over the phone. Or I certainly used to.

It's easy for most girls to communicate with another girlfriend. But guys don't seem to have that same relationship with other guys. They don't really talk about their emotions so much. They talk about more external things, and engage in external activities, like group sports. I don't think I've ever met a guy who sits and yaks on the phone, like a chick does, to another guy. Maybe a gay guy does, but it's usually to a girlfriend.

Guys have a harder time expressing themselves and their emotions. Guys also have egos that need to be nurtured, because they're very worried about growing up and being men, and performing as men. There's a lot of pressure on them.

I'm still talking more about how things were maybe twenty years ago. If a guy was introverted and shy, that was a real dilemma for him. He couldn't talk to anyone about it. But he could find a way to express himself. If he couldn't do it verbally, he could express his emotions, do wonders for his ego, and make himself be seen, in the eyes of others, as having some worth — just by getting shit-hot on the fucking guitar. Guys seem to be more focused; their concentration is better on mechanical things. Women seem to be more easily distracted.

I'm not really particularly impressed if you're a Jewish keyboard player or a Protestant bass player. I mean, just fuckin' play it.

♦ **AJ: Are you still talking twenty years ago?**
♦ CH: Yeah, but these are characteristics that are inherently male and female. I'm not saying that these characteristics can't cross over to the other gender, but in general they are distinctly male and female.

As far as the question of why there aren't more female rockers — hey, you know what? *I don't know.* I've asked the same question myself, for

years. "Why aren't there more chicks doing this?" I thought, "I'm not working in a shoe store; I'm not a waitress. I'm in a rock band. What could be better?" I never could understand; why are so few women doing this?
♦ **AJ: Well, now there is an explosion of girls and women in rock.**
♦ CH: Right, now there's an explosion. And now my feelings are starting to change about the whole thing. I'm finding that it's put some interest into the rock scene. It's like a new voice. Earlier on, when chicks were in bands, they seemed to ape the way that men did it. They sang in the same heavy metal voice. They had the same hard edge. They belted. They screamed. Or they were folky. But now it's interesting, because there are tons of girls in bands. It's not even an issue anymore.

I don't like polarization of the community. Black America, now, is totally segregated. It's never been so polarized before. It's the same with gay America. What's next? The yellow pages, the blue pages and the pink pages. There's no mix of the cultures. Can't people just be people? Can't we be men and women? Do we have to keep qualifying it endlessly with Black, Lesbian, Catholic? Can we please be part of the human pageantry? It's what I've always longed for, and it's what I've always tried to strive for, in my own life.

I'm not really particularly impressed if you're a Jewish keyboard player or a Protestant bass player. I mean, just fuckin' play it.
♦ **AJ: I actually see less of the identity politics — "I am a gay, black, blah-blah-blah" — from kids now.**
♦ CH: Yes. I reckon there's got to be a big backlash coming, and it's going to come from these kids that you're talking about. My dyke friends and I have talked about it a lot lately; most of them are fuckin' disgusted with the reductions of identity politics. You can't pick up a gay magazine without looking at endless sex aids and paraphernalia. It's become very seedy. Most people find the whole thing a bit smug or embarrassing.
♦ **AJ: It's embarrassing because it's so self-conscious.**
♦ CH: I don't walk around like, "Hi, I'm a heterosexual with a penchant for vaginal intercourse." Can't people just get on with their private lives? Can't you have some sort of personal life which is sacred to you?
♦ **AJ: I think that we can now, because of conscious progress towards removing the stigma and shame from these aspects of identity.**
♦ CH: I applaud all the changes. But now is

Pretenders (1980), *Pretenders II* (1981) and *Learning to Crawl* (1984).

the time when it has to be reassessed, before people my age, and even younger, start looking like real old fuddy-duddies for being so stuck in the politically correct agenda of the moment.

First you can't say colored; you have to say black. Then you can't say black; you have to say —

♦ **AJ: — African-American.**

♦ CH: Basically, as people, I think everyone's still pretty fuckin' confused; maybe more so than ever before. Women have never really seemed to understand their own sexuality. I'm not saying that men do, either, but women have never understood their own cycles, and have never gotten in tune with the cycles and subtle rhythms that govern their lives. Instead, they constantly try to bend their female biological condition according to their own will.

♦ **AJ: What exactly are you talking about?**

♦ CH: Well, I'm talking about birth control, for example. There's no point in thinking you're a liberated woman because you're on the pill, if you consequently behave like a man. You have to learn your own true nature, and follow it.

♦ **AJ: Well, what's a woman's true nature? That can be kind of confusing.**

♦ CH: If a woman is going to have an active sex life, and she doesn't want to become pregnant, she's going to have to govern it according to when she's fertile and when she's not. That sort of thing.

♦ **AJ: You don't believe in birth control?**

♦ CH: I don't think it's something to believe in. It's a drug, a tool.

♦ **AJ: What about condoms?**

♦ CH: Condoms haven't helped women understand their own nature. They've been a deterrent. When they teach sex education in school, they show you how to use birth control, but they don't show you how to understand your own cycles. A woman doesn't know when she's on or when she's off.

♦ **AJ: Nowadays, because of AIDS, kids are taught that they have to use a condom.**

♦ CH: I'm not talking about prevention of diseases. I'm just talking about knowing your true nature.

♦ **AJ: Well, as an astrologer, and as someone who also does yoga and things like that, I really believe in cycles, and listening to your inner self.**

♦ CH: That's what I'm talking about. If a woman was instructed, from an early age, to be totally in tune with her cycles, then she'd have a sense of how her body works, and when she's fertile. But as soon as one babe started taking birth control pills, they all had to. Because the "sexual revolution" meant, for a woman, that the man she was after was going to go elsewhere for what he wanted if she wouldn't deliver it.

All I know is that since I got interested in rock'n'roll music, I've never heard a woman be an innovator on the guitar, like Jimi Hendrix, Jeff Beck, or any of the great guitar players.

If all the women were adhering to the same system, saying "We have to do it when we want to do it, or we have to make amends during certain times of the month." If it was up to the woman to dictate when sex could happen, things would be a lot different.

♦ **AJ: Well, women are now starting to own sexual power for themselves. When there's an attitude that only men like sex and women don't, then you do have the problems you're** describing: sex becomes something for women to trade. But that's changing for the younger generation. I think now, more than ever, women have a much more informed view of their sexuality, and men don't think of women's sexuality as such a mystery.

♦ CH: For a long time, women aped the behavior of men. When birth control pills were first available to teenagers, teenage girls just tried to keep up with the boys. "If you're going to have sex with me, and it doesn't mean anything to you, and I'm going to be nursing a broken heart for two weeks—that's not going to happen again. Next time I'm going to be prepared for it. I'm going to treat it as lightly as you did."

A lot of women were very promiscuous, against their own nature, because they wanted to avoid being hurt. They were aping the behavior of men.

♦ AJ: That sounds like the '70s, particularly.

♦ CH: I'm not saying that using all these artificial means of contraception isn't good. They are good means of contraception, but they are not good ways for a woman to understand the subtlety of her own spiritual and sexual nature.

♦ AJ: How old were you, when you first had a child?

♦ CH: 28, 29.

♦ AJ: That's not so young. Obviously, before that you were either using some kind of birth control or you were very lucky.

♦ CH: Well, no. Throughout that time, I was like everyone else.

♦ AJ: And did you feel, then, that birth control was damaging, or did you feel that it was a necessary part of the process?

♦ CH: No, I was just concerned with getting on with doing my thing. All I'm saying is that now, looking at it objectively, wouldn't it be better just to understand your sexuality from the start? To know what restrictions you have, how you have to behave?

♦ AJ: Hopefully both men *and* women will start to think like that.

♦ CH: I'm just saying that I think a lot of women's liberation has been, I think, falsely accredited to the simple fact of women having changed due to other things. A lot of those changes coincide with the ad-

vent of birth control. Now, 30 years later, women are saying, "Wow, did we get a lot of things wrong." Theoretically, that is. I think a lot of feminists are saying that.

There is something to be said for what have traditionally been female values and female interests. For a long time, they were rejected. Women said, "No, we're equal." But we quite clearly are not equal to men. In many regards we are opposites to men. We should be *treated* equally, in terms of value and respect. But we don't have equal facility, in many regards. We're different. That's now being recognized, and everyone thinks that's fine.

I'd be bummed if a guy didn't offer to carry my guitar. I hate carrying shit.

♦ AJ: Before, the goal was to be equal—but with male rules. And now it's, "Wait a minute, maybe we can be equal, but we don't have to throw out female rules or perspectives."

♦ CH: Exactly.

♦ AJ: The fact is that women can be now strong, while bringing in their own rules, even about sexuality. For instance, there is the typi-

The Hynde family (l. to r.): Christy (Chrissie); Bud, dad; Terry, brother; Dee, mom (1950s).

cal male rock'n'roll star that has this unbelievable excess of sexual relations. Mick Jagger, or someone like him, can fuck 50,000 women, and you can imagine the psychic damage it can do to somebody to use sex as that kind of validation.

♦ CH: Yeah, but for guys it's different. They can just get their rocks off, for a bit of a laugh. It doesn't work like that with women.

> "Why aren't there more chicks doing this?" I've thought, "I'm not working in a shoe store. I'm not a waitress. I'm in a rock band. What could be better?"

♦ AJ: But don't you also think that attitude damages men, too? They have the highest suicide rate; especially when they get older, after 40.

♦ CH: I think you have to understand what your natural inclination is, but you also have to try to stay on top of it. We can't be ruled by our desires, because they are really our enemies.

♦ AJ: In light of what we've said about male sexual prerogatives and that rock'n'roll attitude, do you think there is a difference in goals and attitude for the women now getting into rock?

♦ CH: I think there is a big difference. But I'm not really qualified to say, since I'm not one of the women getting into rock bands now.

♦ AJ: But you're a woman and you're in a rock band.

♦ CH: I got into rock because, when I was a teenager, I loved the renegade, outlaw, anti-establishment, rebellious aspects of it. I also loved music and I loved singing. The whole thing looked pretty fuckin' attractive to me. Remember, when I was 14, it was just when the Beatles started.

It was unprecedented when bands started to actually become millionaires. Rock bands didn't have money. This life of luxury that we associate with rock bands and supermodels didn't exist then. You didn't get into it because you were looking for a career. You got into it because you *didn't* want a career. Or that's certainly why I got into it. I had no goals. I didn't want a career. I was very much a product of the '60s. Total re-

jection of my parents' values.

♦ AJ: You mean a rejection of materialism and—

♦ CH: Yeah. People who were raising their families in the '50s still got married and had 2.5 kids, a couple cars—by the end of the '60s, we wanted nothing to do with that kind of life. It looked like we didn't have to, so we weren't going to.

Rock was a small-time affair then. There weren't videos; there was nothing like that. It's a completely different thing that we're talking about now.

♦ AJ: Now it's less about the music, and more about the mechanisms of fame?

♦ CH: Right. Let's just talk about chicks. A lot of them probably just want to be a "big star." They'll do it through dance, or they'll do it through pop music, or by being a supermodel; however they can get in there. However they can get their faces seen. Some people are still very driven musically, and have a real musical aspect. Some people aren't that musical, but they get into it because they like the social aspect of it. That's the thing with rock music. It encompasses all these things.

These days, if you want to actually make it in a band and become really successful, I suppose the things that you have to attend to are the things that have to do with your *image*. Those things are a lot more important now than they ever were. There was a time when you'd listen to songs, and it was very much like how you read novels. You might have read every novel that Graham Greene ever wrote, but you had no idea what he looked like, and you'd never really thought about it. It's the same with songs. There were songwriters, but you didn't see their faces. The singers interpreted the songs.

That way I think happens to be out of step with today, where you're supposed to put all your cards on the table and tell who you fucked last week, and how good it was. I have my life, and it's not open to the public. I'm only known for making music. In the good old days, you'd just get the record, and maybe there would be a picture of me on the record. But I never used to read interviews with, say, Dionne Warwick in 1967.

♦ AJ: That glamorization process kills a lot of art. Of course, you can also say there's an opposition, in the new little pockets of fresh air that bubble up from the underground all the time, to this focus on fame and glamour.

♦ CH: What I'm saying is, now a person can go out and sell themselves. These days, it's a media game, isn't it? It's a media dictatorship

that we've got. If you want to play the media, and you're good at it, then the music itself isn't really the vehicle to get you to the top. You can actually do it just by working the media. There are a lot of people who are very, very famous, but everyone only knows that they're very, very famous. They don't actually know what that person does. A lot of people's fame outweighs what they actually do.

What I'm getting at is that if a chick gets into a band now, there's all sorts of reasons why she might. I imagine that if you're getting in a band, you're already thinking about, "Well, I'm going to have to do videos." And I suppose, if you're in America, "Do I want silicone implants?" Which, to me, is pretty damn contrary to anything I would have thought feminists were all about. But there you go. They've all got 'em.

♦ **AJ: No, they don't all have them. I mean, Courtney Love allegedly does, but I wouldn't call her a feminist.**

♦ CH: I'm just talking about feminist women. I'm not even talking about rock bands. But you're talking about an opposition to all this fame and glamour.

♦ **AJ: I'm saying that there is a whole underground that you're not even reading about, which is what, in a certain sense, rock music used to be about. I've noticed quite a few pockets of resistance with their own political agendas—they're against all the bloated excesses of mainstream rock.**

♦ CH: I'm counting on them. I really am. I think that the new generation is going to be a lot more like the first six months of 1977 was, for the lucky few who can break away from the other horrors of growing up in this day and age.

> **I don't walk around like, "Hi, I'm a heterosexual with a penchant for vaginal intercourse."**

♦ **AJ: Part of what makes me hopeful is a more relaxed attitude towards sexuality, which in this case I see going along with the fact of more women coming into rock music, and being strong about their own roles.**

♦ CH: Incidentally, I wasn't just talking about women rockers, when I mentioned breast im-

The Pretenders (l. to r.): Andy Hobson, Chrissie Hynde, Adam Seymour and Martin Chambers.

plants. I'm talking about show business. I'm talking about Janet Jackson—the entire Jackson family. Every Hollywood actress.

♦ **AJ: Absolutely. This is mainstream.**

♦ CH: The girls in Heart. Stevie Nicks. Everybody. Everybody but me!

♦ **AJ: Well, that's why you're admired by a lot of these younger kids—and by me. That's why you're a pioneer.**

♦ CH: The whole idea of being in a rock band, in the first place, was to say, "Hey, I'm an ugly duckling, fuck you." The point was to be noncompetitive, to say, "I don't have to prove anything. This is me. I walked in here, off the street, and this is it. I'm not an actor. I'm in a rock band. I'm not going to compromise myself to look or be something to make you accept me." That's what rock was to me.

Now there have been a lot of other women in rock. A lot of the women whose stuff I really like at the moment have paid a big tribute to Madonna, for example, saying that she kicked open doors.

♦ **AJ: What do you think?**

♦ CH: I think she was a great disco queen.

♦ **AJ: Do you think she kicked open doors?**

♦ CH: No, I don't. I don't know why people pay such tribute to her. She had a lot of great disco records, and certainly sustained that for a long time. Again, she was a girl who wanted to be a star. If she could have done it through dancing, if she could have done it through acting, she would have—she just wanted to be up there. She chose the kids-from-*Fame* route. And it

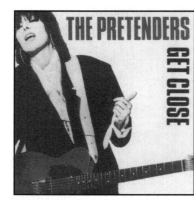
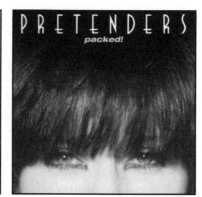

Get Close (1986) and *Packed!* (1990).

worked. But it was never rock'n'roll. So I wonder what these rock'n'roll chicks mean when they say she kicked open doors.

♦ **AJ: I don't know anybody who uses her as a role model, actually. She's mainstream and synthesized.**

♦ CH: Oh, I know. But I read somewhere that Liz Phair said, "I wouldn't be here if it wasn't for Madonna." I was like, "Whoa!" Because I have a lot of time for Liz Phair. I don't mean to say that I dislike Madonna.

♦ **AJ: I don't either.**

♦ CH: She has certainly made a huge impact. And now she's being out-Maddonaed by Courtney Love, which is amusing, if nothing else.

♦ **AJ: Courtney is almost like the stereotype of the male rock star, in a female body. What do you think?**

♦ CH: I like the Iggy Pop-ness of her: being loaded, and just out of her mind. I guess she's entertaining. I saw the band [Hole], and I thought they were good. I thought—"Well, if I just walked in off the street and saw them, and didn't know who they were, I'd think, 'wow!'" I thought they were good fun, but it wasn't the most mind-boggling show I've ever seen in my life. It didn't warrant as much attention as she's gotten. But, again, she's just playing the media game.

I don't know what Liz Phair was talking about, but if it meant that you pull your pants down and then everyone cheers… you can kick down that door, but I ain't goin' through it.

♦ **AJ: That's why you're admired. You stuck to deeper principles.**

♦ CH: Hey, I like my life. I got into this so I could be left alone, do what I want to do, and goof off. You don't have to know who I'm sleeping with. I'm most certainly not going to publicize it. That's *my* thing, and I certainly wouldn't

use it to further myself or make myself look more colorful. Although it certainly would do that, if I started opening my mouth. But the kind of person that I would be into wouldn't appreciate that kind of gossip very much. Cool people like their privacy.

♦ **AJ: Do you believe in monogamy? Do you believe that women are more monogamous?**

♦ CH: I don't know if I'd call it a belief. But I think that, inherently, women are most certainly more monogamous, by their very nature. There's no question. A man can, literally, go out and just knob anyone, then come in and say, "Look, it didn't mean anything." And he means exactly that. A woman doesn't believe him, because she can't understand that; it can't happen to her. If she goes out and has sex with someone, it means something to her. It means something emotionally, and it gets into her psyche.

♦ **AJ: How do you think that difference can be reconciled, without a lot of pain? Or do you think that kind of dissonance is just inherent in relationships between men and women?**

♦ CH: I don't know. What's interesting, to me, is looking at some other cultures, in which men have more than one wife, and trying to understand how this works. Is the feeling of being possessive of someone, and wanting someone to yourself, because of our cultural programming? Or is that inherent to us? It's hard to say, isn't it?

♦ **AJ: Yeah. Although I would say that the cultures in which men have more than one wife are exclusively cultures where women are second-class citizens, and do not have power within the society.**

♦ CH: We're bewildered by it now, because we know how capable we are. But at the time when the social mores that those women are bound to first sprang up, they might have made some kind of sense that we could understand. We don't even know what the origins of a lot of these customs are. We can trace them back to religious texts, but I don't think that's necessarily going to give us an accurate read-out on this. I mean, why are women circumcised, if you can call it that? Millions of them are, and they perpetuate it themselves.

◆ **AJ: But isn't that like saying that in slave cultures, the slaves perpetuate the system themselves?**

◆ **CH:** Well, it's the women who circumcise each other.

◆ **AJ: Right, but in slave cultures, those who are enslaved have usually been recruited to enslave each other. Once a race or a gender has been so denigrated, and made powerless, it's easier to make them turn on themselves; that's why women can be so competitive with each other.**

As for female genital mutilation, it is purely and simply the means to enslave and make "impotent" the female gender—for the exclusive use of the male. It does nothing for women except sometimes to kill them (the operations are brutal) or, at the very least, kill off their sexual feelings.

◆ **CH:** I only heard about the practice within the last ten years; I never had heard of it before. There seems to be a lot of attention focused on it now. We have a lot more Africans here than there are in America; in certain parts of London, there are thousands of girls at risk. They're sent back to wherever they come from, for six weeks. It's a very widespread practice.

Think of it this way: I don't think any of those girls are playing the guitar. I'm not saying that you have to have balls to play guitar, but you've got to have something down there.

◆ **AJ: Women have balls; they're just higher up... I do wonder about the issue of sexuality and competition. You're a prominent woman; you're famous, talented and smart. Do you find that your male peers are competitive, or threatened? I think women of our generation have a bit of a harder time with men who are over 40. You often see older men marrying younger, less powerful women.**

◆ **CH:** There are also a lot of women my age who are with younger men. I think this is going to become very commonplace. People no longer get married by a certain age. They don't stay married for any particular period of time, there's no real structure to relationships, there don't seem to be any restrictions; so why shouldn't anyone, of a sexually active age, i.e.,

an adult, enter into any kind of relationship with any other adult?

Again, it's a recent thing; up until very recently, marriage was structured a certain way. A woman got married when she was 23, to a man that was 25. And then he dumped her when she was 48. That, fortunately, is not going to be our problem. We didn't get married when we were 23, and it hasn't really mattered.

> **I've never understood why women say they're younger than they are, it doesn't make them look good. I add a couple of years to my age. I think it makes being vegetarian look good. If I say I'm 45, someone will think, "Hmm. Maybe there's something to it." But if I say I'm 35, they're going to say, "Well, it hasn't done _her_ any favors."**

I'm 43. In my daily life, I'm more likely to meet guys who are in rock bands. There was a time when most of them were older than me. At this point, most of them are probably younger than me. But I've stayed interested, pretty much, in the same thing. So it's gone from meeting guys who are older than me to meeting guys that are younger than me. There's nothing too fuckin'

The Last of the Independents (1994) and *The Isle of View* (1995).

Chrissie, at age 32, with second child; outside hotel in Florida on tour.

has to be good in bed. I think that makes a guy fuckin' roll over and want to go to sleep. Men are probably not as sexually motivated as they ideally would be, because they feel like they're under scrutiny all the time.

◆ **AJ: Have you actually encountered this reaction?**

◆ CH: It's just a general observation. I think men are shrinking away from the responsibility of having to keep their women satisfied and happy. It's a new one for men; in the past, that didn't really come up.

◆ **AJ: It didn't come up because men didn't feel that there was any expectation of satisfaction.**

◆ CH: Yeah. The man could be a total bastard, and never fuck his wife. But she wasn't going anywhere.

All of this change is healthy. But with so many reassessments being made, people are just confused as to what they are supposed to do. Social rules have been abandoned. Not once in my life have I thought, "Christ, I'm getting up there; I should get married." Or, "Am I going to be left on the shelf?" Nothing like that has ever occurred to me. I've never had feelings like that. Have you?

◆ **AJ: No. I love being older. There are some women who are still stuck on that age thing. They refuse to say how old they are.**

◆ CH: What's the big deal? It's not classified information. I've never understood why women say they're younger than they are, to tell you the truth, because it doesn't make them look good. If I have to go one way or the other, I add a couple of years to my age. I think it makes being vegetarian, which I've been since 1969, look good. If I say I'm 45, someone will think, "Hmm. Maybe there's something to it." But if I say I'm 35, they're going to say, "Well, it hasn't done *her* any favors."

Do you know what I was saying about how different society is now for older women? Traditionally—

◆ **AJ: Traditionally if you were a forty-year-**

mystifying about that.

◆ **AJ: You don't think there's anything wrong with having a relationship with a younger man, do you?**

◆ CH: No. There's nothing wrong with it.

◆ **AJ: You were married or in a long-term relationship with two men whom you had kids with. Two men who were also famous rock stars, your peers. Did you find that there was competition with these men?**

◆ CH: Well, they were very different. There was possibly competition in one case, and maybe not in the other. I've found that it's just kind of boring to listen to someone else doing business on the phone all the time. Maybe that has nothing to do with them being in the same business, but you don't want it in your face all the time, and people in rock bands conduct their business from home. That can be tedious.

◆ **AJ: Did you find yourself being competitive?**

◆ CH: No. I never felt competitive.

◆ **AJ: I find that women are less competitive, and men's egos can be very fragile.**

◆ CH: I think men are having a hard time, at the moment, because there's so much emphasis in the media on satisfying women. You see it in women's magazines and men's magazines. I don't think any man wants to feel like he's being judged by his performance, or that he has to deliver, and

old woman, you were washed up.

♦ CH: Society had some structure then.

♦ AJ: But that structure, for a woman, meant that she had to kiss off any sex life or love life after 40, because she didn't count anymore.

♦ CH: Well, quite.

> I feel very obligated to publicly say that I'm a pothead, and fuck you. I'm growing it, I'm smoking it, and I *will* smoke it, if I want to… that's why I say, legalize pot.

♦ AJ: So who cares about the structure? Because if things still worked like that, we'd be in a very poor position.

♦ CH: There's some security in structure. But I'm not saying it's good. All I'm saying is that now it's a free-for-all age. There's not much structure; there's been a breakdown of the family structure, that's for sure. People are scared. They aren't quite sure how hands-on fathers should be, if they should even be involved; is the nuclear family ideal or not; should women be just looking after the kids?

Personally, I just wonder why, on god's green earth, can't gay couples adopt children? And what's to guarantee that, say, an unmarried couple won't stay together forever and be wonderful parents? Can everyone lighten up, a little bit, around here?

♦ AJ: Right. I don't mind the breakdown of the traditional nuclear family structure. The breakdown of compassion, politeness and respect toward other people—that's what I find scary.

♦ CH: That's very scary. That's part of this change we're describing. But… I'm smoking dope while—

♦ AJ: I wanted to ask you about that.

♦ CH: I'm probably going to get slower and slower here.

♦ AJ: That's okay. I read this article on you in *High Times*, and it's rare for women to come out and be public like that about their support and use of pot. Usually, women end up in the position of being the moral guardians of the mainstream.

♦ CH: I do feel like the moral guardian of the mainstream; that's why I say, legalize pot. I haven't heard any good reasons why it shouldn't be legal. So if there aren't any good reasons why it shouldn't be legal, legalize it. What's wrong with it?

I don't think of it as a drug. It's an herb, and I smoke it a lot. It's an enhancer that can enhance anything, like a meat tenderizer. I smoke it to get to sleep, too. I just like it. I don't know if it's necessarily good for me; it's probably not any better for me than a hot water bottle. It's probably not good if it's abused, like anything else—like drinking too much tea, which I drink far too much of. I don't see pot as any more harmful than that.

I'm not saying that you *should* use pot. I'm just saying that if you want to, then do it. And *say* you do it, because no one has given me a good reason why it shouldn't be legal. The reasons why it supposedly shouldn't be legal are all very dubious reasons, based in economy, and all the wrong things.

♦ AJ: Exactly.

♦ CH: I do feel like a moral guardian. Why should people be doing time for selling pot? I feel very obligated to publicly say that I'm a pothead, and fuck you. I'm growing it, I'm smoking it, I'm getting it however I can to smoke it, and I *will* smoke it, if I want to. Why shouldn't I? I feel I should say that on behalf of the people who have gotten busted for doing the same thing. If you see a social injustice, that's founded in utter bullshit, of course you're going to at least say that you notice the problem. ♦ ♦ ♦

discography

The Isle of View (1995)
Last of the Independents (1994)
Packed! (1990)
The Singles (1987)
Get Close (1986)
Learning to Crawl (1984)
Pretenders II (1981)
Pretenders (1980)

equipment list

Fender Telecaster guitar, Gibson J100 12-string acoustic guitar, old Martin acoustic guitar, Jim Dunlop wah wah pedal, MXR compressor pedal, Rat distortion pedal, Boss chorus pedal, original Marshall amp head, 2x12 cabinet

June Millington
Fanny

June Millington was born in the Philippines. After moving to California in the early 1960s, she formed a succession of all-girl bands with her sister, Jean. By 1969 their band Fanny had become the first all-women rock band to be signed to a major label. June left Fanny in 1973; by 1975 she had become involved in the nascent womyn's music movement. She toured as a solo artist through the '80s and co-founded the non-profit Institute for the Musical Arts in 1987, where she works as Artistic Director, produces albums, and teaches. For information about IMA, call (707) 876-3004 or write to P.O. Box 253, Bodega, CA, 94922.

◆ **ANDREA JUNO: Fanny was *the* pioneering female rock group. I discovered Fanny when I was 16, and the band was a bright light and inspiration to me—the first women rockers I knew about. When did it all start?**

◆ JUNE MILLINGTON: It started in the Philippines, the first time I heard someone play guitar.

◆ **AJ: How old were you?**

◆ JM: I was just about to turn 13. When I was in seventh grade, my parents put me and my sister Jean (who's a year younger) in a convent to study for a year. It was a horrible year for me—except for the fact that I heard somebody playing guitar. I didn't know what it was, but, like a sleepwalker, I got up out of my seat and followed that sound down the hall. There was this other young girl, playing guitar. I was just spellbound. It was like the secrets of the universe had suddenly been revealed to me, and there was hope.

Five or six months later, we moved to California, where the folk thing was still happening. Jean and I had played ukuleles before, so it was easy for us to get into folk. We went to hootenannies, and all that. Then the Beach Boys hit, which changed our ideas about music. We had boyfriends who were in bands, and next thing you know, we're playing their electric guitars. Some other girls heard about us, and said, "Let's start a band."

◆ **AJ: Did you take lessons?**

◆ JM: No. I just picked it up naturally, because I was so attracted to it. I *had* to play the guitar.

At first, Jean and I both played guitar. But when we started a band—which was called the Svelts—in Sacramento, I told her, "I want to keep playing guitar, so *you* play bass." Since I was the big sister she had to listen to me. It actually turned out to be a really good call; she's a great bass player.

◆ **AJ: Did you get a lot of pressure that you shouldn't play guitar—that it wasn't "feminine"?**

◆ JM: Yes, we did. The pressure we got wasn't so much about guitar, but that we shouldn't be in bands, because it wasn't socially acceptable. What would we do when we went out there? It made us suddenly independent—iconoclastic, rebellious figures. It was okay to play acoustic guitar, but to play electric guitars and be in a band was heavy-duty.

The interesting thing is that it gained us an entree into society that we hadn't had previously. Here we were, half-Filipino and half-American; we had just moved to the United States, so we didn't have any friends. We were good students, well behaved and all that stuff. But there was the juxtaposition of having this rock'n'roll side to us that hardly anybody else knew about.

They were very different worlds. We'd go to school and be well-behaved, and get good grades—and then we'd go rock out. It definitely

June Millington at Olivia Records' 20th anniversary party.

was our ticket to freedom.

♦ **AJ: What did your family think of the two of you playing rock?**

♦ JM: My mom always supported anything that made us happy. My dad was kind of distant, but he expressed a reservation about us being able to support ourselves — in fact, he was right.

I'm the only person alive who was at the beginning of both women in rock and womyn's music.

I'd always wanted to be a doctor. I thought I was going to be a surgeon. Of course, my father thought it would be great if I became a doctor. I went pre-med at U.C. Davis, and I went to Ber-

keley for a quarter. But then we ended up going to Hollywood, and we were always doing gigs. I guess it was just the call of the wild.

♦ **AJ: What was it in you that bucked the pressure about playing?**

♦ JM: Well, I really feel it was destiny. Jean and I both wanted to be in the first all-girl band to make a record and become known. In high school, I used to sit in class and — while listening to the teacher and doing my work — I would doodle all the time: "the Svelts, the Svelts, the Svelts." It was like my mantra.

We concentrated very seriously on doing our music. A lot of people don't realize that we worked really hard in Fanny. We rehearsed every day, when we weren't on the road. We had very little time off. We were *extremely* well disciplined — which brings on another kind of pressure. But that was the only way we could make it. We were not a band like, for example, the Runaways, which was created by some guys who thought it would be great to get a bunch of young girls, call them the Runaways, and

The Svelts (l. to r.): Kathie, June, Cathy, and Jean.

with Big Brother and the Holding Company, very much in the hippie Grateful Dead mode. They were pretty well known in San Francisco.

I met practically all the girls in the other bands (except for the Ace of Cups), and if somebody quit a band, we would call each other. Our band finally ended up as an amalgam of girls from those three bands, and that was the band that went to Los Angeles. We had the lead guitar player from the California Girls; I was playing rhythm guitar then. I just wanted to play a little guitar and write.

teach them how to play.

We started the Svelts in '65. We got a record deal in '69. We had been playing professionally even before that, doing the acoustic thing. We had practiced incessantly and played at all these gigs and clubs—we had a number of years on the road. We were writing songs, and were very focused. I really feel like it was rock'n'roll manifest destiny, and we were chosen to do that.

♦ **AJ: You also had the inner strength required to make good on that destiny; considering that there were no earlier female rockers to model yourselves on, what you did was very unusual.**

♦ JM: Our mother was always proud of us. That made a big difference. Having two sisters together in the band meant that it was still family, and we gave each other a lot of support.

It was definitely not easy. A lot of girls did leave the Svelts, so it was hard to keep the band together. It was *really* difficult to get a girl drummer; they were the ones that quit the most, because the most far-out thing you could do as a girl was to actually sit behind the drums and play. It was a major heart attack for us whenever we had to start looking for another drummer. There were maybe four all-girl bands that started in northern California at about the same time, so we wound up with a synchronistic deal.

There was our band, the Svelts; a group in Palo Alto called the California Girls; a group in Atherton called the Freudian Slips; and the Ace of Cups, in San Francisco. They were friends

♦ **AJ: Was this band still the Svelts?**

♦ JM: Actually, it became the group Wild Honey. In one of our phases when we were looking for a drummer, Alice de Buhr, who had been in a girl group in Iowa, called Wild Honey, came out to play with us. When she was a senior in high school she discovered that she was a lesbian, and her parents put her in a mental institution right before she graduated. They considered her to be totally sick. She couldn't even graduate with her class.

She came out to California with her lover, and joined our band. We had her, Jean, Addie Clement (the lead guitar player from the California Girls), a girl named Brie Berry who played percussion, and me.

♦ **AJ: Were the women supportive of each other?**

♦ JM: Oh, yeah. We were supportive of each other, for sure—once we found out about each other. We were all in the same lifeboat, whether we knew it or not.

♦ **AJ: Joan Jett said that when she was in the Runaways, she felt that women were attacking her a lot; she didn't feel much of a support system.**

♦ JM: With whom? Women in the band?

♦ **AJ: No; with women in general, in the public. There was a strong sense of competition.**

♦ JM: Well, that's probably true. I thought you were talking about other women musicians. In general, women reacted just as men did. There's always going to be some resistance to anything that's brand new and has heretofore been considered inconceivable. But overt hostility? No, I don't think I felt that much. We took the resistance with a grain of salt.

The Runaways might have had such a different experience because they were created by somebody else; they didn't necessarily come together as kindred spirits.

♦ **AJ: They also seemed to have a far more titillating image, as well as an unavoidable novelty factor.**

♦ JM: That was definitely in the package. I remember sitting backstage at the Whisky-a-Go-Go, having a discussion with the guys who were putting the Runaways together.

We'd go to school and be well-behaved, and get good grades and then we'd go rock out. It was our ticket to freedom.

♦ **AJ: Was that Kim Fowler? He's usually credited with creating the band.**

♦ JM: Yes, that was him. He was eccentric. People took him seriously, but he was also seen as something of a comic buffoon character. Everybody just sort of *tolerated* him. I was at a party once, up in the Hills, and he made an announcement that if everyone gave him $5, he would have

somebody give him a blowjob in front of the whole party. That's the kind of thing he was known for. People said, "Oh, yeah, that's Kim."

He and this other guy actually started Musicians' Referral Service, which everybody was excited about. It was the first time anyone had organized rock musicians at all. He had a small office down on the strip, and you could go down there and put your name on a list. He helped people find each other.

♦ **AJ: Did you actually go to the Musicians' Referral Service?**

♦ JM: Well, Nickey Barclay did; in fact, that might be how she found us when we were looking for a keyboard player. We went through a lot of changes very quickly.

We had moved down to San Jose. We had a manager—a woman manager—and we were playing gigs. We made a couple of trips down to Los Angeles to play at open-mike night at the Troubadour, where everybody went. The first time we played, nothing happened. The second time, our manager had gone around to all these different people's offices and beat the bushes, so more people came. A couple of days after our gig, when we were literally minutes away from walking out the door of our motel, we got a phone call—just like in a movie. It was Richard Perry's secretary, and she had heard us play.

♦ **AJ: Who is Richard Perry?**

♦ JM: Richard Perry is now this incredibly big record producer. At the time, he was staff at Warner Brothers. His name was known in L.A. because he had produced "Tiptoe Through the

Front and back panel of Fanny's first record, *Fanny* (1970).

207

Photo: Tom Hanley

Fanny driving around on a pony cart in London in the summer of 1973 (clockwise from l.): Jean Millington, Alice de Buhr, June Millington, and Nickey Barclay.

seen. He thought we were going be like the female Beatles.

◆ **AJ: When did you sign this contract?**

◆ JM: 1969. Right after we signed, Richard flew off to London to record Ella Fitzgerald. It's a totally unknown album; the idea was that she would do Motown hits with this London string section. [laughs] They did it in London, because it was cheaper, and then came back to mix the stuff. That Ella Fitzgerald album was my introduction to the studio process. I spent every minute I could in the studio, just watching Richard manipulate these tracks; I was fascinated. He'd change the bass part, delete this or punch that in. I couldn't believe it. I realized what kind of control you could have in the studio. It's like an alchemist's playground.

◆ **AJ: Were you also recording while you were learning about producing and engineering?**

◆ JM: Well, once we got the record deal and were living in Los Angeles in "Fanny Hill," our house on Marmont Lane—Addie quit the band. Now there was a huge problem. Jean and Alice decided that *I* was now going to play lead guitar, and we had to find either another guitarist or a keyboard player. For about a year we flew girls in from Texas, St. Louis, or wherever, just to audition them. Of course, that was charged against our recording account. We were getting a monthly stipend from Reprise Records, which was soon to become a subsidiary of Warner Brothers. Richard told them, "I am the producer; trust me. We're going to make a lot of money off of these girls."

We were working really hard, practicing every day, and looking for a replacement. While we were bringing in all these girls to try them out, Richard was using us to get into every major studio in Los Angeles; he was trying to get his producer's job underway. He dragged us around to check out all these studios and different engineers. We were auditioning girls, so they came along. We were laying down tracks and

Tulips," by Tiny Tim. He had also just worked on Captain Beefheart's *Trout Mask Replica* album. He went on to produce Barbra Streisand, and the Pointer Sisters' big hits. He's really big.

Anyway, he had a track record, but he wasn't a major producer yet. His secretary called because *she* had liked us. She asked, "What are you doing?" We said, "Well, we're just about to leave town." And she said, "Hold on, I'll call you right back—don't go anywhere!" She called back about ten minutes later. "I talked to my boss. He said you should go down to Wally Heider's studio; he wants to audition you before you leave town."

We got in our bus, which was this old renovated school bus we'd gotten from our dad. It was painted blue on the outside and orange on the inside. We drove over to Wally Heider's Studio B, set up our equipment, and played for Richard Perry for 20 minutes. On that basis, he got the record company to sign us—sight-unlearning how to record.

By the time we found Nickey, a year later, we were totally ready; we were *primed*. We had gotten on-the-job training. We rehearsed for two or three months, and recorded the album. *Boom.*

♦ **AJ: How old were you then?**

♦ JM: I was probably 20, 21.

> We had what we wanted; we had a record deal. We were *infamous*. All the other bands and musicians totally adored us. We were riding around in limos, and we felt like our major hit was just around the corner. But I lost it.

♦ **AJ: You really entered the star-making machinery at a young age. What happened once the album came out?**

♦ JM: Our lives changed completely. Once you actually record an album, you have to back it up. Your life is subject to what that record needs, in order to make the sales to support it. So from that point on, we were on the road all the time—about 85 percent of the year. When we weren't on the road, we were rehearsing or recording. We had no personal life any more.

♦ **AJ: What did that do to you?**

♦ J M: I fell apart, after three years. I had a nervous breakdown. I was too young to handle that kind of pressure. We had what we wanted; we had a record deal and we were cutting records. We were *infamous*. All the other bands and musicians totally adored us. We were riding around in limos, and everybody wanted to stay together and record another album. We felt like our major hit was just around the corner. But I just lost it. I was a nervous wreck.

♦ **AJ: Did you get sucked into drugs or alcohol?**

♦ JM: Oh, no, not at all. I was doing yoga every day, and I was a strict vegetarian. In fact, I was much cleaner than I am now. I drink coffee. Back then, I didn't even do that.

♦ **AJ: That kind of healthy discipline is rare for someone so young—particularly back then. One tends to associate that era with hedonism and overindulgence.**

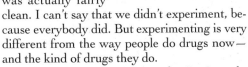

Fanny Hill, Fanny (1972).

♦ JM: The band was actually fairly clean. I can't say that we didn't experiment, because everybody did. But experimenting is very different from the way people do drugs now—and the kind of drugs they do.

Before we moved to Los Angeles, I quit smoking marijuana, because it made me too paranoid. Then there was a phase, in L.A., when I liked smoking hash. That was around the time that we were hanging out with the band Little Feat. We were close with them; George Lowell was one of my best friends. They were signed to Warner Brothers also, so we would rehearse next to each other at the movie sound lot. They would come over to our house all the time and we would just jam, night and day.

We were very well disciplined, and we didn't do a lot of drugs. I tried to eat well and sleep well, and all that stuff. But I'm the type of person who is questing for inner truth. I was so young that I didn't know I wasn't getting what I needed, in terms of finding my way in the world and the universe. I know that sounds like an extravagant statement.

♦ **AJ: I don't think so.**

The Svelts.

Charity Ball, **Fanny** (1971).

♦ JM: I think that was the basis of my nervous breakdown. My personal life had fallen apart, and that was coupled with the feeling that I was not, *spiritually*, going in the right direction for me. I might not have been able to articulate it, but that's what I felt. Suddenly I realized—and this was the worst irony of all, the blow that totally pushed me over the edge—*that Fanny didn't really mean that much to me*. The idea of having success with Fanny, when the landscape of my inner life was so bare and Kafkaesque, was as if a cruel joke had been played on me. Fanny was just about to become successful. We were already, in many people's minds, a success. But it meant nothing to me. It was dry and bitter. I just couldn't take it, and I fell apart.

I made a deal with the band, and with Roy Silverman over in our management, that I would stay until we found a replacement for me.

♦ AJ: You didn't play on *Rock'n'roll Survivors*, right?

♦ JM: No, but I found Patty Quatro, who played on that album.

♦ AJ: Suzy Quatro's sister?

♦ JM: Yeah. We did a gig in Detroit, and the band that opened for us happened to be Patty Quatro and her brother's band. They lived in Grosse Pointe, Michigan, where they had grown up. We were watching this girl playing guitar, and I turned to the other girls in our band and said, "That's her—that's my replacement." They said, "Go talk to her."

She agreed to audition, and then she agreed to join the band. There was a six-month switchover. I taught her my parts, and then I left.

♦ AJ: What did people around you think of your being in the band, and being on stage? Did that contribute to your breakdown?

♦ JM: Oh, we didn't care, because we'd already been through five years of that shit before we even got to Los Angeles. In order to survive, to make it to the other side of the tunnel, you had to not think about what other people thought. It didn't matter. You couldn't take any of that personally.

♦ AJ: It also sounds like you gave each other a lot of mutual support.

♦ JM: Oh, yeah. We were like family. I'm still in touch with everyone who was in the band back then. My sister is an herbalist now, and Alice de Buhr, the drummer, calls her from Arizona. She does the herbs that Jean recommends. She also visits us, when she's out here. I see Patty in Los Angeles every once in a while. The only person I don't really see is Nickey, and that's because she doesn't want to be seen. She lives in London, under an assumed name, we understand.

♦ AJ: What happened to her?

♦ JM: I don't know. Brie happened to see Nickey playing with a band in London. She went up to say hello, and Nickey said, "Don't you dare tell anybody who I am—it's between you and me. I'm a woman from Ireland now." She was speaking with an Irish accent. This is a big joke with us, now. She completely changed her persona, and so did her husband, who was one of our roadies. Brie was so blown away when Nickey said that, and then she turned around, and there was Seagraves. She didn't expect him to have done the same thing, but he said, "Hello, Brie," in this brogue.

The idea of having success with Fanny, when the landscape of my inner life was so bare and Kafkaesque, was as if a cruel joke had been played on me.

♦ AJ: That's the husband?

♦ JM: Yes. Every once in awhile, we'll turn to each other and go, "Hello, Brie." [laughs] Now I've let you in on our little secret, but I don't know what her new name is or anything.

But it was very much like family then. We

could clearly see that what we were doing was a tough gig. We were the first ones. We had to give each other pep talks, all the time —

♦ **AJ: What kind of things did you encounter that you needed pep talks about? Nowadays, female rockers still talk about pressure, but you must have been running a much harder gantlet.**

♦ JM: A lot of times, after we'd play, people would come up to us and say, "You're not bad for chicks." That was supposed to be a really high compliment.

Let's just start from there. That, to us, was an insult, but that was the terrain. And from there, everything was downhill. The climate was not agreeable. It was just not acceptable for girls to go out there and rock out. But the interesting thing was that we also knew, through experience, that the second they actually heard us and understood that we were good and really committed, there would be a switch. All of a sudden, they would be majorly in love with us. So we saw how close the tension between attraction and repulsion is. They're different sides of the same thing.

The same person who said, "What are you girls doing? This is bizarre. You look like guys —" would be ranting and raving the next second, thinking we were the best thing in the world.

♦ **AJ: How did men react to you?**

♦ JM: They'd want to go to bed with us. Everybody was constantly trying to pick us up. Most of us in the band got our information about music by asking people to show us things, or by jamming with them. A lot of times, guys thought we were coming on to them.

♦ **AJ: Was there a lot of free-form sexual activity at the time? Did you girls take that up?**

♦ JM: Not so much. A little, but not anything like what someone might fantasize about the rock star life: you could get laid, have orgies, have sex night and day with both men and women. Not at all. I was monogamous the whole time I was in Fanny. I never slept with anyone on the road.

♦ **AJ: You had a relationship?**

♦ JM: Yeah. I did.

♦ **AJ: How did that person deal with —**

♦ JM: Well, that's what I was referring to when I said I didn't have a personal life anymore — I never saw her. That was the problem. It basically fell apart because I was not there. But that doesn't mean that I went crazy when I was on the road. I went crazy when I had a nervous breakdown.

Right after we got to Los Angeles, when we had the record deal and we were looking for the

From June's scrapbook: photograph of Fanny and Barbra Streisand (right) from the *Circular*.

other guitar player, I started to feel very insecure, because I really didn't want to play lead guitar. But I was also insecure about something else. Some of us in the band were lesbians, and we wondered if that was going to be a problem. So that was another pep talk. "Well, let's go out with guys again."

♦ **AJ: Just for a front?**

♦ JM: No. I really did go out with guys; I slept with a number of them. It wasn't just to put up a front. I was really into them. But that's just not who I was.

♦ **AJ: But at that time, wouldn't there have been negative repercussions if you just expressed who you were?**

♦ JM: Within the industry, I think they just knew.

♦ **AJ: I heard a rumor about a famous singer who came out publicly in the '70s, when she thought that things were more liberal and open —**

Fanny Hill EP featuring "Young and Dumb" and "Knock on my Door" (1972).

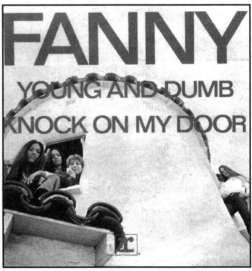

June Millington

◆ JM: No, we would never have done that. It was understood that you just couldn't do that, back then.

◆ **AJ: —and it really hurt her career. Well, what about attempts to sexualize the band? A number of women, even today, talk about the pressure they get from the major labels, who want them to wear sexy little things and pose provocatively.**

◆ JM: It was only at the end of my involvement in the band that they were trying to do that. Our manager and producer were both only concerned that we stay together as a band, record the albums and go out on the road. They understood that if people could see us play, *that* was the important thing. You didn't need to sexualize it. Just the fact that girls were up there playing was enough of a shock.

It's not a shock anymore, so people go to level two now, which is to sexualize it. Level one was just: a girl would get up there, and it didn't matter what she was wearing. She was playing. That was the deal.

◆ **AJ: It does seem, though, that the impulse to sexualize female rockers is inescapable, even if it doesn't succeed with every band. In your time, that happened with the Runaways.**

◆ JM: Yeah. That was a whole other bag.

◆ **AJ: Right. What about groupies? Did you ever get women groupies?**

◆ JM: Oh, sure. We had girls and boys. Some of them became our really good friends; groupies are people, too. The only difference between them and us was that we could play. They couldn't—that's why they were groupies. [laughs] They did the next best thing. They hung out with the people who were doing it.

◆ **AJ: That's a great way of looking at it. What did you do once you left the band?**

◆ JM: I moved to Taconic, New York, which is on the tip of Long Island. I got about as far away from everything as could be.

I was friends with Eliott Randall, who had a band called Randall's Island (he played the solo on Steely Dan's "Reelin' In the Years"). I would go into the city and jam with Eliott and with the guys in Sha-Na-Na, because he used to do lots of gigs with them. I wanted to jam with different people, and start to become known as a musician—not as that "girl player," lead guitarist in Fanny. That was really important to me. I needed to be anonymous and just prove myself.

◆ **AJ: Did you want to be a studio musician?**

◆ JM: Well, not necessarily. I simply wanted to be respected just as a player, not as that girl in Fanny. It was really a big deal to me. I holed up at this place by the ocean, and just listened to a lot of Stevie Wonder and pre-New Age music. Then I'd go into the city and jam.

Eliott told me about this guy in Woodstock, NY who was looking for a guitar player, so I went and checked him out. He turned out to be Tim Moore, who was an incredibly gifted songwriter. I joined his band for maybe three months, and moved to Woodstock. That was very, very good for me. The Band was still there. Dylan had just left Woodstock, but there was still a lot of energy there. I joined another whole family community of musicians, singers, songwriters, and artists.

◆ **AJ: How did you make a living?**

◆ JM: I played gigs whenever I could. I was a starving artist, just like everybody else. I didn't make any money off Fanny. All that money went to expenses. I was so happy to get away from the band, I didn't even ask for severance pay. I think I left with six or seven hundred dollars in my pocket. I just subsisted on nothing. Sometimes I would go into the city, and a whole bunch of us would jam, and I remember one time when we put a cabbage in a pot and boiled it; we all ate that one cabbage. I didn't care.

I wanted to expand, as a person and as a musician. That's all I wanted to do. I was reading

Zen Mind and *Beginner's Mind*, trying to start practicing. I took those books very seriously. I was trying to cultivate a certain frame of mind; I bowed to the trees in Woodstock. It might have looked really strange to other people, but it was keeping me alive. I mean, my mom was just so happy I didn't commit suicide. She would call me up and ask, "Are you eating, June? Junie? How are you doing?"

♦ **AJ: Is she Filipino?**

♦ JM: Yeah. That first year in Woodstock was really, really great. It was the first time, in North America, that my body felt aligned with the Earth. I hadn't felt that since I was a little girl in the Philippines, running around in the trees and on the beaches. Some things clicked for me, internally, and that was the beginning of my healing. I had the time and space to adjust to whatever spiritual practices I was moving towards, and expand my mind.

At the same time, I got involved with the whole beginning of womyn's music. I'd become friends with Cris Williamson. So there was this juxtaposition of living in Woodstock, going into New York where I had this other band, and going on the road with Cris.

♦ **AJ: Isn't that like night and day? You got into womyn's music, which is usually kind of soft and folky, after being a pioneer in hard rock.**

♦ JM: Yeah. I'm the only person alive who was at the beginning of both women in rock and womyn's music.

They call me and Jean the godmothers of women in rock.

♦ **AJ: That's amazing. How did you get involved in women's issues? What led you to those kinds of ideas?**

♦ JM: Well, right around the time I quit Fanny, I met this woman, Jackie Robbins, who was in a band in upstate New York. She and I became lovers, and we lived together in Woodstock. She got a phone call from a friend of hers, who was going to record an album. She wanted Jackie to play bass on this album, so she sent a tape.

Jackie put on the tape. I was doing other things around the house; it was just another tape

Jean Millington

to me. But it sounded really good, and all these people were totally *losing it* on the tape—there was this *incredible* excitement! They were screaming after every song. Well, it was Cris Williamson playing in some church.

♦ **AJ: Wow. That's history.**

♦ JM: That was my introduction to Cris Williamson and womyn's music. Jackie was asked to play on Cris's album, *Changer and the Changed*. They were recording it in Los Angeles for this brand-new record company, which was going to be run by all these women. So Jackie went off to L.A.

Meanwhile, Jean had come for a visit that month, or a month earlier. Fanny had recorded *Rock'n'Roll Survivors*, and then the band had *finally* split up. It was over. Jean had come to New York to see David Bowie, who had been a boyfriend of hers, and she also came to visit me in Woodstock. While she was in Woodstock with me there was this horrible snowstorm. No one could go anywhere. She got a phone call from L.A., and they said, "One of your songs from *Rock'n'Roll Survivors* is heading up the charts with a bullet. You'd better get back here, because we can make money off this!"

♦ **AJ: Which song was it? "Butter Boy"?**

♦ JM: Yeah. She wrote that about David, by the way.

Fanny (1973).

♦ **AJ: David Bowie?**

♦ JM: Yeah.

♦ **AJ: No!**

♦ JM: Yeah.

♦ **AJ: That's so wild! "Butter Boy" is one of my favorite songs.**

♦ JM: Well, as soon as Jean could get the next plane out, she went to Los Angeles. She called me up from there and said, "Listen, you've got to do me a favor. Would you just go on the road with me one last time? I don't want to do this tour with Patty Quatro, because that would be too rock'n'roll; I want more of a funk thing." I said, "Okay, just one tour. Three weeks." She agreed. The management agreed. I went to Los Angeles and we rehearsed. Brie was our drummer this time.

♦ **AJ: So it was something of a Fanny reunion?**

♦ JM: We called it the Fanny's Last Gasp Tour. It was spring of '75; we ended in Juneau, Alaska on July 4th. I had started another band in New York, called Smiles, a seven-piece pre-disco funk-salsa band. Part of my deal for the

Fanny's Last Gasp Tour was that I could bring the percussionist from Smiles, plus my roadie, on tour. This band that we got together for the tour started to sound really good, and we started to write songs together. We decided to start this *other* band that was also all women, from the band that had done the tour. We called it the L.A. All-Stars. Smiles was sort of on hold, but everyone had their own life in New York City anyway.

♦ **AJ: Was the band in L.A. more rocking?**

♦ JM: Oh, yeah. It was rocking; it was rock and funk. While we were getting the L.A. All-Stars together, Jackie was in Los Angeles, starting to rehearse with Cris for *Changer and the Changed*, the album they were recording. It turns out that Cris had been a major fan of mine when I was in Fanny. So now, of course, she wants me to play on her album. I hadn't met her yet, but I got this tape, and I was supposed to practice with that. I was like, "Okay, it's fine. This sounds really nice," and I played my parts on her album. But I was totally into the L.A. All-Stars.

We had just gotten an attorney, Michael Lippman, who was also David Bowie's attorney. We went to the lawyer's offices, and were just about to sign this record deal, when the record guys turn to me and Jean at the last possible second—I mean, we had our pens in our hands. They go, "By the way, we decided we don't want you to call yourselves the L.A. All-Stars. We want you to call yourselves Fanny." I just lost it. There was no way I was going to let this band be called Fanny, because it *wasn't* Fanny. I knew what would happen. We'd get on the road, and they'd want us to play Fanny songs. They would never even listen to the L.A. All-Stars.

♦ **AJ: How sleazy!**

♦ JM: I know. So, we didn't sign the record deal. It cost me and Jean $1200 to turn down that deal. We had to pay it out of our own pockets. All of a sudden, because we didn't do that deal, the wind was taken out of our sails. The L.A. All-Stars broke up.

Cris had recorded *Changer*, and things didn't

wind up working out with her first band, so she asked me to go on the road with her. I kept saying no. We were just starting to become friends. We hadn't really become friends during the album; I just walked in and did my parts, and everyone gave me a standing ovation, because I actually did it in one session, working with all these women who didn't know what they were doing. I was the first person that walked in who knew what to do.

◆ **AJ: Well, you're a pro.**

◆ JM: It was a big deal to them. These women were from Washington, D.C. Their goal had been to either start a record company or start a restaurant. [laughs] It didn't matter to them which one—it was just an adventure.

◆ **AJ: What is this record company?**

◆ JM: Olivia.

◆ **AJ: Wow—the famous Olivia!**

◆ JM: They were all on the same softball team, and they had this idea that they would start some sort of a women's company. Cris just happened to be in town, and she said, "What about a record company?"

◆ **AJ: This is right at the epicenter of a really important movement. This is history!**

◆ JM: I know. We both happened to be in L.A. at the same time. I was doing the L.A. All-Stars and Cris was doing *Changer*, but none of it worked out for us, in terms of the people we were working with. Finally I said, "Oh, okay, I'll go on the road with you." I was like, "God, this music is really lightweight—it's *acoustic*."

> **A lot of times, after we'd play, people would come up to us and say, "You're not bad for chicks." That was supposed to be a really high compliment.**

But getting up onstage with Cris was really good for me. It changed my life around. Especially at that time, the excitement was so palpable. There were people of all ages, older women and kids. Everyone was just so happy and excited, and I really didn't feel the sexual objectification that I had gotten before. I had been totally objectified! I hadn't even realized that was such a big deal; I was just so used to it. It was a psychic barrage.

Running, solo LP (1983).

Playing with Cris was like a vacation for me. *She* was the star. She was getting all the attention. Nobody knew who I was, and *nobody cared*. Behind her, I could doodle and do anything I wanted. She adored that I was there. It was great. Interestingly enough, I was also able to learn some things from her about humanity, feminist principles, and other things I didn't know about yet because I had been so hardcore, just trying to get along in this world and do my rock thing. My edges hadn't been softened yet.

◆ **AJ: What kind of things did she open up for you?**

◆ JM: I was really headstrong then. I wouldn't listen to the lyrics much. I would only listen to the tag, the groove and the guitar parts. I didn't know how to get into that second level of not just singing the lyrics but actually *living* them.

◆ **AJ: Which lyrics are you talking about?**

◆ JM: Any song. Let's take "Heaven Is In Your Mind." I remember Cris once saying to me, "Why can't you listen to the lyrics to that song?"

◆ **AJ: What's the song about?**

◆ JM: "Oh, brothers and sisters, will you be united, will the silence remain till the end of time?" It's sort of a cosmic song about peace, everyone living together and not fighting, being in harmony, and so forth. Cris was basically saying to me, "Why can't *you* be in harmony with everything? Why are you just trying so hard all the time? Why are you always pushing and being so aggressive? Just slow down a little bit. Don't be so rough. Don't be so hard. Don't be so anxious."

◆ **AJ: How did these lyrics compare to the**

ones you wrote in Fanny?

♦ JM: Well, I wrote "Think About the Children," for example; that's a pretty soft and quiet tune. Or "You've Got a Home"—that's a quiet song.

♦ **AJ: But how about on a feminist level; was there attention paid to—**

♦ JM: No. We didn't know anything about feminist principles at all. All we knew about feminism was that the idea seemed to be that you could do whatever you wanted to do, which we felt like we were doing already. Of course, there are so many levels to feminism; that's just level one, the tip of the iceberg. But we hadn't lived yet. We were like 19, 20. How are you even going to know these things at that age? But I think Cris was *born* knowing a lot. I was kind of a hassle for her to work with, because I was so headstrong and all over the place. But she flat-out told me that I was worth it.

On that first tour, nobody had any money, so we were all squished together in this little station wagon Cris had borrowed from a friend. Cris, Jackie and I were sitting on the front seat, with the equipment crammed in back. In the middle of the tour, I'm driving through Iowa, and Cris keeps telling me not to drive so fast. I keep forgetting, and driving fast again. Finally she just gets furious at me. We stop at this really small café; it's just like a Norman Rockwell painting. There are a few tables, and all these guys in coveralls sitting at a small counter. Cris lights into me.

She is totally pissed. I just can't keep it to-

Cris Williamson, *The Changer and the Changed* (Olivia Records, 1975).

gether; why can't I remember not to speed up? Slowly but surely, all the heads in this little café are turning.

♦ **AJ: Was she yelling?**

♦ JM: She was talking very loudly, giving me this super-big dressing-down.

♦ **AJ: That's kind of ironic, since she was telling you to slow down and be more peaceful.**

I was at this Olivia Records meeting. I remember thinking to myself, "There's a lot of talent here, but who's going to take care of business?"

♦ JM: Well, she was asking me, essentially, why I couldn't be more mindful. Now that I have done the Buddhist practice, I understand what she was saying to me. I couldn't keep my mind on any one thing. I would be driving, and then I'd forget I was driving, and in a second I'd be driving 82 miles an hour because I was thinking about something else.

♦ **AJ: You disconnected from the moment.**

♦ JM: But I stayed on the *point*. While she was telling me all this, I started to cry—and that was a really big shift for me. I didn't cry because she was yelling at me. It was because I realized that all my life, nobody had cared enough about me to really tell me the truth, and deal with my headstrong, impulsive nature. But she was meeting me head-on, saying, "We've got to deal with this, because I want to work with you. You're worth it. I'm telling you this because I want you in my life. We're going to have to work this out." It was the first time anybody had said that to me.

It was like I had moved on to a higher level—level two. After that, I had a conversation with Cris in L.A. and she said, "I'm going to be a really clear mirror for you." I didn't know what she meant, at the time. But she was true to her word. She tries to mirror back exactly what I'm putting out. At the same time, she gives me information so that I can *see* what she's mirroring back to me—which is myself.

♦ **AJ: Is she a centered and evolved person?**

♦ JM: Well, she's got her own stuff to deal with. But I think she was born knowing certain things, and she helped give me the tools to start me on that path. Some years later I had another next great teacher, the Dalai Lama.

♦ **AJ: How did that happen?**

♦ JM: It started in Madison, Wisconsin, the first time he did the Kalachakra Initiation. I followed him around like a groupie. I did the Lam Rim. I went for the teachings in Middlebury. This was in '81, way before he got the Nobel Prize. But the time we're talking about was six years before that, in '75.

With Cris, it was actually an equal energy exchange, because I was able to give her something too. She was totally freaked out by the fact that she became an instant star in the womyn's music genre, which was exploding then. It threw her off, and was very difficult for her. But now she had me as her ally; whatever happened with her in the womyn's music scene was lightweight compared to what had gone on with Fanny. She could totally lean on me. She could throw anybody my way, and I could handle them. I think she learned a lot from me about how to handle that kind of energy, that onslaught. She had to realize that if you get up on that stage, there's a payback: that adoration. I told her, "These people are coming up to you after the show, with whatever it is they're going to lay on you, because you got up onstage. You've got to take responsibility for it."

You've got to basically tai-chi with it. It's not *you*. You're the statue that's up on that platform. You can also be *off* the platform, watching that person everyone's adoring—that's you at the same time. It's a strange terrain, and it takes a while to get used to it, so you don't get so blown away that you can't even do your work anymore.

♦ **AJ: You have to remember that what's presented to the audience is a mask.**

♦ JM: Exactly. That's what I taught her. Now it's twenty years later, and we're pretty much on a par. We're learning things together. We're good friends.

♦ **AJ: You're still involved with each other's work?**

♦ JM: Oh, yeah. I worked on her last album, and she's on the advisory board here at the Institute for the Musical Arts in Bodega, California. IMA is the non-profit organization I started for women in music. We have a recording studio and a performance space. It's like the Musicians' Referral Service, except it's for women all over the world.

♦ **AJ: Is it also for all different kinds of women's music?**

♦ JM: Yeah. Any woman from anywhere, any

June and Jean (pregnant) with Bonnie Raitt (far left) in the studio (1979).

time. We're not separatists. We're trying to think at least seven generations ahead.

♦ **AJ: When did you start this?**

♦ JM: I think '86 is when Ann and I started to really think seriously about putting it together. Ann Hackler is the executive director, and she's also my lover and partner. She encouraged me to do it. She was the director of the Women's Center at Hampshire College, in Massachusetts, so she knew a little bit about organizing things. At one of the very first meetings in L.A. that Olivia had, right after my first tour with Cris—

♦ **AJ: Olivia Records?**

♦ JM: Yeah. They were a commune, basically. A co-op. They put out a call for women of color to come to a meeting, so they could tell us about Olivia and get us involved.

I was at this meeting. I remember thinking to myself—I didn't say this out loud—"There's a lot of talent here, but who's going to take care of business?" That's still a big problem. You need agents, managers and producers. In womyn's music, it's very difficult to find people with the experience and confidence to take those positions—almost impossible.

♦ **AJ: That's true; across the board, you don't usually find women on the business side of things.**

♦ JM: Right. Well, after that meeting, years roll by, and now it's 1986. I still have this voice nagging in my head. "Somebody's got to put something together to help all these women out. They've got to get organized. You have all these musicians and singers and songwriters, and they're all really talented, but it's just so disorganized. Everyone's always reinventing the

Photo: Negra Olcese

June in Woodstock, NY (1978).

wheel and starting from ground zero." Finally the voice got loud enough, and I said, "I really don't want to do this; I do not want to start a non-profit organization. But I guess I've got to do it." It's just like what happened with Fanny. [laughs]

I talked to Ann about it, and I also talked to Angela Davis, who's a friend of mine. Ann said, "What you need to do is just write all your ideas down on paper." Angela said, "Just go ahead and do it. You certainly have my support." She was on the founding board. I wrote a seven-page tome, Ann and I took it to a professional grant-writer in Boston who narrowed it down to a two-page statement of purpose, and that was the gen-esis of IMA. I started doing small benefits to raise money, just to pay for the attorneys' fees and everything it took to set up the 501 [c] 3.

◆ **AJ: The nonprofit status.**
◆ JM: Yeah. Ann and I moved back to Cali-fornia, and kept doing more benefits, getting more people involved. I told all of my musician friends about it, and asked them what they all thought. Everyone thought it was a great idea. But 99 percent thought I was nuts. They thought it would never happen, because it was such a

big undertaking. "What? You're going to start an organization for women, and it's going to be a school? *What*?"

◆ **AJ: Do you mainly teach engineering?**
◆ JM: We teach everything. We don't have a set agenda. We try to just respond to the needs, and what we need right now is information. Technical. Management. Booking. How to record an album. How to perform. How to write a chart. One of the things we do is teach record-ing workshops. Real basic stuff.

A lot of women come through these doors, and they know not one thing about the record business. I say, "Do you know anything about publishing?" and their eyes start rolling. They don't know what I'm talking about. Once they're here, they're not only learning all these basic methods and techniques—they're networking and finding each other.

◆ **AJ: Is it a collective?**
◆ JM: No, I wouldn't be involved in a collec-tive. The spirit of it is collective, and it sort of ends up working that way. But I'm way too im-patient to wait for everybody to make a deci-sion. [laughs]

◆ **AJ: Do you produce the records?**

♦ JM: Yes. I'm taking time off from mixing right now, as a matter of fact.

♦ **AJ: What kind of music is usually recorded there? Is it hard punk, or—**

♦ JM: I'll do anything that comes through the door. It's non-judgmental, in that sense. A woman named Sandice Alaska just did a demo here. She was very, very punky, and the stuff is great.

♦ **AJ: You mentioned these recording workshops. How do you run them?**

♦ JM: We have a performance center here, which also doubles as a studio where we record. It's a huge room. We have performances about every other week, and the person who gives the performance usually gives a workshop the following day. There's a question-and-answer period during the course of the performance.

Just about everyone I know in womyn's music has played here. Linda Tillery and the Cultural Heritage Choir, Rhiannon, Cris and Tret Fure. Barbara Borden, who's a drummer, did a one-woman show here just a few months ago, which was *incredible*. The stuff that comes through here is awesome, and we video everything so it's all on tape. Plus we've got the recording studio, so we help women do their demos, and we've also helped women do albums. We've put out maybe seven albums so far.

♦ **AJ: What's the record label called?**

♦ JM: Oh, whatever they want to call it. I have my own record company too, called Fabulous Records. A couple of people have released albums through that. We decided to have meetings with different women to find out what we need to offer; we had our first meeting of this kind last fall. There were eleven of us there. We decided that what we really need is an in-house record label. So it looks like IMA is going to have a label called RPM: Real People Music. Right now we're working on the rough mixes of a whole bunch of stuff that we're recording.

When we played at the Michigan Womyn's Music Festival this year, we asked for donations for RPM. We gave everyone who donated more than $25 a cassette with rough mixes of the Slammin' Babes, Nancy Vogl, and Lynn Vidal (who's also in our band the Slammin' Babes). Yes, we are called the Slammin' Babes. I'm 47, and I am a slammin' babe.

♦ **AJ: All right!**

♦ JM: Another thing that's important about IMA is in our statement of purpose, which specifically states that our target population is women, especially women of color and single mothers. I realized, when I was on the road playing womyn's music, that not only is it hard for women to exist in this society—we're disenfranchised to begin with, and if you're a musician-singer-songwriter, it's even worse—but if you're a single mother, it's almost impossible.

I did a lot of solo gigs, playing womyn's music all over the country. A lot of times I'd have an opening act, and every time it was a single mother, I'd sit down with her and say, "God, you're great. What's happening? What are you doing?" And she'd say, "I don't know. I don't have any money, and there's child care; I sent a tape to Olivia (or Redwood, or Rounder, or whatever), and I never even got a reply. It's so discouraging." With IMA, they have a place they can call or send something to, and somebody will talk to them. They can come here and do some workshops, or fly in and do a demo, and get some support. It's a safe place.

It's like the '90s version of the collaborations we were doing with the Svelts and other girl groups in the '60s—the Dark Age of women's music, when there was nobody. There was a small article on us in *Ms.* magazine last year, and we got phone calls from all over the country. Some people just wanted to know that we really did exist. That's all they needed, to have someone pick up the phone and say, "Yes, this is IMA; yes, we are here."

♦ **AJ: You've been such an inspiration in so many ways; I hope you don't mind my saying this, but you're one of the grandmothers of—**

♦ JM: I'm one of the grandmothers of women

Ticket to Wonderful, **June & Jean Millington's latest album (1993).**

in rock. Actually, they call me and Jean the god-mothers of women in rock.

♦ **AJ: Godmothers? That's even better.**

♦ JM: Someone made that up, and we loved it, so we adopted it. It's funny, because Jean and I will listen to the stuff women rockers are playing now, and we'll go, "God, this sounds like our rehearsals in the garage in 1966." It's wild. Nothing's really changed. I mean, the lyrics are different, but the energy is totally exact—and the sound is the same as what we were doing back then.

♦ **AJ: Now it's more of an attempt to have lyrics that women can totally relate to.**

♦ JM: Right. That's really where the big shift has been—in our minds. ♦ ♦ ♦

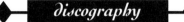
discography

♦ ARTIST ♦

Mother's Pride, Fanny (1973)
Fanny Hill, Fanny (1972)
Young and Dumb, Fanny, EP (1972)
Charity Ball, Fanny(1971)
Fanny, Fanny (1970)
"I'll Never Be the Same," solo B-side
   with Andy Williams' single "Last Tango
   in Paris" (during Fanny years)

♦ ARTIST/PRODUCER ♦

Ticket to Wonderful, June and
   Jean Millington (1994)
One World, One Heart, June Millington
   (1988)
Running, June Millington (1983)
Heartsong, June Millington(1981);
   "When Wrong Is Right" co-produced
   with Leslie Ann Jones and
   Jackie Robbins
Ladies On The Stage, June and Jean
   Millington(1977) co-produced with
   Tom Sellers

♦ PRODUCER ♦

Glass House, Kathryn Warner(1994)
Live At IMA, Gwen Avery (1993)
Big Big Woman, Rashida Oji (1993)
Share My Song, Melanie de More (1993)
Honey On My Lips, Pam Hall (1992)
Lumiére, Cris Williamson, co-produced
   with Cris Williamson (1981)
Fire In The Rain, Holly Near (1980)
Strange Paradise, Cris Williamson (1979)
Brick Hut, Mary Watkins(1978)

equipment list

In the Svelts (circa 1965-68): Fender Mustang guitar, Gretsch Countryman guitar, Gibson J-50 acoustic guitar, Vox amp on swivel stand, Fender Bandmaster amp; **In Fanny (circa 1969-73):** Gibson ES 355 stereo guitar, Gibson Les Paul original sunburst guitar, Gibson Les Paul Jr. chartreuse guitar for slide, Fender Stratocaster guitar, Fender Telecaster (occasionally), Gibson J-50 acoustic guitar (stolen on tour in NYC in 1980), Fender Twin amp, Traynor amp, Leslie speaker (adapted for guitar), Mateuse glass wine bottle neck cut for use as a slide, metal spark plug remover fitted to little finger at auto supply store for use as a slide, Dyna-comp compressor pedal, Boss chorus, delay, and octave-divider (Octaver OC-2); **Presently:** Gibson Les Paul Sunburst guitar, Fender Stratocaster guitar, Guild Bluesbird guitar, Gibson Les Paul Jr. chartreuse guitar (replacement for original), Montana M18-4 acoustic guitar (on loan from Cris Williamson and Tret Fure), Roland GP-8 amp through old Shure Vocal Master head powering a Yamaha monitor cabinet with 15" speaker (result is digital through analog), Gallien-Krueger 250 ML amp head, Korg AX30-G ("AmbiChorus" setting) for acoustic guitar, Dean Markley Pro-Mag pickup on acoustic guitar, Maxima Gold strings (made in Germany, gold-plated), passive DOD A-B box to swtich between Les Paul and Stratocaster guitars without noise, cable with "off" pin at the end to switch between Les Paul and Bluesbird guitars without noise, Boss Octave Divider (Octaver OC-2), active Morley A-B/C box; **In Production:** 3 Alesis ADATS: 16 tracks digital, TASCAM MSR-16: 16 tracks analog, Alesis BRC for full synchronicity between ADATS and MSR-16 for a total of 31 tracks after striping, TASCAM DA30 for digital mix-down, TASCAM M-3700 board: 32-channel and automated with eight subs and six auxiliary sends.

Healing Herbal Borders

Mexican Poppy (*papaver*)
Introduction
Associated with: skin
Part used: rhizome, seeds

The juice extracted from the Mexican poppy has a highly caustic effect used straight for warts and diluted for skin irritations externally. The dried plant is a weak opiate and helps to reduce pain and induce sleep. The seeds have a strong purgative effect. They also have a somewhat sedative and narcotic effect if the seeds are smoked. The seed oil was formerly used in place of castor oil.

Jack in the Pulpit (*arisaema triphyllum*)
Jarboe
Associated with: lungs, skin
Part used: root

It is an effective expectorant in that it acts on the membrane of the lungs altering the quality and increasing the quantity of its secretions. This results in the discharge of fluid or semi-mucous matter from the trachea or lungs through coughing or spitting. This herb is also good for treating throat maladies such as soreness, dryness, laryngitis, sensitivity, coughing and constriction. It can also be used externally for sores, boils, ulcers, skin irritations, and tumors.

Juniper (*juniperis communis*)
Tribe 8
Associated with: kidneys, stomach
Part used: berries

Primarily a urinary tract herb, most frequently used for cystitis and urethritis. Juniper contains among other oils *juniperin* that stimulates stomach secretions i.e. hydrochloric acid and pepsin therefore helping the digestive functions. Juniper should not be used when there is a kidney infection or chronic kidney weaknesses, as the oils are excreted in the urine and can be irritating to most inflammations. Juniper can also be used as a diuretic by helping to keep the sodium to potassium ratio in balance, thereby preventing water retention.

Cinchona (*cinchona officinalis*)
Joan Jett
Associated with: liver, stomach, heart
Part used: bark

Also called quinine, this herb has a very wide influence over the entire nervous system due to its general tonic effect. It prevents fermentation and putrefaction (decomposition). It is an excellent gargle and throat astringent. Small doses of cinchona increase saliva, gastric juices, heart activity, cerebral functions and excretion of waste matter. On the other hand, large doses may cause physical discomfort, vertigo, headache and temporary deafness.

Dandelion (*taraxacum officinalis*)
Kathleen Hanna
Associated with: stomach, spleen, kidney, liver, bladder
Parts used: root, leaves

The main purpose of the dandelion is as a diuretic which increases both the water and waste products in the urine. All parts of this plant have a stimulating effect on the liver and aids liver or spleen congestion. As a bitter, it is believed to work by stimulating digestion as a result of activating the bitter taste receptors on the tongue. Stimulation of these receptors activates a number of digestive properties including the secretion of digestive juices. Dandelion contains more vitamins, iron and other minerals, proteins and other nutrients than any other herb. It has a long history of use in the treatment of anemia, primarily due to its high nutritive content.

Lady's Slipper (cypridium pubescens)
Valerie Agnew
Associated with: nerves, heart
Part used: root, rhizome

It is almost a pure nervine and relaxant. Its action is slow, yet it influences the entire nervous system. It affects such ailments as depression, anxiety, insomnia, epilepsy, tremors and neurosis. It is an excellent analgesic for pain. It is also beneficial for inducing sleep and relieving female problems such as cramping.

Yellow Rhododendron (rhododendron)
Lois Maffeo
Associated with: nerves
Part used: root, rhizome

Much like lady's slipper, it is a nervine used to relax and calm the nervous system to bring on a peaceful state of mind.

White Bryony (bryonia alba)
Naomi Yang
Associated with: liver, spleen
Part used: root, berries

It prevents constipation, congestion of the liver, lead poisoning, diarrhea, and intermittent fevers. It works by removing waste matter from the liver and bile ducts. Use with caution since the roots and berries can be extremely toxic.

Sorrel (rumex acetosa)
Kendra Smith
Associated with: kidney, stomach
Part used: root, leaves

It acts on the urinary tract and is good for renal (kidney) diseases and especially scurvy due to its high content of vitamin C. It is very beneficial for muscle cramps and spasms and externally for skin diseases. If used in excess, sorrel can be poisonous or irritating to the kidneys.

Ragwort (senecio aureus)
Phranc
Associated with: bladder
Part used: leaves, flowers

Alpine ragwort is the most effective of all ragwort species. It contains considerable amounts of *rutin*, well known as a factor in increasing capillary strength. By increasing capillary strength, its function in reducing hemorrhoids and hemorrhages is very well documented.

Peony (paeonia alba)

Candice Pedersen
Associated with: bladder, liver
Part used: root

It is not certain how this herb functions to relieve melancholia and panic states. It is also used as a uterine astringent that causes the uterine lining to constrict thereby helping cases of excessive menstruation.

Hops (humulus lupulus)
Bettina Richards
Associated with: nerves, stomach
Part used: leafy conical flowers

It is perhaps the ideal remedy for a nervous stomach; its aromatic bitterness acts to stimulate and redefine stomach functions; its sedative effects help in relaxing the individual and dampening the sympathetic nervous system. It is not certain as to its effects in initiating sleep, but it may help with the production of *serotonin*, a brain compound which induces sleep. It contains at least two antibiotic substances both effective on staph and other skin bacteria. This is the reason why it is used in making beer since it retards spoilage.

Garlic (allium sativa)
Chrissie Hynde
Associated with: stomach, colon, kidney
Part used: bulb

Garlic's sulfur compounds are antibacterial, antifungal and antiviral. It prevents the sticking of blood cells therefore preventing hypertension. Its sulfur content helps with the detoxification of harmful toxins that accumulate in the fatty layers of the body by water solubilizing them and making it easier for the body to excrete.

Bindweed (convolvulus sepium)
June Millington, Healing Herbal Borders
Associated with: liver, intestines
Part used: root, flowers

Used as a purgative, it cleans waste matter from the liver, gall ducts and alimentary canal and helps reduce inflammation of mucous membranes. It also helps with the normal peristaltic (contractive) action of the bowels. In large amounts, bindweed can cause constipation and should not be taken for extended periods of time.

Information supplied by: David I.F. Miller, Nutrition Consultant/Herbalist, NYC.